ROLLING THUNDER
IN A GENTLE LAND
THE VIETNAM WAR REVISITED

OSPREY
PUBLISHING

ROLLING THUNDER

IN A GENTLE LAND

THE VIETNAM WAR REVISITED

Editor Andrew Wiest

First published in Great Britain in 2006 by Osprey Publishing,
Midland House, West Way, Botley, Oxford OX2 0PH, United Kingdom.
443 Park Avenue South, New York, NY 10016, USA.
Email: info@ospreypublishing.com

A CIP catalog record for this book is available from the British Library.

ISBN-10: 1 84603 020 X
ISBN-13: 978 1 84693 020 6

The authors, Bui Tin, Kenton Clymer, R. Blake Dunnavent, Bernard Edelman, Ronald B.
Frankum, Jr., Jeffrey Grey, Daniel C. Hallin, Le Ly Hayslip, Arnold R. Isaacs, Lam Quang
Thi, John Prados, Gordon L. Rottman, Lewis Sorley, Martin Windrow, Andrew Wiest, have
asserted their right under the Copyright, Designs and Patents Act, 1988, to be identified as
the authors of this book.

Page layout by Ken Vail Graphic Design, UK (www.kvgd.com)
Index by Alison Worthington
Maps by The Map Studio
Originated by United Graphics, Singapore
Printed in China through Bookbuilders

06 07 08 09 10   10 9 8 7 6 5 4 3 2 1

For a catalog of all books published by Osprey please contact:

NORTH AMERICA
Osprey Direct c/o Random House Distribution Center
400 Hahn Road, Westminster, MD 21157, USA
E-mail: info@ospreydirectusa.com

ALL OTHER REGIONS
Osprey Direct UK, P.O. Box 140, Wellingborough, Northants, NN8 2FA, UK
E-mail: info@ospreydirect.co.uk

www.ospreypublishing.com

PHOTOGRAPH CREDITS
Title page: © Tim Page/Corbis.
Page 6–7: Australian War Memorial, Michael Coleridge, EKN/67/0103/VN. The complete
photo is on page 158.
Map on endpapers: Vietnam Archive, Texas Tech University.

ACKNOWLEDGMENTS

During my years studying the Vietnam War I have incurred many intellectual and physical debts that can never be fully repaid. First I would like to thank Anita Baker and Ruth Sheppard, the editors at Osprey, for dreaming up this project and for trusting me to take it to fruition. They have worked tirelessly, and were open to my suggestions about taking this project down a somewhat less than traditional road. I would also like to thank all of my colleagues at the University of Southern Mississippi for their continued support. At the risk of slighting some I would like to single out Charles Bolton, Phyllis Jestice, William Scarborough, Bradley Bond, Kyle Zelner, Mary Beth Farrell, Suzy Steen, and Michael Neiberg for special thanks. In one way or another they each made my life easier or served as sounding boards for this project. As usual our indispensable administrative assistant Shelia Smith was central to my success in so many ways. I completed this project while serving as a Visiting Professor in the Department of Warfighting Strategy at the Air War College. I would very much like to thank Col. Stef Eisen, Lt. Col. Jeff Hood, Dan Huges, Adam Cobb, Toshi Yoshihara and the wonderful students of Seminar 16 for their friendship and help during this very enjoyable year. I also owe a debt of gratitude to the Vietnam veterans with whom I work. They brought me to the study of the Vietnam War and always serve both as my guides on my Vietnam journey and as my conscience. Though I work with so many veterans, again I will single out a few for special thanks: John Young, Courtney Frobenius, Tran Ngoc Hue, and Pham Van Dinh. Finally as always my thanks go out to my family, especially my wife Jill, for first instilling in me the desire to write and then allowing me the time to do so.

DEDICATION

This book is dedicated to my beloved children Abigail and Luke.

CONTENTS

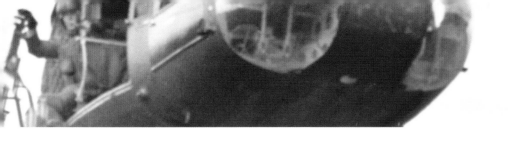

CONTRIBUTORS

Bui Tin was born in 1927 near Hanoi. At the age of 18, he joined Ho Chi Minh's revolution, fighting against both French and American troops and Pol Pot's Khmer Rouge. He was in the VN People's Army from 1945 to 1982, and in the Communist Party of Vietnam from 1946 to 1990, and in 1975 he was present in Saigon to accept the surrender of the South Vietnamese government. Following demobilization in 1982, Bui Tin became a defense and foreign affairs analyst for *Nhan Dan*, the Communist Party's official newspaper, and was named editor-in-chief of the Sunday edition of *Nhan Dan* in 1988. Tin began harboring doubts about communism, and on a visit to France in 1990 he elected to stay abroad to work for the restoration of freedom and democracy in Vietnam. While in exile in Paris, he has written several books including *Following Ho Chi Minh* (1999), *Vietnam: La face cachée du régime* (1999), and *From Enemy to Friend: A North Vietnamese Perspective on the War* (2002). He writes for many newspapers, and has participated in numerous conferences on the Vietnam War.

Professor Kenton Clymer, who received his Ph.D. from the University of Michigan, chairs the History Department at Northern Illinois University. He is the author of five books, including most recently a two-volume history of United States relations with Cambodia, *The United States and Cambodia, 1872–1969: From Curiosity to Confrontation* and *The United States and Cambodia, 1969–2000: A Troubled Relationship* (2004), which won the Robert H. Ferrell Book Prize from the Society for Historians of American Foreign Relations.

Professor R. Blake Dunnavent received his BA from Abilene Christian University in 1990. He received his MA and Ph.D. degrees from Texas Tech University in 1998. His major field is American history, with a concentration on military and naval history. He joined the faculty at Louisiana State University in Shreveport in fall 2002. His publications include *Brown Water Warfare: The U.S. Navy in Riverine Warfare and the Emergence of a Tactical Doctrine, 1775–1970* (2003).

Bernard Edelman served as a broadcast specialist/correspondent for the US Army in Vietnam in 1970. He co-curated one of the first exhibits of the artwork of veterans in 1981, and was named by Mayor Ed Koch to serve on the New York Vietnam Veterans Memorial Commission, for which he edited the volume *Dear America: Letters Home from Vietnam*. He was associate producer of the documentary feature film based on his book, and co-produced a documentary short, *Memorial: Letters from American Soldiers*, which was nominated for an Academy Award. He currently works for Vietnam Veterans of America.

Professor Ronald B. Frankum, Jr. earned his Ph.D. from Syracuse University. He was formerly archivist of the Vietnam Archive at Texas Tech University and is currently an assistant professor of history at Millersville University of Pennsylvania. He is author of *Silent Partners: The United States and Australia in Vietnam, 1954–1968* (2001) and co-author of *The Vietnam War for Dummies* (2002), and *Like Rolling Thunder: The Air War in Vietnam, 1964–1975* (2005).

Professor Jeffrey Grey is Professor of History in the School of Humanities and Social Sciences, University College, Australian Defence Force Academy in Canberra. He holds the degrees of Bachelor of Arts (Honors) from the Australian National University (1983) and Doctor of Philosophy from the University of New South Wales (1986). He is the author or editor of 22 books in the fields of Australian and comparative military history, and has published numerous articles, chapters and reviews in these fields. In the academic years 2000–02 he held the Major General Matthew C. Horner Chair in Military Theory at Marine Corps University, Quantico.

Professor Daniel C. Hallin is Professor of Communication at the University of California at San Diego. He holds a Ph.D. in Political Science from U.C. Berkeley. His books include *The "Uncensored War": The Media* and *Vietnam* (1986), *We Keep America on Top of the World: Television News and the Public Sphere* (1994), and *Comparing Media Systems: Three Models of Media and Politics* (2004). The latter book received the Goldsmith Book Award of the Shorenstein Center on Press and Politics, as well as the Diamond Anniversary Book Award of the National Communication Association.

Le Ly Hayslip spent her early life living through the horrors of war-torn Vietnam. She left the country and moved to the United States in 1970, where she still lives. Following a visit to Vietnam in 1986, she founded a non-profit relief organization that provided housing, education, and medical care for Vietnamese children and villagers. She is the author of two best-selling books, both memoirs: *When Heaven and Earth Changed Places* (1989) and *Child of War, Woman of Peace* (1992). In 1990, she received the PEN non-fiction prize for *When Heaven and Earth Changed Places*. The books have been made into the critically acclaimed film *Heaven and Earth* (1994) directed by Oliver Stone. She has received many honors for her charity and humanitarian work. She organizes and leads groups of US veterans and citizens on trips to Vietnam. She established the Global Village Foundation in 2000, which honors individuals and organizations for their humanitarian contributions and peace efforts. Her co-author **Dien Pham** was a translator for the South Vietnamese Army and now lives in the United States.

Arnold R. Isaacs reported from Vietnam for the *Baltimore Sun* from June 1972 until the final US evacuation of Saigon on April 29, 1975. He subsequently wrote about the war's closing years in *Without Honor: Defeat in Vietnam and Cambodia* (1983). Isaacs is also the author of *Vietnam Shadows: The War, Its Ghosts, and Its Legacy* (1997). In recent years, as well as writing, he has traveled widely, teaching journalism in the former Soviet Union and elsewhere.

Lieutenant General Lam Quang Thi was born in the Mekong Delta of South Vietnam and fought for the Army of the Republic of Vietnam. He was awarded the Vietnam National Order, Third Degree; the Vietnam Gallantry cross with 17 combat citations; the US Legion of Merit; and the Korean Order of Chung Mu. He holds a French Baccalaureate Degree in Philosophy and an MBA from Golden Gate University in San Francisco. He is the author of *Autopsy – The Death of South Vietnam* (1986) and *The Twenty-Five Year Century: A South Vietnamese General Remembers the Indochina War to the Fall of Saigon* (2002).

Dr. John Prados is a project director with the National Security Archive. Prados holds a Ph.D. from Columbia University and focuses on presidential power, international relations, intelligence, and military affairs. He is author of a dozen books, including *Hoodwinked: The Documents That Reveal How Bush Sold Us a War* (2004), *The Blood Road: The Ho Chi Minh Trail and the Vietnam War* (1998), and *The Hidden History of the Vietnam War* (1995). He has edited several titles, including *White House Tapes: Eavesdropping on the President* (2005) and *America Confronts Terrorism* (2002). He has contributed chapters or articles to numerous other works. Prados is a contributing editor to *MHQ: The Quarterly Journal of Military History*, and a contributing writer to *The VVA Veteran*.

Gordon L. Rottman entered the US Army in 1967, volunteered for Special Forces, and completed training as a weapons specialist. He served in the 5th Special Forces Group in Vietnam in 1969–70 and subsequently in airborne infantry, long-range patrol, and intelligence assignments until retiring after 26 years. He was a special operations forces scenario writer at the Joint Readiness Training Center for 12 years and is now a full-time author, living in Texas.

Lewis Sorley is a third-generation graduate of the United States Military Academy at West Point, and also holds a doctorate from the Johns Hopkins University. He has served on the faculties at West Point and the Army War College, and with tank and armored cavalry units in Germany, Vietnam, and the United States. He is the author of two biographies, *Thunderbolt: General Creighton Abrams and the Army of His Times* (1992) and *Honorable Warrior: General Harold K. Johnson and the Ethics of Command* (1998); and two historical studies, *A Better War: The Unexamined Victories and Final Tragedy of America's Last Years in Vietnam* (1999) and *Vietnam Chronicles: The Abrams Tapes, 1968–1972* (2004).

Professor Andrew Wiest is Professor of History at the University of Southern Mississippi, where he co-directs the Vietnam Studies Program and the university's Center for the Study of War and Society. In the academic year 2005–06 he was a Visiting Professor in the Department of Warfighting Strategy at the United States Air Force Air War College. He has previously served as a Visiting Senior Lecturer at the Royal Military Academy, Sandhurst. He is the author of many books, including *Haig: The Evolution of a Commander* (2005), *The Vietnam War, 1956–1975* (2002), *War in the Age of Technology* (edited with Geoffrey Jensen, 2001), and *Passchendaele and the Royal Navy* (1995).

Martin Windrow was born in 1944 and educated at Wellington College. Since the 1970s, he has worked in book publishing as a commissioning and art editor specializing in military and aviation history, and is currently a freelance editor and writer working from his home in Sussex, England. He is an Associate of the Royal Historical Society and of the Foreign Legion Association of Great Britain. In 2004 his major study *The Last Valley: Dien Bien Phu and the French Defeat in Vietnam* was published to critical acclaim in Britain and the USA.

CHRONOLOGY

1861		French forces capture Saigon
1883		France establishes a "protectorate" over Annam and Tonkin and rules Cochinchina as a colony
1890		Ho Chi Minh is born
1930		Formation of the Indochinese Communist Party
1940	June	France falls to Germany
	September	Japan occupies Indochina, but leaves French colonial administration intact
1941		Formation of the Viet Minh
1945	March	Japanese take over French administration in Indochina
		Bao Dai proclaims Vietnamese independence under Japanese auspices
	August	Japanese capitulation
		Japanese transfer of power to the Viet Minh
		Bao Dai abdicates power
	September	Ho Chi Minh proclaims Vietnamese independence
		British forces land in Saigon; they soon return authority in the South to the French
1946	March	French/Viet Minh accord recognizing Vietnam as a "free state" within the French Union
		French troops authorized to return to the North
	May	French/Viet Minh agreement begins to break down
	November	French warships bombard Haiphong
	December	Viet Minh forces withdraw from Hanoi – war begins
1947	October	French launch Operation *Lea*
	November	French launch Operation *Ceinture* against the major Viet Minh base areas
		George F. Kennan, writing under the pseudonym X, publishes the doctrine of Containment
1948		"War of the roads" on Tonkin/China border
1949	March	Bao Dai signs agreement making Vietnam an "associated state" within the French Union
		Creation of the Vietnamese National Army
	October	Mao Tse-tung takes over China
1950	June	Korean War begins
	October	French defeat in Cao Bang
	December	General Jean de Lattre de Tassigny takes command of French forces
1951		Viet Minh forces launch sustained attacks in the Red River Valley which fail, at a high cost
1952	January	General Raoul Salan takes command of French forces
	October	French launch Operation *Lorraine*
1953	May	General Henri Navarre takes command of French forces

	October	France grants Laos full independence as a member of the French Union
	November	Prince Norodom Sihanouk declares Cambodia's independence from France
		French launch Operation *Castor* and reoccupy Dien Bien Phu
1954	March–May	Battle of Dien Bien Phu
	May 7	French defeat at Dien Bien Phu
	June	Bao Dai selects Ngo Dinh Diem as prime minister
	July	Signing of the Geneva Accords
1955	July	Diem renounces the Geneva Accords
	October	Diem becomes president and declares the Republic of South Vietnam
1956	April	US Military Assistance and Advisory Group (MAAG) takes over the training of the South Vietnamese armed forces
1957	October	Fighting breaks out between the forces of Diem and the Viet Minh
1959	May	Under the guidance of Colonel Vo Bam, North Vietnam begins moving men and supplies down the Ho Chi Minh Trail
1960	December	Formation of the National Liberation Front, dubbed the Viet Cong by its enemies
1961	April	Bay of Pigs invasion of Cuba
	May	Kennedy approves sending Special Forces to South Vietnam and approves the "secret war" in Laos
	June	Kennedy and Khrushchev meet in Vienna
1962	February	US Military Assistance Command, Vietnam (MACV) is formed in Saigon under General Paul Harkins
	March	Launching of the Strategic Hamlet Program
	July	First members of the Australian Army Training Team Vietnam arrive in South Vietnam
1963	January	Battle of Ap Bac, a critical failure of arms for the Army of the Republic of Vietnam (ARVN)
	June	Monk Thich Quang Duc immolates himself on a Saigon street corner, symbolizing Buddhist protest against Diem's rule
	November	Diem is overthrown and killed in a military coup
		Assassination of President John F. Kennedy
1964	April	North Vietnam decides to infiltrate units of the North Vietnamese Army (NVA) into South Vietnam
	June	General William Westmoreland takes over command of MACV
	August	Gulf of Tonkin incident
		US Congress passes the Gulf of Tonkin Resolution, giving President Lyndon Johnson a free hand in the coming Vietnam War
	November– December	Viet Cong attacks on American interests in South Vietnam
1965	February	US begins Operation *Rolling Thunder*, the sustained bombing of North Vietnam

	March 8	First US combat forces arrive at Da Nang
	May	1st Battalion, Royal Australian Regiment arrives in South Vietnam
	October–November	Battle of the Ia-Drang Valley, first major clash between US and NVA forces and first major use of airmobility
	December	US establishment of the River Patrol Force
1966	November	Operation *Attleboro*, a major search-and-destroy operation northwest of Saigon
	December	Number of US forces in Vietnam reaches 385,000
1967		The year of the "big unit" war, in which US forces seek to attrit the power of the VC and NVA
		North Vietnamese and Viet Cong efforts to fight in the countryside and draw US forces away from the urban areas in preparation for the Tet Offensive
	January	Operation *Cedar Falls*
	February	Establishment of the Mobile Riverine Force
	February–April	Operation *Junction City*
	May–October	NVA siege of the Marine base at Con Thien, just south of the Demilitarized Zone
	November	Battles for Dak To and Hill 875
	December	US forces reach 500,000
1968	January	77-day siege of the Marine base at Khe Sanh begins
	January 31	Tet Offensive begins
	February	After the military victory of Tet, Westmoreland requests 206,000 additional troops; this action eventually sparks a chain reaction of change
	March	My Lai massacre
		Johnson announces that he will not seek re-election
	May	Peace talks open in Paris
	June	Westmoreland replaced by General Creighton Abrams
	August	Riots and Democratic National Convention in Chicago
	November	Richard Nixon elected president
		SEALORDS campaign to cut off Viet Cong waterborne supply lines begins in Mekong Delta
1969	March	Secret bombings of Cambodia begin
	May	Battle of Hamburger Hill
	June	Nixon announces first troop withdrawals, inaugurating his policy of Vietnamization of the war
	September	Ho Chi Minh dies
	October	Largest anti-war demonstrations in US history
1970	March	Prince Sihanouk overthrown by Lon Nol in Cambodia
	May	US/ARVN forces invade Cambodia
		US National Guard forces kill four demonstrators at Kent State University in Ohio
	December	US forces in Vietnam down to 335,000

1971	February–March	ARVN forces invade Laos in Operation *Lam Son 719*
	March	Lt. William Calley convicted of mass murder at My Lai
	November	1st Australian Task Force withdraws from South Vietnam
	December	US forces in Vietnam down to 156,000
1972	February	Nixon visits China, sparking North Vietnamese fears of abandonment by their allies
	March–April	North Vietnamese Easter Offensive
	April	Operation *Linebacker I*, the concentrated bombing of North Vietnam, begins
	May	Nixon visits Moscow
		Nixon announces the mining of Hai Phong harbor
	August	The last US combat forces leave South Vietnam
	September	ARVN forces retake Quang Tri Citadel
	October	South Vietnamese President Nguyen Van Thieu rejects peace treaty
	December	Operation *Linebacker II* begins
1973	January 27	Peace agreement signed, ending American involvement in the Vietnam War
	February	Cease-fire agreement reached in Laos
	March	Last US troops leave South Vietnam
		US POWs return home
	November	US Congress passes the War Powers Act
1974	January	Thieu declares that war has begun again
	August	Nixon resigns
		Congress announces sharp cuts in support for South Vietnam
	December	80,000 people have died in the ongoing fighting in South Vietnam, making it the most costly year of the war
1975	January	North Vietnamese forces overrun Phouc Long Province
	March	North Vietnamese forces launch invasion of South Vietnam
		President Thieu announces decision to abandon the Central Highlands
	April	Battle of Xuan Loc
		Operation *Frequent Wind*, the evacuation of Saigon
	April 30	Saigon falls
	August	Pathet Lao forces take control of Laos
	December	Khmer Rouge forces take control of Cambodia
1977	January	President Jimmy Carter pardons US Vietnam War draft evaders
1978	December	Vietnam invades Cambodia
		Thousands of "boat people" begin to flee Vietnam
1979	February	China invades Vietnam
1982	November	Vietnam Veterans Memorial unveiled in Washington, DC

Chapter 1

Introduction
An American War?

Professor Andrew Wiest

The Vietnam War is alive and well. Though the American phase of the conflict began nearly 50 years ago, which ranks it as ancient in a world increasingly obsessed by technological developments that come and go at a blinding pace, the United States and the world still struggle to come to terms with Vietnam and its aftermath on a daily basis. Reminders of the Vietnam War litter the cultural landscape of the United States, ranging from movies that seek to redefine the conflict to the formation of a burgeoning number of veterans' organizations in which graying men and women seek to remember and honor the events of their youth. In truth, the Vietnam War sits at a critical nexus in time, precariously balanced between the vivid clarity of the present, and the hazy half-light of history, a quality that imbues the war with all of the attributes of historical conundrum. Certainly Vietnam was not a "good war," in the mold of World War II. Yet on the other hand, Vietnam also was not simply the war of "baby killers," and the abject defeat of popular myth. Indeed, Americans, both those who lived the war and those to whom the conflict is ancient history, are engaged in a raucous debate over the very nature of the Vietnam War – a debate charged by and understood in light of living in a world where other "Vietnams" seem inevitable. The debate is freewheeling and wide-ranging, so much so that some effectively question whether or not America "really" lost the Vietnam War at all. However, one of the most difficult and oft-forgotten cultural reminders of America's war serves to set the entire conflict in a different and more disturbing light. Across the nation, from Los Angeles to Washington, DC, there exist vibrant and proud communities of Vietnamese émigrés. While Americans can console themselves through cathartic and nearly endless arguments over the nature of the Vietnam War, the Vietnamese community – the South Vietnamese community – is afforded no such luxury. They have no nation to which they can return. Their defeat was total – brooking no argument about the nature of the end of the Vietnam War.

Ho Chi Minh, founder of the Indochinese Communist Party and leader of the Viet Minh struggle against both the French and later the Americans. While revered by many in Vietnam, in the wake of the Vietnam War the historical interpretation of Ho's career has become more complex. (Topfoto)

Southeast Asia

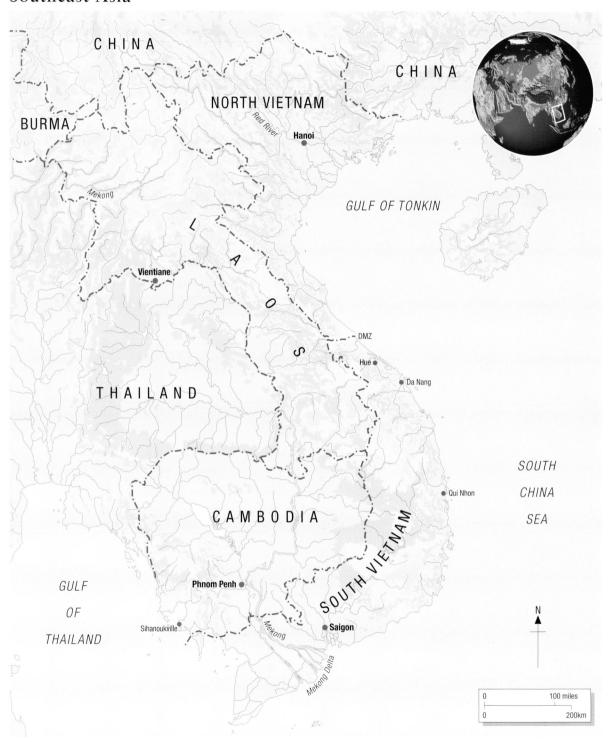

General Creighton Abrams, here pictured second from right visiting the 3rd Division at Phu Bai in July 1967, took over command at MACV in June 1968 and instituted the successful "one war" strategy. After the war Abrams would be instrumental in reshaping the American military, an action that had far-reaching consequences. (Vietnam Archive, Texas Tech University)

The societal flotsam and jetsam – arguments, academic debates, and innumerable cultural signposts – are reflective of a war that, though somewhat tiny in relative terms and rather distant, served as a pivotal turning point in American and world history. America entered the conflict united and self assured, ready to accomplish great things in an effort to defend democracy against a Soviet/Communist foe that seemingly equaled Hitler in barbarity and ferocity. However, America exited the conflict beaten and internally fractured, forever altering the long-cherished belief in American exceptionalism. In the United States the social after-effects of the cataclysm were varied and all-pervasive – ranging from a newfound mistrust of the government to an unfinished Civil Rights Movement, one that left inequities behind but buried so deeply that some only came into sharp relief in the destruction of New Orleans after Hurricane Katrina in 2005.

In a military sense, the consequences of Vietnam were no less thoroughgoing and dramatic. Smarting from the indignity of defeat, the US military revolutionized its thinking about war after 1975 and moved toward a maneuverist doctrine based on the primacy of technology. A key statement of this new philosophy was the Powell Doctrine, which called on the United States only to fight short, decisive wars that enjoyed the support of the American people – in other words, wars like the Gulf War, that were everything that Vietnam was not. At a more basic level, General Creighton Abrams, who had served as Commander of Military Assistance Command, Vietnam, championed a "total force" policy that sought to integrate America's reserve forces fully into its active military.

Simply put, Abrams never wanted the military to go to war again without calling up the reserves as it had in Vietnam.[1] Abrams was successful in his quest, which had unintended results so far-reaching that they became apparent only in late 2004, during Operation *Iraqi Freedom*. Lieutenant General James Helmly, Chief of the US Army Reserve, sent shock waves through the military by contending that, due to manpower costs associated with its lingering active role in Iraq, a legacy of Abram's total force policy, the reserve was a "spent force."[2] A true legacy of Vietnam, Helmly's memorandum sparked wide-ranging debates regarding the war in Iraq, with some pundits calling for a withdrawal of American forces while others began agitating for a renewal of the draft. Indeed, from the narrowly military to the broadly cultural, the consequences of the Vietnam War are alive and well in all aspects of American life.

VIEWPOINTS

In the glacially paced world of academic history, Vietnam remains very much a "current event." The historiography of the field is primordial, as a varied group of historians, journalists, and war participants rush to construct the historical orthodoxy of the conflict. It is indeed a heady time for the protagonists in the academic struggle of the printed word, who work in what is arguably a military historian's paradise. In what other conflict are there still important battles awaiting major historical treatment, much less true understanding? In what other conflict does a sea of recently opened documentary evidence exist that still awaits exploration? Thus, while historians and reporters of other conflicts sift through the same documents again, in search of some neo-revisionist gem, historians of the Vietnam War are engaged in the hustle and bustle of learning even to ask the right questions about their war.

A trip to the local bookseller will indicate that, while books devoted to the Vietnam War still lag behind in number compared to the historical attention lavished on World War II and the American Civil War, the field is burgeoning. Thus even though the historiography of the Vietnam War is only in its formative stages, there already exists a rich collection of books, some rightly regarded as classic works of history, that serve to define the debate regarding the nature of the conflict. Again indicating that the war in Vietnam defies historical norms, the historical debate began even before the arrival of American combat units on the scene. Bernard Fall's *Street Without Joy*, released in 1961, chronicled the French experience of war in Indochina and served as a warning to many in the United States. The debate concerning the Vietnam War continued during the conflict and has only gained in intensity since. Today books on Vietnam topics ranging from Special Operations to political machinations are legion.[3] As a result, though American motivations regarding the conflict remain in doubt, the historical dogma of the war is becoming clear. The mighty United States had misjudged the conflict in Vietnam at every level, from a flawed grand strategy based on ill-founded truisms of the Cold War to an over-reliance on technology and mass to overcome what was, in the end, a war of wills.

Captain Tran Ngoc Hue and his American advisor Bob Jones. The cooperation evidenced by the close advisor/counterpart relationship in South Vietnamese units indicates the complexity of the Vietnam War – at once both an American war and a Vietnamese civil war. (Andrew Wiest)

However, the task is far from complete, leaving much of the traditional history of the Vietnam War yet to be written. The main weakness of the current historiography is, perhaps, the tendency to view the conflict solely as an "American war." Indeed, the conflict in Vietnam was anything but an "American war." It began long before the US Marines ever splashed ashore at Da Nang, and it lingered long after the last "freedom bird" lifted off from Tan Son Nhut airbase outside Saigon bound for "the World." The Vietnam War was vast, involving several nations. It was complex, at once a war of colonialism, nationalism, insurgency, civil war, and a critical moment in the global Cold War. Until American historiography expands fully to encompass the true complexity that was the Vietnam War, our understanding of the conflict will remain flawed and incomplete. It is one of the goals of *Rolling Thunder in a Gentle Land* to consider the Vietnam War more globally. While the present study cannot pretend to answer all of the questions surrounding the war, it can help, at least, to introduce those questions and thus serve as a springboard for further research.

VIETNAMESE ROOTS OF WAR

Any effort to understand the Vietnam War should start neither in Washington DC nor in Paris, but in the recesses of Vietnam's distant past. An ancient nation that relies on the Confucian values of family and honor, and where the semi-feudal autonomy of the village is paramount to life itself, Vietnam is something of a historical conundrum. Remote and seemingly insignificant, the nation of hard-working peasants has repeatedly found itself the object of violent superpower attention. Long before Japanese, French, and American interference in their affairs, the Vietnamese struggled for nearly 1,000 years to stave off China's unrelenting efforts to swallow up its neighbor to the south. In the process the Vietnamese developed a warrior culture and a tradition of fighting long wars against hopeless odds – an ethos that would serve them well in much shorter conflicts to come.

After prevailing in the millennium-long struggle against China, the Vietnamese continued their own expansionist "move south," and took control of the Khmer areas in the Mekong Delta, including modern day Ho Chi Minh City (Saigon). To this day, even the casual tourist quickly discerns that Ho Chi Minh City is culturally different from Hanoi, reflecting a brash surety and speed of life that is somehow lacking in the more culturally homogenous north. Deep cultural divides, especially evident between the Vietnamese and the various Montagnard tribes of the highland regions, would leave Vietnam susceptible to ethnic and civil strife, and would serve to weaken Vietnamese resistance to coming foreign incursions.

Motivated by religion, strategic impulses, and outright greed, the French, in part due to overwhelming technological superiority, were able to secure rule over Vietnam by the mid-nineteenth century. Sometimes benevolent, but often brutal overlords, the French more or less attempted to administer Vietnam for profit.[4] As a result, a majority of the nation's sturdy peasants descended into landlessness and poverty, representing a vast potential pool of supporters for a call for independence – a dangerous reservoir of discontent that would remain in place until the advent of true land reform. Under French rule, Vietnamese nationalist groupings, initially led by the traditional mandarinate, came and went – often suffering brutal repression at the hands of the colonial authorities. Though there were several operative strands of nationalism, some of which looked to Japan for support, all suffered the same dismal fate.

Fractured and ineffective, Vietnamese nationalism seemed to stand little chance of overall success. The long odds, though, did not daunt young Ho Chi Minh, who believed that he had found the secret to nationalistic success in the theories and teachings of Marxism while living abroad in Paris and Moscow. Upon his return to the area, Ho worked to found the Indochinese Communist Party, which initially was but one of a cacophony of exiled Vietnamese nationalist voices raised against the continuation of French rule. Over time, though, the discipline and single-minded determination of the Communists saw them rise to dominance, sometimes brutally, among the Vietnamese nationalist groups.

The fortunes and nature of Vietnamese nationalism changed quickly as France succumbed to German aggression in June 1940. By 1941, the French colonial leadership had bowed to Japanese pressure, ceding much of its control over Vietnam. Only the Indochinese Communist Party, now operating under and through the umbrella organization known as the Viet Minh, had truly avoided the maelstrom of French purges to emerge as a nationalist counter to what amounted to French/Japanese joint rule. Certainly other nationalist groups were represented within the Viet Minh that stood against the French and Japanese. Equally certainly the last Nguyen emperor, Bao Dai, seemed a logical focal point for nationalist sentiment. However, the Communists and the Viet Minh bulldozed all in their paths, and coopted what they could not defeat. Thus the Viet Minh were the only real force that stood against the Japanese, and, though their military efforts were rudimentary at best, they earned Ho Chi Minh increasing amounts of American support. As their own rule collapsed in the area due to defeat in the Pacific, the Japanese proved unwilling to leave Indochina in the hands of Europeans, and jailed the French colonial leadership. The Viet Minh stepped into the resulting power vacuum and emerged in titular control of Vietnam at war's end.[5]

STRUGGLE OF DECOLONIZATION, REGIONAL CONFLICT, OR CIVIL WAR?

For a number of reasons, the French chose to attempt to reassert their authority over their lost colonies in Indochina following the close of World War II. There were periods of meaningful negotiations with the Viet Minh, and the support of the United States for France was not a foregone conclusion, but war erupted in Vietnam nonetheless – a war that would end in French defeat and presage direct American involvement in the region. However, the path taken to the wider war was indirect and indistinct – in a country fatefully located at the confluence of several of the operative forces of the postwar world.

The Vietnam War can certainly be seen as a legacy of the untidy conclusion to World War II. In addition, though, the war must be taken as part of a broader

A Montagnard woman and her children. The place of the Montagnards within Vietnam has long been a source of ethnic strife and discord. Even so, as with the remainder of Vietnam, to the Montagnards village life remains central to the formation of their cultural identity. (Andrew Wiest)

General Douglas Gracey, commander of British forces in Vietnam in 1945. Gracey refused to recognize the Democratic Republic of Vietnam's claim of sovereignty and was instrumental in aiding the French return to power in the southern portion of Vietnam. (Imperial War Museum, IND3551)

trend of decolonization throughout the world. The leading European colonial powers, Britain and France, had been exhausted by their labors during World War II and would be unable to retain control over the vast parts of the globe that had traditionally been under their suzerainty. Such matters would seem of little concern to the United States, which stood avowedly against European colonialism. However, the situation was much less clear-cut than this, since the United States relied on the support of the nations of western Europe in the emerging Cold War, and since many of the nationalist movements in European colonies were also openly communist. Thus Vietnam would fall victim to two of the prime motivating forces of the late twentieth century – decolonization and the Cold War.

Often the lesser, but still fundamental, contexts of the Vietnam War are swallowed up by the all-pervasive influence of historical concentration on the clash of superpowers in a Cold War struggle by proxy. It is important to note, though, that the conflict was a signal moment within the history of decolonization, and deserving of study in that light. In a complex web of events the British, who had a vested interest in the validity of colonial rule in the area, were critical to the initial re-imposition of French rule in Vietnam.[6] In addition, the concurrent British experience of war against insurgency in Malaya would form a critical backdrop to French failure in Vietnam and would serve to inform the coming American war in the area.[7]

The Vietnam War must also be understood as a regional conflict, encompassing the end of the French colonial regimes in Laos and Cambodia – with devastating results. Independent civil wars, proxy wars for the world's superpowers, and regional conflicts involving both ignored border violations and outright wars of conquest, the struggles in Laos and Cambodia are just as complex as the historically daunting war in Vietnam. A bit further afield, Thailand saw the rise of communism in neighboring states as a fundamental threat; as a result, its government sent a division of troops to the aid of South Vietnam and became fundamentally involved in the "secret war" in Laos. In the main, the complex regional nature of the Vietnam War has been the subject of relatively little historical inquiry, aside from individual moments in the conflicts such as the infamous "killing fields" of Cambodia.

The Vietnam War may also be considered in an even broader regional context, involving the complicated motivations and fears of nations bordering the Pacific Ocean. South Korea, New Zealand, and Australia were quite concerned about the potential threat posed by the continued spread of communism in the Pacific basin, and chose to join the United States in the struggle to defend South Vietnam. The South Koreans, hoping both to thwart the expansion of communism and to work more closely with their American protectors, sent the largest allied force to South Vietnam, eventually reaching a high of 48,000 in 1969. The South Korean forces performed well, but at a high price, for increasing Korean demands for funding from the United States led to a widening rift between the two allies.

Australian infantrymen supported by tanks move out of fire support base Kyke during a combined operation in December 1968. The presence of forces from Australia, New Zealand, and South Korea in the Vietnam War indicated the conflict's regional nature. From the "killing fields" of Cambodia to protests in the streets of Sydney, the Vietnam War would affect societies and lives across the Pacific basin. (Topfoto)

Australia began its commitment to South Vietnam early, sending the Australian Army Training Team to the area in 1962 to aid in training the forces of the Army of the Republic of Vietnam. The elite unit, made up of soldiers from Australia and New Zealand, remained in Vietnam until 1972, giving it one of the longest service records of the entire war. As the conflict grew, Australia and New Zealand sent increasing numbers of troops, culminating in the deployment of the 1st Australian Task Force in 1966. As the fighting lingered on, the Vietnam War and its attendant draft became ever more controversial in Australia, involving the nation in a period of discord and societal reform.

In light of this information, viewing the Vietnam War through a regional lens becomes important in the effort to achieve a fuller understanding of the conflict. In a narrow sense, ranging from the fact that the Ho Chi Minh Trail snaked through Laos to the involvement of Australian forces in the struggle, the regional nature of the fighting directly affected the outcome of the war in South Vietnam. In a wider sense, the claim can be made that the fighting in Vietnam was only one part of a war that spread through the entirety of Southeast Asia. Finally, the fighting in Vietnam played a major role in the political development of regional powers as far away as Seoul and Sydney.

Another critical context of the Vietnam War that often gets lost in the superpower shuffle is that the war in Vietnam itself was in many ways a brutal civil war. Western history of the conflict often wrongly asserts that the Viet Minh were the only true Vietnamese nationalist force of the time, and that their victory was predetermined. However, as American involvement in the war waxed and French influence waned, the political situation in Vietnam became increasingly

Ngo Dinh Diem, controversial first president of South Vietnam, here inspecting disarmed paratroopers after an attempted coup against him in 1960. Hand-picked by his American backers, Diem initially made great strides in uniting the new and strife-wracked nation of South Vietnam. However, Diem's dictatorial bent would lead to his downfall, and years of chaos for the fledgling nation. (Topfoto/AP)

unpredictable. While the Viet Minh exerted strong control over the North (where French colonialism had always been at its most shallow), many subsidiary nationalist groups in the South abhorred communism and its leader, Ho Chi Minh. Political choices were fundamentally intertwined with religious preferences, family and village loyalties, and economic class, but those choices were nonetheless real.

After the French withdrawal from the conflict, South Vietnam – in many ways a French colonial construct – fell under the bumbling, ham-fisted and American-supported rule of President Ngo Dinh Diem. Though he initially made great strides in taking control of a country that never really asked to exist, Diem's successes paled in comparison to his tragic flaws – flaws so great that Diem's successors, and indeed South Vietnam as a whole, seemed historically destined to failure.[8] However, devotion to a non-Communist Vietnamese nationalism ran deep within many communities in the South, especially among the Catholic minority and the middle class. That South Vietnamese nationalism was so porous, leaving reservoirs of indifference or outright support for the North Vietnamese, does not mean that South Vietnamese nationalism did not exist or that it was predisposed to failure. Certainly the South Vietnamese state and the ARVN were imperfect.[9] Even so, South Vietnam fought on for 25 years, and the ARVN lost more than 200,000 dead. After the close of the conflict, the North engaged in a costly purge of the South, leaving tens of thousands dead and imprisoning hundreds of thousands under hard labor for nearly a decade. In addition, millions chose to flee the fall of South Vietnam and the economic misery that followed.

In the end, then, the Vietnam War was, in many ways, a true civil war. Understanding the mechanism of the defeat of South Vietnam, a state that was neither totally an American puppet nor simply predestined to ultimate failure, is vital to a complete understanding of the war as a whole.

AMERICAN ROOTS OF WAR

Though the myriad levels of nuance surrounding the Vietnam War are critical to a deeper and more accurate understanding of the conflict, to most the war remains quintessentially an American war – and quintessentially an American defeat. Within this wider rubric of the American war in Vietnam, several certainties exist. The war was one of the lengthiest conflicts in United States history, beginning with the arrival of the US Marines on March 8, 1965, and ending with the signing of a peace agreement on January 27, 1973. The war was costly in terms of both blood and treasure. More than 58,000 Americans died during the conflict, and another 300,000 were wounded. Financially, with the exception of World War II, Vietnam was the most expensive war in American history, carrying an estimated price tag of $167 billion.[10] Despite this investment, the war ended in defeat, for the United States failed to achieve its prime strategic objective of defending and sustaining an independent South Vietnam.

The facts of American involvement in Vietnam raise obvious questions that serve to cloud the US military and political effort in a mantle of gray. Perhaps the most glaring is why the US chose to become involved in a war supporting the re-imposition of French colonialism in a country that was so distant and seemingly unimportant? A second, equally vexing question follows on from the first: after choosing to fight, how did the world's greatest superpower, fully capable of defeating the mighty Soviet Union, fall to ignominious defeat at the hands of the peasant army of a Third World nation?

The answers to such questions, disturbing answers that sometimes seem unsatisfying, can be found in matters of context. It was the complex context of the Cold War clash of superpowers that transformed Vietnam into the ultimate tragedy: a war that the United States had to enter, but could not hope to win.

The world must have seemed a quite disturbing place in 1946 as Americans, demobilizing after years of effort in World War II, wondered if they now faced an enemy even more frightening than Germany and Japan. Eastern Europe had fallen to Communist rule, and the territorial ambitions of the brutal leader of the Soviet Union, Joseph Stalin, seemed to know no bounds. In dire economic straits, the electorates even in many of the victorious powers of western Europe seemed vulnerable to the siren call of communism. Making matters worse, revolutions sprang up across the globe in the territories ruled by the now weakened European colonial powers. It was a situation in which the United States could not fall back into its familiar position of isolation – the threat was too dire.

To American policymakers, the nature of the threat was clear enough – they believed that communism was monolithic in nature. Across the planet, Communists worked together, under the leadership of Moscow, in an effort to destroy capitalism and achieve global domination. The threat was unified and very serious – dividing the globe into black and white, east and west: a bi-polar world that served as a superpower battleground. The stunning ideological clarity of the Cold War served the United States well in the ensuing bitter and protracted struggle. Fear of annihilation, fear of the Soviet steamroller that had flattened the vaunted Germans, was a powerful motivator that arguably eventually propelled the United States to ultimate victory. However, the black-and-white view of the Cold War world also blinded the United States to many of the deep subtleties that existed during the conflict, especially among nations yearning to throw off the yoke of European colonialism.

From the Congo to Vietnam, the colonized desired freedom and seized the opportunities presented by European weakness in the wake of World War II. Though driven by nationalism and local ethnic realities, many of the groups seeking independence also turned to communism as their ideology of choice. To US policy planners, these independence movements in the main seemed but a piece of the growing global Communist conspiracy, movements that had to be halted in their tracks.

As the frightening new geopolitical age dawned, America struggled to come to terms with how to deal with such an unprecedented threat. The answer was found in the failings of Neville Chamberlain in the Munich Conference in 1938. Appeasement had not forestalled the coming of World War II; dictators, it seemed, could not be bought off or swayed from their aggressive goals. Instead, the United States quickly inaugurated a new policy of Containment. First articulated by career foreign service officer George F. Kennan and announced to the world in the 1947 Truman Doctrine, which pledged that the US would "support free peoples who are resisting subjugation by armed minorities or by outside pressures," Containment called for halting Soviet/Communist expansion anywhere it occurred in the world.[11]

The Cold War and America's new role as the policeman of the world became infinitely more complex in 1949, when the Soviets ended the American nuclear monopoly by detonating their first atomic bomb. Containment itself suffered a dramatic defeat when China fell to the Communist forces of Mao Tse-tung. Americans faced for the first time the specter of the "Domino Theory." If Containment was allowed to fail, Communism would spread to surrounding countries, leading to a domino effect that would eventually threaten the United States itself. The scenario seemed to be playing out according to script when North Korea invaded South Korea on June 25, 1950, and overt Chinese involvement in the conflict became apparent.

The American ideological epiphany had wide-ranging implications. As the Cold War progressed and deepened, the United States, which had stood against the re-imposition of European colonial regimes under President Franklin D. Roosevelt, now found common cause with the French and their efforts to subjugate Vietnam. The fact that Vietnam was distant and posed no threat, and that the war was being fought for a nationalist cause, meant little. Ho Chi Minh and the Viet Minh were Communists; the French, though they were fighting for colonialism, were also fighting on the side of Containment. Thus the war in

President Harry Truman, who in 1947 announced to the world his "Truman Doctrine," the clearest example yet of the emerging American policy of Containment. First articulated by George F. Kennan, Containment would be a fundamental policy building block leading to American involvement in Vietnam. (NARA)

Vietnam lost its shades of gray and stood in stark relief as an important moment of the Cold War.

In his inaugural address of 1953, President Dwight Eisenhower stated that "the French soldier who dies in Indo-China, the British soldier killed in Malaya, the American life given in Korea" were lives lost in the same great struggle, in which "freedom is pitted against slavery; lightness against the dark."[12] A shadowy war in a faraway land had become an integral part of the wider American construct of the Cold War, and the journey to the American war in Vietnam had begun.

In 1953 Vietnam remained, at best, a side issue in a wider Cold War focused mainly on Europe, but events slowly pushed the fortunes of the tiny nation into the forefront of the American consciousness. French failure in Vietnam, epitomized by the Battle of Dien Bien Phu in 1954, resulted in the landmark political settlement of the Geneva Accords. In the agreement Ho Chi Minh

President Dwight Eisenhower (one from right), seen here with John Foster Dulles, Winston Churchill, and Anthony Eden at the White House in 1954. Under the presidency of Dwight Eisenhower the meaning of Containment became clearer. Communists across the planet, whether in Korea, Vietnam, or the Congo, were representatives of the Soviet Union and were fighting the same war against capitalism. (Topfoto/AP)

received control over Vietnam north of the 17th Parallel, while French forces regrouped in the South, prior to an election that was meant to reunify the country in 1956. The scheduled election never took place, partly due to the American decision to halt the advance of communism in the area. As a result, the 17th Parallel hardened into an international boundary, separating Communist North Vietnam from the American-backed regime of Ngo Dinh Diem in South Vietnam.

Even as the United States staked its own claim in South Vietnam, the overall Cold War picture continued to worsen. In 1957, the Soviets launched Sputnik, not only inaugurating the space race, but also demonstrating that their mighty ICBMs could now visit destruction on the United States in mere minutes. In 1959, Containment suffered another devastating defeat, this time much closer to home as Cuba fell to Communist revolution under Fidel Castro. The attempt to retake Cuba at the Bay of Pigs in 1961 failed miserably, leaving the new American President, John F. Kennedy, vulnerable. Only five months after entering office, Kennedy was bullied by Soviet Premier Nikita Khrushchev at their initial summit meeting in Vienna. The experience left Kennedy sobered, believing ever more certainly that checking the expansion of communism was paramount to the very survival of the United States. The shaken president confided to James Reston of *The New York Times* that "now we have a problem in making our power credible, and Vietnam is the place."[13]

COLD WAR FLASHPOINT/HOMEFRONT BATTLEGROUND

The exact details of the American road to war in Vietnam are in many ways secondary to a full understanding of the important context of superpower conflict that focused the attention of the United States on Vietnam in the first place. American power and prestige had been caught up in the fate of a regime in South Vietnam – an arguably inefficient regime with little overall chance of survival. As that regime lurched toward crisis and possible defeat, Kennedy (and later President Johnson as well) had to increase American involvement in the conflict to avoid the presumed disaster that would befall a renewed failure of Containment. The inexorable move to war under Kennedy was somewhat subtle, involving seemingly unending political machinations and a slow increase in support, in terms of money, equipment, and advisors for the ARVN. Even so, to most American observers South Vietnam seemed to exist perpetually on the edge of collapse amid ever-changing governments, a growing Viet Cong insurgency and an increasing threat of more direct intervention in the conflict by North Vietnam.

The final step on what was perhaps an inevitable American road to war fell to President Lyndon Johnson. Having achieved military freedom of action in the area

President John F. Kennedy and Soviet Premier Nikita Khrushchev in June 1961. Shaken by the failure of the Bay of Pigs invasion of Cuba, and under relentless pressure from the Soviet Premier, Kennedy remarked, "Now we have a problem in making our power credible, and Vietnam is the place." (Topfoto/AP)

President Lyndon Johnson. Though drawn into the Vietnam War, President Johnson was a "New Dealer" at heart and longed to make America more inclusive through implementation of his "Great Society" program. Johnson's focus on the homefront was instrumental in his efforts to fight a limited and flawed war in Vietnam. (Vietnam Archive)

by steering the Gulf of Tonkin Resolution through Congress, Johnson and his Secretary of Defense Robert McNamara in 1965 reacted to Viet Cong provocation and to credible intelligence that South Vietnam was in imminent danger of collapse by launching a sustained series of airstrikes on North Vietnam and beginning a graduated escalation of commitment of US ground forces to South Vietnam. It is rather ironic that it was President Johnson who decided to commit US ground forces to the conflict – the culmination of Cold War reasoning regarding the fate of South Vietnam. Johnson, in fact, was not a "Cold Warrior" by trade, which would bring a final and critical context of the Vietnam War into play.

President Lyndon Johnson was a Franklin D. Roosevelt "New Dealer" at heart, and longed to transform American society even further through the implementation of what he termed the "Great Society." Simply put, Johnson preferred to utilize the political capital inherent in the consensus that he inherited to achieve economic and social change in the United States, including the transformational Civil Rights Movement, rather than risk that political capital in war. Thus Johnson chose to fight the Vietnam War quietly and cheaply, relying on a draft and never calling up the National Guard or the reserves, rather than truly rallying the nation behind his geopolitical cause. As a result, amid the social turmoil of the Great Society, ranging from race riots to the rise of the counterculture, Americans also found themselves embroiled in a distant conflict that they did not fully understand. The myriad strains proved too much for the

American body politic to bear. Best exemplified by the turbulent events of 1968, Americans began to question why they were involved in a war that seemed to involve government prevarication at best and war crimes at worst. Americans wondered why their cities burned in racial violence in the summer, why the massive younger generation seemed to have spiraled out of control, why the Democratic National Convention exploded into a police riot, and why the economy was in a shambles.

One of the central maxims of the Vietnam War is that American soldiers "won all of the battles," but that "America lost the war." Though this maxim is somewhat misleading, it does accurately indicate that any effort fully to understand the American experience of the Vietnam War must involve a study of the "homefront context" of the conflict. Indeed, the American experience in Vietnam cannot be divorced from the swirling nexus of events that formed the troubled decade that was the 1960s.

CONCLUSION

In the end, then, the Vietnam War was a conflict of myriad complexities. It was a colonial war and a regional war. It was a total war and a limited war. It was a civil war, an insurgency, and a conventional war – and indeed it varied from one form to another at different times and in different places. It was a war in mountains, jungles, or open rice paddies, depending on the location of the battlefield. It was a war of high technology and no technology. It was a war of airpower and a war of footpower. It was a helicopter war and a brown-water war. It was a war won on the battlefield and lost on the homefront. One thing that the Vietnam War was not was simply an American war. It was a war of varying and mutable contexts – a chameleon of constant change. The greatest American failure in the conflict was a failure to understand context. For far too many important American planners, the Vietnam War had but one context – the black-and-white context of the Cold War. Such a context begged an inexorable, singular military logic and solution, one that was so overly simple that it proved to be no solution at all.

The main goal of this book is to place the Vietnam War in its proper contexts. Though *Rolling Thunder in a Gentle Land* cannot pretend to answer all of the nagging questions that still surround the conflict, it can at least begin to pose new questions that have too often been left unasked or ignored. Through the work of a unique collection of historians, journalists, and war participants *Rolling Thunder in a Gentle Land* also seeks to spark historical debate and research by searching for new contextual answers to questions that many historians had thought long since answered – sometimes calling for a needed revision of the historical orthodoxy of the conflict. Thus the present study proposes to take fresh looks at several of the most important aspects of the Vietnam War, and hopes to demonstrate that the field remains one of the most vibrant and important available to future historical inquiry of all types, by scholars and laymen alike who seek an opportunity to help define a war of unending complexity.

Chapter 2

The French Indochina War
1946–54

Martin Windrow

The United States' involvement in Vietnam may be traced most directly to two almost simultaneous victories by Asian Communist armies in late 1950. In mid-October, French troops suffered a shocking defeat along Route Coloniale 4 in northeast Tonkin, at the hands of Communist Viet Minh insurgents newly invigorated by Chinese aid; and in late November, Communist Chinese troops intervened massively in North Korea, launching their first offensive against US forces just south of the Korean–Chinese border. In the face of these two attacks – interpreted as warnings of a coordinated, aggressive Communist Chinese regional strategy – America reappraised her previously semi-hostile policy towards France's long struggle to reestablish her rule over her prewar colonies in Vietnam, Laos, and Cambodia, which had begun following the Japanese surrender in August 1945.

In the space available here, it is only possible to attempt the briefest of summaries of the main phases of this eight-year war – largely in North Vietnam, the arena of major operations – and of the character of the French forces involved.

THE BACKGROUND

The Chinese example had inspired a small Communist Party as one strand of the prewar Vietnamese nationalist movement; but after the crushing of two brief, bloody uprisings in 1930, most of the insurgent leadership – including Ho Chi Minh's Communists – operated from exile in China and elsewhere.

German victory over France in June 1940 left the collaborationist Vichy regime powerless to resist pressure on her Indochinese colonies from Germany's ally Japan. Japanese demands culminated in use of French airfields and *de facto* occupation in 1941, although the weak French colonial garrison retained nominal responsibility for internal security. By November 1941, the Japanese Southern Army were planning for the imminent attacks on Allied territories in East Asia and the Pacific from headquarters in Saigon.

Cho Ben, November 10, 1951: Operation *Tulipe* was the immediate road-opening overture to General de Lattre's ambitious Operation *Lotus*, to retake the city of Hoa Binh outside the southwest perimeter of the Red River Delta. Here legionnaires of III/13th Half-Brigade ride M5A1 Stuart and M24 Chaffee tanks of the 1st Light Cavalry *(Chasseurs à cheval)*. Note particularly the terrain each side of the narrow dirt road; these abrupt, heavily overgrown limestone peaks or *calcaires* are characteristic of Tonkin, and offered the Viet Minh magnificent cover for observation and ambush. On many occasions the French armor and artillery, confined to a two-vehicle front at most, had to fight from the road surface itself. (ECPA)

Ninh Hoa, January 1946: an M5A1 Stuart tank of 501st Combat Tank Regiment, 2nd Armored Division, negotiates the bank beside a blown bridge during General Leclerc's reoccupation of Cochinchina and southern Annam. Even those pre-1945 bridges which escaped sabotage were inadequate for most military traffic: few spans could take more than 6 tons' weight – less than that of an M8 armored car, an M3 half-track, or a loaded 2½-ton truck. (ECPA 11066-G10)

From 1942 to 1945, a Communist underground controlled from inside China was established in the forested hills of northern Tonkin (North Vietnam), under the in-country leadership of Vo Nguyen Giap – a talented student of Mao Tse-tung's Chinese Communist guerrilla doctrine. Giap risked only minimal attacks on the Japanese, however; the Vietnamese Communists – ostensibly members of a broad nationalist front, aided by Chiang Kai-shek's Chinese Nationalists and Western agencies – concentrated on creating safe base camps and a clandestine political infrastructure. Their relative freedom to pursue this task became absolute in March 1945 when the Japanese – their leverage over France destroyed by Allied advances in Europe – disarmed and imprisoned the French colonial garrison. The Communists exploited this power vacuum with extraordinary energy and success; and following the abrupt Japanese surrender in August 1945, Ho Chi Minh proclaimed the Democratic Republic of Vietnam in Hanoi on September 2. The Northern Communists worked ruthlessly to marginalize and eliminate all other parties to the nationalist coalition, and Giap's People's Army seized both Japanese and French arsenals. Meanwhile, in Cochinchina (South Vietnam), a separate Communist group, in loose association with Hanoi, exploited a situation of anarchy.

France had very few troops in Asia in 1945; the Potsdam Conference had decided that the Japanese north of the 16th Parallel (in Tonkin and northern Annam) would be disarmed by the Chinese Nationalists, while those in the South would be handled by the British. Both forces began to arrive in mid-September 1945; the British division was accompanied by a small French advance party, and

The French Indochina War

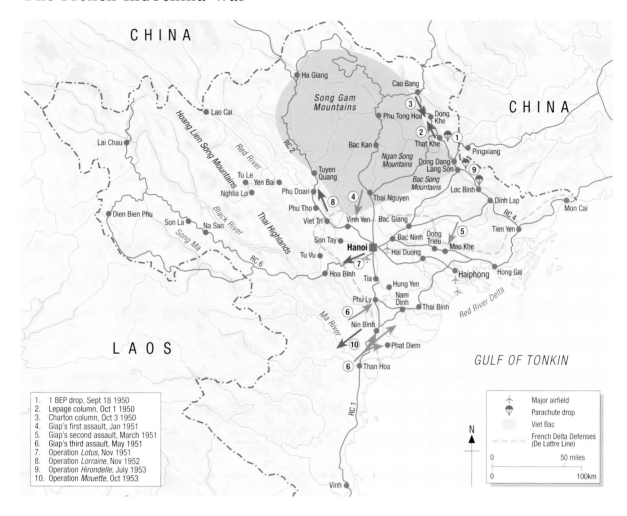

1. 1 BEP drop, Sept 18 1950
2. Lepage column, Oct 1 1950
3. Charton column, Oct 3 1950
4. Giap's first assault, Jan 1951
5. Giap's second assault, March 1951
6. Giap's third assault, May 1951
7. Operation *Lotus*, Nov 1951
8. Operation *Lorraine*, Nov 1952
9. Operation *Hirondelle*, July 1953
10. Operation *Mouette*, Oct 1953

Major airfield
Parachute drop
Viet Bac
French Delta Defenses (De Lattre Line)

0   50 miles
0   100km

over the next six months 30,000 French troops were gradually shipped in to Saigon to replace the British.

General Leclerc quickly established freedom of movement and control of the South's major towns and roads, but never the pacification of the countryside, where widespread banditry by many disparate groups continued. While the small Southern Communist units at first mainly targeted the Cao Dai and Hoa Hao[1] sectarian militias, general insecurity was endemic throughout the French-ruled South, and Communist links with the independent North steadily improved.

Meanwhile, in Tonkin the Communists were increasing their grip, unhindered by the Chinese Nationalist occupation, whose leaders were bribed to remain passive, and to hand over large numbers of weapons. While the Chinese delayed their withdrawal until after the opium harvest, Chiang Kai-shek agreed to French advance parties landing in the Red River Delta in March 1946. These established

North Vietnam, with some major operations mentioned in this chapter.

Southern Annam, 1946: a squad from the Legion's 2nd Foreign Infantry Regiment, with motley uniforms and British weapons, pose with locals outside their primitive "fort" – an old brick pagoda reinforced with logs. Such posts were seldom assaulted directly during the early years. One exception was Phu Tong Hoa on RC 3bis in northern Tonkin, whose earth walls were attacked by two Viet Minh battalions – with, for the first time, 75mm artillery – on the rainy night of July 25, 1948. The 104 men of 2nd Company, I/3rd Foreign Infantry Regiment were partly overrun, but eventually drove off their attackers after two hours of close-quarter fighting inside the fort. The only surviving officer – 2nd Lt. Bevalot, just 15 days in-country – still had 39 legionnaires on their feet when Lt. Col. Simon's relief column finally fought its way through multiple ambushes to arrive three days later. (Charles Milassin)

an uneasy control in an enclave around Haiphong and Hanoi, side by side with Giap's Communist units. While negotiations dragged on, the Communists built up their infrastructure and armed strength. They established large concealed base areas with substantial facilities – north of the Delta in the hills of the "Viet Bac" (the provinces of Cao Bang, Ha Giang, Tuyen Quang, Bac Kan, Thai Nguyen and Lang Son), and south of it in the "South Delta Base" (Thanh Hoa, Nghe An and Ha Tien provinces).

In May 1946 the Chinese Nationalists began to withdraw; French troops from the South tried to advance rapidly in their wake, but in the monsoon rains Giap moved a lot faster across country than the road-bound French. The Communists seized control of much of the North, wiping out the weak non-Communist parties; henceforward the name "Viet Minh," once that of the broad nationalist coalition, would be synonymous with the Communist movement. In November 1946, an armed clash between Viet Minh and French troops in Haiphong prompted the French commander-in-chief, General Jean-Étienne Valluy, to unleash his forces. Naval gunfire killed many civilians in Haiphong; street fighting soon spread to Hanoi, which the French controlled by December 21. Ho Chi Minh's government and Giap's troops – about 30,000 strong – withdrew to their base areas in the hills, and war broke out with varying intensity all over Vietnam.

THE COURSE OF THE WAR

Viet Minh regional forces (and a few independent regular units) in Cochinchina, the Central Highlands, and the narrow coastal belt of Annam were controlled and coordinated from Hanoi.[2] A constant war of guerrilla pinpricks all over South and Central Vietnam distracted and dispersed the French Far East Expeditionary Force (CEFEO), but before 1954 this fighting was less intense than that involving the Chu Luc – Giap's main force regulars in Tonkin. It was mainly in the North, where the Viet Minh had enjoyed their priceless 18 months of undisturbed preparation and *de facto* government, that major and identifiable campaigns were fought; and for that reason the following chronology focuses on events in that region, with the briefest accounts of only a few of the most significant actions.

1947

General Valluy launched major operations *Lea* (October) and *Ceinture* (November) against the Viet Bac, inflicting heavy losses; but the Viet Minh regrouped in the heartland. French posts were established on the Chinese frontier. Operation *Lison*, with Montagnard support, defeated VM in the

CEFEO security operations in the cultivated deltas posed mobility problems that would become familiar to US troops in the 1960s. These paratroopers of a Colonial battalion were photographed during Operation *Citron/Mandarine* in the Bamboo Canal sector of the southern Red River Delta in September–October 1951. The two phases involved 14 and 17 battalions respectively, of the Legion, Colonial paratroopers, engineers, artillery and Navy riverine forces. After 16 days, the CEFEO claimed 1,150 Viet Minh killed and numerous prisoners; French losses were 127 dead, 363 wounded, and 28 missing. (ECPA T51-165-R66)

A truck burns while smoke still rises from the cratered road; the fairly relaxed poses of the soldiers show that this is a banal mining incident, rather than an ambush. The roads serving the forts along the Tonkin/China frontier were subject to repeated sabotage and ambushes in 1948–50. The catastrophic destruction of the September 3, 1949 convoy over 6km of RC 4 at Luong Phai Pass was achieved by four VM battalions with mortar and light artillery support; 52 trucks and armored vehicles were destroyed and more than 100 troops killed, besides unknown numbers of civilians. By 1950 the cost of maintaining the posts along RC 4 between Lang Son and Cao Bang was becoming unsustainable. (SPI via Howard Simpson)

highlands between the Red and Black rivers which thereafter would remain quiet until fall 1951.

1948

No major maneuver operations took place; troops were dispersed in small posts for local security. The "War of the roads" was initiated on the Tonkin/China border, as the VM repeatedly ambushed convoys serving French posts along RC (Route Coloniale) 4 and RC 3bis, and mounted probing attacks on small garrisons.

1949

The French achieved some success in cutting rice supplies from the Red River and Mekong deltas to Viet Minh heartlands. Emperor Bao Dai's nominally independent government of South Vietnam was installed in March. By April VM regulars totaled 32 battalions, plus 137 of regional troops; Giap continued limited attacks on posts and communications in the highlands from March to July. In August the leak of a report by General Georges Revers, on the feasibility of withdrawal from the Tonkin border country to an enclave in the central Delta, caused a major scandal and delayed decision. Giap formed the first regular quasi-division, Regimental Group 308 in August. The "War of the roads" intensified; and VM 174th Regiment destroyed a major convoy on RC 4 on September 3. In China, the Communist victory led to the proclamation of the People's Republic in Beijing in October. The arrival of the first Chinese supplies allowed Giap to begin transforming 25,000 regional troops into regulars (see page 39, note 2), and to increase the size of battalions, adding heavy weapons.

"The disaster of RC 4" (September–October 1950)

The commander-in-chief, General Marcel-Maurice Carpentier, planned withdrawal from the main frontier garrison of Cao Bang and a "telescoping" of the line of posts southeastwards down RC 4, for early October. Giap forestalled him: his newly Chinese-trained and equipped regular battalions were to be blooded in a major operation to destroy Cao Bang and all the smaller frontier garrisons. Assembling up to 20 battalions with light artillery support, Giap struck on September 16.

Colonel Dang Van Viet's reinforced VM 174th and 209th regiments – about ten battalions, with artillery – wiped out the two-company Legion garrison from II/3rd Foreign Infantry at the key post of Dong Khe by early on September 18. This success placed the VM astride RC 4 well southeast of Cao Bang. On the same day, a Legion parachute battalion, 1BEP, was dropped at That Khe, the next main post to the south, but was unable to fight its way up to Dong Khe. On October 1, Lieutenant Colonel Lepage arrived up RC 4 with 3,500 Moroccan *Tirailleurs* and *Goumiers*, as well as local troops. With the Legion paras, this column pushed north once more. On October 3, Lieutenant Colonel Charton was ordered to start south from Cao Bang, with his 1,500 legionnaires (III/3rd Foreign Infantry) and *Goumiers*.

By the night of the 3rd, both columns had been blocked and torn apart in a series of major ambushes on the narrow, twisting road through forested mountains. Both were forced to abandon their vehicles and take to the jungle crags west of RC 4; by the time they managed to link up on the evening of October 7, both had taken very heavy casualties. The survivors were ordered to abandon their wounded with volunteer medics, and to disperse in squad-sized parties to infiltrate through the forest to That Khe, where three more companies of paratroopers were dropped on October 8. Before That Khe was abandoned on October 10, only some 300 men had reached the post. In all, only about 600 survivors of the Lepage and Charton columns and the paratroopers ever reached safety; many smaller post garrisons were wiped out, and of the 6,000-odd total casualties, some 4,800 were listed dead or missing.

This unprecedented French defeat caused panic in Hanoi. Other garrisons simply fled before any threat approached; and at Lang Son, the major depot for the whole border region, they abandoned enough weapons and ammunition to equip a complete VM division. Rear-echelon officers began burning documents and evacuating their families; and the whole Tonkin/China border territory was abandoned to the Viet Minh, from the border crossing at Lao Cai on the Red River in the west, to the coast just north of Mon Cai in the east.

1950

An assistance pact between the VM and Chinese was signed in April in Beijing; arms supplies allowed formation of the first VM support companies with recoilless guns (RCLs) and 120mm mortars. The VM introduced mass conscription in Tonkin and Annam in May, and regulars began training in Chinese camps, bringing the Chu Luc to about 50 regular battalions. The 304th, 308th, and 312th divisions were formed between January and October, with about 9,000 men each. In May the first US MAAG arrived in Saigon; the first modest aid followed in June. General Wei Guo-quing led a large Chinese military mission to the Viet Bac. In October a successful VM offensive on RC 4 led to French withdrawal from the Chinese border region, and a crisis of morale in October (see above).

Hanoi, October 23, 1951: General Jean de Lattre de Tassigny (left – wearing a mourning band for his only son, killed at Ninh Binh on May 29), reviews a Foreign Legion guard of honor with visiting US General Lawton Collins. De Lattre's skilful personal wooing of the US media during a visit to America played a part in securing public support for greatly increased US aid from 1951. (SHAPE)

General Boyer de Latour took command in Tonkin, forming *Groupes Mobiles* – motorized brigades with one artillery and three infantry battalions, an armor squadron, support, and services – in anticipation of VM assaults on the Red River Delta (November). General Jean de Lattre de Tassigny arrived as joint military C-in-C/high commissioner, and restored morale in December. The first VM artillery units undertook training in China.

1951

Between January and March the VM 316th, 320th and 325th divisions were formed. Giap launched major assaults on the Red River Delta's perimeters at Vinh Yen in January, Mao Khe and Dong Trieu in March and April, and the Day River, May–June. General de Lattre defeated all three attacks, killing nearly 20,000 VM regulars. As a result, Giap was severely criticized by the Party Central Committee for throwing away perhaps half his regular infantry. Throughout the year, the French worked to construct belts of concrete posts – known as the "De Lattre Line" – around the Delta perimeter and Haiphong base areas, and to improve airfields. The US aid flow increased massively. One VM division advanced south across the Red River against the post of Nghia Lo in the Thai Highlands in September, but in October was defeated by French paratroops and US-supplied aircraft. General de Lattre was diagnosed with inoperable cancer in October; he launched the Operation *Lotus* offensive via RC 6 and the Black River loop and recaptured Hoa Binh, southwest of the Delta in November. Giap assembled three divisions around Hoa Binh and access routes; other regulars infiltrated the Delta to aid regional regiments in December.

Defense of Na San air–ground base (November–December 1952)

Commanded by paratroop Colonel Gilles, 12 battalions of paratroopers, Legion, North African, and local infantry were flown in to fortify a ring of hills about three miles across, closely surrounding the airstrip. These were backed by an inner ring of strongpoints, with 120mm mortars and 105mm artillery. Misled as to the size and morale of the garrison, Giap launched assaults by elements of VM 308th, 312th, and 316th divisions on three nights between November 23 and December 2. Captured outer strongpoints were quickly retaken by counter-attacks from the inner ring; French artillery inflicted heavy casualties, and – thanks to the lack of Viet Minh howitzers or antiaircraft guns – the French Air Force maintained resupply and casualty evacuation flights. French losses were modest, and the air–ground base concept seemed vindicated; it would be repeated, notably at Dien Bien Phu.

1952

General Raoul Salan replaced General de Lattre as C-in-C, and launched a major operation to clear Hoa Binh access in January; the results of this attempt persuaded him to order withdrawal from Hoa Binh, which involved a hard fighting retreat through February and March. Security operations continued in the Delta, May–October. The VM extended conscription to Cochinchina during the summer; for the autumn–winter campaign season, Giap had some 110,000 regulars in 117 battalions, with heavy mortars, 75mm mountain guns, and RCLs. He sent the 308th, 312th, and 316th divisions south across the Red River to open a new front in the Thai Highlands in October; small French garrisons north of the Black River were soon eliminated. The French installed an "air–ground base" in the hills around the Na San airstrip south of the Black River in October–November. General Salan launched Operation *Lorraine*: 30,000 men thrust northwest up RC 2 from the Delta, aiming towards VM depots around Phu Doan, and across the rear lines of Giap's army in the Thai Highlands (October–November). This operation failed to divert Giap. Other VM units infiltrated the weakened Delta defenses, and *Lorraine* was forced to withdraw in November. In November–December the Na San air–ground base successfully repulsed major attacks (see above).

1953

Giap's three divisions continued to maneuver in North Laos, threatening Luang Prabang and the Plain of Jars (April), and forcing heavy French reinforcement, which strained reserves and airlift capacity. Giap decided to withdraw to base areas in May. General Henri Navarre replaced Salan as C-in-C in May. Major security operations in the Delta and Annam continued. In July, the paratroop Operation *Hirondelle*, against VM depots at Lang Son, was successful. China supplied the VM with 48 105mm howitzers by October. Operation *Mouette*, south out of the Delta, weakened the VM 320th Division in October–November. General Navarre's main object was to build up the Vietnamese National Army (ANV) in multi-division operations in southern Annam; but signs of a renewed VM threat to the Laos border, and the hope of drawing Giap into costly attacks against strong firepower under air cover, prompted Navarre to launch Operation *Castor* – airborne implantation of an air–ground base at Dien Bien Phu in the Thai Highlands, 180 miles from the Delta airfields – on November 20. Three-plus VM divisions, supported by 351st Heavy Division artillery, began the march to the Thai Highlands in response between November and January. The VM also undertook a diversionary attack from Annam west into central Laos, December–March.

1954

Between January and March, the Dien Bien Phu garrison, holding a perimeter approximately seven miles by three miles, was increased to some 10,000 men in 12 infantry battalions with artillery, tanks, and fighter-bombers. Sorties through the surrounding hills were driven in. General Navarre opened Operation *Atlante* in southern Annam on January 20, with 28 battalions, mainly ANV, planning to commit 53 battalions by May. A disappointing ANV performance contributed to the offensive bogging down. The VM responded by attacking weak French forces on the High Plateau around Kon Tum, Pleiku, and An Khe in February–March, and intensifying activity by Delta regionals. Dien Bien Phu fell in May (see opposite).

Substantive talks began at the Geneva Peace Conference on May 8. General Navarre was dismissed on June 4, followed closely by the fall of the French government on June 12. The new French Premier Mendèz-France declared his intention of achieving cease-fire within one month. Operation *Auvergne*, a French tactical withdrawal from the southern third of the Red River Delta, was

Tu Le, October 20, 1952: Major Marcel Bigeard's mixed-race 6th Colonial Parachute Battalion make a 40-mile forced march through the hills to the Black River, with two Viet Minh regular regiments at their heels. Dropped into the path of Giap's 1952 thrust through the Thai Highlands before its strength became clear, the unit was written off as lost; but they managed to shepherd small garrisons to safety, for the loss of about 100 paratroopers in rearguard actions. The Viet Minh stuck their heads on poles along the track, and left the wounded to die where they lay. (SPI via Howard Simpson)

Defense of Dien Bien Phu (March–May 1954)

With Chinese aid and advice, Giap assembled 28 battalions and 30,000 supporting troops in the hills around the camp, with 36 105mm, 24 75mm guns and 50 120mm mortars dug in and concealed, plus 36 37mm AA guns and numerous lighter weapons. The major bombardment opened with devastating effect on March 13. The French counter-battery plan failed badly; VM shelling and AA fire made the use of the airfield precarious from the first, and would close it altogether on March 28, stopping casualty evacuation and limiting all resupply and reinforcement to hazardous parachute drops. Sacrificial VM human-wave night assaults overran the first two outlying hill positions on March 13/14 and 14/15, and the perimeter proved too extended for counter-attacks. Piecemeal parachuted reinforcements brought the total garrison to about 15,000 by early May; this barely permitted the continued defense of the closer hill strongpoints against repeated assaults, and intense fighting lasted throughout April. Viet Minh losses were around 30,000, mostly to the camp's stubborn artillery; this attrition prompted the call-up of untrained boys from as far south as south Annam. Despite this, French air support proved ineffective, and resupply steadily failed as the perimeter shrank. On May 7, the camp fell, and the 9,000 surviving troops passed into captivity.

successful, but *Groupes Mobiles* 100 and 42 were defeated in the Central Highlands in June–July. The cease-fire took effect on July 27; under the Geneva armistice terms, France was required to evacuate North Vietnam to the 17th Parallel on October 9. The VM released its French prisoners between August and October; of the 9,000 prisoners taken from Dien Bien Phu, only about 3,900 survived four months' captivity.

1955–56

In May 1955, Vietnam was partitioned at the 17th Parallel, between the Democratic Republic in the North and the new Republic of Vietnam in the South. In October, Ngo Dinh Diem was named president of the Republic of Vietnam with US support. The last French troops left South Vietnam in April 1956.

STRENGTH AND COMPOSITION OF FRENCH FORCES

To occupy and pacify the whole Indochinese peninsula – North, Central, and South Vietnam, Laos, and Cambodia – the CEFEO had only about 50,000 men at the end of 1946. In 1947, when the World War II enlistees of the initial reoccupation force had to be repatriated just as campaigning began in Tonkin, the CEFEO faced a crisis of manpower. One central difference between the French and US expeditionary armies was that the former was restricted, by legal and political constraints, to volunteers: no French conscripts could be sent to Indochina unwillingly. Metropolitan Army conscription provided France's NATO forces in Germany, and the only conscripts who went to Vietnam were individual volunteers who chose a tropical war over the safe boredom of European garrisons. During 1949, the CEFEO numbered about 150,000; strength peaked at about

190,000 by late 1951, and fell to about 174,000 by mid-1952, where it remained until the end of the war. To achieve even these figures had required raising units from a number of different sources, of variable value.

From the first, this "dirty war" was widely unpopular in a France demoralized, impoverished, and politically divided by the traumas of defeat, occupation, and liberation in World War II. On the one hand, the French Communist Party was a powerful force in postwar politics and the labor unions; left-wing propaganda and obstruction were relentless. On the other, their recent humiliations made conservative French politicians and soldiers hotly determined not to compromise over the reestablishment of France's power and prestige in her overseas empire.

While some (usually non-infantry) units of the Metropolitan Army were sent to Indochina, with regular cadres leading individual volunteers from among the conscripts, the majority of white French infantrymen, paratroopers, and gunners were provided by the volunteer Colonial regiments – a separate organization, long-established to garrison Asian and sub-Saharan African colonies. Once in Indochina, all these units recruited large numbers of Indochinese, who soon came to provide up to half of their enlisted men, a proportion of senior NCOs, and a few officers. The Colonial regiments had a long-founded culture of energy and independence; many units maintained a high combat reputation until the very end, particularly the Colonial parachute battalions but also mixed-race infantry units. Black units – most of them designated *Tirailleurs Sénégalais*, and raised in France's West and Central African colonies – also belonged to the Colonial corps, but were not of comparable value. They suffered from a generally lower quality of leadership and from discriminatory treatment; a few units did well, but most were wastefully neglected, being dispersed in static defenses.

These units are not to be confused with the *Armée d'Afrique*, which historically had garrisoned the North African colonies, and which also provided many units for the CEFEO. The regular infantry of the *Régiments de Tirailleurs Algériens* and *Marocains*, and the light infantry of the smaller *Tabors de Goumiers Marocains*, were largely recruited among the robust Berber highlanders of the North African mountains. Products of an age-old warrior clan culture, they had distinguished themselves in Italy in 1943–44. Each unit had a minority of native officers and senior NCOs and, when well led by white cadres sympathetic to their culture, they proved effective, at least up to 1951; thereafter morale and reliability began to decline.

Some 35 percent of the CEFEO's European manpower and the majority of its white infantry was provided by the Foreign Legion (Légion Étrangère). By 1952 the Legion had nearly 20,000 men in Indochina, in twelve infantry battalions, a light armor regiment, two amphibious tractor battalions, two parachute battalions, and numerous specialist support and service companies. About half of them were Germans; in the early years a majority were World War II veterans, but by about 1952 most of these had served out their five-year contracts. However, many veteran German senior NCOs re-enlisted, continuing to provide excellent leadership in units which might include men of dozens of nationalities with very

Mon Cai, January 18, 1951: legionnaires peer from a watchtower in the Red River Delta defenses. This example seems to have concrete skinning over old brick, and predates the massive "De Lattre Line" construction effort later that year, which was prompted as much by fears of a Communist Chinese conventional invasion as by hopes of stopping Viet Minh infiltration. A 235-mile arc of 1,200 prefabricated concrete blockhouses, proof against 155mm shells, were built in groups of three to six around the outer perimeter of the Delta; an inner belt 35 miles long protected the Haiphong base areas. This program required some 2,950 metric tons of concrete to be delivered every single day for a year. It completely absorbed French engineer assets and resources and much of the local economy, and was a huge financial drain. (Képi Blanc)

variable military backgrounds. The Legion's long and fiercely prized culture of discipline, self-sufficiency, and loyalty to the corps rather than France herself, was generally successful in turning this raw material into first-class infantry. They were at their best in the major operations of 1951–54.

At the height of the war in 1953, the CEFEO's regular ground units numbered about 52,000 Frenchmen, 30,000 North Africans, 19,000 Foreign Legion, 18,000 West Africans, and 53,000 Vietnamese locally recruited to the Colonial, Legion, and few Metropolitan units. There were an additional 55,000-plus irregular local auxiliaries in attached or autonomous units, giving a grand total of some 228,000 men. Frenchmen thus represented less than 25 percent of the total, though the

Evacuation airlift from Na San airfield, second week of August 1953. Operations in the almost roadless Thai Highlands in 1952–54 depended fundamentally on air transport, including requisitioned civilian freighters like this British Bristol 170. Before the Viet Minh acquired 37mm AA guns in 1954 the insertion, maintenance, and extraction of "air–ground bases" proved practical, although the evacuation of Na San – considered no longer useful – forced the garrison to abandon a great deal of equipment: 34 vehicles and more than 300 tons of supplies and fuel. Reportedly, not all of this materiel was destroyed in time, and some was salvaged by the ever-resourceful Viet Minh. (ECPA TONK 53-6202)

great majority of the leadership; and about half the troops facing the Viet Minh in French uniform were actually Vietnamese. Some of these had, inevitably, been infiltrated by VM agents, but others boasted a genuine pride in membership of prestigious French units. Their quality covered a wide spectrum, depending largely upon that of their French cadres – which was often high.

In 1951 General de Lattre energetically sponsored formation of the Armée Nationale Vietnamienne. He and all subsequent C-in-Cs were sharply aware of the need to create a parallel Vietnamese force to take over static defense and local security tasks, freeing CEFEO assets for a maneuver force strong enough to confront Giap's regular divisions. (In January 1954 the Delta's internal posts alone were still tying down some 82,000 CEFEO personnel.) Although on paper the ANV exceeded 160,000 men by the end of 1953, the combat value of its units varied widely, from good to useless. Most conscripts were unwilling and sketchily trained, many of the Vietnamese officer corps were half-hearted (if not actually corrupt), and the French cadres were withdrawn from most units far too soon.

The shortage of solid junior leaders bedeviled the CEFEO. While replacements for French troops repatriated after their two-year tours were routinely rotated to Indochina, replacements for battle and other casualties – remarkably – were not: successive C-in-Cs had to beg and argue for additional drafts to make up these annual losses (which amounted in 1952 to 587 officers, 1,756 senior NCOs, and 2,132 enlisted men). The multinational nature of the CEFEO, the steady drain of casualties, and the effort from 1951 to raise the ANV overwhelmed the available numbers of French junior officers and senior NCOs; by January 1954 some nine percent of total French manpower were serving as cadres with Indochinese units. Many infantry battalions had little more than half the 18 French officers and 80 senior NCOs that they needed; the average age of battalion officers was too high (in 1953 the average lieutenant was 32), and many were transfers from non-infantry branches.

Apart from its weakness in manpower, the CEFEO before at least 1951 suffered from chronic shortages of all types of equipment and weapons. France's NATO commitments enjoyed priority, and her armed forces were strictly forbidden from diverting any of the limited flow of US aid pre-1951 to fight a colonial war of which the US government disapproved. The higher direction of the war was mired in a confusion of political and bureaucratic responsibilities, and procurement of all necessities was lethargic and inefficient. For the soldiers it was a beggar's war, fought with elderly, patched-up, and hand-me-down weapons, vehicles, and uniforms. In 1946–51 units received a "lucky dip" of small arms and crew-served weapons, of different nationalities, calibers and ages, and a virtual museum of war-weary and improvised vehicles. By 1953 US aid had greatly improved this situation, but this gain was counterbalanced by Chinese aid to the Viet Minh.

Lack of mobility

Operations throughout the war were restricted by the rudimentary road networks upon which the CEFEO was dependent for virtually all movement apart from limited riverine and coastal insertions. Narrow dirt roads formed tenuous corridors through the hills, forests, swamps, and paddies, constantly vulnerable to sabotage and ambush, and to flooding during the summer monsoon. Few airfields other than those around Hanoi/Haiphong and Saigon were capable of taking heavy traffic, and the transport fleet was quite inadequate for strategic support; even in mid-1953 it totaled just 49 C-47s and 15 Junkers Ju 52 trimotors in the whole of Vietnam. The US loan of a few C-119s had only temporary benefits. The helicopter played no part in transporting troops and materiel; even by 1954 the numbers of French helicopters in Indochina could be counted in tens, and these were dedicated almost exclusively to casualty evacuation.

The French command

All French C-in-Cs were crippled by France's political instability (there were 19 administrations during the war, none of them with any truly coherent Indochinese policy); and their subordinate commanders were hampered as much by the lack of continuity in strategic planning as by shortage of resources. Some C-in-Cs concentrated on Tonkin, where Giap's main force regulars, slowly maturing in their safe refuges, represented a major long-term threat to the northern colonial heartland of the Red River Delta. Others attempted to wrestle with the southern Viet Minh's constant guerrilla activity in Cochinchina, the colony's economic engine room. None were free from political and commercial pressures when making these choices.

In 1946–50, most French generals – denied our hindsight, or any recent historical model – lived in a mental world shaped by prewar colonial experience, and by the European campaigns of 1943–45. Few of them recognized a wholly new type of adversary – though this failure to grasp that they faced a people in arms, inspired by a national idea, was not universal: by the time he left Indochina early in 1947, General Leclerc was already advising negotiation at any price. His aide Jean Lacouture would write: "I never met any well-informed man down there who had any doubt about the necessity of negotiating the conditions for an inescapable Vietnamese emancipation with the Viet Minh, who were the only serious spokesmen." Such realism was not widespread, however.

Most French regular soldiers did not at first rate the guerrillas as dangerous enemies: they were back-shooters who murdered the unwary and the isolated, but no threat to combat-ready units. Before 1951, professional officers remained convinced that if they could bring the VM to battle then they could defeat them without difficulty, and those who served in the South failed to recognize the much greater threat posed by Giap's nascent regular army in Tonkin.

Morale and effectiveness

Chronic guerrilla activity stretched most of the CEFEO throughout Indochina as "sector" troops, scattered in groups of small, usually one-company posts along vulnerable roads, to provide an illusory local security. This dispersal and defensive posture were bad for the unit cohesion, morale, and efficiency even of good troops like the Legion, and had worse effects on African and local units. The modest reserve of "intervention" units was largely restricted to a few individual parachute battalions based at Hanoi and Saigon, initially dependent on a couple of dozen Junkers Ju 52s. For tactical air support, the CEFEO initially had only a handful of old World War II fighters, inherently unsuitable for the task. (Even when US aid reinforced and updated the Air Force, tactical support was handicapped by the lack of the necessary ground/air forward control links, and by a constant shortage of trained aircrews.)

The routine missions of sector troops included "road-opening" patrols, to neutralize overnight mining and to repair the endlessly sabotaged roads and bridges. In the thickly inhabited and cultivated deltas, traffic and small guardposts were repeatedly attacked by guerrillas. Sector troops responded with sweeps which rarely brought the VM to combat, but cost a constant hemorrhage of casualties from sniping, mining, and boobytraps. Exhausted and frustrated, the troops were provoked into brutalities; indiscriminate use of firepower in inhabited areas, and the destruction of villages under an official policy of collective retaliation for guerrilla activity, were effective recruiting sergeants for the Viet Minh.

The shock of the defeat on RC 4 and the retreat from the Tonkin Highlands in October 1950 was stunning, and brought a new realism to the French view of the Chu Luc. In 1951 the overconfident Giap handed General de Lattre morale-building victories by his premature assaults on the Delta; thereafter US material aid allowed the assembly of more motorized *Groupes Mobiles*, and the paratroopers too were gathered into three-battalion *Groupes Aéroportées*. However, Giap's error in committing his regulars to open-country fighting would not be repeated; and the 1951 victories in turn bred French overconfidence in the

potential of their new motorized and airborne brigades, armor, and airpower in 1952–54. In fact, despite their often high fighting quality, the *Groupes Mobiles* remained fatally road-bound once they ventured into close country outside the Delta. The *Groupes Aéroportées* were still capable of only hit-and-run operations, limited by an improved but still inadequate airlift capacity; and the Air Force ground-attack squadrons were too few, and too poorly controlled, to make a decisive difference. In any case, by the time the CEFEO had built up these new assets they had lost too much ground, too many men, and too many battles; and the disaster at Dien Bien Phu finally broke France's national will.

* * *

The imminent partition of Vietnam prompted at least 600,000 refugees from Tonkin and northern Annam to flee to the South during 1954, the majority of them Roman Catholics. These co-religionists were favored by President Diem's new US-supported regime, thus aggravating the rifts in an already disunited society.

In the North, the establishment of a Communist government was far from a bloodless process. In 1955–56, the regime pursued an ill-considered ideological program, brutally destroying age-old social structures in the Delta lowlands and the tribal highlands alike. Widespread famine followed, and serious armed uprisings south of the Red River Delta at the end of 1956 were ruthlessly crushed. The death toll in the first two years of Ho Chi Minh's government is variously estimated at between 30,000 and 100,000 men, women and children.

Na San, December 1, 1952: 3rd Colonial Parachute Battalion successfully counter-attack strongpoint PA24, captured the previous night by Viet Minh Regiment 102 "Ba Vi" from Giap's crack 308th Division "Viet Bac." During this assault the courageous photographer Jean Péraud – who would not survive capture at Dien Bien Phu in May 1954 – accompanied Captain Hovette's 23rd (Indochinese) Company. The tactics employed successfully at Na San failed at Dien Bien Phu. The latter was a much larger perimeter, overlooked by Viet Minh-held hills, and attacked by a larger army newly equipped with 105mm howitzers and 37mm antiaircraft guns. The consequent closing of the airfield at Dien Bien Phu proved decisive. (ECPA T52-211-R53)

Chapter 3

Fight for the Long Haul
The War as seen by a Soldier in the People's Army of Vietnam

Bui Tin

THE REALITY OF COMMUNISM

The Communist Party regarded the People's Army of Vietnam (PAVN) as its most salient instrument. In its interpretation of Marxism and Lenin–Stalinist doctrine, the Party considered the class struggle as the engine for developing society, and it regarded violence as the midwife for bringing this new society to life. The Party followed the teaching of Mao: "power comes from the barrel of a gun." The Communists regarded armed struggle, from guerrilla warfare to regular combat with main force units of the People's Army, as the determinant tool of the proletariat and the Party. One uses this tool to seize power.

Ho Chi Minh came to political maturity in Moscow, where he lived from 1924 to 1938, aged 34 to 48, under the absolute power of Stalin. This was when the majority of Stalin's bloodiest purges took place. Here Ho developed his belief that the Communist Party was the sole authentic revolutionary force and that all other parties were reactionary forces that needed to be removed.

Applying this precept, Ho Chi Minh in 1945 viewed with suspicion all the Vietnamese political parties which were then competing with the Communists. These included the Vietnam Nationalist Party, Dai Viet (Great Viet), Duy Dan (People's Party), Vietnam Cach Menh Dong Minh (Vietnam Revolutionary Party), Lap Hien (Constitutional Party), and the Trotskyists. In spite of their having fought in the anti-colonial resistance war against France, these parties were regarded by Ho as reactionary forces, as traitors and lackeys of foreign countries, which had to be eliminated. He considered the dictatorship of the Party as the only legitimate patriotic force, and believed that it alone should raise an army and direct the military struggle.

The period of the resistance war against France (1945–54) was the stage on which the Communist Party displayed its patriotism. As it strove to achieve

North Vietnamese soldiers entering Saigon on April 30, 1975. (Topfoto/Roger-Viollet)

Military zones of South Vietnam

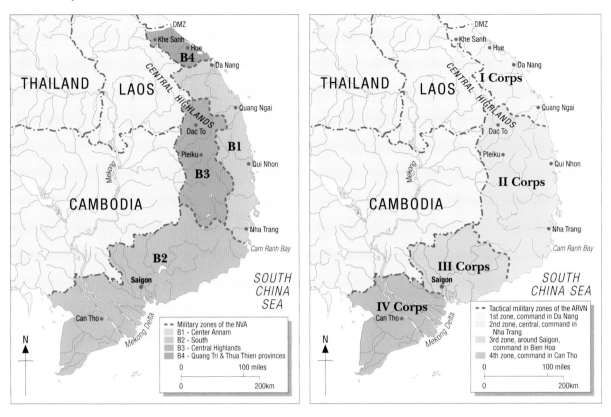

independence and unity for the people, the Party promoted cooperation among social classes and religious groups. It hid the proletarian nature of the Party and the Communist view of "religion as the opium of the people." It also hid its plans for land reform until 1953, and its intention to eradicate capitalists and discriminate against ethnic minorities.

Regarding foreign relations, the Party accentuated relations with other European colonies (French, English, Dutch, Portuguese) and non-aligned countries. The Vietnamese resistance against France was seen as avant-garde in a worldwide movement to liberate the European colonies, a position that helped to disguise the Communist nature of the struggle. After the Geneva conference, thanks to the provision allowing for the free movement of people between North and South Vietnam, more than a million and perhaps as many as 1.6 million northerners moved South. The majority were government officials, well-to-do families, intellectuals, and Catholics. Fewer than 100,000 southerners regrouped in the North, despite the fact that three million people lived in the Southern liberated Zone V and in Nam Bo. The Communists, presuming that war would take place and that the scheduled national elections mandated by the Geneva Accords would not be held, had issued directives to hide caches of weapons in the

Southern mountains and jungles, and had arranged for thousands of cadres to remain in the South.

After the mandated election did not take place in July 1956, the Party Central Committee secretly passed Resolution 15 in 1959, which called for waging war across the land, building the Ho Chi Minh Trail, and sending small, armed groups and weapons to the South. At the same time, the Party was creating a fuss about Saigon breaking the terms of the Geneva Accords, canceling the general election, and executing Viet Cong sympathizers. It condemned the United States for replacing France as the new colonial power intent on ruling the South.

Hiding behind the People's Liberation Front and the Liberation Army, and then, later, behind the Provisional Revolutionary Government, Hanoi always pretended that the fight against the imperialist lackeys was a spontaneous, home-grown movement. As part of this propaganda ploy, the Communists created two parties (the Labor Party and the People's Revolutionary Party) and two armies (the People's Army and the Liberation Army), but Hanoi always explained, at least to those inside their ranks, that there was only *one* Party and *one* Army. Hanoi never officially admitted that the People's Army of Vietnam was operating in the South, since this was prohibited by the Geneva conventions. They justified their prevarications by arguing that the 17th Parallel was a temporary demarcation, not a national boundary. Since a people cannot invade their own country, the PAVN soldiers in the South were presumed to be fighting on their own soil.

In the end there were two different, but closely combined, wars in the South. One involved the PAVN and one involved the NLF, and both need further explanation.

THE NATIONAL LIBERATION FRONT

In the beginning, the war was largely a guerrilla action. The terms "Viet Cong" and "VC" were used by the South Vietnamese and Americans to describe members of the National Liberation Front, which consisted of guerrillas or local-area Southern soldiers and secret agents. Throughout the war, Hanoi disguised the fact that the NLF was controlled from the North. In doing this, they intended to make everyone believe that these Southern forces were an indigenous, homegrown movement which had no direct connection with the Vietnamese Communist Party and the Communist internationalist movement. This was part of Hanoi's general strategy to hide the true Communist nature of its regime.[1]

This strategy was one example of the North's successful use of psychological warfare. It allowed them to claim that the NLF forces in the South were purely legitimate and patriotic. Hanoi, while maintaining this strategy, could plausibly deny that the NLF was directly connected to the Communist movement and proletariat internationalism.

The PAVN

The war in the South began as a guerrilla war, utilizing NLF forces. In time it became a war fought by the PAVN. It is important to understand how this

The last US troop withdrawal at Tan Son Nhat air base in Saigon on March 29, 1973. Bui Tin, Chief of the North Vietnamese observer team speaking with the last American soldier to board the plane, Army Master Sergeant Max Beilke. Tin said to Beilke, "I hope you return as a tourist, you are certainly welcome!" In a sad twist, Beilke was killed at the Pentagon on September 11, 2001. (Bui Tin collection)

transformation took place, and a brief history of North Vietnamese forces in the Vietnam War follows.

April 1959–December 1963

Hanoi recruited soldiers who lived in the South and regrouped them to the North in 1954.[2] The majority of them made up the 350th, 324th, and 325th divisions. Broken into smaller platoons and companies, they were given crash courses for two to three months in the Phu Quy forest (Nghe An) and then sent back into South Vietnam. Together with the local forces, they made up the original core of the military forces of the National Liberation Front, known as the Viet Cong.

December 1963–January 1968

After President Diem was assassinated in 1963, Hanoi sent improved People's Army units to the South, including 12 battalions and eight regiments.[3] These soldiers, commanded by General Nguyen Chi Thanh and other generals such as Le Trong Tan, Chu Huy Man, Tran Do, and Hoang Can, greatly fortified the regional command structure and increased tenfold the antitank and armored-vehicle weapons and other weapons used against helicopters, as well as the machine-guns (57mm) available to the Southern forces.

After the Tet Offensive, February 1968–1971

The troops in the South suffered debilitating losses during the Tet Offensive. Their bases in the countryside and cities were destroyed. The NLF was virtually eliminated as a fighting force, and it could no longer replenish its ranks, due to the speed of the South's and USA's pacification and counter-attacks. The North had lost the initiative in the war. Troops lost at the village and district levels had to be replaced by soldiers from the North. While much of the fighting was taking place outside of South Vietnam, in Cambodia and southern Laos, there were no great battles in the South.

1972

After the US had withdrawn four-fifths of their troops, there was a great change in troop strength between the two sides compared to previous years. South Vietnamese air and artillery firepower were definitively reduced. The North began sending entire divisions to the South, along with heavy artillery and hundreds of tanks, which were deployed on three battle fronts: Loc Ninh, An Loc, north of Saigon; the Central Highlands, around Dakto and Pleiku; and Quang Tri-Thua Thien, around Dong Ha and Cam Lo. The Quang Tri-Thua Thien front was commanded directly by the Central High Command. For the duration of the three offensives (February, May, and September) the situation remained inconclusive. Hanoi did not succeed in its intended goal to seize and hold one or two provinces on each front. Quang Tri City was captured, but then retaken by the Southern army. The North was only able to hang on to one district at each front: Loc Ninh, Tan Canh-Dakto, and Cam Lo.

After the Paris Peace Accord, February 1973–December 1974

Following the signing of the Paris Peace Accord, the United States withdrew its troops, exchanged prisoners, and drastically reduced aid to the South. No longer being bombed, the North enjoyed a period of peace. In August 1974, after Richard Nixon had resigned due to the Watergate scandal, Hanoi decided to vastly increase her military strength in the South, deploying her entire arsenal and mounting an offensive aimed at ending the war with a decisive victory. The number of liberation troops in the South was doubled compared to 1970. All the Southern militarized zones possessed units of division strength. In addition, there were still four infantry divisions in place in the North, along with three more infantry divisions in the process of being created, with the ultimate aim of building four army corps (each corps possessing three divisions and one armored brigade). During this time, the Ho Chi Minh Trail was widened and opened to truck traffic. This newly improved supply route to the South doubled the speed at which ARVN outposts could be surrounded and destroyed, such as Thuong Duc in Quang Nam province; Tong Le Chan, in the Central Highlands; and Dong Xoai, east of Saigon.

December 1974–April 30, 1975

During the final five months of the war, the transport and supply highway was upgraded. A Cuban construction crew was brought in, along with heavy road-building equipment. The oil pipeline was extended to Loc Ninh. The first battle to kick off the offensive was staged at Dong Xoai. This was followed by battles at Phuoc Long, and after that, at Ban Me Thuot, on March 10, which led to President Nguyen Van Thieu's decision to abandon the Central Highlands. This launched the total offensive, leading to the fall of Hue, then Da Nang, then Nha Trang and Cam Ranh, and then Xuan Loc. Finally, the Ho Chi Minh campaign began at 0:00 hours on April 29, with four army corps moving to take over Saigon on April 30. The last battle in the war, fought in Long Xuyen (Chau Doc province), ended at 9:00 am on May 2, 1975.

TYPICAL SOLDIERS FIGHTING FOR NORTH VIETNAM

Due to the nature of the Vietnam War, the North Vietnamese fielded two fundamentally different types of soldier, both of which are explained below.

The typical PAVN soldier

He is called "Bac," meaning "North" and comes from a peasant background.[4] Bac is of small build, weighing about 46 kilos (105lb), and about 1.54m tall. He completed the seventh grade (middle school), and has never before traveled outside his village. He has good endurance, from working in the fields as a young boy, herding buffaloes, tilling the soil, planting rice, and watering the paddies in the sun and rain, knee-deep in mud. A member of the Communist Youth League (the only youth organization in North Vietnam), he "volunteered" for the Army when he was 17, as did all of his classmates. His parents were worried, knowing that Bac had a good chance of being sent to fight in the South. On average, only two or three of every ten soldiers who went South came back. Yet they managed to wear smiles on the day he left his village – when flowers and heroic songs and

Bui Tin on the Ho Chi Minh Trail, in the west of Binh Dinh province in September 1971. US bombs were dropped from high-speed planes flying at more than 2,000m onto a trail "as thin as a thread," only 5m wide. Therefore it is unsurprising that only 0.23 percent of the US bombs dropped actually hit the Trail. (Bui Tin collection)

high-sounding speeches were given. Their smiles gave way to tears and suffering only in private, when the night came.

Bac spent eight months in intensive training, learning to use rifles and light machine-guns, throwing grenades, detonating mines, killing opponents in close combat with a bayonet. He went on marches three times a week, each 25 kilometers long, first carrying 20-, then 30-kilo knapsacks. In his last two months of training, he was deployed to the mountains and forests, spending long, stormy nights in the monsoon rains.

Bac was indoctrinated by political cadres every Saturday morning for two-hour lessons on patriotism, on the political values and heroic deeds of the Communist Party, on Uncle Ho, on the high discipline and morality of the People's Army soldier, on socialist doctrine, on the Soviet Union and its socialist allies, on imperialism, which was now in its death throes, and on his ignoble and poverty-stricken Southern brethren, who were enslaved under the yoke of the Americans.

Every morning and afternoon Bac listened to the People's Army radio station and read the People's Army newspaper for about half an hour. When he was still in the North, Bac periodically received news from his family. After his deployment to the South, contact with his family was cut off.

The division between North and South Vietnam was demarcated along the narrow Ben Hai river at the 17th Parallel. What was supposed to be a temporary partition, established by the Geneva Accords of 1954, came to be known as the demilitarized zone. There was no contact across the zone, no connecting roads or highways, no mail delivery or telephone lines between the two sides. Once a unit of the People's Army had crossed the demarcation line, there was nowhere for them to run to. They had no home base to fall back to. They might get lost, die in the jungle, or be captured from the rear, but their retreat was cut off.

Indoctrination and persuasion, combined with stealthy coercion techniques, were the two basic approaches used to build the fighting spirit of the People's Army. When surrounded by ARVN forces, frightened under B-52 bombardments, losing his wits as his unit's position was destroyed six or seven times over, witnessing his comrades' bodies scattered over the battlefield, Bac had no choice but to advance to his post and continue fighting, even when facing what he knew could be the last minute of his life.

The typical Viet Cong soldier

He is called "Nam" and is a peasant from the Mekong Delta. His father and uncles were all engaged in the nine-year anti-colonial resistance against the French. Nam's revolutionary roots "evolved from the maquis" in 1946. After finishing middle school, Nam was recruited by his uncle, who had been liberated in the "general uprising" at the end of 1959. Nam's uncle was an "infiltrated" Communist Party member, who had previously been a high school teacher. He owned a small radio that he used expressly for listening to broadcasts from Hanoi every morning and evening, always taking the time afterwards to discuss current events with the young people in the village. Nam was enlisted into a Viet Cong guerrilla unit in his rural district and trained for three months in using guns, grenades, anti-personnel mines, and antitank mines. He learned the art of camouflage and how to observe and follow ARVN and US military movements. He became particularly adept at night maneuvers and ambushes.

When coordinating with PAVN units from the North and with other regular divisions from the military region, Nam, along with his unit, was responsible for reporting on the situation in his area and describing the surrounding topography. He scouted enemy outposts and analyzed the standard operating procedures of the troops in his area. He fought, ate, and slept with his comrades from the North. He became the eyes and ears for these friendly units; he was responsible for carrying off the wounded, burying the dead, and hiding captured military equipment and other war booty.

PAVN TACTICS

Hanoi exploited the political weakness of the Army of the Republic of Vietnam by condemning it as a "lackey" army, created by the French. Their high-ranking officers, trained by the colonialists, carried the stain of French defeat at Dien Bien Phu. From the viewpoint of Vietnamese society, the ARVN was a compromised political force.

By contrast, the motto of the liberation forces was "Fight for the long haul; control and concentrate on the high point in each battle." Soldiers were directed to fight a swift and intimate battle on a well-prepared battlefield. They should isolate the vulnerable points of the enemy, study them well, and rehearse the battle in advance, if possible. They should concentrate their forces and strike swiftly to overwhelm an enemy that might have two, three, or even four times as much manpower and firepower. The attack should be based on the element of surprise and timed to occur during the night, ending before dawn.

After the Gulf of Tonkin incident, the US Air Force began to bombard North Vietnam, and American troops prepared to land in South Vietnam in 1965. Considering this a grave matter, the Central High Command met to discuss the situation in December 1964. Everyone agreed that the upcoming war would be difficult. Uncertain of the outcome, General Van Tien Dung, the commander of the Joint Chiefs of Staff, discussed the parallels to Korea in 1951 and how the introduction of American troops there had changed the situation, making it unfavorable to the North Korean Army, which had retreated all the way to the Chinese border. The military leaders wondered if they could prevail. The average height of the American soldiers was 1.70m. They weighed 65 kilos – far more than the average Vietnamese. They were well fed and well supplied. Their firepower overwhelmed what was available to the North. The PAVN had to develop tactics that would counter these advantages.

General Giap tried to reassure his colleagues, but he himself was obviously worried. He thought the United States was prepared to send between 100,000 and 150,000 troops and so the war was going to be hard-fought. The PAVN needed to prepare well for the first battle, to test their strength and draw important lessons from it. They needed to fight in close quarters, strike swiftly, and take advantage of the element of surprise. If the United States sent more than 200,000 troops, the situation would become critical. With this American troop strength alone, they would have more soldiers than the PAVN regular forces. At that time, no one could predict that within two years the American troop strength would exceed half a million.

General Nguyen Chi Thanh volunteered to go South to write a military manual to counter the American troops and find a solution to this threat. Headquartered in the Tay Ninh forest, General Thanh assumed his role as representative of the Politburo, overseeing the regional command of General Tran Van Tra. General Thanh commanded and closely observed the first battles against the Americans in the Western Highlands, Zone 5, and then in eastern Nam Bo. After these battles, he dictated his Five Military Essays, each more than 10,000 words long. The Essays were transcribed by Major Mai Quang Ca, General Thanh's personal secretary, and cover the following topics:

1) The United States is Rich but Not Strong (February 1965);
2) The Bitter Dry Season of the American Army (written after the battles of Dat Cuoc, on August 11, Dau Bang, on December 11, and Pleime-Ia Drang, in November 1965, from which the movie *We Were Soldiers* was drawn);
3) Take Them by the Belt and Kill Them (February 1966);

From right, Bui Tin the journalist/ highest officer accepts the surrender of General Duong Van Minh "Big Minh," and his government. Fourth from right is Prime Minister Va Van Mau. Photo taken April 30, 1975 at the Presidential Palace in Saigon, the war being finally over. (Bui Tin collection)

4) Destroying their Pacification Program (the end of 1967); and

5) Five Precious Lessons from a Great Victory in the Dry Season (written after the battles of Attleboro, in October and November 1966, *Cedar Falls*, in January 1967, and *Junction City*, from February to April 1967).

General Thanh[5] drew five important lessons from his essays:

1) always take control; pick the best location and the most propitious time for battle;

2) force the enemy to fight *our* battle *our* way;

3) always attack and move, concentrate and disperse rhythmically; cover, camouflage, hide, and disguise well, using subterfuge to fool the enemy;

4) fight in close range and fast; fight ferociously; terminate the fight quickly (a battle should last only 15 to 20 minutes; a campaign should last only from three to five days); and

5) the commander should understand the topography of the battlefield well; he should go to the exact location to study the terrain and understand his enemy's modus operandi; he should anticipate the conduct of the battle using different plans, concentrate his firepower, and open fire from a high elevation to overwhelm the enemy.

General Thanh's Essays were disseminated immediately to the People's Army and Liberation Army. They were broadcast from Hanoi and read slowly so the different units could copy them down. In March 1966, General Thanh issued a directive to all rank and file troops on the front. He commanded them to "attack the Achilles heel" of the Americans. This involved expanding the use of sapper units, which he had decided would be a determining force in the war. The Achilles heel of the Americans was the command posts from which they directed their best and most versatile forces. These included the airfields, their officers' quarters, embassies and consular offices, military depots, and communications centers. Attacking their Achilles heel involved launching missiles, placing bombs and mines, and creating the most damage with as little force as possible. The Achilles heel strategy called for creating well-trained, well-equipped sapper units, who were demolition experts, well-versed in martial arts, and masters in the arts of camouflage, climbing, swimming, and subterfuge. When executing the Achilles heel strategy, just one sapper or sapper unit could achieve the same results as a larger force. At a cost of a few hundred dollars, one could destroy dozens of ARVN or American soldiers or a plane, or a communications center costing several million dollars. From the standard unit of a sapper company (1964–65), there were developed entire divisions made up of sapper battalions (1967), which were later used for the Tet Offensive and on from there until the end of 1974. Two sapper regiments paved the way for the final offensive in the war, occupying in advance all the important bridges and transportation points leading into Saigon. In each military region there was even a water sapper company, chosen from fishing villages along the coast, which was equipped and trained to attack boats and ships, docks, pier storage areas, and ports.

Elements of PAVN strategy

The general strategy of the People's Army was to coordinate the military, political, intelligence, and diplomatic fronts closely. This involved the three regions of the battle zone: the countryside, the mountains, and cities; the three forces deployed in the war: guerrillas, regional, and regular forces; activities in the North and the South; and the battle front in Vietnam with the anti-war movement in the United States.

The People's Army used regular forces and modern weaponry, but fought with guerrilla tactics. Its divisions, with no home bases, slept on hammocks in the forest and were always on the move (with the exception of the battle at Dien Bien Phu, which was set up by the French as a stationary defense post). In the liberated areas, contested areas, and areas that were temporarily occupied, our forces were dispersed among the general populace like the spots on a leopard. Whenever we engaged in aerial combat with an American plane, the contest was one-on-one, or, at most, two-on-two, never involving more than four planes. Pilots were instructed to pick a propitious moment, as directed by radar, rise suddenly to tail an enemy plane, fire an air-to-air missile, and then land quickly.

The People's Army relied on Soviet and Chinese weapons, but always followed its own tactics (after 1960[6]). China advised Vietnam to operate solely with guerrilla tactics, in platoon- and company-sized units, to operate by ambush, to wait for opportunities. The Soviet Union, even more strenuously, advised Vietnam to do

The journalist Bui Tin sat at the presidential desk at noon on April 30, 1975. His dispatch began with the words: "I am seated on the first floor of the Presidential Palace in Saigon just liberated…" (Bui Tin collection)

away with advanced weapons, because the United States was a superpower with overwhelming technological firepower; so there was no way the Vietnamese could confront them. In spite of this advice, Vietnam always maintained her own ideas regarding tactics and strategy. We asked for money from our two "big brothers," since Vietnam was a bastion of the Socialist camp, fighting for its security and sacrificing on the frontline. The "brothers" had a duty to supply all the necessary materiel needs for Vietnam's survival. However, due to our differences over strategy, Vietnam only received specialists in technology, organization, and military training from China and the Soviet Union. No outsiders were present in meetings about command structure, military campaigns, and combat. Many Chinese and Russian military leaders were upset about not being apprised of Hanoi's military plans and activities. This is why Russian Air Force Commander Pavel Batisky, the chief of the Soviet air defense, complained that when visiting Vietnam at the end of 1971, he had not been briefed on the great offensive in early 1972, which the North was preparing at the time of his visit.

For the reasons stated above, Vietnam did not allow foreign officers to enter South Vietnamese battlefields. (This rule held true except for a cell of three North Korean psychological warfare specialists, who came in April 1967 to the mountainous area around Binh Dinh to drop leaflets and use loud speakers to propagandize the South Korean units who were fighting there, but to no avail. There were also about 30 Cuban officers and military engineers who were sent to Vietnam in 1973 by Fidel Castro, with ten bulldozers, to help fortify the Ho Chi Minh Trail.) On the whole, North Vietnam was not aided by any foreign combat units, either in North or South Vietnam. This allowed Hanoi to protest vociferously the half-million American troops operating in the South. Recently, China has provided some inflated figures regarding the number of troops they deployed in Vietnam. In reality, there were little more than 60 advisors at Dien

Bien Phu commanding the campaign, divisions, and ground artillery. China's most important contributions were guns and ammunition for the infantry, artillery shells, mortars, and about a hundred military transport vehicles, which were driven by Vietnamese soldiers from Bang Tuong, a small town near the Chinese–Vietnamese border, to the battlefield.

The Chinese inflated their importance when they claimed that 200,000 to 300,000 Chinese troops had fought in the American air war. In truth, the Chinese supplied about 40 gun squads, belonging to 12 battalions, and four regiments of air defense, along with several corps of army engineers and various transportation, communication, logistics, and medical units. These rotated through the country in two-to-three-month cycles, from 1966 until 1972, when they were recalled. They were stationed north of the Hong River, at the request of the People's Liberation Army of China, who wanted their troops "to get combat experience suited for modern warfare and learn about the activities of the American Air Force." At Vietnam's request, the Chinese soldiers lived in the jungle away from Vietnamese population, to avoid trading between the two peoples and the formation of relationships between the Chinese soldiers and local women. The local Vietnamese disdained the Chinese for being on a "wild turkey shoot." The Chinese expended great amounts of ammunition, shooting skyward while reciting Mao's slogans and waving his little red book over their heads, but they never downed a single American aircraft.

HANOI'S VIEW OF US FORCES AND STRATEGY

In mid-1965, the North Vietnamese Military Training Department began producing documents showing America's strengths and weaknesses. Their strong points were listed as technology, firepower, and mechanization. Their weak points were weather, terrain, and people – the three basic unities in Sun-Tzu's military manual. For the United States, the geography and tropical weather of Vietnam, along with US public disapproval of the conflict, were all unfamiliar and unfavorable. The documents also compared American troops unfavorably to the French Army, and stated that French troops (Legionnaires, Euro-Africans) were bold and daring, more understanding of the local society and terrain, and more experienced and specialized.

Other American weaknesses perceived by Hanoi's Joint General Staff included the fact that their fighting objective was not clear. They often met with dissension, including protests from the anti-war activists back home in America. Their rotation cycle was too brief, so they felt unsure of themselves at the start of their deployment and then, after acquiring experience, they started to think about how to play it safe, so they could return home to their families unharmed. Another important weakness was the fact that the number of combat soldiers was actually only one-fifth or one-sixth the total number of US soldiers deployed in Vietnam. Accustomed to rely on air and artillery firepower, Hanoi believed that even these combat soldiers were afraid to fight at close range; they lost their spirit fast without air or artillery support.

Bui Tin shaking hands with General Westmoreland in April 2002. Westmoreland remarked "From enemies, we are now friends... We are defeated only in our country." (Bui Tin collection)

In the opinion of Hanoi's leaders, the United States had made an error when they signed the peace treaty with Laos in Geneva on July 23, 1962. Hanoi viewed Vietnam, Laos, and Cambodia as an integral battlefield that could not be separated. They cultivated Laos as a friendly country and the Pathet Lao, the Communist revolutionaries in Laos, as close brethren. The governments of Vientiane and Phnom Penh were neutral, if not leaning toward Hanoi. Hanoi capitalized on the unmarked and ill-defined border between Vietnam and Laos. With sparsely populated border areas, inhabited only by a few primitive tribes, Hanoi could bring in troops and weapons at will. They were free to establish a North–South lifeline for transporting weapons and men to the battlefield in the South.

Another mistake made by the Americans was their misjudgment of the role the Chinese played in the war. The Americans unrealistically assumed that the Chinese would intervene on the side of North Vietnam if the country were attacked. At the end of 1963, the Joint General Staffs of Hanoi and Beijing had signed an agreement that if the US attacked North Vietnam by air, land, or sea, then this attack would trigger a response in kind; in other words, a Chinese engagement by air, land, or sea. In October 1963, the Chinese chief of their General Staff, Lo Rui Qing, led a group of military officers to Hanoi and into military Zone IV to study the battlefield and coordinate the plan for a Vietnamese-Chinese counter-attack. Chinese Air Force cells were flown to airfields at Noi Bai, Kep, and Hoa Lac (Ha Tay province). The United States might have been aware of these developments, but the CIA didn't seem to realize that in mid-1964 China unilaterally cancelled their pact with North Vietnam. Afterwards, as Mao said to a group of Vietnamese generals, including Le Quang Dao, "When we signed the military agreement with Vietnam, our generals were too eager." (General Dao repeated this remark when the China–Vietnam border war exploded in 1979. This was during a meeting of the Office of the Central Committee, which I attended.) Mao had decided not to intervene in Vietnam because he realized that China's involvement in Korea in 1951 had cost the country dearly. China could not afford to be involved in another war outside her borders. Later, General Dao Dinh Luyen, commander of the Air Force, told me that even China's limited engagement in the war was of little use. Chinese pilots were hampered by the language barrier. They could not understand directions from ground controllers speaking Vietnamese, and it proved too slow to have the commands translated.

Hanoi's General Staff also believed that the Americans had erred by not logically deploying their troops. As General Hoang Minh Thao, commander of the Central Highlands between 1971 and 1975, who later served as chairman of the High Military Institute from 1976 to 1990, told this author in Hanoi in 1989: "The Americans only needed to use one or two divisions, plus one ARVN division, stationed in the Quang Tri-Thua Thien area, to seal the border between North and South. This would have allowed the ARVN troops in the South to concentrate on fighting and pacifying the rear base. A transfer of the superior weapons and firepower of the Americans to the ARVN units would have been far more cost effective, as the Americans had a tendency to overkill." General Thao was my commander in the 304th Division from 1950 to 1954. In his opinion, the Americans didn't need a half-million troops. They could have prevailed with a far smaller number of soldiers, and by adopting this more effective strategy, they would have reduced their losses, damped down the protest movement in the United States, and built a less dependent, far more effective ARVN fighting force. This strategy would have minimized the destruction of lives and unnecessary violence, which engendered an environment of hatred and degradation in South Vietnam. The massive influx of American troops also spawned a myriad of unintended consequences – black markets, prostitution, drug addiction, unwanted Amerasian children – all of which could have been avoided or minimized with fewer troops, more logically deployed.

Finally, it was Hanoi's opinion that America made another crucial blunder in squandering its air superiority. Its expenditures for aircraft, bombs, and ordnance were enormous, and yet the military advantage was abysmally low. In my opinion, the United States could have accomplished its military objectives in Vietnam with one-fourth the manpower and one-tenth the number of bombs in both regions. The military impact would not have been less. In fact, I believe it would have been greater with a considerable reduction in the deployment of ammunition and bombs (five times the amount dropped on Europe in World War II). This would have mitigated anti-war sentiment in the United States and anti-American sentiment around the world, and it would have avoided the kind of political fallout that came from accidentally bombing Bach Mai hospital in Hanoi in December 1972, a civilian target with no military value.

Alternative strategies

In 1977, General Le Trong Tan, the Chief of Staff, and I were on a military mission to Moscow, Berlin, Warsaw, and Beijing. During a private talk, I asked him: "You told me the Americans had committed a blunder in fighting 'a rich man's war,' relying on their weapons and firepower. They didn't know how to fight a war searching for the enemy's vulnerabilities and striking his Achilles heel. So if you had been the American Chief of Staff, how would you have fought the war?"

He smiled and said, "A slight shift in strategy, nothing earthshaking, would have made all the difference. The Americans needed to deploy no more than a division of troops in the Dong Hoi panhandle [Quang Binh province] slightly to the north of the 17th Parallel, supported by a fleet of ships off the coast. They could have declared that this American incursion into North Vietnam was limited in scope, both in terms of time and space. Not offensive in nature, it was required merely to prevent the People's Army of the North from infiltrating into the South." General Tan went on to explain, "This strategy would have been lethal, because China would have sat idly by, while our troops were pinned down, defending our rear in the North, which, of course, was our main and unavoidable priority. The military configuration of the war would have flipped. The impetus of the fighting in the South would have reversed itself. The United States with impunity could have invaded and withdrawn, invaded and withdrawn, with its mobility guaranteed by the covering fire of the Seventh Fleet."

I recall that during the period from 1964 to 1965, when General Vo Nguyen Giap made numerous visits to Military Zone IV, headquartered in Vinh, he feared

General Le Trong Tan, chief of staff, VPA, at the airfield Liang Khuong near Dalat City in the Highlands in July 1980. In 1977, Tan commented, "The Americans needed to deploy no more than a division to occupy the Ding Hoi panhandle temporarily. China would have sat idly by while our troops were pinned down, defending our rear in the North – our unavoidable priority. The configuration of the war would have been flipped completely." (Bui Tin collection)

General Giap and Bui Tin on the Mekong River in May 1975. Giap had earlier remarked, "We must find every means to defeat the American troops in South Vietnam and force them to de-escalate the destructive air war in the North... Above all, we must avoid their launching a ground war in North Vietnam, no matter how limited." (Bui Tin collection)

our vulnerability should the United States and its ARVN allies occupy the panhandle area south of the Gianh River. Every year he carried out military exercises intended to counter this threat. General Giap described his fears to the military editors of the People's Army newspaper, where I worked: "We must find every means to defeat the American troops in South Vietnam and force them to de-escalate the destructive air war in the North," he said. "Above all, we must avoid their launching a ground war in North Vietnam, no matter how limited." Giap knew that any advance by American troops into the North would have flipped the military situation on its head. This prospect worried him more than any other military engagement.

So why did the Americans not take the ground war to the Ho Chi Minh Trail? I have traveled down the Trail many times, beginning with my first trip, when I transported materiel in a bamboo basket strapped to my back. On my next trip I graduated to carrying supplies by bicycle. Finally, I traveled down the Trail with mechanized transport divisions. The force dispatched to guard the Trail, the Truong Son High Command, was no larger than the equivalent of two army corps. Their responsibilities included running a fleet of trucks, along with repair shops and storage depots. This small number of soldiers managed an incredibly complex operation which included communications centers, scout- and guide-posts, an army corps of engineers, land-based antiaircraft units, an oil pipeline, traffic controllers, cells of Vanguard Youths, field hospitals, casualty transport units, rest houses, kitchens, movie projection units, and a troupe of actors.

In 1975, when I again found myself moving past the 32 military stations that dotted the Ho Chi Minh Trail, I overheard the soldiers exclaiming with relief, "The Americans bombed us fiercely, but they never allowed their infantry to attack or occupy the Trail. Even if they had occupied just one small segment, this would have caused us tremendous grief."

In Hanoi in 1989, during the 30th anniversary of the construction of the Ho Chi Minh Trail, known as Route 559, Mr. Dong Sy Nguyen, who was promoted from colonel to lieutenant general at the end of the war, and who had served as the commander of 559 and, afterwards, as prime minister of Vietnam, confided in me: "I was scared to death that the Americans would use their infantrymen to seize even a small portion of Route 559. This would have complicated our lives enormously. The soldiers stationed in the outposts along the Trail were adept at managing the logistics that kept it running, but they weren't combat experienced. Under attack, they would have scattered like bees from a hive. Transportation would have been interrupted, and we had no idea what we could have done to recover. This would have enormously impacted the battlefield in the South."

"The Americans could bomb as much as they wanted," he said. "That hardly bothered us at all. According to our statistics, out of every 100 bombs that were dropped, only 0.23 percent hit the road, which means that the Americans needed to drop a thousand bombs to get two of them on the road. Our repairs were quick. We used the exploded dirt and rock to repave the Trail. The Americans dropped their bombs from an average height of 2,000m, from bombers traveling at high speed. They were targeting a road that was a mere four to five meters wide. From their position high in the sky, the Americans were trying to attack a target that for them was as thin as a thread. No wonder the massive numbers of bombs they dropped on us served so little purpose." In 1971, when the US and the ARVN forces launched the *Lam Son* campaign, attacking the Ho Chi Minh Trail in southern Laos, it was too late, the Trail by then had branched into numerous byways, circuits, and shortcuts. The invasion created no noticeable decrease in the amount of tonnage transported.

Could America have won the war?

In my opinion, as a former officer in the People's Army, the idea that "America could never win the Vietnam war" is only half right. It is true that the United States could not have won this war totally. But the Americans could have avoided the great loss they incurred, both for themselves and for the Saigon regime. If the United States had not over-estimated the potential response of the Chinese, if they had not so gullibly signed the peace accord with Laos in 1962, if they had sent their infantry to occupy the panhandle south of the Gianh River, if they had occupied a small segment of the Ho Chi Minh Trail ... the outcome might have been very different.

Take a look, for example, at that period when we incurred the greatest losses in South Vietnam and could no longer replenish our forces without sending troops from the North. I am referring to the time immediately following the Tet Offensive, when our bases in the cities and countryside had been exposed and destroyed. This period, lasting from the Tet Offensive until the middle of 1971, coincided precisely with the time when the Americans were precipitously pulling

Bui Tin with General Nguyen Cu, commander of the sapper units of the NVA, taken in September 1989 in Hanoi. (Bui Tin collection)

out their troops and reducing their firepower. The ARVN were supposed to pick up the relief, but what happened instead was that their morale took a nosedive. The Americans thereby gave us a great escape route and a quick way to regain our force and position. We were able to overcome our most difficult period, and by 1972 we had regained enough momentum to start our final offensive. It was also during this time that the Western press began talking about our inevitable victory and the sure defeat of the South Vietnamese.

In military strategy, one needs to seize opportunities and press on to victory while the enemy is down. Contrary to this wisdom, I believe that the United States gave up and withdrew while it was winning. This happened even before Washington had started befriending Beijing in mid-1972.[8]

Now, looking back at the war, I realize that we had the good fortune to be exceptionally lucky. Watergate was heaven-sent for Vietnam. Nixon's resignation meant that his commitment to the war went unfulfilled. Ambassador Harriman had been careless when he signed the Laos Accords in 1962, which prevented the United States from attacking our route to the South. The intelligent but undemanding and ignorant Henry Kissinger (an assessment delivered to the

People's Army newspaper by Le Duc Tho in May of 1973) was also a gift from heaven. In a Politburo meeting at the end of December 1974, Mr. Pham Van Dong repeated Kissinger's remarks after he had toured the Vietnam Revolution Museum in Hanoi. "You see here how our people defeated the Yuan Chinese three times [from 1279 to 1368]. So do you think the United States will return to Vietnam for another round?" "No, once was enough," came Dr. Kissinger's quick and matter-of-fact reply.

Thieu's decision to abandon the Western Highlands on March 13, 1975 was another unexpected boon. No one could have predicted that. The fact that the United States Congress turned down Thieu's request for another $1.5 billion in aid, when it had already expended $60 billion in the previous nine years, was another stroke of luck. This was not something we expected from a democracy that cherished the political precepts of freedom and progress for Vietnam.

THE PRICE OF WAR

In the ranks of the People's Army, opinion differs today about the American war, whether it was worth the price, or whether victory came at too great a cost. An order was issued during the battle of Dien Bien Phu, forbidding the commander from reporting to his superior the number of dead and wounded falling in the fight. Only when the battle was over were these numbers revealed. From my observation, the winners incurred twice the number of dead and wounded as the losers. Later, during the American war, the North Vietnamese losses were far greater.

Right after its victory, the Communist Party deliberately forgot about the oft-promised reconciliation and concord. They began to apply the cruelest policies of occupation, as dictated by the class struggle. They imprisoned roughly 300,000 officers and government officials, and created the biggest tragedy of our time: the exodus of the boat people. Truly, they squandered their hard-won victory!

At the beginning of 1975, the Party decided to liberate Cambodia and Laos (but was chased off by the Khmer Rouge). They even prepared their intelligence agents, spies, and sapper units to go to Bangkok, until they realized, to their immense regret, that the Thai Communist Party was too weak to implement any plan to liberate Thailand and the rest of Southeast Asia. For the Party, the mission of the Communist Internationale would always take precedence over the needs of the people.

Today, many of the North Vietnamese veterans who fought in Cambodia and Laos under the ironic name of the "Volunteer Army of Vietnam"[9] feel embittered by their experience. Many have come to realize that they were mere pawns of the Vietnamese Communist Party, intent on fulfilling its hidden international agenda to color the countries of Indochina red. The word "volunteer" is even more painful when one realizes that not a single high-ranking cadre lost a child in Cambodia. This honor was reserved for the sons and daughters of the peasants, the "pariah" class of the regime.

One of the most ironic and painful things for us to realize is that there has never been a true democracy in Vietnam. The government never reports anything to Congress, even to the Central Committee of the Communist Party, regarding its strategic intentions or the losses incurred in a war. After the American war, the imprisonment of 300,000 Southerners was not even discussed in the Congress, either in the Central Committee or in the Politburo. In America, the Pentagon had to report each week the number of dead on the battlefields of Vietnam. More than 200 casualties, and the public would have grown restive. As General Westmoreland told me during a conference in Chicago in 1998, "I understand the military talent and ability of General Giap, but if he had been an American general, Congress and the American public would have had his job long ago!"[10]

I believe that although heaven was on the side of the North Vietnamese during the war, the Communist utopia will not last long. Heaven is just. When living kindly, one will reap goodness. When sowing wind, one will reap tempest. Communism has reached its glorious goal, but in the process, it has bankrupted itself, both in theory and in deed. Its goal to build a society without exploitation is contradicted by its cruel and inhumane practices, its violence against its opponents, and its embrace of class struggle and war.

Chapter 4

The Road South
The Ho Chi Minh Trail

Dr. John Prados

In many important ways, the Vietnam War can be viewed as a race. One example of this is the story of the Ho Chi Minh Trail, the supply line that Hanoi created to sustain its forces and those of the National Liberation Front in South Vietnam. In this case, the race featured the Democratic Republic of Vietnam's efforts to build the Trail against those of the United States and South Vietnam to block the borders and coasts, in essence to isolate the battlefield in South Vietnam. This race, an epic struggle between the two sides, had a great deal to do with the final outcome of the conflict.

Others have dealt with the origins of the insurgency and the course of the fighting in South Vietnam. But that insurgency required sustenance, and this became the origin of the Trail. On Ho Chi Minh's birthday, May 19, 1959, senior Lao Dong Party officials summoned Colonel Vo Bam for a private meeting. Bam, chief of the Army Agricultural Department, was an engineer officer familiar with previous supply operations, and became the sparkplug in what began as a covert operation. Instructed to gather a special unit consisting solely of Vietnamese of the South who had gone North after the 1954 Geneva Accords, Vo Bam created the 301st Battalion, several hundred soldiers who were equipped with untraceable French weapons left over from the Resistance War and uniformed like peasants. The unit moved to the Vinh Linh sector of the DRV, just above the Demilitarized Zone that separated North and South Vietnam. There they began to survey and explore the land, looking for a path they could use to infiltrate South Vietnam. Hanoi's orders were to carry stocks of weapons and accompany a certain number of cadres – the initial mandate was for 7,000 weapons and 500 men – that would bolster the insurgency.

Vo Bam found peasants from villages west of Vinh Linh – tribesmen from the hills along the Annamite mountain chain – to be useful guides, and walked the ground. Soon he had identified a possible route for a trek. In June 1959, the Vietnam People's Army sent the first marching party out to the South. That party

North Vietnamese carry supplies along the Ho Chi Minh Trail in this undated photo taken by North Vietnamese photograper Trong Thanh. Thanh spent five years taking photos along the Ho Chi Minh Trail. He carried his cameras, hundreds of rolls of film, and developing chemistry, and wore his processed negatives around his waist as a belt 24 hours a day. (Empics/AP)

remained exploratory. Early in August, an ecstatic radio message reported the actual first delivery of arms to Southerners of the Interzone V military region, which encompassed the coastal area of the South starting from about Quang Ngai province. Only a few dozen rifles were involved, but they were the first of a flood of men and weapons.

The journey down the Trail was not an easy one until very late in the war. (TRH Pictures)

The Trail's history is that of a race because Hanoi's initiative did not take place in a vacuum. Though the DRV conducted its early efforts as a covert operation, Saigon – and US observers – quickly developed their own suspicions. The route of Hanoi's trekkers went west through the Annamite foothills, skirted the Demilitarized Zone for fewer than 20 miles in Laos, and entered South Vietnam at the corner where the DMZ meets the Laotian border. Then the marchers proceeded through the hills above Khe Sanh, and crossed Route 9 near that place. The Army of the Republic of Vietnam maintained a garrison at Khe Sanh of a reinforced battalion, and those troops patrolled the area. Vo Bam's men took precautions to be sure. They left nothing behind, not even a cigarette butt, and put down mats to leave no footprints crossing roads like Route 9, which they did only at night. But soon enough the ARVN found traces of passage, and high officials of the Diem government told the Americans that the guerrillas had started a major offensive. By the summer of 1960, enough evidence had accumulated for Saigon to complain to the International Control Commission which monitored compliance with the 1954 Geneva agreements. Then the South Vietnamese captured a couple of men from the seagoing counterpart to Vo Bam's land infiltration unit.

Americans were aware of these developments, and increasingly concerned about infiltration from the North. Blocking the borders of South Vietnam along both landward and seaward sides was first listed as an objective in plans drafted in 1960 and remained, with variations and permutations, part of every subsequent strategy devised during the war. The goal would be enshrined beginning with the Kennedy administration in 1961, whose theory of counterinsurgency assumed guerrillas require an outside base. By these lights, blocking access by sealing borders and water routes isolated the battlefield, enabling the counterinsurgents to mop up the guerrilla fighters.

Thus began the race. Hanoi soon decided the infiltration route skirting the DMZ was inadequate, and reconfigured the Trail to connect with roads in Laos, running down the western side of the Annamite mountains. This required sweeping away the Laotian army units guarding several posts in the area. This task had been accomplished by the spring of 1961 when Group 559 – Vo Bam's command for the Trail, named for the month and year when the project began – sent People's Army regulars, plus DRV border security units and local troops, into Laos to spearhead the move. Laotian military strongman Phoumi Nosavan unwittingly contributed to the success of the maneuver by pulling his best troops out of the Laotian panhandle to use in his coups d'etat and political maneuvers in northern Laos.

The Americans countered with a junk patrol off the Vietnamese coast and a border defense initiative. In 1961, Edward Lansdale suggested a "Northwest

The Ho Chi Minh Trail

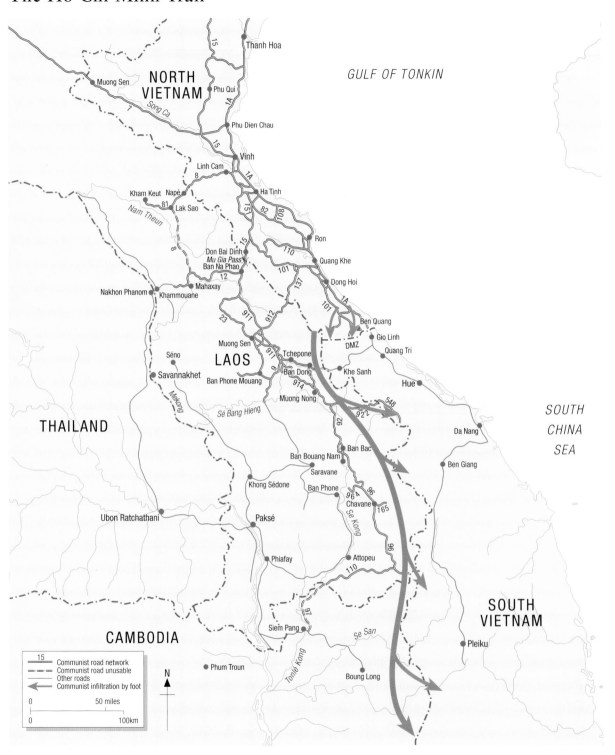

Frontier Force," essentially a border scout program, which the CIA later put together, and the agency's own Saigon station began to arm and train Montagnards in the Central Highlands. This initiative, originally the Village Defense Program and later the Civilian Irregular Defense Groups under military tutelage, aimed partly at self-defense but also tried to keep an eye on the mountain trails that entered South Vietnam from its borders.

Vo Bam proceeded to systematize his infiltration network. At first working under appalling conditions, where the marching parties had to carry forward food to camp sites, then return to pick up their loads, the People's Army soon created "way stations," permanent installations at intervals along the route of march. The high command committed the 98th Engineer Regiment to trail maintenance. The 301st Battalion, strengthened, became the 70th Regiment and built the first little piece of what became the Trail. The People's Army cleared the Laotian side of Route 9 as far as Ban Dong, a little over 20 miles west of Khe Sanh. South Vietnamese troops patrolling around that village discovered one of Vo Bam's stations in early 1961 and captured records showing that 2,800 persons had already passed through it. Border security still left much to be desired. In fact, in May 1961 alone Hanoi dispatched a party of 500 cadres, led by Major General Tran Van Quang, deputy chief of staff of the People's Army. For a time Quang served as deputy senior commander (under a Liberation Front figure) of the war in the South.

Washington tried a large solution, championed by then-deputy national security advisor Walt W. Rostow, who was also a primary exponent of counterinsurgency doctrine. Rostow wanted to get the Southeast Asia Treaty Organization to activate one of its contingency operations, Plan 5, that provided for a multinational occupation of the Laotian panhandle that would presumably seal off the Trail. One of Rostow's objectives on the Taylor-Rostow mission of November 1961 would be to survey the area of operations for and sound out SEATO allies on Plan 5. Nothing was right at the time. The SEATO alliance turned out to be a hollow shell, not actually obliging member nations to go to war, and covered South Vietnam only loosely as a "protocol" state. Plan 5 itself actually envisioned only a very small US contingent, with the overwhelming bulk of forces to be provided by SEATO nations not willing to become involved. Even the logistic network that would have been necessary to implement Plan 5 did not exist. Rostow continued to encourage variants – "Plan 5+," even "Plan 6," and Washington deliberations included talk of making necessary preparations. When the Kennedy administration briefly deployed US Marines to Thailand in 1962, in connection with new Geneva negotiations, their activities in that country, which backed up the Lao panhandle, included surveying the Thai roads needed to supply Plan 5 troops and even some of the required engineering work.

The US Joint Chiefs of Staff were not enthusiastic about the SEATO contingencies. They evaluated local forces as insufficient for an effective intervention, even if men could be supplied. The Chiefs produced a US contingency plan that would have used three divisions of American troops (129,000 men) to

A North Vietnamese Army patrol in the forest south of the Ho Chi Minh Trail in 1968. Ingenuity and tenactiy enabled the Trail to be built and maintained through this terrain. (AFP/Getty Images)

hold a defense line across the DMZ and the 17th Parallel through Laos to the Mekong River. President Kennedy, who rejected the Taylor-Rostow mission's recommendation to send 8,000 American soldiers to South Vietnam, had no intention of approving the JCS plan.

All this left the action up to the American CIA and military people in Saigon, and their Diemist allies. Diem had promised to commit a number of his new Ranger companies to the Northwest Frontier Force, but he never did. The CIA's "mountain scout" project began as a stopgap alternative. By 1963 there were 76 posts along the borders with 3,860 troops. As for the Montagnards, Diem had no confidence in their ability to seal the border. He once lectured General Maxwell

Taylor at length about the supposed childlike nature of the tribesmen. The CIA compensated; they tried to organize blocks on *both* sides of the border. In South Vietnam, the CIA and Army Special Forces took quite the opposite tack from Diem on the 'yards, as the CIDGs were familiarly known, and used them to considerable effect. In the Laotian panhandle, the agency and Special Forces attempted to establish Project Pincushion, a CIDG-like program among tribes inhabiting the Bolovens Plateau. The agency also started Project Hardnose, which aimed to gather better intelligence on the Trail by recruiting tribesmen into teams to watch the roads.

Hanoi stood still for none of this. The DRV continued to step up its use of the Trail. From march groups composed entirely of officer-level and specialist cadres, that characterized some groups in 1961–62, Hanoi began sending even larger numbers, including ordinary soldiers. In September 1961, the Politburo approved a People's Army proposal for long-term assistance to the Liberation Front. Over the next two years, this would include sending South 30,000 to 40,000 troops who were Southerners in the DRV.

The needs of the war in the South formed only part of the reason for the movements. Another was the desire to improve the Trail itself. Hanoi could see the major South Vietnamese military build-up the Americans began funding in 1961, plus the American advisors and combat support units that flooded the South to sharpen the ARVN combat edge. The National Liberation Front felt the pressure, yet continued to strike important blows against Diem, all the while demanding more help from Hanoi. By late 1961, the 3rd Truck Transportation Group of the People's Army's rear services department had begun delivering supplies to a point above Tchepone. That was far from the whole job but it was a start.

Stopping was never an option. Hanoi instead debated whether to maintain the Trail as an asset that could theoretically be hidden – an actual network of trails, four to six feet wide, capable of handling bicycles and marching parties; or to expand it to a road, passable by vehicles, bicycles, and people. Vo Bam personally briefed Ho Chi Minh on the Trail's status in May 1962. Part of the debate hinged upon whether to employ artillery in the South, namely guns of up to 75mm. This implied the commitment of the People's Army, since the National Liberation Front lacked any specialized artillery units. Artillery meant prime movers, which meant trucks. In 1964 the People's Army dispatched a survey team to examine this question. The options were still on the table when the Gulf of Tonkin incident took place.

THE CONTEST BEGINS

Those who marched the Trail believed in the Northern dream of reunification. That was why they were willing to endure the hardships of the Trail and the field, and the tribulations of a military campaign that never ended. In 1962–63, when the Americans and Diem started the "Strategic Hamlet" Program, something Hanoi termed "special warfare" and regarded with apprehension, the counter was to further increase the flow to the South. Control of Group 559 by a committee of the Lao Dong Party gave way to regular command of the People's Army general staff.

The number of soldiers actually assigned to the group doubled to 4,000 by 1964. Important bases, particularly near Tchepone, were already carefully defended. The number who moved on and completed the trek to the South averaged 4,000 to 5,000 a year in the early 1960s. With additional "probables," the annual average rose to 12,000 in 1964. Vietnamese official histories put the number at 40,000 having completed the trek by the end of 1963, including 2,000 senior cadre or technical specialists.[1] In a sense, the increases in cadres matched the growth in US advisors, whose numbers increased from 685 to 22,000 between 1960 and 1964. Liberation Front forces multiplied at a rapid rate due to this mutual escalation. In early 1964, Hanoi decided to adopt the road option for its further improvements, which entailed sending 1,000 more engineering troops, plus heavy construction equipment, down to work with Group 559. In addition a massive road improvement program began in the DRV improving the road approaches to the Annamite mountain passes at Mu Gia and Nape, which became the major entry points to the Trail. Tchepone, inside Laos on Route 9, became a major transit base for the network.

Within months US U-2 spyplanes over Laos captured their first pictures of heavy construction equipment along the Trail, evidence that would be shown to President Lyndon Johnson at a National Security Council meeting. On March 17, 1964, after that meeting, the president approved a directive (NSAM-288) that permitted South Vietnamese military forces to make cross-border forays into Laos (without their American advisors) as well as reconnaissance teams, complete with US leaders and aerial resupply. At the end of April, the NSC listened again as US intelligence briefed developments in even greater detail. As a result, the Johnson administration resolved to induce the Royal Laotian Government to begin a bombing campaign against DRV targets on the Trail.

Washington had already begun scaling up its own level of effort, providing capability for scout patrols. At the end of 1963, the US command MACV created its Studies and Observation Group, which took over all manner of special warfare activities, from CIA commando missions against North Vietnam to patrols along the Laotian border. Forays against the Ho Chi Minh Trail itself were soon included on its menu of activity. The first of the cross-border missions was *Leaping Lena* in June 1964, carried out by Project Delta of the 5th Special Forces Group because SOG had not yet gotten up to speed. In *Leaping Lena*, five South Vietnamese commando teams parachuted into Laos, two of them above Tchepone, the rest south of Route 9. A handful of survivors made it back to friendly positions; the rest disappeared. Americans decided that the patrols had failed because no US troops had been present to exert leadership and lend their field skills. The SOG formula became one of using teams whose indigenous troops had a backbone of several SOG Americans.

The Laotian Air Force had its main base at Savannakhet, where Route 9 reached the Mekong. General Thao Ma, its commander, had been willing to use his propeller-driven T-28 aircraft against the Trail from the previous year, but the US denied permission to use the planes for that purpose at that time. That changed in 1964, though the Americans at first refused to furnish bombs, imagining rockets and machine-guns would be sufficient. In Washington, JCS planning papers were prepared that estimated ridiculously small numbers of air sorties sufficient to neutralize various targets. The bomb limitations disappeared soon enough, and US aircraft were added, for an extended aerial interdiction campaign that would endure through the remainder of the war. Presently the Laotian Air Force would be redirected to the war in northern Laos, leaving the Americans to fight the Trail.

Hanoi had not stood still either. In August 1964, around the time of the Gulf of Tonkin incident, it sent Infiltration Group 53 down the Trail. The 400 men of the party, arriving in Quang Tri, became the 808th Battalion. This was the first constituted unit to use the Trail. That fall and winter, the North Vietnamese followed with their 95th and then 101st regiments, which arrived in the South in February, arrayed against the Central Highlands. Road-watch teams put in place by the CIA to monitor the Trail counted 185 trucks headed South in December, rising to 311 in February 1965 and 485 the following month. Aerial photography showed gasoline tanker trucks for the first time. American naval aircraft made their first strike on the Mu Gia Pass on February 28, 1965.

That April, the DRV defense minister, General Vo Nguyen Giap, summoned General Phan Truong Tue, until then minister of transport, and asked him to assume command of Group 559 in addition to his other duties. His ministry had the resources for expanding the "Truong Son Strategic Supply Route," as the North Vietnamese called the Ho Chi Minh Trail. Tue made a start by sending down 1,000 specialists with 30 pieces of heavy construction equipment, plus 1,500 more volunteers. When the monsoon rains hit, he sent 300 more engineers and another 2,000 volunteers, many of them women from Ha Tinh province. The role of women in building and defending the Trail became so important that General Giap himself eventually visited the women's volunteer units to acknowledge their contribution.

By the end of 1965, there were 10,000 to 12,000 Vietnamese directly involved in maintaining or extending the Trail, and an equal number engaged in moving supplies. Group 559 became a strategic rear services unit under the People's Army General Department of Rear Services. The department also created Group 665 to coordinate troop movements South and the transport of badly wounded soldiers to hospitals in the North. There were a half-dozen truck battalions, two bicycle transport battalions, and one boat transport battalion. The initial network, now the 70th Transport Group, had been supplemented by the 71st and 72nd groups: one to extend the Trail down into Cambodia, the other to build connections into South Vietnam. By June 1966, the Truong Son network had both arrived at the Cambodian border and penetrated into South Vietnam's A Shau valley. The construction teams had been building roads at the rate of 60 miles a month.

Ever more complex, the Trail became a heavily articulated network connecting a number of nodes, "way stations" in the idiom of the day, or as the Vietnamese called them, *binh trams*. Each camp had command and political department leaders, sections of engineers for road repair, mechanics for vehicle maintenance, security, antiaircraft defense, communications and supply. Between the *binh trams* were multiple camouflaged routes, with especially difficult passages, or "choke points" – like the Mu Gia Pass – given redundant pathways. The whole thing functioned like a sophisticated switching system, with the forward echelon of Group 559 as the dispatchers, routing each convoy down the safest open route. At this time, Group 559 had 18 engineer battalions, four antiaircraft battalions, 45 communication stations, plus other support units running several dozen way stations. It also controlled an additional four antiaircraft battalions whose sections were deployed to defend key points along the Trail.

In 1965, Group 559 transported almost as many supplies as had passed down it in all the years since its creation. The flow of men had increased as well. Considering the fact that the trucks could move only in dry weather – during monsoon season marching became the only means of transport – that amounted to a considerable feat.

MARCHING THE TRAIL

Until very late in the war, travel down the Trail was never easy. The realities are illustrated by the experience of Le Cao Dai, a Vietnamese chest surgeon assigned to a field hospital Hanoi decided to send South, to the tri-border junction of Vietnam, Laos, and Cambodia. Dai would be deputy director of the surgical department. Designated Group 84, the hospital deployment would be the largest action of this kind Hanoi had undertaken at this point in the war. The unit had to be broken into three different marching parties, and there were endless headaches trying to figure out how to divide up its 1,200 crates of medical equipment. Leaders pulled in doctors and nurses from hospitals all over the DRV, and trained right in Hanoi, under relaxed rules the People's Army implemented in 1966. Dai's marching party, the last of three, left for the South on February 27. They trucked as far south as the Mu Gia Pass, each vehicle responsible for its own food and water. Dai, though a senior officer, often washed dishes for the party on his truck, while others prepared the food, did the cooking, or set up camp. At one point, in Quang Binh province, they had to wait three days for flood waters to recede before they could cross a stream, and finally only crossed with the aid of a tow-truck. At another, they were held up by a crippled gasoline tanker that blocked the narrow road. It took a week to reach the command post of Group 559, Headquarters R. Dai crossed "Grandmother Gia" – the Great Pass – on March 8. Afraid of detection, drivers were told to use no lights. They joked, "This is a war between the blind and the deaf." A Group 559 officer sent along as guide warned, "This is the most 'shocking' road in Indochina." The convoy made it to "0-50," Group 559's forward echelon center, on March 15. There a cadre advised them that walking was the best way to progress further. Indeed, soon after leaving the base, the truck hit a bad spot and overturned when the driver fell asleep at the wheel. Everything had to be made right. At Tchepone, they found the village

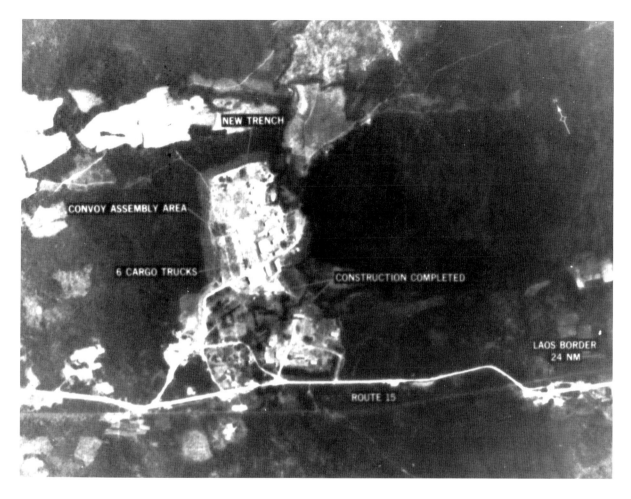

NEW TRENCH

CONVOY ASSEMBLY AREA

6 CARGO TRUCKS

CONSTRUCTION COMPLETED

LAOS BORDER
24 NM

ROUTE 15

completely destroyed. At Ban Dong, Dai had to perform surgery on a wounded soldier, his first on the Trail. The local commander asked if they had encountered US Special Forces.

Dai's group eventually reached a point in South Vietnam near Khe Sanh in late March, after three weeks on the road. Yet Dai's infiltration group had traveled in style compared to early trekking parties, who often took several months to reach such distant parts as the Mekong Delta. Even with improved road conditions, the challenges remained: wild animals, malaria, diseases born of exposure, miserable rain, poor food. All of that apart from the US bombing or the troopers of SOG. At least a hospital possessed medical supplies, which most march groups quickly ran out of and could never restock. Almost everyone who traveled the Trail contracted malaria. The ravages of hunger, the land, and the Americans exacted more losses. And the cost could be quite severe – when Hanoi sent down its 52nd Regiment, the unit departed the Xuan Mai training center 2,800-strong but reached the Mekong area with just 1,200 soldiers. The Trail was truly a test of endurance for the supporters of reunification.

A convoy staging area in North Vietnam on Route 15 to Laos in 1964. This photo was used by Robert McNamara in a presentation to the Senate Foreign Relations Committee on March 3, 1966. (TRH Pictures)

ESCALATION

The Vietnam War changed completely in 1965. That was when the Americans sent their big battalions, when Lyndon Johnson made his fateful decision to commit ground troops, when the *Rolling Thunder* air campaign began. This also became the year that the United States' effort to isolate the battlefield attained full speed. The Laotian bombing, known as *Steel Tiger*, became a high-intensity interdiction effort, combining reconnaissance bombing with targets identified by cross-border operations and those directed by Forward Air Controllers. General Westmoreland created Operation *Tiger Hound*, flying out of Khe Sanh, in which some of the first Air Force FACs flew over the Trail and put fighter-bombers against everything they saw.

The ground element was not wanting either. By 1965, the SOG had established a training and supply network (50 tons of equipment per month were moving just on SOG accounts), set up an air arm, and perfected its headquarters organization. Colonel Clyde Russell, SOG commander, was anxious to get into the field. Colonel William H. McKean, of the 5th Special Forces Group, had taken over the CIDG program. Both had a lot to work with. By September 1965, there were 1,300 Americans in 5th Group, leading 24,400 Montagnard strikers, 25,000 local defense militia, and 1,900 Montagnards in the mobile strike forces. McKean also had a special mission unit called Project Delta. The SOG had 336 Americans, 370 third-country or contract troops, like the redoubtable Nung fighters, reinforced by another 1,800 soldiers in Colonel Tran Van Ho's Strategic Technical Directorate.[2] Already building toward a peak strength that would approach 10,000, SOG had ground, maritime, and air capability.

In the spring and summer of 1965, Colonel Russell laid plans for cross-border operations against the Trail in Laos. These had to be coordinated with William H. Sullivan, the US ambassador in Vientiane, and up the chain of command. General Westmoreland had his doubts, principally arising from the difficulty of his relationship with Sullivan, but these were eventually worked out. The operation acquired the codename *Shining Brass*. To assuage Sullivan, Westmoreland agreed to start with two sectors in the southern reaches of Laos, and not to permit his patrols too far into the country. From the other side of the Pacific, the Commander-in-Chief, Pacific, Admiral Ulysses S. Grant Sharp, pressured Westmoreland to get going on patrols out along Route 9 toward Tchepone.

By this time, Colonel Donald Blackburn had taken over SOG, and put the finishing touches on an operational concept that had several phases. In the first, a few patrols would scout the uplands inside the border and the Laotian wilderness. For the second, SOG would begin to saturate its area of operations with reconnaissance teams. In the last, patrols would be backed by mid-sized Hornet Forces and larger Hatchet Forces, 100-man operational groups with some staying power, who could pin the adversary, then leave them to be smashed by air attacks. On October 12, 1965, the Joint Chiefs of Staff informed Westmoreland that President Johnson had approved the concept and the first phase of execution.

Colonel Blackburn was ready. A few days earlier, he had flown Reconnaissance Team (RT) Iowa up to Kham Duc. It made initial familiarization

Ho Chi Minh Trail extensions, 1966–67

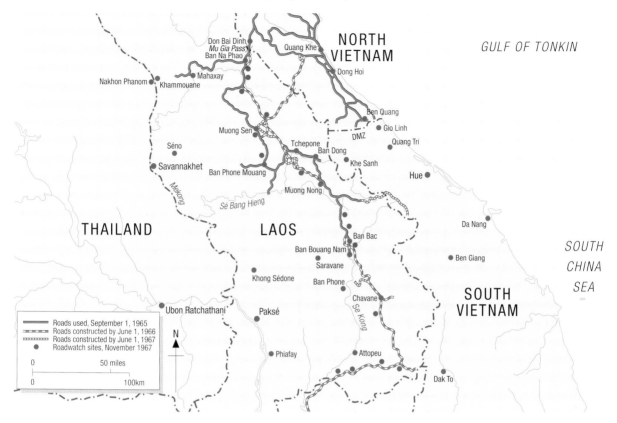

patrols around this Special Forces camp. When Blackburn received approval for *Shining Brass*, RT Iowa moved to Dak To in the Central Highlands and began to scout out to the border. Its first offensive patrol found a North Vietnamese camp for the bombers to hit. Before the end of the year, five RTs had begun patrolling and results were deemed excellent. Working in "Indian Country," as the regions dominated by the North Vietnamese were familiarly called, was always both exotic and highly dangerous. Simple physical survival and movement in the bush remained arduous, with challenges ranging from elephant grass to snakes, to malarial mosquitoes, to the land itself. And then there were the North Vietnamese. A constant contest took place between the SOG teams – finding new ways to get into Indian Country and survive there – and the Vietnamese – organizing surveillance and defense of the territory. Helicopter insertion would be SOG's mainstay, a method that remained problematical throughout the war.

The SOG reached full stride under Don Blackburn. Before he left in 1966, it had grown to 3,500 troops. It organized the terrain into theaters, north, central, and south, each under a subordinate headquarters. Thus Command Control North led operations toward Tchepone, and Command Control Central operated out of the Central Highlands. Later, when cross-border operations against

Cambodia were added in Operation *Daniel Boone*, a Command Control South led that initiative. The RTs (nicknamed "Spike" teams) were attached to the Command Control elements. SOG created "Forward Operating Bases" from which the RTs would work. Khe Sanh, Kham Duc, and Dak To all became FOB locations. During 1966, the SOG air wing flew 442 missions in South Vietnam alone, moving 13,893 passengers and 2,450 tons of cargo. Insertions of RTs were usually accomplished by South Vietnamese Air Force helicopters backed by army gunships and Air Force fighter-bombers. Occasionally teams or elements of just a few specialists parachuted into more distant operating areas. In a typical period, July 18 through September 26, 1966, there were 36 patrols, including three by Hornet Forces and one where a Hornet Force reinforced a Spike team.

When Colonel John K. Singlaub took over SOG around this time, the system was fully functional. Singlaub headed SOG until after the Tet Offensive, and he innovated in certain ways. One was his effort to improve communications with the Spike teams by setting up a relay station on a high mountaintop in Laos, enabling the teams' line-of-sight radios to report from far in the field. Another was an emphasis on parachute insertions. A third was his adoption of non-lethal gas as an aid in neutralizing landing zones before the introduction of the scouts. Also of key importance was the struggle behind the scenes to enlarge SOG's area of operations and its authority to operate deeper into Laos.

Inserting the Spike teams became the major headache in the SOG effort. The land offered obstacles to US technology and strategy, just as it did for Hanoi. There were only a few FOBs, and except for Khe Sanh they were well inside South Vietnam. The sectors of interest to the US command were remote from these bases, usually covered by triple-canopy jungle with few clearings for helicopters to land, and likely to be occupied or watched by the People's Army or their Laotian political allies. Hanoi's troops developed simple but effective ways to communicate news of landings, even without radios. Individual guards posted around clearings, water sources, trails, or potential camp sites had a warning code, firing a number of shots from their rifles to betoken the message. Hanoi's troops could react swiftly. Even the half-dozen or so aircraft typically employed for a SOG insertion made a great deal of noise, telling Vietnamese scouts to look out for something, and setting in motion the whole warning sequence. Colonel Singlaub's experiments with methods of insertion formed a logical tactical response to SOG's difficulties, and was a practice his successors continued, albeit without ever achieving an ideal method. It is instructive that the most successful Spike team leaders, notably Sergeant Richard Meadows, actually insisted on walking to their assigned patrol zones whenever possible. The land of the Trail remained "Indian Country" throughout the war.

Hanoi's forces also made quite conscious maneuvers to improve their dominance in lower Laos and the transportation routes. For one, they systematically eliminated bases that were well positioned to launch SOG forays. This was clearly a motive for the North Vietnamese assault on A Shau Special Forces camp in February 1966. Two *binh trams* soon appeared in the hinterlands cleared by the A Shau battle. In due course, the sector became a Liberation Front base area. In Laos, the People's Army kept continuous pressure upon Royal Laotian Army posts in the panhandle or the Bolovens Plateau. The siege of Khe Sanh, whatever its other effects, also eliminated an FOB patrol base. When the Vietnamese overran the Kham Duc camp in May 1968, the northernmost remaining launch point for Spike missions went with it. While extending the Trail, Hanoi consciously cleared its flanks.

All of that effort had one aim and one aim only – to sustain the Truong Son Strategic Supply Route and use it to augment the People's Army in the South. Observing the rapid increase in US forces under Westmoreland, Hanoi greatly reinforced its own troops in the field. The infiltration flow increased despite US bombing and the efforts of SOG. The battlefield had not been isolated. Seventeen regiments of People's Army regulars went South during 1966, along with a plethora of specialist units, including artillery, armor (for the first time), air defense, engineer and medical units, plus many individual replacements. More than 60,000 troops in all made the trek, and the major march to battle of the People's Army. The next year replacements would predominate among infiltrators, with just a few regular regiments. Renewed infiltration by regular formations, such as in the period from late 1967 to early 1968, when two fresh divisions moved South (to besiege Khe Sanh and strengthen forces near Hue), heralded a major strategic maneuver, the Tet Offensive.

People's Army truck convoys heading up Route 15 to the Mu Gia Pass, February 9, 1967. This montage shows 26 of the 130 fully loaded trucks counted by photo interpreters. The previous day another 75 trucks had been counted. (TRH Pictures)

NO PLUG IN THE FUNNEL

Washington's concern to isolate the battlefield never abated. If one thing did not work, another might be tried. As early as 1962, supplemented by a May 1964 analysis, Walt Rostow had set out the basic options menu. Patrol operations and bombing had both been mentioned and both were in progress. Rostow had also advocated a range of "intermediate" possibilities. These included blocking the neck of Indochina from the Mekong to the South China Sea, airborne raids to occupy Trail segments for short periods, or a more permanent occupation of an "airhead," as at Dien Bien Phu. Rostow considered Tchepone the most suitable objective for an operation like that. Every one of these options was explored as the Vietnam War wound on.

The blocking option, of course, had been the course in the original SEATO Plan 5, no doubt where Rostow picked up his enthusiasm for it. The Joint Chiefs of Staff had proposed to use the strategy in their own war plan for Southeast Asia at about the same time. That had remained a contingency until 1965, when President Johnson considered broadening US participation in the war and sent Army chief of staff General Harold K. Johnson out to survey the situation and propose a strategy. General Johnson came back with the blocking option, which he estimated would require five US or SEATO divisions, along with many engineer units and 10,000 extra South Vietnamese workers. Not only did President Johnson not wish to approve that many US troops in Vietnam at that point, many in the US Army – Westmoreland among them – considered that the engineering resources to implement the scheme simply did not exist. Though this was less well known at the time, the port and supply capacity to back an effort of those dimensions also did not exist in 1965. Later that year, when the 1st Cavalry Division (Airmobile) began deploying to South Vietnam, its commander proposed a novel strategy that would have had the division enter Thailand instead of Vietnam, then make attacks across the Laotian panhandle. They would catch the North Vietnamese against cover forces Westmoreland would post along the Vietnamese border. Westmoreland rejected the proposal on both logistic and diplomatic grounds. Thailand still lacked the necessary logistic infrastructure, while, under the 1962 Geneva Agreements, Laos was supposed to be neutral and no American troops were to be inside it. South Vietnamese General Cao Van Vien again proposed a blocking force in 1965–66, but one to consist of five ARVN divisions. Johnson never warmed to this possibility either, and General Vien never had to explain how he would be able to motivate five of his divisions and free them from their territorial ties to use them in the remote theater that would have been necessary.

In late 1965 the blocking position idea was revived by scientists of the Jason Group, which advised the US government, in the form of what became known as the "Strongpoint Barrier System," or more familiarly, the "McNamara Line." Military officers opposed the concept as a dangerous diversion of troops from mobile operations, but President Johnson approved it in 1967. Less ambitious than the old JCS war plan, the McNamara Line sought to have half a loaf: instead of physically occupying all the terrain below the DMZ and out to the Mekong,

NVA engineers fill marshy bomb craters and cover with bamboo mats.

the defense line would cover only those parts inside South Vietnam, with the Laotian side covered by a virtual presence: sensor systems that would identify adversary troop movements and enable them to be attacked by air. To limit troop requirements, the portion of the Line in the Vietnamese lowlands was thinned to where it consisted only of independent strongpoints, with minefields and cleared terrain in the intervals. Planners ruled out any effort to craft a defensive position that actually connected Khe Sanh to the Line in the lowlands. Even with much of the garrison duty handed over to South Vietnamese troops, McNamara Line requirements pressed against US force levels in South Vietnam. After the Khe Sanh siege in 1968, there would no longer be any pretense that the McNamara Line blocked anything other than the sector just below the DMZ.

Another possibility was to harass and perhaps block the Trail with ground troops, not in the numbers of a blocking force, but in sufficient strength to disrupt Hanoi's infiltration flows. General Westmoreland proposed two different versions of this idea: *High Port*, which provided battalion size operations, and *Fire Break*, a somewhat larger operation. Westmoreland saw a division-size operation also, *South Paw*. None of these would have entered Laos with enough steam to affect the Trail very much. In 1967, repeatedly frustrated, Westmoreland slated a series of operations he called *York*, intended to clear the Vietnamese side of the border enough to furnish a platform for *El Paso*, an invasion of Laos. When President Johnson learned of *El Paso*, he reacted with such fury that General Westmoreland quickly informed Washington that *El Paso* was simply an advance plan for something that could be tried in late 1968 or in 1969 if there were a change in national policy. Several months later, as US troops plus some from the ARVN relieved the siege of Khe Sanh, Saigon commanders attempted to plot pursuit operations with South Vietnamese across the border toward Tchepone. Again Washington ruled out the idea, and pursuit was confined to objectives within South Vietnamese boundaries.

General Westmoreland's most intense attempt at obtaining permission to block the Ho Chi Minh Trail came in April 1967, in the context of President Johnson's deliberations on Westmoreland's first request for more than 200,000 reinforcements. Westmoreland returned to Washington for the key meetings at the White House. Johnson wanted to know what Westmoreland would do if he got the troops he wanted. The general briefed a concept for invading Laos. This time Walt Rostow opposed him, advocating instead an invasion of the DRV. Westmoreland in turn described why Rostow's latest idea was not practical. It was after this inconclusive discussion that Lyndon Johnson approved the construction of the McNamara Line. Back at Saigon headquarters, Westmoreland mused to subordinates that he had wanted to go to Tchepone but could never get the ticket.

The invasion option came back again during the Nixon administration. A policy paper compiled for the President during the summer of 1970 came back with a range of options identical to those given to presidents Johnson and Kennedy, everything from covert operations to multinational forces to an invasion. By 1970 the Trail so bristled with armament that only the last of these options had any feasibility at all, but not much since political opposition to the war had by now forced the withdrawal of many US troops, while a law now existed prohibiting US troops from being sent into Cambodia or Laos. Nixon decided to attempt an offensive using South Vietnamese troops without even their US advisors, and he convinced President Thieu to go along with the gambit.[3]

Thieu refused to approve final execution when his astrologer reported the time not propitious for a decision, but the CIA covertly induced the astrologer to reverse himself. It might have been better had Thieu's original hesitation prevailed.

US commander General Creighton Abrams had a similar reaction;[4] he actually called off the US preparatory operation at a certain point, but was ordered to proceed. On January 30, still a week before the onset of the South Vietnamese offensive, called *Lam Son 719*, communications intelligence revealed clear indications that the Route 9 Front, the People's Army command for the Tchepone area, expected the attack.

These trucks were destroyed while stationary, by a strike by US fighter-bombers in July 1966.

South Vietnam began its offensive on February 8. The ARVN troops included some of the best units in the Army – the 1st Division, the 1st Armored Brigade, Rangers, Airborne, and later Marines. The troops thrust into Laos as far as Ban Dong, where they halted. Any North Vietnamese not already in position to receive *Lam Son 719* now had plenty of time to move. The People's Army began a series of strong counter-attacks, including, for the first time, large tank formations. The South Vietnamese were put under heavy pressure, made a symbolic heliborne assault near Tchepone, then pulled out of Laos. By late March, the South

Vietnamese offensive had collapsed. Two elite ARVN divisions lost a third of their strength, the Ranger units more than half, with significant losses elsewhere as well. Saigon claimed major losses inflicted on the North Vietnamese, but within days the truck convoys were moving unimpeded on the Trail, and in the meantime the supplies had simply been pulled into a battle in which the South Vietnamese were defeated. The accomplishment was nothing like what the Nixon administration claimed.

A DEFINING EXPERIENCE

No longer the lifeline of desperate men and women, the Trail became the highway to Hanoi's victory. Roads became three-lane blacktop, numerous supply depots of 10,000-ton capacity appeared. Tanks, trucks in unprecedented numbers, petroleum pipelines, daily traffic equal to what had previously been seen only at peak periods, all sustained the major offensive Hanoi launched in 1972. The decision for this offensive had been made at conferences held to review the results of the *Lam Son 719* campaign. North Vietnam did not achieve final victory in 1972, and the Trail went on fueling the forces in the South after the Paris Agreements of January 1973, which marked the American departure. Hanoi shifted to a conventional style of operations, the hallmark of the war from 1972 on, and the resilience of the Trail is evident in the fact that it proved equal to the task of moving the much greater amounts of supplies necessary for those operations as well. Different Vietnamese sources record that 1,777,027 tons of supplies went down the Trail during the war, and that 823,164 tons of that amount moved between the beginning of 1974 and the April 1975 fall of Saigon. Thus almost half the volume of transport for the entire war moved South during its very last phase. They had not been stopped either by air, or SOG, or an invasion of the supply lines.

Was the Trail necessary? For a conventional war it certainly was. For the guerrilla warfare of the early 1960s, probably not. But the question cannot be answered in a vacuum. The Liberation Front could have fought on its own, sorely pressing the Saigon government for a decade or two, absent any outside action, and the outcome might have been the same. But political decisions for escalation, on both sides, upped the ante. In 1965, when Hanoi committed regular forces to the war, the Trail became important. By 1967–68, with major DRV forces in the South, the strategic supply route was necessary. After 1971 it became vital.

A different question is that of the relative importance of the Trail versus seaborne transport, at first to points along the Vietnamese coast, later to Sihanoukville in Cambodia. The sea was an important alternative avenue, especially during the middle period of the war, but never a substitute for the Trail. In the early years, the junks and small steamers employed in the traffic carried only a small volume of materiel – actually comparable to the Trail at that time. The land route, however, had considerable potential for expansion, while the sea became increasingly dangerous as Saigon and the Americans organized a naval patrol of the coast. Moreover, the Trail could be used by large numbers of infiltrators which the seaborne route could never accommodate. When the traffic shifted to Sihanoukville in 1966, volume went up tremendously, but declassified documents indicate that that avenue shut down in the summer of 1969. A major controversy on this matter raged in US intelligence circles. The CIA analysts eventually decided that Cambodia had been the key for NVA supply in the Mekong and lower parts of South Vietnam, but for manpower there was no substitute for the Trail. Evidence indicates that the Cambodia traffic was most important in upgrading the Liberation Front weapons to a new generation of small arms and heavy weapons. Without them, the war would still have continued. Sihanoukville could not substitute for the Trail.

Finally, the physical achievement of building and maintaining the Trail was an enormous one. The Trail became the crucible for a generation of Northerners. The labor and sacrifice, and the losses, affected everyone. The fight to close the Trail framed the experience of many Americans and even more South Vietnamese. The tactics, techniques, and the desperate gambits challenged skills as well as morale. On every side the Ho Chi Minh Trail would be a defining experience of the Vietnam War.

Chapter 5

The War outside Vietnam
Cambodia and Laos

Professor Kenton Clymer

President John F. Kennedy explains the significance of stopping Communist expansion in Laos at a press conference on March 23, 1961. (Cecil Stoughton/John F. Kennedy Presidential Library, Boston)

In August 2005, the United States and the Lao Democratic People's Republic marked the 50th anniversary of official relations. The event was marked, among other things, by a soccer match between officials from the American Embassy and the Lao Ministry of Foreign Affairs (won by the Ministry of Foreign Affairs by a score of 3–2). The Laotian-American singer Ketsana Vilaylack returned to her native country for a concert; and the embassy organized a photographic exhibition. These events symbolize a remarkable shift in the Laotian–American relationship: in 1975, the American contingent at the embassy in Vientiane was reduced to a skeleton staff, headed by a chargé d'affaires. Today there is an ambassador, and the relationship is back to normal. In Cambodia the transformation has been even more remarkable. Shortly before the Khmer Rouge victory in April 1975, the American embassy in Phnom Penh closed down entirely. Diplomatic relations were restored only in 1993.

It was no coincidence that American diplomatic representation either disappeared or was dramatically reduced in these countries in 1975, for that year marked the end of the Vietnam War. In the previous 25 years there had been intense American involvement in Laos and Cambodia, almost entirely as a result of the Cold War and, more directly, the growing conflict in neighboring Vietnam. Prior to the Cold War, neither the Cambodian nor Laotian parts of French Indochina were of much official interest to the United States. The Americans had long maintained a consulate at Saigon, and prior to World War II American officials would occasionally travel to Cambodia and Laos. At least one military intelligence officer investigated airfields in Cambodia. Otherwise, interest was limited to intrepid tourists who visited the recently "discovered" Angkorian temples, hunters who contributed to the depletion of the wild water-buffalo population, and missionaries from the Christian and Missionary Alliance. Arriving in Cambodia in 1923, the missionaries were the only Americans to reside permanently in the kingdom, but their presence was small.

COMMUNIST REBEL AREAS
22 MARCH 1961
NORTH VIETNAM
HANOI
LUANG
PRABANG
THAILAND
LAOS
ROADS
150
MILES

Laos and Cambodia

CHINA

NORTH VIETNAM

CHINA

PHONG SALY

Red River

BURMA

HOUA KHONG

Hanoi

LUANG PRABANG

GULF OF TONKIN

Pha Thi
HOUA PHANE
(SAMNEUA)

Luang Prabang

Mekong

XIANGHOANG
Plain of Jars

L

SAYABOURY

VIENTIANE

A

BORIKHANE

Vientiane

O

KHAMMOUANE

DMZ

S

Tchepone

SAVANNAKHET

THAILAND

VAPIKHAM
THONG

CHAMPASSAK

SÉDONE

ATTOPEU

SOUTH
CHINA
SEA

SITHANDONE

ODDAR MEANCHEY

PREAH VIHEAR

STUNG TRENG

RATANAKIRI

SIEM REAP
Angkor
Siem Reap

BATTAMBANG

Tonle Sap

KOMPONG THOM

CAMBODIA
Kompong Thom

KRATIE

MONDOLKIRI

N

PURSAT

KOMPONG
CHHNANG

SOUTH VIETNAM

KOMPONG CHAM

GULF

OF

THAILAND

OUDONG
MEANCHEY

KOH KONG

KOMPONG
SPEU

Phnom Penh

KANDAL

PREY
VENG SVAY
RIENG

TAKEO

KAMPOT

Mekong

Chantrea

Saigon

0   100 miles

0   200km

During World War II, there was little American involvement in Laos or Cambodia. There was one American air raid on Phnom Penh, and apparently American forces in India assisted the French underground in Laos by sending in some supplies, though that ended after the Yalta Conference in February 1945. Some American guerrilla units entered Laos early in 1945 to fight the Japanese.

AMERICAN INTEREST IN INDOCHINA GROWS

After World War II, two factors marked American foreign policy in Southeast Asia. One was a residual anticolonialist ideology that President Franklin Roosevelt had embodied to an unusual degree for an American president. In 1944, he commented that the Indochinese people were worse off after 80 years of French occupation. After Roosevelt's death in 1945 such sentiments diminished notably, particularly as anti-communism came to overshadow other factors. Of most concern to the United States was Ho Chi Minh's Viet Minh resistance to the French in Vietnam. Toward the end of World War II, the Americans had worked cooperatively with Ho against the Japanese, and some American intelligence officials developed a favorable view of the Vietnamese leader. But Ho was a Communist, and as the Cold War developed it became almost impossible for the United States to cooperate with him, despite the Americans' acknowledgment that he was a popular leader. Instead, the Americans supported the French. Thus when the United States first recognized the quasi-independent countries of Cambodia and Laos (along with Vietnam) in February 1950, it was because of the Cold War. Most notably it was because of the recent "fall" of China and the perception that international communism threatened all of Southeast Asia, particularly in Vietnam, where the Viet Minh was gaining on the French. The United States wanted to show support for the recent (and largely specious) French claim that these countries were "independent" within the French Union, hoping to ensure a stronger will among the people to resist communism. In important respects, then, the very beginning of American relations with Cambodia and Laos was directly related to the war in Vietnam – though in this case the French war which the Americans were about to inherit.

Although the United States recognized the Cambodian government of King Norodom Sihanouk (whom the French had elevated to the throne in 1941 at the age of 18), it did not trust the government to resist communism and thus was uncomfortable with efforts to force the French out. But in 1953 Sihanouk, faced with considerable pressure from armed anti-French rebels called Khmer Issaraks (who had been active since the late 1940s), led an ultimately successful royal crusade against the French. Making major gains in that respect in 1953, the Geneva Conference of 1954 (best remembered for the decision to divide Vietnam temporarily) marked the final recognition of genuine independence for Cambodia, as well as Laos.

During the conference, one of the most contentious issues involved representation for the resistance movements in all three Indochinese countries. The Viet Minh could hardly be denied an important place, since they controlled much of Vietnam. In Laos, there were Vietnamese "volunteers" and the indigenous Communist Pathet Lao, while Cambodia had the Issarak resistance along with Viet Minh elements. Ultimately, the Lao and Cambodian resistance groups were not allowed to take part in the conference. Even without them there, Chinese Prime Minister Zhou Enlai argued that these groups embodied considerable popular support and that, at the very least, their aspirations deserved some official attention. For a time it appeared that the conference might collapse over this issue. In the end, Zhou made an important concession: he acknowledged that the situations in Laos and Cambodia were not the same as in Vietnam, and he was therefore prepared to recognize the governments of each, provided American military bases were not allowed. He did, however, insist that in Laos there be regrouping areas in Phongsaly and Sam-Neua provinces for the Pathet Lao. The Cambodian delegation strenuously resisted a similar proposal for the Issaraks, arguing that whatever resistance and revolutionary movements existed in the country were really Viet Minh, and not indigenous. Though this was not an entirely accurate depiction of Cambodian reality, the Cambodians successfully resisted attempts at any kind of division or even mention of the Issaraks. The United States admired Cambodia's tenacity in this respect.

THE EARLY STRUGGLE TO KEEP CAMBODIA AND LAOS FREE FROM COMMUNISM

American actions with respect to Laos and Cambodia following the Geneva Conference were remarkably similar. The fundamental consideration was to try and prevent Communist domination of the two countries. Toward this end, the United States upgraded its diplomatic representation in both countries to the embassy level and sent its first ambassadors. It also provided considerable economic and military assistance to each and, over time, took over from the French (who bitterly resented the American intrusion) the training of the armed forces. Even as the Geneva Conference was in session, American pilots began secretly dropping supplies into Laos. The United States feared that Laos might become the first domino, and was determined to prevent that from happening. With the conclusion of the conference, the United States immediately began to pay for, supply, and train the Lao military, establishing a new organization, the Programs Evaluation Office (PEO), as a cover for American military involvement and to get around the Geneva Conference's prohibitions against foreign military personnel in Laos. American military officials, who had technically resigned from the military and were assigned Foreign Service Reserve Officer status, moved into Laos with the PEO. An American general was in charge, though he reported to the ambassador. The CIA airline, Civilian Air Transport, later renamed Air America, provided air transport and dropped propaganda leaflets.

Despite American efforts to keep Laos in the Western camp, in 1956 Souvanna Phouma's government opened talks with the Communist Pathet Lao (led by Souvanna Phouma's brother, Souphanouvong) which the following year

This cartoon reflects Cambodian suspicions that the United States supported Souvanna Phouma's overthrow of the Soviet-backed Kong Le. *Le Sangkum*, No. 18, January 1967, p.11. Cartoon by Huy Hem.

produced a coalition government. The former Pathet Lao provinces returned to government control, and in 1958 the Pathet Lao made considerable electoral gains. Consequently, the Dwight Eisenhower administration undertook efforts to sabotage the coalition government: it cut off economic assistance, forcing Souvanna Phouma to resign. The pro-Western Phoumi Sananikone replaced him, and American aid resumed. But the Pathet Lao resumed armed resistance.

In Cambodia, the United States also supplied economic and military assistance, largely paying for the country's armed forces and establishing a Military Assistance and Advisory Group, something the Americans had not been allowed to do in Laos. But despite American support, Sihanouk soon opted for a non-aligned, neutral course in international affairs. In 1956, much to the distress of the United States, he visited "Red" China, and two years later the two countries established diplomatic relations. Adding to American displeasure was Sihanouk's antagonism toward the Ngo Dinh Diem administration in South Vietnam, which the United States supported as an alternative to Ho's North Vietnam. This was in part due to Sihanouk's concern that the Diem government, as well as another American ally, Thailand, was supporting his political nemesis, Son Ngoc Thanh, and the dissident Khmer Serei (Free Khmers). In the context of the Cold War and the beginning of armed resistance movements in South Vietnam, it is not surprising that the United States not only found Sihanouk irritating but adopted as official policy a provision to support anti-Sihanouk dissidents under certain conditions.

In the late 1950s, there was American involvement in at least one of the several plots against the prince (Sihanouk having abdicated as king so that he could take a more active part in political affairs). Early in 1959, American agents helped supply Dap Chhuon, a former Sihanouk confidant who had lost the favor of the prince and had gone into opposition. An American intelligence officer, Victor Matsui, was involved in sending supplies to Chhuon from South Vietnam. The plot collapsed, Sihanouk's forces killed Chhuon, and the evidence of both South Vietnamese and American involvement came to light.

In Laos, the Americans had succeeded in replacing a leader they did not like. In Cambodia they did not, at least in part because Sihanouk was enormously popular throughout most of Cambodia. After the plots came to light, the United States backed away from efforts to overthrow him and tried to convince the Diem government to do the same. But Ngo Dinh Nhu, brother of the South Vietnamese prime minister and the official in charge of conspiracies, paid little attention to American pressure, and the plotting continued.

As the fighting resumed in Laos, the Americans increased their assistance. In December 1959, when Phoumi Sananikone proved to be politically unreliable, the CIA encouraged a military coup that brought Brigadier General Phoumi Nosavan to power. The next year, the CIA rigged an election to prevent any Pathet Lao electoral victories. Although Phoumi Nosavan seems to have allowed Pathet Lao leaders, including Souphanouvong, to escape from prison, the Americans were, by the middle of 1960, generally optimistic about Laotian developments. That is,

President Richard Nixon meets with Prime Minister Souvanna Phouma in the Oval Office, October 21, 1970. (NARA)

they were optimistic until the American-trained Captain Kong Le led another coup in August 1960, denounced the corruption that had resulted from American assistance, and proclaimed a neutral government. Souvanna Phouma emerged again as the prime minister. When Souvanna Phouma elicited aid from the Soviet Union and again entered into talks with the Pathet Lao, the United States cut off aid and then tried to convince Souvanna Phouma to change course. When the Laotian leader refused, the United States actively sought to overthrow him, in part by supporting the ousted Phoumi Sananikone, who had mounted a resistance movement of his own in southern Laos. In December 1960 General Phoumi's forces, with full American backing, resumed control in Vientiane, but only after a battle that resulted in 500 civilian casualties. With Soviet help, Kong Le and his Pathet Lao allies retreated to the Plain of Jars, where they defeated government forces and drove them out of the area. An American aircraft, flying over the Plain of Jars, was struck by machine-gun fire. "This was the first incident in Southeast Asia of a USAF aircraft flown by active-duty military pilots being struck by communist ground-fire."[1] It would not be the last.

By the end of the Eisenhower administration, there was serious concern that, despite the massive American aid, Laos might well be taken over by the Communists. Soviet assistance to the Pathet Lao had increased markedly, and nearly half of the country was in their hands.

John F. Kennedy was determined to show resolve in Laos, not because the country itself had much strategic significance, but because he surmised that Communist leaders around the world would be watching his response carefully. One possibility was to send up to 60,000 American troops into the country, with nuclear weapons available for use if necessary. Though Kennedy did not opt for this extreme measure, he did authorize covert military missions, based in Thailand, to enter Laos in support of the government. He also upgraded the PEO to a MAAG. There began to be American casualties, as the Royal Lao Army, despite large amounts of American supplies and training, proved that it was no match for Pathet Lao forces.

With Lao military ineptitude evident, the Americans turned to the Hmong, the people who lived in the highlands. The Hmong historically had little liking for the lowland Lao, who in turn considered them uncivilized and inferior. Fortunately for the Americans, the Hmong also had little love for the Pathet Lao or their Viet Minh allies. The Americans soon discovered an aggressive Hmong lieutenant colonel in the Lao armed forces, Vang Pao, and began to cultivate relations with him. This was the beginning of a longstanding, and ultimately tragic, relationship between the Americans and the Hmong. But for the moment, the Kennedy administration turned to diplomacy to solve the Laotian conflict, having determined that if there was to be a war, it ought to be in Vietnam.

A cease-fire took effect on May 11, 1961, and a few days later a new Geneva conference convened to tackle the Laotian situation. After considerable posturing on all sides, the conference reached an agreement on July 23, 1962. Souvanna Phouma was once again in charge of a neutral government, and Kennedy was

American diplomat Chester Bowles meets with Norodom Sihanouk in January 1968. The meeting improved relations between the two countries temporarily but did not result in the restoration of diplomatic relations. *Kambuja*, No. 35, February 15, 1968.

pleased. Laos had been removed, it appeared, as a Cold War issue. His attention turned to Vietnam.

In Cambodia, meanwhile, there was no civil war, and for a time relations between the United States and Sihanouk were relatively good. But as the war in Vietnam began to grow in the early 1960s, tensions with Sihanouk increased once again. Overflights into Cambodian airspace, ground incursions, and especially the bombing of border villages intensely angered Sihanouk, who had long been convinced that the American involvement in Vietnam was both misguided and doomed. He had no love of Vietnamese communism and often suppressed domestic leftists, but he believed that American involvement only increased the likelihood of Communist domination of Southeast Asia. As he put it a few years later, "The best way to create Communists is to bring in Americans where there aren't any [Communists]. Americans attract Communists like sugar attracts ants."[2]

In November 1963 Ngo Dinh Diem was overthrown and murdered. Sihanouk immediately suspected American involvement in the coup and, while he had no affection for Diem, feared that the Americans might have a similar fate in store for him. He decided to distance himself further from the Americans, and so on November 19 he ended all American military and economic assistance. President Kennedy was himself assassinated three days later, the situation in South Vietnam unraveled, and early in 1965 President Lyndon Johnson made the fateful decisions leading to a large-scale American war in Vietnam.

CAMBODIA AND LAOS DURING THE AMERICAN WAR IN VIETNAM

As the war heated up, attacks along the Cambodian border only increased. One of the most serious occurred at the border town of Chantrea on March 19, 1964, when 17 Cambodians were killed. Some informed observers believed that the attack was a deliberate provocation by American military officials who did not want to see relations improve between Cambodia, on the one hand, and South Vietnam and the United States, on the other, since improved relations tended to curb military activities along the border. Diplomatic relations were not broken, but American influence in Cambodia was virtually nil. The final break came the following year, after four American Skyraider aircraft bombed two Cambodian villages on April 28, 1965, killing one 13-year-old boy and wounding several other people. It was the last straw for Sihanouk. A few days later he broke off diplomatic relations, saying at the time that if the Americans would stop the attacks on border villages, he would restore relations. Diplomatic relations between the United States and Cambodia had become a casualty of the raging war in Vietnam.

In Laos, the Americans initially abided by the Geneva Accords and withdrew their military personnel. The North Vietnamese did not, however, and within a few months the United States was once again providing support to the Royal Lao

Royal Lao forces guard the approaches to Luang Prabang against the Pathet Lao in 1970. (Fred Eisenhauer)

The US air attaché, Colonel Bob Tyrell, in civilian clothes, standing beside the RLAF commander, General Thoa Ma, at Wattay Air Base, Vientiane, in 1966. The United States was not supposed to have military personnel in Laos at this time, so Tyrell was officially working for the US embassy in Vientiane, but in reality he supervised the air operations in the country, acting as a local USAF air commander in Laos. General Thao Ma, a charismatic and popular commander with the RLAF, would later be involved in a failed coup in October 1966. He then fled to Thailand before trying to return to Laos seven years later. In this second coup attempt, his aircraft was shot down and he was killed. (Albert Grandolini collection)

Army, as well as to Vang Pao's Hmong forces. The MAAG was reconstituted as the Requirements Office (it was placed in the US Agency for International Development), and building up and training of the Hmong army of 9,000 men was turned over directly to the Central Intelligence Agency. American pilots flew reconnaissance and combat missions from bases in Thailand. The fighting was mostly on the Plain of Jars, as the Hmong army grew to 30,000 men. The American objective was to prevent the Communist forces from moving across the Plain and on to the capital, Vientiane, only 100 miles to the south. American concern in Laos was directly linked to the escalating war in Vietnam. If the Pathet Lao succeeded in capturing Vientiane, the government they would install would certainly insist that another major American bombing campaign – the effort to cut off North Vietnamese infiltration into South Vietnam along the Ho Chi Minh Trail in Laos – end. Thus the war on the Plain of Jars was not just symbolically important: it was strategically linked to Vietnam.

By 1964, the Pathet Lao controlled the Plain, which then became a "free fire" zone and led to increasing levels of American bombardment against Pathet Lao positions. The Americans backed Royal Lao Army and Hmong units to try and retake the Plain. C-47 gunships firing thousands of rounds per minute entered the war. By 1970, B-52 strategic bombers were also employed. Sometimes the massive firepower was sufficiently devastating that Vang Pao's army captured the Plain, but despite fighting bravely, his forces were ultimately no match for the battle-hardened Pathet Lao and North Vietnamese, who always managed to recapture it.

Despite the huge amount of bombing (the Plain of Jars became "the most intensely bombarded place on the face of the planet")[3], American involvement remained secret until 1970. The bombing ended only in 1973. Although American officials testified that the bombing did not target civilians, in fact the 50,000 villagers living on the Plain of Jars suffered immensely. Between the massive bombings and the attacks by gunships, civilians could not persist for long. Those who were not killed fled in droves and became refugees.[4]

As for Vang Pao's army, it fought bravely, but also suffered very high casualties. Soon the army of 30,000 was reduced to about 20,000, and Vang Pao increasingly had to draft boys as young as 12. The Hmong villages were hemorrhaging. When the bombing ended in 1973, Vang Pao's army was doomed. He held out until 1974, and the following year the CIA evacuated him and his family, along with several thousand other Hmong, to Thailand. Soon tens of thousands of other Hmong followed them.

Some aspects of American involvement in Laos were even more directly related to the American war against North Vietnam. The top secret Lima Site 85, on Pha Thi mountain, served as a radar station to guide American planes bombing North Vietnam. But in March 1968 the North Vietnamese overran the base, resulting in "the largest single ground combat loss of US Air Force personnel in the history of the Vietnam War." Twelve men were killed or captured. Only seven escaped.[5]

Also, beginning in 1965, the United States began massive bombing campaigns in southern Laos to try and stem the flow of personnel and materiel down the Ho Chi Minh Trail. Despite the immense bombing, the North Vietnamese steadily improved the Trail to increase its capacity for moving supplies to the South. They learned to adapt, often in ingenious ways, to the bombing. The number of soldiers and amount of supplies coming down the Trail increased annually. Frustrated at their inability to stop the infiltration, the United States in February 1971 organized a South Vietnamese invasion of southern Laos to cut the Trail near the town of Tchepone. Operation *Lam Son 719*, however, mainly revealed the weakness of the South Vietnamese military. Their troops could not match the military expertise of the North Vietnamese who were waiting for them. In the end they had to retreat from battle, some escaping by hanging to helicopter skids, having lost more than 200 Americans and 1,700 South Vietnamese dead. It was a major setback, even though as many as 20,000 North Vietnamese also died, most in the intense bombing supporting the attack. By the time the bombing over Laos ceased in 1973, the United States had dropped about 2.1 million tons of bombs, the equivalent of all conventional explosives dropped on both Germany and Japan during World War II.[6]

If Laos was involved in the shooting war in Vietnam from the very beginning, Cambodia's involvement was for several years minor, though only by comparison. After the break in diplomatic relations in 1965, the Australian ambassador to Cambodia, Noël St. Claire Deschamps, ably handled American interests in Phnom Penh for the next four years. Virtually all of the American matters he addressed involved the Vietnam War. American sailors crossed into Cambodia waters and were captured. American pilots ejected or shot down over Cambodia and taken into custody. American and South Vietnamese intelligence teams entered Cambodia covertly; they sometimes killed Cambodians and sometimes became

A satirical Cambodian view of American military actions along the Cambodian–Vietnamese border. *Kambuja*, No. 44, November 15, 1968, p.143. Cartoon by Huy Hem.

Look at those folk, the nearest is Giap and farther away on my left is Pham Van Dong!

casualties themselves. And, as always, there were military incursions into Cambodia as American and South Vietnamese chased after fleeing Vietnamese Communist forces, while American planes and artillery in Vietnam targeted villages across the border thought to harbor NVA forces. The American Special Forces worked with anti-Sihanouk Khmer Serei personnel and probably played a role in inserting them into Cambodia. Vietnamese Communist forces utilized Cambodian territory as a sanctuary and acquired supplies there, at least to some extent with the complicity of Cambodian government officials. North Vietnamese forces entered South Vietnam through Cambodia. Just how important Cambodia was to the Vietnamese Communists was a matter of debate in American circles. Some informed Americans thought that they used Cambodian territory only sporadically, that most of their supplies came from places other than Cambodia, and that the Cambodian infiltration route was minor. Others thought Cambodia played a major role in their strategy.

By late 1967, Sihanouk himself was increasingly worried about Vietnamese Communist use of his territory, and he began to seek better relations with the United States. Early in 1968 he told a high-level American diplomatic team led by Chester Bowles that he would not object to hot pursuit of fleeing Vietnamese Communists into uninhabited Cambodian territory by American forces. There was movement toward restored relations, but in the end Lyndon Johnson did not make the one pledge necessary at that point to restore relations: a promise to recognize and respect Cambodia's current borders.

That pledge came, ironically, from the new president, Richard Nixon, who had long sought a more aggressive military policy toward NVA/VC forces in Cambodia and who was soon to begin the devastating secret bombing of that country. But he also reestablished relations with Sihanouk, in part because restoration of relations would suggest to the world that the Cambodian leader had changed his mind about the inevitability of an American defeat in Vietnam. The secret bombings began before diplomatic relations were established, and there were few protests from Phnom Penh about it, suggesting to some that Sihanouk himself must have acquiesced in, if not actually encouraged, the bombing. The prince did not commiserate with those Vietnamese who died in the attacks, but it seems unlikely that he approved of the bombing. He had agreed to hot pursuit in uninhabited areas of Cambodia, but bombings by B-52s was scarcely akin to chasing soldiers across the border. Most likely Sihanouk restored diplomatic relations in spite of the bombing. Despite American claims to the contrary, the bombings were not in unpopulated areas, and hundreds if not thousands of Cambodians died.

THE CAMBODIAN CIVIL WAR

In March 1970, Lon Nol and Sirik Matak organized a coup to depose Sihanouk while the prince was out of the country. The degree of American involvement has long been debated, with no definitive answers emerging. Sihanouk himself always believed that the CIA was behind the action, but most scholars are not convinced. It does seem probable, though, that American military intelligence officials in Vietnam had foreknowledge of the coup, and perhaps assured the plotters of American support. These officials had long disliked Sihanouk, whose

US ambassador Emory Swank meets with Cambodia's new leader, General Lon Nol, shortly after the ouster of Norodom Sihanouk in 1970. *Cambodge Nouveau*, No. 6, October 1970, p.7.

protests about actions along the border had led to restrictions on what they could do. Over the years they had resented efforts to improve relations with Sihanouk, lest the restrictions increase. They had probably sabotaged efforts in the past to improve relations. So they are the prime suspects on the American side. Whatever the degree of American involvement was, the Nixon administration was not displeased with Sihanouk's ouster. As Nixon's aide H. R. Haldeman wrote, it was "all right with us."[7]

Shortly after the coup, American and South Vietnamese troops invaded Cambodia to destroy the Vietnamese Communist headquarters. The invasion succeeded in reinvigorating the anti-war movement at home, driving the Vietnamese deeper into Cambodia, and in general destabilizing Cambodia. All of these developments resulted in tragedy: for the first time, Cambodia was fully engulfed in the Vietnam War, compounded with a brutal civil war. The Cambodian Communist opposition (the Khmers Rouges, as Sihanouk called them), only a nuisance in 1969, was growing, ironically in part due to the deposed Sihanouk's call for his countrymen to join the opposition.

The United States fully supported Lon Nol's Republic of Cambodia. Initially little more than a "sideshow," as William Shawcross termed it,[8] the Nixon administration

Women soldiers in a photo taken shortly after the ouster of Norodom Sihanouk and the American invasion of Cambodia in 1970. The photo appeared on the cover of the Cambodian government's magazine, *Cambodge Nouveau*, July 1970.

Lon Nol's soldiers pass out weapons to Cambodian villagers shortly after the ouster of Norodom Sihanouk and the American invasion of Cambodia. The picture appeared on the back cover of the Cambodian government magazine, *Cambodge Nouveau*, July 1970.

came to view the survival of the Khmer republic as vital. The United States therefore stepped up the bombing, increasingly in direct support of Lon Nol's beleaguered forces. By the time it was finally stopped by Congress in 1973, tens of thousands of Cambodians lay dead. Estimates of deaths range as high as 300,000, though 150,000 is probably closer to the truth.[9] Henry Kissinger himself now accepts that 50,000 probably died.

The war in Cambodia was a disaster for which Lon Nol bears considerable responsibility. Personally directing the military campaigns, Lon Nol proved his incompetence. The most disastrous campaign, Chenla II, was designed to reopen a major highway between Phnom Penh and Kompong Thom in August 1971. It turned into a rout: 3,000 of Cambodia's best troops were killed, while 15,000 left the field in disarray. It was the last major campaign mounted by the Republic of Cambodia.

The peace agreement with Vietnam in January 1973 did not apply fully to Cambodia; the North Vietnamese told Henry Kissinger that, while they could influence events in Laos, they could not deliver the Khmer Rouge. A cease-fire in Cambodia lasted scarcely a week before fighting resumed. The Khmer Rouge nearly overran the capital in the summer of 1973, and were stopped only by massive American bombing. Somewhat surprisingly, the government survived for nearly two more years, propped up by American support. But many Americans knew that the government forces were doomed. On April 17, 1975, the Khmer Rouge marched victorious into Phnom Penh. The war was over, but calamity lay ahead.

In diplomatic terms, the great tragedy of this period was the United States' failure to engage Sihanouk in negotiations. From 1971 on Sihanouk offered numerous times to meet with the Americans to try to arrange a settlement, but the Americans always declined. They had no objection, they said, to including Sihanouk in a final settlement, but they would only support negotiations between Sihanouk and Lon Nol, to which Sihanouk would never agree. The Chinese urged the Americans to change course, as did John Gunther Dean, the last American ambassador in Phnom Penh before the Khmer Rouge victory. By the time Kissinger was willing to talk with Sihanouk (in February 1975) it was much too late. In April the Khmer Rouge entered Phnom Penh and renamed the country Democratic Kampuchea (DK).

With the collapse of Cambodia and South Vietnam, the non-communists in the Laotian government of national unity fled the country. Soon the Pathet Lao was completely in charge. By the end of 1975, they had ended the centuries-old monarchy and established the Lao People's Democratic Republic. A notable difference from the two other Indochinese countries was that in Laos, the final transfer of power proceeded without military action.

POSTWAR POLICY

With the change in government, most Western aid to Laos ended, and it took the new government several years to cope with the many problems that beset the war-ravaged country. Hmong resistance continued for two years in the northern parts of the country. There was nothing approaching the killing fields of Cambodia, but there were re-education camps for former government officials and attempts were made to collectivize agriculture, limit private commerce, and hold mandatory political education sessions. All of this proved unpopular, however, and by the end of the 1970s the government had eased up. Even so, by the mid-1980s, perhaps 350,000 people (10 percent of the population) had fled, including a large portion of the intelligentsia, thus setting back Lao development.[10] Despite this, by the late 1980s Laos had made considerable advancements in agriculture, education, and health services.

From the Lao perspective, a major concern during these years with the United States were the thousands of unexploded American landmines scattered through the country. Every year several hundred Lao died (and continue to die) from exploding mines. Before the United States reestablished ties with Vietnam, the Lao–American connection was also useful for contact between the United States and Vietnam. For the United States, the leading concern was with American soldiers lost in Laos whose remains had not been recovered. In the 1980s Laos began to permit some joint teams to investigate sites to recover remains, and the United States allowed some humanitarian assistance to reach Laos. Thus the official relationship began to warm in the 1980s, and despite some disputes over Lao opium production there were no major confrontations between the two

countries. In 1992 the two countries exchanged ambassadors once again, and today the relationship is quite good. American tourists can now enter Laos by obtaining a visa at the airport. In November 2004, the United States Congress authorized normal trade relations between the two countries.

Whatever problems Laos faced in the years after the end of Vietnam War, they were minor compared to the tragedy that unfolded in Cambodia when Pol Pot's killing fields began. By the time the Vietnamese Army drove the Khmer Rouge from power at the end of 1978, an estimated 2.3 million Cambodians (some 30 percent of the population) had perished.

During these years, the United States certainly never supported DK, but there was a scarcely whispered awareness that DK – despite its monstrous policies – served an American interest by preventing the spread of Vietnamese (and by implication Soviet) influence deeper into Southeast Asia. The United States supplied DK with very limited humanitarian assistance (the chemical DDT to fight malarial mosquitoes). Otherwise there was no contact. By 1975, and more so by 1976, news of Khmer Rouge atrocities was beginning to become known, and the following year the new president, Jimmy Carter, known for elevating human rights into a major factor in American foreign policy, condemned DK as the "worst violator of human rights in the world today." But when Vietnam ended Khmer Rouge rule with its invasion late in 1978, the United States condemned it even if it meant liberation for the suffering Cambodians. When China retaliated against Vietnam with a military invasion in February 1979, the United States raised little objection.

Despite Carter's expressed concern with human rights, his administration's approach to events in Cambodia was based purely on geopolitical considerations. The United States viewed Vietnam's invasion and occupation of Cambodia as an

US cluster bombs still litter the Laotian countryside. From 1964 to 1973 the United States dropped about 2 million tons of bombs along the North Vietnamese Army's supply route known as the Ho Chi Minh Trail, in the jungles of eastern Laos. (Topfoto/Imageworks)

extension of Soviet influence, since Vietnam and the Soviet Union had recently signed a treaty of friendship. This meant a diminution of China's influence, since China had been close to the Khmer Rouge. Since the United States was on increasingly good terms with China (full diplomatic relations were established early in 1979), the United States considered Vietnam's victory and DK's defeat a geopolitical setback.

Consequently the United States (along with China and Thailand) determined to undermine the Cambodian government installed by the Vietnamese, the People's Republic of Kampuchea (PRK). With Carter's National Security Advisor, Zbigniew Brzezinski, leading the charge, the United States encouraged China and Thailand to resuscitate the Khmer Rouge remnants. The United States itself assisted smaller, non-Communist resistance groups, and even assisted the Khmer Rouge directly by providing food for them (along with all refugees) in the Thai camps. The Americans also concentrated their relief efforts along the Thai border, where thousands of Cambodians had fled, and refused to supply aid to those Cambodians still living inside the country. Although relief was certainly needed along the border, the refusal to supply it within Cambodia was a political decision.

As reports of widespread famine inside Cambodia emerged, Congress pushed for meaningful assistance inside the country, and Carter then allowed some relief to flow through Phnom Penh. But it remained American policy to destabilize and weaken the

PRK. As Stephen Solarz (D-NY) and others noted at the time, little thought was given to what would happen if the PRK collapsed. Did the administration care if the result was a resumption of brutal Khmer Rouge rule? Apparently not.

Carter and his two Republican successors, Ronald Reagan and George H. W. Bush, continued to supply the non-Communist opposition forces, particularly after 1982 when, under Chinese and American pressure, they merged with the Khmer Rouge to form the Coalition Government of Democratic Kampuchea, which the Khmer Rouge dominated. At the United Nations, the successive American administrations voted to seat the Khmer Rouge, rather than the PRK.

By the late 1980s, American policy toward Cambodia was becoming a political issue. Why, the critics asked, did the United States in effect support the murderous Khmer Rouge? Whatever the shortcomings of the PRK, was it not infinitely preferable? Was it worth undermining the PRK when the consequence would likely be a return to the killing fields? Continued assistance to the resistance forces seemed even less defensible when, in 1989, the Vietnamese finally withdrew their army from Cambodia. Criticism of American policy gained considerable popular force after Peter Jennings' documentary account, *From the Killing Fields*, which appeared to show direct American contact with the Khmer Rouge, aired on ABC television. Peter Rodman, an official in the Reagan administration, expressed the government's dilemma well: "Our trying to ride two horses – opposing both Phnom Penh and the Khmer Rouge – was a risky gamble. How could we possibly overthrow the one [the PRK] without removing the main barrier to the dominance of the other [the Khmer Rouge]?"[11]

Faced with mounting criticism, the Bush administration then changed course and, withdrawing its support from the coalition government, announced that its first priority was to prevent the return of the Khmer Rouge. This change initially angered China, but thereafter the United States, working with the other permanent members of the Security Council, as well as with Indonesia, Japan, and others, sought to end the conflict. The result was United Nations-organized elections in 1993 that discredited the Khmer Rouge and set the stage for the eventual disappearance of the organization. The United States then restored full diplomatic relations with Cambodia.

The restoration of relations with Cambodia, and the upgrading of relations with Laos, symbolized the real end of the war in Vietnam. American involvement in both countries was deeply related to the war from the beginning, and once the Americans had withdrawn their troops from Vietnam, they continued to oppose the united Vietnam, something most evident in Cambodia. Today, there continue to be some tensions and disagreements between the United States and these countries, and some more extreme American factions seek regime change. But for the most part, the differences are what one might expect in times of normality. For now, there is peace in Indochina.

The author wishes to thank Dr. Judy Ledgewood for providing the Cambodian magazines from which several of the photographs and illustrations in this chapter were taken.

Chapter 6

A View from the Other Side of the Story

Reflections of a South Vietnamese Soldier

Lieutenant General Lam Quang Thi

In a divisive and lengthy conflict, such as the Vietnam War, it is often difficult to distinguish myths from realities. Douglas Pike, the late Vietnam historian, once compared the efforts to understand Vietnamese affairs to peeling layer after layer from an onion, in search of an elusive core. Thus, it is not surprising that there are many myths related to the Vietnam conflict. From the perspective of a South Vietnamese officer, perhaps the most common and galling public misperception concerning the conflict is the idea that Ho Chi Minh was merely a patriotic leader who fought his whole life for the independence of his country. In reality, the situation was more complex, for Ho was also a hard-core Marxist whose goal it was to transform Vietnam into a satellite of the Communist bloc. Ho's devotion to a Marxist ideology became clear during the bloody land reform of the 1950s – in which an estimated 500,000 landowners perished – which was an inevitable result of the Marxist doctrine of class warfare. Ho's successors also had more than national unification in mind, and were bent on a Communist takeover of surrounding nations. At the convention of the North Vietnam Labor Party held on February 11, 1974, for example, Le Duan, first secretary of the North Vietnam Communist Party, exposed the objective of the Communists when he called for strenghtening the "aid to the revolution in South Vietnam to proceed toward the reunification of the Fatherland." It was also Duan who openly called for the "fulfillment of international duty toward the revolution in Laos and Kampuchea" – in other words aid to the continuing Communist revolutions in those countries.

The second myth is that the South Vietnamese population was sympathetic to the Viet Cong (VC). In my opinion, nothing could be further from the truth. The failure of the VC during the 1968 Tet Offensive, for example, was due largely to

ARVN soldier in action. This award-winning photograph by Nguyen Ngoc Hanh, ARVN, was taken during an operation in Bong Son valley in MRII in the mid-1960s. It shows the courage and determination of the South Vietnamese soldier in the face of the enemy. (Photo courtesy Nguyen Ngoc Hanh)

Road-opening operation in Red River Delta, North Vietnam, 1948. During the Indochina War, the Vietnamese National Army operated at battalion level and was mostly assigned static defensive missions including road-opening operations. (Photo QLVNCH/*Quan Su 4*, ARVN/*Military History 4*)

the loyalty of the population toward the government. Popular uprisings in the cities and urban centers that the VC expected would support and bring to fruition their Tet Offensive simply did not materialize. In fact, in Hue, the VC summarily executed more than 4,000 people whom they accused of opposing the "revolution." Yet, according to *Newsweek*, the VC could not have attacked Saigon and other cities without at least the passive support of the population. According to this line of reasoning, a good portion of the population in the South during the American Civil War must have been sympathetic to General Sherman's army.

A more serious myth, in my opinion – and the main topic of this chapter – is that the ARVN was an army of incompetents and cowards. The most important fact which can be used to refute this assertion is that the South Vietnamese armed forces lost well over 200,000 dead during the Indochina Wars. In proportion to population, that was equivalent to some 2.5 million American dead. An army that did not fight would not have incurred such exorbitant losses. The ARVN actually has a much longer history than many in the West realize, tracing its lineage back to the foundation of the Vietnamese National Army under Emperor Bao Dai in 1950 – a force that played a growing military role in the First Indochina War. When, as a young second lieutenant, I reported to the newly created Vietnamese artillery battery in NVN in early 1952, the Viet Minh were hurling entire divisions, supported by artillery regiments, on embattled French forces defending the Red River Delta. When, in May 1954, General Vo Nguyen Giap sent three infantry divisions supported by one artillery division against the French *camp retranché* of Dien Bien Phu, the Vietnamese National Army still operated at battalion level. The same army lived on after the partition of Vietnam and became the ARVN. Thus, after nearly two decades of continuous combat, something never witnessed by US forces in any war, it was this same army which stood its ground and convincingly defeated NVN's finest divisions in their ill-fated 1972 Easter Offensive. Having proven its mettle in the most dire of situations, the ARVN only went down to defeat three years later due to the nearly complete withdrawal of US support for their beleaguered cause.

To make an objective, equitable, and informed judgment on the South Vietnamese Army, it is necessary to study its history, its role in nation building, its performance on the battlefield, and also the true causes of the 1975 disaster. Yet some American self-appointed pundits, including former Vietnam veterans, intentionally or by mistake, choose instead to make hasty judgments based on film footages of isolated actions or unconfirmed and even distorted stories, and to slander an army that fought and died for the cause of freedom. "It is a pity," wrote Harry F. Noyes, an Air Force veteran of Vietnam, "that many veterans of the Vietnam War have joined radical agitators, draft dodgers and smoke-screen politicians to besmirch the honor of an army that can no longer defend itself. To slander an army that died in battle because America abandoned it is a contemptible deed, unworthy of American soldiers."[1]

ARMY OF THE REPUBLIC OF VIETNAM

To study the morale and motivation of the South Vietnamese Army, it is necessary to go back to its origins, and the sociopolitical environment in which it was created.

On March 8, 1949, a treaty was signed between French President Vincent Auriol and Emperor Bao Dai, recognizing an "independent and unified Vietnam" within the framework of the French Union. This treaty also provided for the

Prime Minister Ngo Dinh Diem receiving the surrender of Binh Xuyen forces in Saigon in 1955. Evicted from Cholon region where they controlled for years prostitution and gambling, the Binh Xuyen armed gangs were defeated in the marshy Rung Sat area near Vung Tau by the troops under Colonel Duong Van Minh (later general and chief of state). (Photo ARVN/*Military History 4*)

creation of a "National Army" which would incorporate the various paramilitary units and religious factions in existence at the time. The Vietnamese Joint General Staff was created in 1952. Four military regions (MR) were also formed, although they handled only administrative functions because all military operations were controlled by French military authorities. The table on page 120 shows the comparative strength of the Viet Minh, the French Expeditionary Corps, and the Vietnamese National Army at the end of 1952.[2]

During the years following the 1954 Paris Accords, Mr. Ngo Dinh Diem, the postwar prime minister, after having consolidated his political power, organized a national referendum. This resulted in the overthrow of Bao Dai and the formation of the First Republic on October 26, 1955, with himself as its first president. The Vietnamese National Army thus became the Army of the Republic of Vietnam.

In the meantime, Mr. Diem undertook the difficult task of taking complete control over his own fledgling nation. In the chaos following Geneva, several important armed groups and militias threatened the nation with anarchy and collapse. Through deft maneuvering and US support, Diem succeeded in overcoming the shadowy, underworld Binh Xuyen forces in Saigon-Cholon and the dissident, militant Buddhist Hoa Hao forces in the Mekong Delta. As a result, Diem halted the immediate threat that faced South Vietnam and welded the ARVN into a more effective force, a force that would quickly grow with the passage of time.

Comparative strength of forces in Vietnam in late 1952

1. FRENCH:	233,826
Expeditionary Corps	174,736
consisting of:	
French	54,790
Legionnaires	19,079
North African	29,532
African	18,153
Native	53,182
Auxiliary Forces	59,090
2. NATIONAL ARMY:	**147,800**
Regular Forces	94,520
consisting of:	
57 infantry battalions	
5 airborne battalions	
3 artillery battalions	
6 reconnaissance armored squadrons	
Various support units	
Auxiliary Forces	53,280
3. VIET MINH:	**425,000**
Regular Forces	270,000
consisting of:	
6 infantry divisions: 304, 308, 312, 316, 320, 325	
1 artillery division	
8 engineer battalions	
Various combat support units	
Auxiliary Forces (Popular Force and Guerrilla)	155,000
consisting of:	
NVN	60,000
Central VN and hauts plateaux	25,000
Inter-Region 5 (south of Central VN)	30,000
SVN	40,000

Before the Communist offensive in 1975, the ARVN, with a total of about 1 million men, consisted of 11 infantry divisions, one airborne division, one marine division, 15 Ranger groups, 66 artillery battalions, four armored brigades, and various combat support units. The Air Force had four air divisions with 1,000 aircraft and 800 helicopters, totaling 40,000 men. The Navy had 39,000 men and was equipped with 1,600 vessels of all sizes organized into one Sea Task Force and numerous riverine squadrons.

After the 1968 Tet Offensive, in which the VC suffered heavy losses, the North Vietnamese Army brought troops from the North to replenish the depleted VC units or to replace them entirely. By 1972, it was estimated that 75 percent of

the soldiers in VC units came from North Vietnam. At that time, the NVA/VC forces in the South amounted to approximately 300,000 men, consisting of 200,000 regular troops and 100,000 local forces. The main regular force consisted of 20 infantry divisions plus various combat support units.

Troops of the Vietnamese Army in combat operations against the Communist Viet Cong guerrillas, 1961. (NARA)

Thus, after the withdrawal of US and allied (South Korea, Australia, and New Zealand) forces under the Vietnamization program beginning in 1971, the ARVN faced the NVA from a presumed position of strength – outnumbering Communist forces roughly three to one. However, in reality the situation was much more precarious, for accepted wisdom contends that government forces must achieve at least a ten-to-one ratio to be able to defeat an insurgency. This is because the greatest portion of that force could not be used to face the insurgents, but instead would be used to protect the populated areas and to safeguard key logistical installations, airports, bridges, and lines of communication.

It is remarkable that the ARVN, under heavy odds, had almost won the war toward the end of 1971. After having destroyed, in tandem with their American allies, more than half of the VC's regular forces during the Tet Offensive, the ARVN rooted out the VC's political and administrative infrastructure in the hamlets and villages of South Vietnam. It is more remarkable that this same army, with pivotal American air support, held its ground and defeated the NVA's multi-division Easter Offensive in 1972, achieving perhaps the biggest single victory of either the Indochina War or the Vietnam War.

THE 1972 EASTER OFFENSIVE

It was indeed the 1972 Easter Offensive that served as the best indicator of the ARVN's potential and the way forward to victory in the Vietnam War. The conflict had changed fundamentally since the beginning of Vietnamization.

ARVN troops attacking VC positions in Hue Citadel during the 1968 Tet Offensive. Eleven ARVN infantry battalions and three US Marine battalions participated in the battle to recapture the Citadel of Hue. ARVN troops suffered 384 killed among the 500 KIAs suffered by all South Vietnamese-allied forces in Hue. (Photo courtesy of Nguyen Ngoc Hanh)

American combat forces were, in the main, gone from the conflict, leaving the ARVN to face both the irregular war in the countryside and the big-unit war of the North Vietnamese. Though American troops were leaving, their massive air support remained behind to work in tandem with their South Vietnamese allies. It was to be a fruitful partnership, American firepower and economic support and South Vietnamese manpower, a partnership that would prove well nigh unstoppable.

For their part, the NVA/VC would no longer choose to run and hide in their cross-border sanctuaries. Instead, Hanoi decided to launch the 1972 Great Offensive to capture SVN by force. In lieu of continuing the traditional Communist strategy of guerrilla warfare culminating in a combination of conventional warfare and popular uprising to overthrow the South Vietnamese government, NVN decided to literally "burn the stage" (*dot giai doan* in Vietnamese) by simultaneously launching multidivisional assaults on three fronts: Quang Tri and Thua Thien provinces in MRI, Kontum province in MRII, and Binh Long province in MRIII. According to the Communists' plans, if these offensives proved successful, Hanoi would use these new bases as a springboard for the final conquest of SVN.

On the northern front, the attack began on March 30, 1972. After heavy artillery preparations on the ARVN's 3rd Division's positions, the NVA's crack divisions, 304, 308, and 324B, supported by one artillery division and two armored regiments, crossed the Ben Hai River, which separated the two Vietnams

The Easter Offensive, 1972

NORTH VIETNAM

DMZ
Dong Ha

Savannakhet

Lai An
Hue
Phu Bai

L A O S

Da Nang

T H A I L A N D

Chu Lai

Quang Ngai
Mo Doc

SOUTH

CHINA

SEA

Kontum

Pleiku

An Nhon
Qui Nhon

S O U T H   V I E T N A M

Siem Reap

Tonle Sap

C A M B O D I A

Ban Me
Thuot

Ninh Hoa
Dac Song
Nha Trang

Da Lat

Cam Ranh Bay

Loc Ninh
An Loc

Phnom Penh

Hat Ninh
Phan Rang

Mekong

Bien Hoa

Saigon

Phan Thiet

Ha Tien

Quan Phu Quoc

Can Tho

Vinh Long

Vung Tau

GULF OF SIAM

Quan Long

Con Son

N

	March 30–31 offensive
	April 14 offensive
	April 5 offensive
	Highway
	Provincial road
	Railway
	International airport
	Airport

0   100 miles
0   200km

ARVN Marines raised the national flag on the Citadel of Quang Tri after its recapture on September 15, 1972. The Citadel of Quang Tri, consisting of a fortress of approximately 500m^2 surrounded by a 5m-thick wall, was defended by an NVA regiment-sized unit. (Photo ARVN/*Military History 4*)

under the 1954 Geneva Accords. This major offensive coincided with the arrival of the first seasonal monsoon storm, which prevented tactical air support to the defending units.

At the time of the attack, the ARVN's regular forces in Quang Tri province consisted of the 3rd Infantry Division reinforced with the 147th Marine Brigade, the 5th Ranger Group, and the 1st Armored Brigade. The 3rd Division was the ARVN's youngest division. The majority of its soldiers were deserters, draft dodgers, and other undesirable elements who had been sent to the northernmost province of SVN as a punishment. It was the fate of this division to receive the brunt of the NVA's bloodiest offensive of both the Indochina and the Vietnam wars.

Under heavy pressure, the 3rd Division, outgunned and outnumbered, had to fall back, first to Dong Ha and then to the next line of defense south of the My Chanh River. This was defended by the Airborne Division (minus one brigade) and one Marine brigade.

During the month of May, the situation was stabilized along the My Chanh River. NVA/VC troops had to stop to await resupply. The weather had improved, and tactical air support and B-52 sorties had taken a heavy toll. In early July, the Airborne and Marine divisions, refurbished and re-equipped, crossed the My Chanh River abreast, to launch the counter-attack to recapture the city of Quang Tri. Although heavily outnumbered – by that time, the NVA's order of battle consisted of the 304th, 308th, 312th, 320th, and 325th divisions – the Airborne on the west of RN1 and the Marine Division on the east, supported by US airpower, had caught the North Vietnamese off balance and quickly regained some strategic terrain north of My Chanh.

Differing from many actions earlier in the war, in 1972 the NVA chose to fight hard to retain their gains and resisted tenaciously. On the night of September 14, the 3rd Marine Battalion of the 147th Brigade blew a hole in the southeastern corner of the Quang Tri Citadel. During the night, the Marines fought block by block, and used hand grenades to destroy the last NVA/VC pockets of resistance. Finally, on September 15, after 48 days of uninterrupted fighting, the Vietnamese Marines, like their US counterparts in World War II on Iwo Jima, raised the national flag on the main headquarters of the Citadel and on its surrounding walls.

Concurrently with the offensive in Quang Tri, the NVA launched a powerful attack on Kontum province in MRII, using the NVA's 2nd and 10th divisions as the main attacking force. Meanwhile, the 3rd Division made a diversionary attack in Binh Dinh coastal province. Brigadier General Ly Tong Ba, the ARVN's 23rd Division commander, skillfully used his armored reserve task force to destroy the NVA's attacking forces and evict them from the city of Kontum after hard-fought street combats.

While the "Tri-Thien" (Quang Tri-Thua Thien) theater was directly controlled by Hanoi's High Command and the offensive in the Central Highlands by the commander of VC's Military Region V, the attack on Loc Ninh and An Loc in MRIII was directed by nothing less than the Central Office of South Vietnam, Hanoi's highest political organ in the South.

After the fall of the district town of Loc Ninh (20 kilometers north of the city of An Loc) on April 7, 1972, the ARVN's Joint General Staff decided to defend

An NVA T-54 tank knocked out in the main street of An Loc in April 1972. Due to lack of experience in combined-arms tactics, enemy tanks and personnel carriers advanced deep into the ARVN's positions without infantry protection and were destroyed by ARVN units and members of self-defense forces. (Photo courtesy of Phuc Dang)

An Loc at all costs. If An Loc fell, nothing could stop the NVA's march into the capital of South Vietnam.

ARVN forces in An Loc originally consisted of the understrength 5th Division, the 3rd Ranger Group, and Binh Long provincial forces. They were later reinforced with the 1st Airborne Brigade and the 81st Airborne Commando Group. These two units were heliborne into an area approximately three kilometers southeast of An Loc, and had to fight off numerous NVA/VC attacks before linking up with the embattled garrison. Total strength of the troops defending An Loc was 6,350 men.

The NVA order of battle consisted of three divisions: the 5th, 7th, and the 9th. These divisions were supported by the 75th Artillery Division, with three artillery and one antiaircraft regiments. Additional combat support units consisted of three tank battalions. The attacking force totaled about 18,000 troops. The 5th and 9th divisions were to take part in the attack of An Loc, while the 7th Division was to destroy the ARVN's reinforcement units trying to link up with the besieged garrison from the South.

The first attack on An Loc began on April 13. (In Paris that same day, Madame Nguyen Thi Binh, the chief of the VC delegation at the peace talks, declared that "within the next ten days, An Loc will be proclaimed the capital of the Provisional Revolutionary Government of South Vietnam."[3]) The attack was launched by the 9th Division, supported by elements of a tank battalion. As usual, the assault was preceded by intense artillery preparation. The attacking forces quickly overran the Dong Long Hill and the airstrip located on the northern outskirts of the city, and forced the 8th Regiment and the 3rd Ranger Group to withdraw toward the center of the city. The NVA infantry, however, was stopped by AC-130s (transport aircraft equipped with fast-firing machine-guns) and helicopter gunships. Due to poor coordination between their armored and infantry units, NVA tanks continued to advance into the city without protection.

The first NVA tank was destroyed at the junction of Dinh Tien Hoang and Hung Vuong streets by three young members of the Self-Defense Forces. A PT-16 tank was set on fire in front of the underground bunker of Brigadier General Le Van Hung, 5th Division commander. A total of seven tanks were destroyed during the first attack.

On April 15, the NVA's 9th Division renewed its attack on An Loc, with the 272nd Regiment in the north and the 271st Regiment in the west. Each of these attacking forces was supported by a tank company. Like the first attack, NVA tanks penetrated deeper into the ARVN's positions without infantry protection. Five tanks were destroyed inside the city; the attack on the west was blunted before it began. As the 271st Regiment entered Xa Cat plantation, four kilometers west of An Loc, and began to deploy in formation for the final assault, the regiment headquarters and one battalion were hit by a direct B-52 strike. The attack on the western wing was cancelled entirely.

The NVA launched their biggest offensive on An Loc on May 11. The 5th Division conducted the main assault directed to the north and northeast, while the

An Loc, May 11 1972, third NVA attack

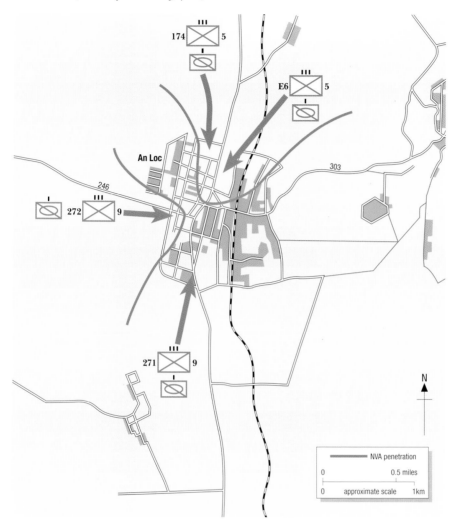

9th Division attacked the west and south sectors of the garrison. The attack was preceded by an intensive artillery preparation, which lasted three hours.

Despite heavy air support, the situation had become critical by 10:00 am. In the northeast, the NVA reached a point only 500m from the ARVN's 5th Division Headquarters. In the west, elements of the 9th Division were stopped 300 meters short of the 5th Division Headquarters.

At that time, General Hung ordered the 1st Airborne Brigade to counter-attack to stop and destroy the two converging columns, which were dangerously closing in on his command post. The street combats raged all day long, and by nightfall the outcome of this seesaw battle remained uncertain.

The next day, the NVA tried to exploit their successes and widen their gaps by launching a new pincer attack, employing the 272st Regiment of the 9th

Division in the west and the 174th Regiment, 5th Division in the northeast. Both of these columns were supported by elements of a tank company.

With efficient tactical air support, the garrison held its ground and repulsed the NVA assaults. By nightfall, it became apparent that the offensive had lost its momentum and that, like the first two attacks, this one had also failed.

Toward the end of May, most of the North Vietnamese antiaircraft defense system had been destroyed by airpower. By early June, helicopters were able to land in An Loc for resupply and medevac. On June 9, the ARVN's 21st Division, reinforced with the 15th Regiment, 9th Division, and supported by the 9th Armored Cavalry Regiment, finally linked up with the garrison of An Loc, after two months of uninterrupted murderous combat with the NVA's 7th Division along Highway 13.

General Paul Vanuxem, a French veteran of the Indochina War, called An Loc the "Verdun of Vietnam." Sir Robert Thompson, advisor to President Nixon, considered An Loc the biggest victory of the Free World in the post-World War II era. Douglas Pike described An Loc as "the single most important battle in the war." Critics of the Vietnam War attributed the success of An Loc to US airpower. But General Abrams, the commander of US forces in Vietnam, had a ready answer: "I doubt the fabric of this thing could have been held together without US air," he told his commanders, "but the thing that had to happen before that is the Vietnamese, some numbers of them, had to stand and fight. If they do not do that, ten times the air we've got wouldn't have stopped them."[4] The South Vietnamese Army and its people did stand and fight.

THE 1975 OFFENSIVE

In the furious battles of 1972, too often ignored by Western historiography, the ARVN showed what it was capable of when backed by US firepower and economic support. However, the situation would be much different in the more infamous battles of 1975. Having tired of the conflict, the US exited the Vietnam War with the promise that it would continue to provide needed support for the ARVN. Instead the United States, in a shocking development to most South Vietnamese, quickly lost interest in the war that had so consumed both its treasure and the lives of its soldiers. Thus in 1975, South Vietnam, a Third World country unable to support the massive logistical appetite of its First World armed forces, faced the NVA onslaught virtually alone. Units could not move due to lack of gas; artillery could not fire due to lack of shells; modern weapons systems remained unused due to shortages at all levels. Abandoned, the ARVN would fall to ultimate defeat.

The Paris Agreement signed in January 1973 allowed the US to "withdraw with honor," but failed to require the withdrawal of an estimated 125,000 to 145,000 NVA troops from the South. Right after the agreement was signed, the NVA activated two engineer and transportation divisions to repair and improve the Ho Chi Minh Trail. Alongside the Trail, the NVA also built a pipeline to bring oil and petroleum to Loc Ninh in MRIII near the Cambodian border. The Communists also built or repaired a sophisticated system of lateral roads which permitted them to bypass our big cities and threaten our flank.

Major General Bui The Lan, Marine Division commander (right), and Lam Quang Thi inspecting ammunition and Chinese rations retrieved from a sunken NVA ship north of Hue, June 20, 1974. The ship belonged to NVA's 5th Naval Regiment based on Cua Viet on the mouth of the Quang Tri River. It was sunk by one round of a 90mm gun from the 17th Armored Cavalry Squadron. (Lam Quang Thi collection)

Shortly before the Paris Agreement was signed, I assumed the function of Commanding General, I Corps Forward Command at Hue. In this capacity, I commanded an army corps task force consisting of the 1st Division, the Airborne Division, and the Marine Division, and was responsible for tactical operations in the two northern provinces of Quang Tri and Thua Thien near the DMZ.

In the middle of the NVA's frantic build-up in preparation for a new invasion, I was very concerned about adverse political developments in the United States. On April 4, 1974, the US Congress cut military aid to SVN for fiscal year 1974–75 from $1 billion to $750 million. Out of this $750 million, $300 million was appropriated as salary for the personnel at the US Defense Attaché's Office in Saigon. Significantly, Israel received $2.1 billion in military aid during the three-week Yom Kippur War in 1973. In other words, SVN, over one year, received 21 percent of what Israel obtained for three weeks. "The economic aid was cut," said President Thieu on a TV broadcast, "the military aid was cut, and we have no means to fight." The president's words were true, for US aid now supplied only a small fraction of what the ARVN required to function in a calendar year. Without adequate aid, the ARVN would cease to be an effective fighting force.

In the summer of 1974, the NVA's 711th Division, reinforced with the 304th Division, launched a powerful attack on Nong Son and overran the district of Thuong Duc, approximately 50km southwest of Da Nang. I received orders to release the Airborne Division to I Corps to counter this new offensive. Although the Airborne Division stopped and beat the 304th on the peaks of the chains of mountains northeast of Thuong Duc, I Corps gave up attempts to recapture the district town.

The battle of Thuong Duc showed that the NVA intended to take full advantage of the new system of roads and of their new strategic mobility to isolate and attack our cities from the rear. This strategy could be called a "strategy of indirect approach," a phrase coined by the famous British military strategist Liddell Hart. This strategy consisted of making a frontal attack with a relatively small force, while making a deep envelopment at the rear. This was made easy, not only by the new road system built after the Paris Agreement, but also by the fact that SVN was a long narrow stretch of territory, at certain areas measuring less than 100km from the mountains to the sea.

On March 10, NVA's 316th Division, reinforced with one infantry regiment, one sapper regiment, and one armored regiment, launched a coordinated attack on Ban Me Thuot in MRII. Despite a heroic defense by the 53rd Regiment of ARVN's 23rd Division and two Ranger groups, the city fell to the NVA when the last battalion of the 53rd Regiment ran out of ammunition and had to disperse after six days of fierce resistance. On March 14, I received orders to release the Marine Division, minus one brigade. The Marine Division was to move to Da Nang immediately to replace the Airborne Division; the latter was to be attached to II Corps in an effort to retake Ban Me Thuot.

Also on March 14, President Thieu made perhaps his most fateful decision of the entire war, and ordered an immediate withdrawal of all forces from Pleiku and Kontum in MRII. The troops from the area were to withdraw under fire, the most difficult tactical action of all, and establish a new defense line roughly linking Ha Tien, Tay Ninh, Ban Me Thuot, and Nha Trang. Thus, due in part to a lack of military aid, President Thieu had chosen to abandon the northern half of his country, MRI and part of MRII, to NVA/VC forces. ARVN forces north of the new demarcation line – depleted, abandoned, and cut off from all support – were to defend three bridgeheads around Hue-Da Nang, Tam Ky-Chu Lai, and Quang Ngai in MRI.

In my sector, the 1st Division, reinforced with the 15th Ranger Group, again had to stretch out to cover the area left by the Marine Division. Making matters much worse, in early March, NVA's newly activated II Corps hurled the 324Bth and 325th divisions against the 1st Division's depleted positions on the high ground southwest of Hue. Though outnumbered, the ARVN forces engaged in dogged and bloody combat on the numerous hills west of Phu Bai airport. Some of these hills changed hands many times during the day. While the 1st Division was barely able to contain the NVA's furious assaults on its left flank, on April 19, without warning, the NVA's 308th Division, reinforced with armored elements, launched a frontal attack on Quang Tri Regional Forces (RF) battalions, and forced them to withdraw to the My Chanh River.

While the NVA's divisions were tightening their noose around Hue, the two southernmost provinces of MRI, Quang Tin and Quang Ngai, were under imminent threat of being overrun by superior forces. On April 23, General Ngo Quang Truong, I Corps Commander, ordered the evacuation of Hue because he judged the situation of the Imperial City untenable and also because he needed the 1st Division and the 147th Marine Brigade in Da Nang to shore up the embattled city's defense. However, a great number of 1st Division soldiers, in lieu of moving south, stayed behind to take care of their families in Hue. The next day, as the 1st Division and the 147th Marine Brigade were disengaging from NVA units around Hue, the NVA began their final assault on Tam Ky, the capital city of Quang Tin province. By afternoon, the city was lost.

On the evening of the 27th, while NVA artillery was firing at Da Nang airport and Tien Sa naval base in preparation for their final assault, General Truong ordered the evacuation of the city. The Marine Division and the remnants of the 1st, 2nd, and 3rd divisions were to be transported to Saigon by sea. Scattered resistance by ARVN units left behind lasted a few more days; by nightfall on March 30, the second largest city of SVN belonged to NVA/VC forces.

After the collapse of MRI and the disastrous withdrawal from Pleiku, the coastal cities of MRII fell one after another. Phan Rang, MRII's last organized defensive position, fell on April 18 after an heroic but desperate resistance of III Corps Forward's task force.

With the fall of MRI and the northern part of MRII, Xuan Loc, Bien Hoa, and Cu Chi became the last defense line against the NVA's advance to the capital. The city of Xuan Loc, in particular, took on a special strategic importance. Located 60km northeast of Saigon, it controlled the vital junction of RN1 and RN20, the two paved highways into Saigon from the coastal cities and from the Central Highlands. To exploit their successes in the northern MRs, the North Vietnamese hurled their entire IV Corps, consisting of three divisions, against the ARVN's 18th Division defending Xuan Loc. The fate of the capital, and of the Republic, hinged on this last vestige of the South Vietnamese resistance. If the

Brigadier General Le Minh Dao, 18th Division commander, talking by radio to his unit commanders in his underground bunker in Xuan Loc, April 1975. The heroic stand of the 18th Division in the last battle of the Vietnam War stunned war critics and redeemed the ARVN's reputation. (Photo courtesy of Phuc Dang, SD18BB)

18th Division troops had panicked and fled, the NVA's forces would have captured Saigon within days. The soldiers of the 18th Division, however, did not flee. They stood their ground and fought for 11 days against heavy odds. The ARVN's stubborn defenders threw back repeated NVA assaults and destroyed many tanks. Brigadier General Le Minh Dao, the 18th Division commander, also skilfully used his reserves to counter-attack attempted penetrations and inflict heavy losses on the North Vietnamese.

On the 19th, the South Vietnamese Air Force, assisted by DAO technicians, dropped one cluster bomb unit from a C-130 transport aircraft on a North Vietnamese concentration area east of Xuan Loc. The CBU is an awesome weapon. It produces a powerful downward pressure that kills anything in its field and causes people who survive the blast to suffocate in the post-explosion vacuum. The bomb wiped out a regiment of the NVA's 341st Division.

Unfortunately, the bomb, while slowing down the NVA attack, did not stop it. On April 21, the 18th Division was ordered to withdraw under heavy pressure to the new defense line, Trang Bom-Long Thanh. There it continued to fight until General Duong Van Minh, the new President of the Republic, ordered the surrender of all ARVN units.

Undeniably, the public reputation of the South Vietnamese Army was, to a certain extent, redeemed by the heroic stand of the 18th Division. "Despite the public image of corruption and incompetence," wrote George J. Weith and Merle

L. Pribbenow, "the ARVN, as shown in the battle for Xuan Loc, was not an army of bumblers and cowards as it is so often portrayed. It was an army that stood and fought with great courage not only on a few well-known occasions like the siege of An Loc, but also in hundreds of little battles whose names most Americans never knew."[5]

After the war, General Dao turned himself over to the Communist authorities. Along with an estimated 400,000 army officers and officials of the South Vietnamese government, Dao was sent to a "re-education" camp. Some were released after a few years, but others were interned as long as 17 years. Dao belonged to the second category. Another 1.5 million were forcibly resettled in "new economic zones" in desolated areas, where many perished of hunger and disease.

When General Duong Van Minh's message of surrender was announced, five army generals, including General Le Van Hung, the hero of An Loc, committed suicide rather than surrender to the North Vietnamese. By choosing to die, these generals upheld the purest tradition of the Confucian warrior.

THE CAUSES OF THE COLLAPSE OF SOUTH VIETNAM

In the West, the most popular historical opinion is that corruption and incompetence were the principal causes of the fall of South Vietnam. Corruption exists in every country, but history does not show that all corrupted regimes are condemned to disappear. Corruption, for example, was rampant in South Korea under military dictatorships, but South Korea did not fall to the Communists; instead it became a strong democracy with a vibrant economy. On the other hand, the South Vietnamese Army demonstrated again and again that it was not an army of incompetents and cowards and that, with adequate US air and logistical support, it could defeat both the VC insurgency and the NVA's regular divisions in unconventional as well as conventional warfare. Tiny and economically dependent South Vietnam could not support the massive military effort needed to defeat North Vietnam and the Viet Cong alone – American support was the key. The defense against the Easter Offensive of 1972 stands out as the best example of what the ARVN could accomplish when truly working in tandem with the United States. In addition, the defense of Xuan Loc demonstrates the dedication of the ARVN, even when fighting with no hope of ultimate victory. It was only after the nearly total American withdrawal from the conflict that the ARVN was doomed to failure. Thus, in the end, it was that American collapse of public support for and withdrawal from the conflict that sealed the fate of South Vietnam. And, in my opinion, it was the lack of a clearly defined mission for US troops and the hostility of the US media toward the Vietnam War that were the main causes of the Vietnam disaster.

Lack of a clear mission

When President Kennedy sent US military advisors to train the South Vietnamese Army in the mid-1950s, he adopted what was known as the doctrine of "graduated response" developed by General Maxwell Taylor, his military advisor and former Chairman of the Joint Chiefs of Staff. Under this strategy, the US would respond in kind to Communist aggression without resorting to nuclear warfare. For example, if the Communists used guerrilla warfare in Third World countries, such as Vietnam, the US would help the governments of those countries to wage counterinsurgency warfare. If the enemy used conventional warfare, tactical nuclear weapons, or intercontinental ballistic missiles, the US would do likewise. Critics of this strategy, however, contend that it is a strategy of reaction rather than a strategy of action.

When the first US Marine units landed in Da Nang in March 1965, the US used what was called the strategy of "enclave." The main mission of US troops was to defend the populated areas, logistical installations, and airports in the coastal areas. Subsequently, General Westmoreland implemented what was called the "search-and-destroy" strategy, sometimes called the "big unit warfare." The objective of this strategy, under Westmoreland's "war of attrition," was to kill as many of the NVA/VC forces as possible and to cause him to lose heart and to cease aggression against SVN. The destruction of one NVA division in heavy engagements at Ia-Drang in the Central Highlands is a good example of this strategy.

When General Creighton W. Abrams replaced Westmoreland after the 1968 Tet Offensive, he stressed a "One War" concept, which, according to Lewis Sorley, would integrate combat operations, pacification, and upgrading the ARVN. In place of "search and destroy," Abrams applied the "clear-and-hold" strategy under which the pacified areas must be permanently held by allied forces.

However, despite all the exotic names given to these strategies, the basic flaw of the US policy in Vietnam was the lack of clarity of mission. As a result, the different strategies used during the war were largely irrelevant. According to former Secretary of Defense James Schlesinger, the use of military power must pass the test of clarity of mission and efficiency. That certainly was not the case in Vietnam.

In retrospect, I believe that the US had only two courses of action in Vietnam. The first was to carry the war to NVN and destroy Hanoi's will to fight. The second was to support the government of SVN in fighting a long and protracted war in the South. The problem was, the US had neither the guts to go North, nor the patience to stay in the South.

I also believe that the Vietnam War should have been fought by the Vietnamese boys, and I am confident that, with adequate logistical and air support, we could have done the job. The defeat of NVN's elite divisions in Quang Tri in MRI, Kontum in MRII, and An Loc in MRIII in 1972 amply demonstrated this fact. In my opinion, the ARVN should have taken over the war after the 1968 Tet Offensive, in which the VC lost over one-half of its war-making potential. Under this scenario, the reduced US forces would have defended the populated areas and logistical installations under the old strategy of enclave. The resulting lower US casualties would have made the war more acceptable to the American public.

Hostility of US media toward the Vietnam War

It is often felt, for one reason or another, that the US media were hostile to the Vietnam War, and endeavored to present the war unfavorably. For example, during the 1968 Tet Offensive, when General Nguyen Ngoc Loan, the chief of police, executed a VC officer who had killed some of his officers and murdered their families, the US media transformed it into a sort of *cause célèbre* for war activists. NBC went into great detail to make the pictures of the execution more dramatic to the American public. Viewers could see the entire footage showing the VC officer lying dead in the street with an enormous pool of blood forming under his head. On the other hand, the fact that the VC murdered over 4,000 innocent civilians in Hue who refused to cooperate with the "revolution," was hardly mentioned.

In Ben Tre province, a US advisor, in response to reporters' remarks about the destruction of the city, stated that it was "necessary to destroy Ben Tre in order to save it." This unfortunate remark has since been used time and again by anti-war activists. Subsequently, it became one of the most serviceable icons in the anti-war movement. This one-sided and irresponsible journalism, coupled with the lack of a clear Vietnam policy, gave rise to a growing anti-war movement in the United States and resulted in the cut of military assistance and the final collapse of SVN.

After the fall of SVN in 1975, military analysts predicted that Vietnam's pro-Western neighbors would fall like dominoes in the face of the seemingly unstoppable NVA's divisions, equipped with the latest Russian and Chinese weaponry.

Thirty years later, no dominoes have fallen. Instead, the Soviet Union has collapsed and the very existence of Vietnam as an independent country is being threatened by its former ally and historical enemy to the north. China's killing of Vietnamese fishermen in the Gulf of Tonkin in January 2005, in fact, has added to a consistent pattern of Chinese southern expansionism: conquest of the Paracel Islands in 1974; invasion of the Vietnam's northern provinces in 1979; subsequent annexation of 8,000 square km of borderland; occupation of the Spratley archipelagoes the same year; and annexation of 12,000 square km of territorial waters in the Gulf of Tonkin (conceded by Hanoi under the 2000 Gulf of Tonkin Pact).

History has a curious way of repeating itself. Concerns over Beijing's new aggressiveness have triggered new military realignments in the strategic Asia-Pacific region. As a result, Vietnam once again has regained its strategic value in US eyes as a missing link in the new containment scheme and a counterbalance to the even greater threat of Chinese expansionism.

However, only a strong and prosperous Vietnam, enjoying popular support and the support of the community of free and democratic nations, can preserve its territorial integrity. In other words, only by implementing genuine political and economic reforms can Vietnam stand up to Chinese bullying and break – in the words of a French historian – this *éternel recommencement* of a history of wars and destruction which has plagued it for so long.

Chapter 7

Caught in the Crossfire
The Civilian Experience

Le Ly Hayslip
& Dien Pham

MOTHERLAND

Vietnam – our Motherland as we call her – is one of the most beautiful countries in Southeast Asia. No matter where in the world Vietnamese people settle down to live, they always long for the day they will be able to return to help rebuild the country, heal the wounds of the civil war, and live out the rest of their lives if possible. Vietnam is a land of rich minerals, raw materials, and sea products, the land of opportunity! Unfortunately, these qualities have historically brought invaders and aggressors from other countries such as China, whose invading forces were driven out of Vietnam in 1788 after almost 1,000 years of domination.

Then the French colonists came, with all the strength of a modernized expeditionary army and an advanced nation behind them, and imposed their regime on Vietnam for another 100 years. With determination and continued resistance, the Vietnamese people finally succeeded in liberating the country from domination and slavery. The battle of Dien Bien Phu in 1954 marked the death of French colonialism. French troops were forced to surrender, and their defeat led to the Geneva Convention and then the Geneva Accords in 1954.

A SOUTHERN PERSPECTIVE OF A VIETNAM DIVIDED

The Geneva Accords established a temporary division of Vietnam into two regions, with the Ben Hai River at the 17th Parallel as the border. The Geneva Convention also mandated a 300-day period for both sides to regroup and relocate their people north and south of the 17th Parallel. A demilitarized zone was created to enable any maneuvers for those purposes. The relocation process was painful: people who moved often had to leave their parents and other loved ones behind. The separations, especially between young couples, mothers and

Our Motherland, one of the most beautiful countries in Southeast Asia. (Photo by James Nguyen)

sons, father and daughters, were agonizing. In my own family, the sorrow and the fear turned my mother's hair almost white in just months. Encouraged and intrigued by the Viet Minh's policy, northbound young men hurried to get married. Often they had very little time with their new spouses and left not knowing that they had babies on the way.

People heartbroken by separations pinned their hopes on the expectation of reunion after two years, as had been mandated by the Geneva Convention. This hope soon faded away, and was replaced by the reluctant adoption of the new government's policies. From this time on, the lives of villagers and peasants were plagued with worry and depression. There were many new rules and regulations to follow and obey. There were many officers and cadres at all levels who loved to exercise their authority and impose their will on the poor people who lived under them. This made life very hard for the ordinary Vietnamese civilians.

CIVILIAN EXPERIENCES

I was born at the end of 1949, in Ky La hamlet, five years before the resistance war against the French colonists ended. My father married my mother in 1925 and had six children, four daughters and two sons. The hamlet was located on a small piece of land in the central coast, one of the most beautiful places in Central Vietnam.

My father was a gentle man who understood life and its values. He taught us how to extract the goods and materials from Mother Earth, and how to preserve the land's fertility after yielding crops, year after year. He also taught us about family duty, how to stay alive in adverse circumstances, how to find a good husband, and how to care for the family happiness. In his leisure time he would tell us stories about the heroic actions of our ancient kings and queens, and taught us to be faithful and loyal to our country.

When we were working next to our mother in the rice paddies, she would teach us about how girls grow to womanhood and how it is necessary for women to show kindness and affection to men; about marital life, and giving birth to children. She taught us about the tasks of bringing the family name forward, of being faithful to husbands and loyal to mothers-in-law. We worked tirelessly and in high spirits in the rice field, swiveling our bodies back and forth, up and down, like machines, in the hot summer or cold winter weather. My mother always reminded us, "If we live in harmony with Heaven and Earth, our lives will be worth living!" Arming myself with this wisdom, I later went into the world without fear, even when faced with great adversity.

When the war ended, people in my hamlet had time to take care of the dead and their spirits. Previously there were so many unknown people who had died and hurriedly been buried here and there on the roadsides or the hillsides; their graves were just heaps of dirt. As Buddhists, we believed that the spirits of those who were lying under these unmarked graves would be forever restless and wandering until the lost souls had a place to rest. So we constructed many tiny pagodas for this purpose. From 1955 to 1960, peasants lived in peace. That was

This shrine in Da Nang is dedicated to the unknown dead of the war. Shrines such as these were constructed to give the restless souls of those lying in unmarked graves somewhere to rest. (Photo by James Nguyen)

a good time for people in the countryside, especially for the younger generations. At that time, the country people were very poor in property, but not in love. With love and care for one another, they began to rebuild their lives – not only families, but also schools, churches, and temples.

The roles of men and women in the countryside have, for centuries, been clearly classified and determined, not by law or any written documents, but by mutual understanding and necessity. Men take care of the spiritual side of the family, perform rituals at ceremonies and celebrations, and do most of the manual labor. They teach their children what they need to know to take over their parents' duties, when grown up. For women, building their family and raising their children are the most sacred jobs. Outside the family, their duties consist of helping neighbors, giving help and condolence to families in need, keeping culture and tradition alive, and helping as much as they can to keep society in good order.

Vietnamese women have the capacity to uphold the family's stability. While the men were out fighting wars, the women who stayed behind were not only looking after the children, but also taking care of their elderly parents and working as replacements for their men in the fields. And when the enemy came, the women were ready and willing to take up arms and fight.

"Last night with young wife before going North." Many young men married in haste before departing to fight, leaving their wives behind. (Chicago, 2004, painting by Tan Thanh Toan, photo by James Nguyen)

CIVILIANS TORN

After the division of Vietnam in 1954, some people who supported the Viet Minh in the war of resistance went North to follow Ho Chi Minh, and some remained south of the 17th Parallel. Most of these who went North were not Communists; often they wanted only to return to their birthplaces, to do their duty to their elderly parents, and to live a normal life. Even this soon became too difficult, as tensions between North and South increased day by day. Aside from these people, there were also the Communists who had, willingly or unwillingly, stayed behind in the South. These were the people who played active roles in the civil war for the sake of Communist ideology. There were five distinct groups who fell foul of the South Vietnamese government:

1) Families of soldiers or civilian servants who went to the North. These families became the main targets of the Southern authorities' harassment. Following any activity or unrest in the area, these families were the first to be summoned and interrogated. In Central Vietnam, where there were many such families, the authorities organized weekly night classes for the family members to "learn about the new government policy, how to denounce the communism and to become good citizens." My brother Bon, two sisters' husbands, and seven cousins were among the people who went North, so we experienced firsthand this fear and frustration. Of course, we were not alone: numerous families from the Ben Hai River to Ca Mau Point found themselves in this hellish situation with no way to escape.

2) Families of young people who left home for the jungles to join the Viet Cong. These families found themselves on the Southern authorities' blacklists. The authorities viewed them with the greatest suspicion, and they tried hard to keep a low profile. They wanted more than anything, to avoid attention from the police or secret agents.

3) People who had followed Ho Chi Minh. These people, who often didn't understand much about politics, had engaged in the war from motives of pure patriotism. They viewed most of the top people in the new government as traitors to the Vietnamese people, since they had once been employed in high-level posts in the French colonial regime. They felt it was their duty to demonstrate their resistance to the new authority.

4) Women whose husbands had been Viet Minh soldiers, who had become widows or single mothers. These women were always under close surveillance by the authorities, and lived in constant fear of maltreatment and harassment.

5) And the last group, but not the least unfortunate: people who supported neither the Communists nor the Nationalists. They gave the Communists credit for liberating the country from French colonial domination, but thought that allowing them to take over the rebuilding of the country was far too risky. As for the Nationalists, the best that could be said was they were better than the alternatives. Unwittingly, these people were a thorn in the sides of both parties.

Government crackdown

It was not long before President Diem ordered his men to crack down on any movements of people which might threaten the stability of his regime. His men had the power to kill or imprison anyone who followed or sympathized with the Viet Cong, as well as members of the parties in opposition. Diem's government created a program to denounce communism, to tar the Communists, and to label them as monstrous and atheists. At night, Diem's people came into the villages to kidnap and murder villagers. Most of their victims, aside from the people in the five groups described above, were members of political parties, or religious factions other than Catholic. Many people in villages, hamlets, towns, and cities were sent to prison, and were never seen or heard from again. The luckier ones ended up in local prisons, or in newly established investigation and torture facilities. Diem's government also started a program called *di dan* (population relocation) to remove dissidents from their homes to camps, usually in remote regions, for hard labor under tight surveillance. These people were also never heard from or seen again, unless they escaped or their families resorted to bribes to enable them to get out.

Retribution

The Viet Cong did not want to be seen as weaker than Diem's people, and would do anything to intimidate people. Death squads were formed. People who were suspected of cooperating with the enemy would be killed without a second thought. There was one such barbaric execution on the common ground of our neighboring hamlet. The Viet Cong dug a hole in the ground and then seated a

Arrests were common during the war, and spread a culture of fear among civilians in Vietnam. (Topfoto/AP)

woman by it, just on top of the fresh earth. Her hands were tied behind her back, and a black cloth was wound around her eyes. The executioner grasped a big knife. When it was the time to perform the killing, he took a few steps back behind the victim. Upon a signal from the squad leader, he swiftly approached the victim and, with all his might, chopped off her head. Perhaps the knife was not sharp enough, as unfortunately he failed to cut the head off completely. The woman died right away, after a loud scream, but her head still hung loosely on her neck, while blood spurted out in all directions.

Right or wrong, those executions did intimidate people very much. And that was the real purpose of these death squads. Some of these executions were done in the open, but most were conducted in secret in many villages across South Vietnam. That was the way the Viet Cong treated people that they thought were their adversaries, spy or enemies – the ones they called Viet Gian.

SWEET RICE AND BEANS

One of the most popular Vietnamese daily meals is sticky rice and beans, known as *xoi dau*. Right after the end of the war, social life in the South of Vietnam, especially in the hamlets, villages, small towns, and cities of Central Vietnam, was very complicated, and often compared to this dish. The regroup and relocate programs created chaos, which affected the lives of millions of individuals. For a short period, everything was so confused that people did not know what to do, where to go, what was wrong, and what was right. People in South Vietnam, not knowing what side they should take, were placed in a very delicate situation: to fully cooperate with the new government, or to silently help the VC and other parties in opposition? To fully cooperate with the new government was unacceptable to some people. Aside from President Diem, most of the other high authorities were familiar faces from the former regime. As for the Communists, there was no reason for people who were not Communists to follow them or to support them in their war against the Nationalists, once the French had gone. To many people, this was an ideological war, and nothing to do with them. It was only much later that Diem and his dictatorship helped them to decide what side to take! So that period when people's feelings were extremely mixed (and always in doubt), became known as the "Sweet Rice and Bean" period; and the areas where those people lived were called "Sweet Rice and Bean" areas. People found themselves standing at a crossroads, not knowing which direction to take, and fearful that any wrong turn would lead to disaster. The South Vietnamese authorities had no tolerance for opposition; as for the VC, they would let people to mind their own business as long as their own cause was approved and supported.

At that time, I was seven years old, walking to school in the rain and cold of winter. One day we found out that our teacher hadn't showed up for three days. We schoolboys and girls went to his house on the morning of the third day, and his mother told us to go home and rest. We didn't find out until much later that he had escaped to Saigon, to avoid the terror of the new government, because he had been

OPPOSITE
A young Vietnamese girl grieves over the body of her mother, killed by a Viet Cong mine on a country road. (Douglas Pike Collection, Virtual Vietnam Archive, Texas Tech University)

suspected as a Viet Cong collaborator. For the rest of that academic year, we had no teacher. But this was by no means a special case: sometimes we had no school at all for the whole year because the place was simply taken over as a temporary "interrogation and torture" camp when there were military campaigns in the areas.

Many peasants became victims of these camps. Those who escaped death by torture often became cripples for the rest of their lives. Families connected in any way with the Viet Cong found themselves in a very difficult situation. Each time government officials visited our house, my poor mother would try very hard to be nice and friendly to them. She would kill fat ducks and young chickens to feed them, and for them to take to their families. Other families in the hamlet, trying to stay on the authorities' good side, would use the same shameful tactic. This strain, along with trying to restrain the children, in case they absentmindedly told the wrong stories to the wrong ears, was a constant burden in that time of chaos and confusion.

Moi, my sister Ba Xuan's husband, went North with my brother Bon and his combat friends. His cousin Chin joined the South Vietnamese People's Self-Defense Force; he later became a secret policeman, after converting to Catholicism. Chin would send his men to terrorize our family, and force Ba Xuan to go out with him. She did, reluctantly of course, and that was why our parents were exempt from going to the torture camps. It was very strange that people walking different paths of life should sit at the same table, eat and drink the same food, while talking, laughing, and treating each other as old friends. But that is exactly what my parents did when they entertained district chiefs, hamlet chiefs, and other prominent community leaders or police officers. And all the while we knew that to receive government officials in our house put our family in even greater danger from the VC.

STRATEGIC HAMLET PROGRAM

In 1961, an already difficult situation for Vietnamese civilians became worse. The Viet Cong uprising had been buttressed by re-infiltration from the North of cadres and troops who had moved there after the 1954 Geneva Accords. In reaction to the rising threat, President Diem and his followers developed the Strategic Hamlet Program, designed to isolate the Viet Cong from the people. The publicity for the program stated that South Vietnamese civilians would be moved from Viet Cong-infested areas to new and better villages, where they would have protection and enjoy freedom. In reality, the program, and later efforts supported by the Americans, often brutally forced villagers from the beloved lands of their ancestors – a disastrous event in the family-conscious Vietnamese culture. Villagers were also compelled to undertake unpaid labor to build the defensive works of the new strategic hamlets, and to work nearly constantly on their upkeep.

For some, the strategic hamlets worked well. Catholic villagers, especially those who had moved South at the time of the Geneva Accords, responded to the program well and built their hamlets into small fortresses. However, for most civilians in South Vietnam the Strategic Hamlet Program was a good idea gone

bad – an abject failure in the critical war for the hearts and minds of the people. Instead of trading life in the lands of their ancestors for security in a new village, the unfortunate people of the countryside usually found themselves lost and forgotten by their own government, women and children tucked away like herds of animals. Instead of being measures of social welfare, the Strategic Hamlets became places to impose and ensure governmental control. Driven from their homes, the residents of the new Strategic Hamlets – even the returning soldiers who had given so much for Diem's regime – found themselves abandoned, betrayed, jobless victims of governmental manipulation. Sadly, then, the onset of the Strategic Hamlet Program heralded a very difficult time for many of the villagers of South Vietnam – a time when villagers, forced from the land that they loved but still without security, became caught in the middle of a brutal war.

Generally Vietnamese people just want to keep to themselves. With their traditional and stubborn unbowed spirit, they won't yield to any foreign or domestic power forced upon their wills without a struggle, open or silent. So when they had to leave their villages for new and strange dwellings at gunpoint, their immediate reactions were astonishment, deep condemnation, despair, anger, frustration, and rebelliousness. Those reactions and feelings did not fade away, but increased in strength in response to new daily strains and difficulties. Only very few of the peasant families moved voluntarily – usually either because they were too poor and had nothing to lose by moving, or they just wanted to seek new opportunities in new places. But for most families in the countryside, to abandon their homes was the last thing they would want to do, in any circumstance. As a result, some people chose to flee into the jungles and join the Viet Cong. Others remained behind, harassed by the authorities and nursing a growing hatred for the government. I would like to relate here some painful cases, which took place in the areas around my native hamlet at that time.

Outside the boundary of Ky La hamlet, many small and isolated hamlets and villages were scattered. In those places lived some very wealthy and eminent persons, whose ancestors had been local people going back many centuries. Among these rich people were Xa Quang, Huong Lich, Huong Y, Cuu Loi, Thong Bang, Truong Phan, Huong Sang, Thu Cu, Thu Bong, and Muoi Ban, some of whom are alive to this day. Being rich, they could afford to live separately away from other people, so they created hamlets and villages of their own. They lived their lives peacefully as law-abiding citizens through both wars, the resistance war against the French and later the civil war. Their motto was "Song thoi nao theo thoi nay" (To live accordingly with the present time). They believed that working hard and paying tax was the best way to create harmony between people and the government. So their family members would work for any regime, in any administration, either to earn a living or just to show sympathy, to be good citizens. Their houses were surrounded by beautiful gardens, orchards, back yards, front yards, and ponds. The outer perimeters were lined with bamboo, palm trees, coconut trees and bushes, and together they made a natural hedge, to form an oasis for each establishment. Those beautiful dwellings were not made in a month, or in a year, but by generations of hard work and cultivation. Those families not only owned the land on which their establishments stood, but lands and rice fields in the area. In addition to that, they had cows and buffalo for labor, and livestock as well. They would generously lend cows and buffalo to anyone in the area when it was the time to prepare land or rice fields for planting or sowing. They lent extra land and rice fields to peasants in the area who owned no or very

OPPOSITE
The Vietnamese peasants tried to continue their lives despite the arrival in their villages of large numbers of foreign soldiers. (David DeChant Collection, Virtual Vietnam Archive, Texas Tech University)

little land. The peasants became tenant farmers, and paid their landlords a percentage of what they harvested from the lands.

In short, these rich families were the pillars of their communities. People looked up to them, and they themselves were very content with life in general. That is, until the disastrous moment when they were ordered to vacate their houses and move away, either to a strategic hamlet or to another village willing to shelter them permanently. Imagine the astonishment and anger that followed this proclamation.

Two years ago, I paid a social visit to Mrs. Xa Quang, a member of one of these families and one of the few survivors of the strategic hamlet program. She is over 100 years old, and has lived with her daughter Nam in a small house next door to my mother's since the day they became refugees. I asked about the time when they were forced to move out of their lovely house in Bai Gian hamlet. How did they cope with the situation? How did they overcome the frustration and sadness of being deprived of their home and birthplace? It was the daughter, Nam, who replied with this sad story:

We didn't have much time to think what was going on! Everything happened as suddenly as thunder and lighting! Bright sky above suddenly darkened in that early morning when the *thong ngon* [interpreter] and a group of American soldiers came with a bulldozer and ordered us to move out! Just like that! "Move out of here, and be quick about it!" That was their order, translated by the interpreter, who was Vietnamese. We did not quite understand what was going on and what we should do, but the bulldozer was already starting to knock down our auxiliary and independent houses, and in the process to fill up our pond with the rubble!

The fear squeezed my heart, numbed my feelings! I did not know what to do, how to act, not at all! I just ran and ran around in the house, too stupefied to think clearly. When I saw my father go to our ancestors' altar to take down everything from there – things so sacred that he would never dare to move them without a good and necessary reason – my reason suddenly came back to me, and I knew for the first time the seriousness and deadliness of the matter! From that moment forward, I tried to shake away my fear so that I could help with moving efficiently. My mother went into the garden to dig out whatever she had hidden there! I also helped my sister Phu to let all our domestic animals out of their shelters, so that they could flee. As for the two buffalo, we led them out to the garden gate and made them run as far as possible. We knew we could retrieve them afterwards; that wouldn't be any problem. The urgent problem now was our stock of rice. It would take the whole day to move that load of rice away. But we did not have the time or the laborers. And that stock of rice was our only resource for the next crop and our daily meal in the days and months to come! What to do? Nothing to do! Nothing we could do, absolutely!

Afterward we just stood transfixed and watched our beloved home demolished before our eyes, our house reduced to rubble. A total devastation

Le Ly Hayslip talking to Mrs. Xa Quang, and her daugher Nam about the strategic hamlets in 2003. (Photo by James Nguyen)

caused by their machine, the bulldozer, and by a bunch of heartless men, those American soldiers and their interpreter!

Nam stopped for a moment to fetch a worn handkerchief from her shirt pocket. Dabbing her eyes with it, she said, "I am sorry! I can't help crying each time I relate this painful story to anyone or even to myself as I retrieve the image of that unfortunate day from my memory. And, you know, it's very strange! I don't know how I still have enough tears to cry after all those years of mourning and crying for our painful destinies and that unbelievable loss!"

"Within an hour our big main house was all in pieces," she continued, after drying her eyes,

And that was the time we ran, with just the clothes on our bodies, and some precious belongings in our hands, to this hamlet, and begged for hospitality. We did come back there afterward, back and forth many times during that day and the next day, to collect what could be collected, but for the time being, it was much too painful for us to look at that heap of broken bricks, cement, lumber, furniture, and hundreds of beloved things, the remains of the house my grandparents and my parents had built with their own sweat and labor – the home where we were born! Then they began to bulldoze the house next door, the house of uncle Lich! The poor man had just stood there motionless since the beginning of the event, right at the hedge that separated our two establishments. He watched the destruction of our house with tears running down his cheeks. Now he turned on his heels and ran swiftly into his house. When he reappeared, all he had brought with him were books – nothing else!

Mr. Lich had been a teacher and a writer, and it was said that he valued his books more than anything else in the world. As for what happened to the other houses and what were their reactions, we did not know in detail, because to cope with our situation alone was already too much for us.

However, when the bulldozer and the soldiers moved to the other side of the hamlet to continue their work, we could hear a great deal of commotion over there. The clearest noises were the *la lang* of the women, the cries for help or to summon people to witness the disastrous scene. Of course, all their cries and protests were ignored. Nobody came, no help was on the way, simply because no one dared.

In all it took the destroyers just one day to raze the whole hamlet to the ground, to erase our beautiful hamlet from the face of the earth. As for our neighbors, they took refuge here and there, in the surrounding areas. Only Mr. Lich, being a teacher and scholar, moved to Saigon to continue his career.

Of what Ms. Nam had told me, I had known some, had witnessed some, but her story still pained the old wounds in my heart. Some months after Mr. Xa Quang moved to Ky La hamlet, he was wounded when he accidentally stepped on a landmine. Both of his legs were mutilated, so afterward he lived the life of a crippled refugee. It was too miserable for him to bear, and he died some years later. In some ways it was fortunate for him because he did not have to suffer through the later deaths of his three sons. Nam herself got married; her husband went North and later was registered as missing in action. So much misfortune for just one family. Because Mrs. Xa Quang had three sons and one son-in-law who died fighting for the Viet Cong and NVA, the government rewarded her with a certificate entitled "Me Anh Hung" (Mother of the Heroes.) Of course she received the reward without any enthusiasm.

As for me and my friends, we did suffer some of the hardships of life in those days, but in different ways. For starters, we children would always do what the Viet Cong or the South Vietnamese troops asked us to do. Helping the Viet Cong was not so difficult: we had just to memorize what they told us, listen and look around our hamlet and report to them afterward. I enjoyed doing things like that; I thought it would add some excitement to my teenage life. I knew that sooner or later I would suffer punishment, but it came sooner than expected. I was put in jail for three days some months after I had completed an assignment. I never had any idea how horrible prisons were; all I knew were stories from ex-prisoners under the French regime. To them, prisons were hells on earth.

I was arrested three times. The first two times I was taken to the Gia Long police station and Thi Tran precincts on Doc Lap Street, both in Da Nang City. The third time I was held at My Thi prison, a kind of POW camp. There were many interrogation and torture rooms, all intended to intimidate the inmates. For a young girl like me, the rooms were deadly horrible and the quiet of the atmosphere was terrible, especially when I could hear the echoes of other prisoners screaming. The presence of torture devices – whips, batons, big pliers, and especially the electric shock devices – made me almost faint from fear. Then there was the slogan, written in big capital and bold characters on the walls: "KHONG CO, DANH CHO CO! CO DANH CHO CHUA!" This means "If you are innocent, they will beat you so hard that you will confess that you are guilty! But if you are already proved guilty, they will torture you until you have to beg for mercy and promise that you will never again dare to do anything wrong against them!"

For three days in prison, I was tortured with electric shocks and other devices. I will never forget the ugly faces who tortured me at the My Thi prison in China Beach. They were inspectors or interrogators and they were old enough to be my father, but they didn't care. They beat me like I was not a human being, but some kind of punching bag. With each question they asked, they would hammer their army boots on to my young body, or turn on the device to send electric shocks through my body, even though I was only 14 years old and could not tell them anything. They even put their sneaky hands into our pants, and tied us girls together to a post near a red anthill, just to enjoy our screaming!

Later some of my friends in Dai Loc told me that they suffered similar shameful and humiliating treatment in other torture camps during the war. These things happened not just in the countryside, but almost everywhere in the country, where there was no law, no voices, and people were powerless. I did vow to give those victims a voice, and empower them to tell their own stories. I was lucky to get out of this hell on earth fast; most of the people in those torture camps died at the hands of the Vietnamese we called "brother." The shame was on the Vietnamese government and our countrymen! They turned their backs on us victims, and let the killers murder their own people.

Before Ky La became a strategic hamlet, the number of resident families was about 15 or 20 at most, with a population of no more than 70 at any given time. The Southern government officials dumped the people from four other hamlets and villages – more than 300 hundred people – into Ky La. What were so many people going to do on this sandy land? The conditions for survival, let alone for health and happiness, were very poor.

The relocation program brought people from remote and mountainous areas into villages or towns near the government military outposts. Suddenly hundreds of thousands of Vietnamese and Vietnamese minorities found themselves homeless, jobless, and voiceless, stranded in strange places without any means of support. Abandoning the native villages for strange places was a very bad thing for our people, but to live on charity from the "invaders" was worse! Most of these people became beggars through no fault of their own.

Villagers and hamlet people were the ones who constantly came into contact with the realities of war; they were the ones who suffered the most, and who bore all of the burdens of the war. My family suffered among many others in those years when the war climbed to its peak, in the 1960s and early 1970s. For

example, to avoid troubles with Chin, my sister Ba Xuan reluctantly agreed to marry him. (She had no choice, but fortunately Chin turned out to be a very good husband and thoughtful son-in-law.) And this case was not unusual: weddings like this occurred every day in the countryside. Chin's colleagues, some of whom had some really twisted streaks, often took advantage of their positions to attend to their needs. The higher their positions, the greedier they were. Being local men, and knowing all the secrets of the villagers, they would use those secrets as blackmail to further their careers.

We villagers not only had to contend with keeping government officials happy, but also had to pacify the local Viet Cong. One day in 1964, my mother and father were working in the paddy rice field, while I was in Da Nang City. By 10 am my mother came home to cook lunch. When she got home, she was surprised to find a house full of ARVN soldiers, all down on the ground with their guns pointing towards Bai Gian village. As soon as my mother stepped into the house, the soldiers apprehended her and took her to the kitchen, where they ordered her to sit still and be quiet about it. Usually when this happened villagers would try their best to send out signals to another village, to broadcast the danger. For this purpose, each family had one or two heaps of dead leaves piled in their garden ready to burn for smoke signals if the weather was fine. Other signals, such as making some kind of noise, or hanging red clothes where they could be seen from afar, would be used on rainy days. But being closely guarded by a soldier, my mother could do nothing but to sit and mourn for her failure to send the warning. She knew this was a crime, according to the Viet Cong, and a life-or-death matter.

That day, unfortunately, there were some Viet Cong in Bai Gian village. Not seeing any signals from my hamlet, they thought it would be safe for them to travel. Usually, they would not travel in broad daylight, except in emergency cases. When this happened, signals to warn them of danger were crucial.

The ARVN soldiers in my hamlet were successful; they got to their ambush places undetected, perhaps in the early morning, covered by the semi-darkness. The hamlet people were totally unaware of their presence until too late! The two Viet Cong in Bai Gian village approached Ky La hamlet, unaware of any danger awaiting them. Surprised by the ambush party, they tried to defend themselves, and then made a quick retreat, but to no avail! One was killed at the scene, and another was seriously wounded and died later.

This was big trouble for the people of Ky La hamlet. They were to be blamed for the deaths of the two Viet Cong, and there was no way to dispute that. But my parents were the prime culprits, not just because of the failure to give the signal, but because many of their nephews were in the military forces and Chin, my sister's husband, was now a policeman, too. According to the Viet Cong logic, my parents should know in advance such movements of the enemy forces.

One night they set up a kind of tribunal, the so-called "Toa An Nhan Dan" (The Court of the People) to bring my mother and some other "guilty" people to that court for "a trial of treacherousness," as they claimed. After they had killed other women and were about to put a bullet into my mother's head, my Uncle Luc

A wounded Viet Cong prisoner being guarded by the AVRN following capture in a village. (Imperial War Museum CT148)

stepped forward and reasoned with the Viet Cong, begging them to stop the killing and telling them that my family had sons and nephews fighting in the war for the Communists. The Viet Cong relented, and released my mother with the order that she must stay in the house and only walk around within 100 yards of our own property until further notice, a kind of house arrest.

Another killing happened not long after that, this one caused by American soldiers. The victim was a peasant, Mr. De, who lived in Bai Gian village. It was raining that day, so he wore a black nylon raincoat, exactly the kind the Viet Cong always used. Actually, those raincoats were common sights, because most of us in those days used them, but perhaps they were not so to the eyes of the American soldiers. In any case, they took him for a Viet Cong cadre, and began to ask him questions. Being illiterate and not speaking or understanding English, he naturally couldn't answer any of their questions, which made American soldiers more suspicious. De was so scared that he did not know what to do other than put up his hands, and stand still, as if admitting his guilt. The soldiers began to strike him with their rifle butts, and to stab him with daggers. They struck him until he could no longer stand up, then continued after he fell over until some of them pronounced the man was dead. Many of the villagers witnessed this incident, but none of them complained, lest they face the same fate. Deaths such as this were not uncommon, but there was no justice for the victims. Some died luckily because their relatives had the courage to claim their bodies, and give them a decent funeral. Most died as unknown persons and their unclaimed bodies would be buried lonely on the side of the road, or in mass graves with other victims, without coffins or ceremonies.

People who lived in the strategic hamlets lost all the freedom specified in the new constitution of the country. Barbed wire, gates, security posts, and guards ensured that no moving in or out could be done without detection. People who wanted to visit relatives or acquaintances in the hamlets were required to have the authority's permission or a pass. The comings and goings of villagers were not only strictly limited but also under close surveillance. All items carried out of or into the villages had to be declared, and their original sources disclosed, if the loads were out of the ordinary. This meant that people in the villages were living in a kind of concentration camp. They were prisoners in their own villages, in their own houses. Not only that, but there were always duties to be performed. Villagers labored day after day to finish and protect the hamlets. Bamboo, pine trees, and palm trees had to be cut down, to make poles and posts. Trenches had to be dug along the village perimeters to protect against any infiltration attempts. These works cost not only time but also money and the properties of the villagers. Bamboo, trees, and other necessities for the construction of these fortified hamlets were obtained from the people in the hamlets, not by asking, but by compulsion. People who had nothing to offer were required to spend more days at work on the project. So much for the life of the people in the countryside in the war! We all know that a person can only die once. But in Vietnam at that time, it was possible to die twice, because living in the Strategic Hamlets was a living death.

AFTER THOUGHT

To this date writers, politicians, policymakers, and supporters and opponents of the Vietnam War are still arguing about who was right or wrong, who won or lost the war in Vietnam? In my opinion, the only ones who truly lost out are the Vietnamese people. They lost so much in the war. Looking back at the war fought on my Motherland I see that 30 years later, recovery is underway. Despite this, the wounds of the war are still there, and it affects the people's daily life deeply! I pray that no more wars like the Vietnam War will be waged in the name of humanity. I hope that movies and books will continue to tell the stories to the world of the horrors of war, and to remind the leaders of the world that war brings only suffering, death, hunger, and disease to humans. The war in Vietnam should be a precious lesson for all of us. It has brought mistrust, hate, and anger into dealings between the USA and Vietnam for years. But recently there is a hope: a light at the end of the tunnel!

In 1996, the USA and Vietnam re-established normal diplomatic relations. President Clinton, in 2000, was the first US president to visit Vietnam since the end of the war in 1975. Recently Prime Minister Phan Van Khai visited the White House, the first Vietnamese Communist leader ever to do so. And 2006 will see President Bush on his way to Vietnam.

Foes become friends. So, did the US win the war and turn Vietnam towards capitalism and democracy? Or did the Communists of Vietnam "take over" the US domino propaganda?

Though the war changed many things in Vietnam, some scenes, such as these people working the rice paddies, remain timeless. (Bentre, South Vietnam, photo by James Nguyen)

Chapter 8

Diggers and Kiwis
Australian and New Zealand Experience in Vietnam

Professor Jeffrey Grey

Australia and New Zealand were the only two Western democratic allies of the United States to send combat forces to the Vietnam War, but they did so for differing reasons, the forces committed were dissimilar in size, and the length of the commitment varied for each. Nor was the Anzac soldier's experience in Vietnam the same as his American counterpart's, and it bore no relation to the depiction of the war in many post-Vietnam War feature films.

In both cases, the army fielded the greatest part of the forces sent to the war, and did most of the fighting. Australia and New Zealand had been involved in operations in Asia more or less continuously since the outbreak of the Pacific War in December 1941, and both armies had acquired a considerable body of experience and doctrine in counterinsurgency warfare through involvement in the Malayan Emergency (1948–60) and the Indonesian–Malaysian Confrontation (1962–66). The Australian services, in particular, were in the middle of a major equipment acquisition program intended to modernize and enhance their capabilities, and while the Royal Australian Air Force and Royal Australian Navy were the more obvious beneficiaries of this process, the army also benefited, most obviously with the development of rotary-wing aviation through the 1960s, a process greatly hastened by the demands of the war in Vietnam.

Both Australia and New Zealand were signatories to the ANZUS Treaty[1], which formalized their alliance and security relationship with the United States, and both were active members of the Southeast Asia Treaty Organization, created in 1955 to counter Communist aggression in the "protocol states" of Indochina. SEATO in fact proved to be a broken reed, and while ANZUS was the crucial element of the defense policies of both countries in this period, it was not invoked to support Australian or New Zealand involvement. Rather, Australia's commitment to Vietnam was based on concerns that the US might prove an unreliable ally in the event of an attack upon

Private Keith Craven, an M60 machine-gunner with Fire Assault Platoon, Support Company, 7th Battalion, The Royal Australian Regiment, pauses in the jungle during Operation *Forrest*. (Australian War Memorial, EKN/67/0150/VN)

United States Army Iroquois helicopters land to collect members of 5 Platoon, B Company, 7th Battalion, The Royal Australian Regiment (7RAR), who have completed the cordon and search of the village of Phuoc Hai, known as Operation *Ulmarra*. Operation *Ulmarra* was part of Operation *Atherton* conducted by 2RAR/NZ (Anzac). This image is etched on the Vietnam Memorial on Anzac Parade, Canberra. (Australian War Memorial, Michael Coleridge, EKN/67/0130/VN)

Australian territory. This in turn was based squarely on the threat posed by Indonesia as a result of the decision to give Jakarta control of the former Dutch (or West) New Guinea in 1961, and by Indonesian conduct of Confrontation, its undeclared war to destabilize the emergent Federation of Malaysia. The United States had supported the Indonesian claim in 1961, over Australian objections, and had informed Canberra that the continuing war in Borneo was not grounds on which to invoke the mutual assistance clause in the ANZUS Treaty. Taken together, these developments seemed to undermine the widely held assumption that ANZUS was a security guarantee, and led the Australian government in 1964–65 to be acutely attuned to American needs in Vietnam. In a widely used analogy, the Australian commitment to Vietnam can thus be seen as a form of payment on the insurance policy that ANZUS was held to represent.

New Zealand's path to involvement in the war was slightly different. Dubbed by one New Zealand official as "consistently the most dovish of the hawks," New Zealand policy over Vietnam was also driven by alliance considerations, but as well as focusing on the United States and the security guarantee implicit through membership of ANZUS, the New Zealanders were also concerned to keep their policy in broad alignment with Australia's. Although the New Zealand government consistently doubted that a military solution to the Vietnam War was achievable, the enthusiastic support in Canberra for American decisions over troop increases and escalation of the war left Wellington with few options other than to follow suit.

Fielding sub-units from its small armed forces, integrated within the larger Australian contribution, New Zealand's participation was tied directly to Australia's. Australia's commitment was likewise tied to that of the Americans, and it would be fair to say that Australia went into Vietnam because it was important to Washington, increased its force contributions several times at American behest, and began to phase out the commitment and withdraw from Vietnam when it became clear that the United States was doing likewise. The interests of the South Vietnamese did not figure large in these decisions.

The first Australians to see service in Vietnam were the original members of the Australian Army Training Team Vietnam. Thirty officers, warrant officers, and sergeants were dispatched in July 1962, and worked with the South Vietnamese within the US advisory effort that by the end of that year numbered around 11,000 personnel. By 1965, the strength of the AATTV had been increased to 100 officers and senior NCOs, employed predominantly in the northern provinces of South Vietnam. The advisors were soon accompanying their South Vietnamese counterparts into action, and the training team incurred the first Australian casualties of the war. This unit was the most highly decorated of all the Australian forces there, its members earning four Victoria Crosses and many Commonwealth, American, and South Vietnamese decorations. Especially in its early years, its members were all long-serving professional soldiers with experience in Malaya, Korea and, in some cases, the war with Japan. After the withdrawal of the main Australian force in 1971, the AATTV remained in South Vietnam, now concentrated and relocated to Phuoc Tuy province, and continued to train South Vietnamese and Cambodian troops until their final withdrawal in January 1973. Across a ten-year commitment, the unit lost 30 killed in action and 122 wounded.

New Zealand also sent two training teams to Vietnam, although not until late in the war. Designated 1NZTTV, a 25-man team was deployed to the National Training Center at Chi Lang in the Vietnamese IV Corps area in January 1971. The facility trained regular, regional, and popular force personnel, and the New Zealanders worked within a centralized Vietnamese training organization. In January 1972 the New Zealand government dispatched 2NZTTV to assist the US advisory effort in training Khmer infantry battalions at Dong Ba Thin near Cam Ranh Bay north of Saigon. This second team remained in Vietnam until November of the same year, assisting in the training of nine Cambodian battalions.

In the course of 1964, President Johnson placed increasing pressure on key allies, such as Britain and Australia, for force commitments to South Vietnam under what became known as the "many flags" campaign. London successfully resisted this pressure, but regional security considerations drew Australia into an increased force commitment, with the result that in 1965, for the first time in the 20th century, Australia and then New Zealand went to war without Britain. Nor were Australian senior officers particularly sanguine about the situation on the ground at this time. Brigadier O. D. Jackson, commander of the AATTV in 1965, recalled his initial impression that "the war was lost from a military point of view … [and] the Viet Cong were thoroughly on top." Even those at senior levels in the

Australian forces who took a more optimistic view believed that, like Malaya in the 1950s, the war in Vietnam promised to be a long and protracted fight.

Following bilateral staff talks in Honolulu in late March, the Australian government announced at the end of April that an infantry battalion would be committed as part of the American build-up then underway. Conscription (called national service in Australia) had been reintroduced in November 1964 as part of a planned expansion of the Army, though at the time without any specific intention that national servicemen would be sent to Vietnam. In any case, the initial call-up would not commence training until June 1965 and was therefore unavailable for overseas service anywhere, and the first battalion to fight in Vietnam was entirely made up of regular soldiers. Arriving in May, the 1st Battalion, Royal Australian Regiment was attached to the US 173rd Airborne Brigade (Separate), located at the massive air base at Bien Hoa, outside Saigon.

The situation in Vietnam was critical, and American units followed an aggressive policy of finding and fixing enemy units and bringing them to battle, in the hope of inflicting heavy casualties. In the context of the immediate danger of a South Vietnamese collapse, this was probably a good short-term strategy, but it brought with it heavy casualties to the allied forces as well, and this posed difficulties for the Australians. The Australian Army was small, and though better trained, was technically less advanced than its American counterpart. The soldiers of 1RAR had not worked with helicopters in airmobile operations before reaching Vietnam, and the resources in firepower and mobility available to US commanders had no equivalent in the Australian setting in which the battalion had trained and exercised. There were also some serious differences between the US and Australian conceptions of operations. Australian doctrine had been honed in

A platoon from B Company, 7RAR, gather around Lieutenant Doug Gibbons for a final briefing before moving out into the jungle east of the 1st Australian Task Force base. 7RAR had only arrived on the troopship HMAS *Sydney* ten days earlier for its second tour of duty in the war zone. This first operation was codenamed *Finschhafen*. (Australian War Memorial, Peter Anthony Ward, WAR/70/0158/VN)

Malaya in the 1950s and emphasized population security and a slow and patient approach to countering insurgency; the US approach emphasized firepower, a reliance on enemy main force units, and the rapid attainment of decisive outcomes. It was not always a happy combination.

The Australians operated throughout 1965–66 in successive operations in the Iron Triangle and War Zones C and D, securing both the facilities at Bien Hoa and denying the enemy access to the capital, Saigon. In September, to give the battalion more punch, the government dispatched M113 armored personnel carriers, combat engineers, and a field artillery battery to form a battalion group. They joined the New Zealand field battery, of approximately 120 men, which the New Zealand government had decided to send in May following requests from Washington. Although New Zealand also had a system of peacetime conscription in place, the soldiers who went to Vietnam were all regulars, and New Zealand society was thus less deeply divided and affected by the use of national servicemen on active service overseas than was to be the case in Australia. As was also to be the case in Australia, however, the New Zealand government continued to receive requests from Washington for increases in the troop commitment to Vietnam, and in 1967 added two infantry companies from The Royal New Zealand Regiment to the Australian Task Force, together with small additional attachments that brought the New Zealand contribution to about 500 personnel overall.

The New Zealand companies were drawn from the infantry battalion based in Malaysia as part of the Far East Strategic Reserve (to which Australia and Britain also contributed), and the first company was dispatched to Vietnam in May 1967 to become an integral sub-unit within an Australian infantry battalion. For the duration of the joint commitment, the battalions that incorporated New Zealand companies were designated as RAR/NZ battalions within the task force (e.g. 4RAR/NZ). A second rifle company, "W" Company, was deployed in December of the same year and maintained thereafter, while a troop from the New Zealand Special Air Service was added to 1st Australian Task Force in December 1969. The RAR/NZ battalions were commanded by an Australian lieutenant colonel, but had a New Zealand second-in-command and several Kiwi appointments at lower levels. Like their Australian and US counterparts, the New Zealanders withdrew their force incrementally, with W Company withdrawn in November 1970 and V Company taken out in December the following year. Across the course of New Zealand's active involvement, 29 officers and other ranks were killed in action, while almost 4,000 men served in various capacities in South Vietnam.

From the outset, the Australian Army's senior leadership believed that the most suitable minimum contribution would be a brigade-size task force, able to operate independently for lengthy periods and be self-sustaining, and the experience with 1RAR in 1965–66 served to confirm this predilection. The clash of doctrine and operating procedures and assumptions between the Australian and US components led to some tensions between the two components, while direct subordination within an American formation undercut the military and political requirements that the Australian force be independent and clearly identifiable as Australian. As

Phuoc Tuy province

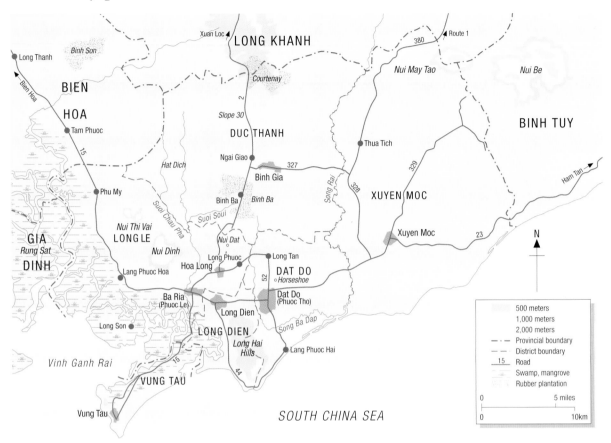

Lieutenant General Sir John Wilton, the Chief of the General Staff, expressed it, while any Australian force would be under US operational control, "I preferred not to be included in an American position. I wanted to have as much independence within the force limitations as I could so I could keep a closer eye on it."

The Australian government had imposed a number of political limitations on the task force's operations, the most important of which was that Australian personnel were not to operate in or over Cambodia, Laos, or North Vietnam (a few in fact did so when attached to US units as individuals). In selecting a province as the Australian area of operations, therefore, a number of factors had to be taken into account. The province could not adjoin either the Cambodian border or the Demilitarized Zone at the 17th Parallel. The Australians were not looking for a quiet or unimportant sector, however, and eventually chose the province of Phuoc Tuy. This had been a highly active area during the French war in Indochina; its importance lay in its position surrounding the increasingly busy port of Vung Tau, linked to Saigon by Route 15. The possession of the port would also make it easier to maintain an Australian line of resupply, and provide an evacuation point should that prove necessary. It was primarily an agricultural province, with considerable stretches of uninhabited country, and population of the province was about 106,000. By 1966 the enemy had several main force regiments and regional battalions in the province, which was largely under enemy control.

The 1ATF of two battalions, an SAS squadron (matched by a New Zealand contribution), and combat and logistical support units, was deployed in May and June 1966, at the end of 1RAR's 12-month operational tour. Throughout the war, the infantry battalions served 12 months in Vietnam before being replaced as units. Personnel in the support units were replaced through individual rotation. The government had directed that the battalions should contain no more than 50 percent national servicemen (to avoid the charge that conscripts were cannon fodder while the regulars sat out the fighting), and this was maintained strictly in terms of reinforcements and replacements during the operational tour. Since the term of call-up was two years, this meant that national servicemen ("nashos" in colloquial terms) spent a lengthy period with their units in training and working up before deploying overseas, improving morale and cohesion as well as capability. Senior regimental officers were all experienced regulars, but a proportion of the junior officers were also national servicemen. Overall, of the approximately 50,000 Australians who served in Vietnam, 17,424 were national servicemen. Of the 501 Australians who died there, 200 were national servicemen.

New command and control arrangements were put in place. The task force answered to an Australian major general, designated Commander Australian Force Vietnam with headquarters in Saigon. Operational control of the Australians was vested in US II Field Force Vietnam, a corps-level headquarters. The commanders' directives from the Australian government were deliberately

Troops of 7th Battalion, The Royal Australian Regiment, dash from a US Army Iroquois helicopter on May 2, 1967, to launch Operation *Lismore*, their first major mission against the Viet Cong. The battalion was swept into the field by 20 American helicopters to begin the operation. (Australian War Memorial, Barrie Winston Gillman, GIL/67/0377/VN)

general, to allow greater freedom of action on the ground. While Phuoc Tuy was designated the Australians' area of operations, they were available for "out of province" tasks at the discretion of higher American command, and indeed during the Tet Offensive and for much of 1968, parts of 1ATF operated in the provinces surrounding Phuoc Tuy. Although part of the thinking behind securing a province had been to enable the Australians to put their own counterinsurgency techniques into practice, initially, at least, 1ATF was deployed on a mixture of main force and pacification operations. The Vietnamese themselves retained responsibility for the populated urban areas, and the provincial military and civil advisory effort continued to be an American responsibility.

Reflecting the small size and limited range of capabilities within the Australian armed forces more generally, 1ATF relied on the Americans to some extent for additional capabilities that it could not deploy from Australian resources. This included medium and heavy artillery fire support, naval gunfire support from ships of the US 7th Fleet, and helicopter support, both troop lift and gunship, and other air support from the base at Bien Hoa. In addition, US and ARVN forces could supplement 1ATF when the occasion required. The Australians also worked extensively with the regional forces and popular forces (RF/PF) within the province, especially from 1969 in keeping with the policy of Vietnamization. As had been the case with the 1st Commonwealth Division during the Korean War, US commanders generally gave their Australian subordinates greater relative freedom to conduct their operations than would have been granted to an equivalent American formation. As Brigadier R. L. Hughes, commander of 1ATF in 1968, noted subsequently, the task force's "method of doing things was different to the way the Vietnamese, the Americans or the Koreans, would do the same things." On occasions, the differences in assumptions and approach led to friction with some senior US officers, including General William Westmoreland, who wanted 1ATF to engage in regular, set-piece engagements with enemy main force units, and looked for high enemy body counts. On the other hand, some senior American officers, such as Lieutenant General Frederick C. Weyand, commanding IIFFV in 1967, thought that allocating formations to designated regions to enable them to really get to know an area paid greater dividends than throwing units around the country in pursuit of the enemy.

The task force's operations between 1966 and 1971 went through a number of phases. The first phase involved the selection of a base area and the establishment of the task force within it. The Australians intended to stay out of the urban areas as much as possible, and selected the area around Nui Dat for their base area. It satisfied all the requirements: it stood between the urban centers and the main concentrations of the enemy, provided clear fields of fire for defensive purposes, was close to Vung Tau for ease of maintenance and resupply, and was centrally located to allow easy access to the province as a whole. This first phase lasted until late 1967, at which time the task force was increased in size to three battalions, Australian armor was committed to Phuoc Tuy for the first time, and much of 1ATF then spent the period from the Tet Offensive to mid-1969 on operations

Armored personnel carriers and a Centurion tank form a laager while members of F Troop, 2 Squadron SAS patrol change into their camouflage uniform prior to reaching the "drop point" to commence a walk-in patrol into the Long Hais. The SAS patrol traveled in normal Jungle Greens to this point to conceal their purpose from enemy agents. (Australian War Memorial, P00966.065)

outside the province. The third and final phase, from mid-1969 until the withdrawal of the force in November 1971, saw operations again largely confined to Phuoc Tuy, with the task force reverting to a two-battalion structure from November 1970 as the US, and hence its allies, began to withdraw from the war.

The first and third phases most closely accorded with the dictates of Australian doctrine for counterinsurgency. In 1966–67, the task force sought to establish and secure its base, deny the enemy main force units access to civilian resources, and deny the enemy's political cadres access to the people. In general, the Australians sought to avoid the destruction of villages or fighting in close proximity to settled areas in a bid to reduce damage and avoid casualties among the local people. The establishment of the base at Nui Dat, however, involved the destruction of two villages located close to the site and the forced removal and resettlement of their inhabitants, albeit by the Americans before 1ATF arrived. The second half of 1966 was largely characterized by operations intended to secure Nui Dat and the lines of supply to Vung Tau, and the operations involved a number of heavy engagements with sizable bodies of the enemy, well illustrated by the battle of Long Tan in August 1966, easily the best-known Australian engagement of the war. It also illustrated the threat posed at this time to the Australian position by strong enemy forces then operating freely within the province.

The base had received sustained rocket fire, apparently aimed at the artillery batteries, and prompting an intensified program of patrols in the vicinity of the base. On August 18, D Company, 6RAR, strength 108 men, was sent to the east of the base to try to locate the firing positions used previously. A large force of Viet Cong and PAVN, in at least battalion strength, heavily engaged one of the platoons, and the intensity of the fire laid down prevented the other platoons from coming to its support. Supported by the artillery batteries in Nui Dat, the company was subjected to sustained heavy fire and repeated assaults over several hours, while a second company from 6RAR with a troop of M113 APCs attempted to get through to them. The besieged company was resupplied with ammunition by helicopter in a torrential downpour. The VC/PAVN forces broke contact and withdrew as darkness fell and the relieving company arrived and engaged elements of the attacking force. Australian losses were 18 dead and 21 wounded. VC/PAVN losses were officially listed as 245 dead, but were probably substantially higher (reflecting Australian reluctance to engage in "body count" games and inflation of VC/PAVN casualties).

The battle demonstrated several things at this stage of the Australians' war. A large VC/PAVN force had maneuvered to within 5,000 meters of the base, illustrating the patchy nature of the intelligence coverage available to the task force's commander. The artillery fire support and the arrival of the APCs had undoubtedly saved D Company, but the vehicles themselves had already seen considerable service, and were old and lacking some equipment. The national servicemen had performed equally with the regulars, supporting the notion that there was little to choose between the two. Having broken contact and withdrawn with their wounded, the VC/PAVN force made a clear escape, and in the following four days of operations the Australians proved unable to locate them. This was the case again in February 1967 when, on two separate occasions, elements of the task force engaged large groups of VC/PAVN forces and inflicted heavy casualties, but were unable to prevent their withdrawal because of the limited means available.

Limited resources, and the unreliability of the local Vietnamese forces at this stage of the war, led to the single worst operational mistake made by the task force: the laying of the so-called "barrier minefield" east and south of Dat Do in 1967. The Dat Do district was a major source of support to Viet Cong main force units operating in the province, and the idea was to block the movement of men and supplies to the VC strongholds in the Long Hai hills, which proved a troublesome area for the task force throughout its deployment. Constructed to run 12km from the Horseshoe position, past Dat Do to the village of Long Phuoc Hai on the coast, protection and oversight of the minefield was to be provided by local territorial units because of the shortage of Australian manpower. The importance of locating and securing minefields had been learnt in the Korean War, but seemingly forgotten by the task force commander responsible, Brigadier S. C. Graham (who had not, himself, served in Korea). Not only did the local South Vietnamese units fail to provide the security needed, but the VC/PAVN forces became highly adept at lifting and removing the M16 anti-personnel mines, and converting them into booby traps for use against the task force itself. As many as 5,000 mines were taken in this way, and between mid-1968 and mid-1970 it was estimated that their own ordnance, turned against them, inflicted fully 50 percent of Australian casualties in the province. The widespread use of mines by the enemy led to the regular attachment of field engineer teams to infantry and armor units on operations. The minefield was finally removed by the task force itself in early 1970, though the mines already lifted continued to be used by the enemy.

Widespread "search-and-destroy" operations the same year had greater effect than the failure to think through the needs and implications of the minefield. Together with "cordon-and-search" operations, aimed at detecting and detaining VC/PAVN political cadres in the villages, the operations in 1967 were intended to degrade the capabilities that the VC had built up so effectively by 1966, when the task force deployed to the province. The problem here was the continuing low level of performance by the South Vietnamese, including the national police, who were charged with harassing and eliminating the Viet Cong infrastructure. These integrated, large-scale operations, running over months, scored some important successes, not least in filling out an extensive intelligence picture of the VC and his capabilities and impinging, at times heavily, upon the Viet Cong capacity to resupply from the villages and to tax the inhabitants. This achievement came at a price in Australian casualties: a four-day operation by 5RAR in the Long Hai hills in February 1967 resulted in seven killed and twenty-two wounded, largely from VC mines and booby traps. In August 1967, in a short but intense action at Suoi Chau Pha, a company of 7RAR suffered six dead, in contact with a company of VC main force soldiers covering the withdrawal of the rest of their battalion. Large numbers of VC were killed, but only five bodies were recovered because the Viet Cong, as was so often the case, carried their dead away whenever possible.

While these operations were short-term successes, they did not provide longer-term solutions to the problems of population security and the VC's freedom of

Two members of V Company, a New Zealand component of the Anzac battalion manning Checkpoint C near Dat Do. They are looking north towards Horseshoe Hill in the distance. (Australian War Memorial, P01661.003)

Members of A Company, 2RAR/NZ, wade through deep water to cross a paddy field southeast of the Australian Task Force base at Nui Dat. The patrol, along the coastal strip of Phuoc Tuy province, was part of a move by the battalion to prevent Viet Cong reinforcements, supplies, and equipment entering the province by sea. (Australian War Memorial, Bryan Campbell, CAM/67/0804/VN)

action once the task force had moved on. As one analysis noted in November 1967, "our operations have not denied the area to the VC because he was free to return after our withdrawal, but he is faced with a major task in restoring this logistic area if he does wish to return." Task force operations were only as successful as the capacity of the South Vietnamese authorities to capitalize upon them and this was limited. The commanding officer of 5RAR, Lieutenant Colonel J. A. Warr, noted that "the speed with which the Vietcong cadres can be eliminated by cordon and searches must be adjusted to the capacity of the government forces to secure the villages against the return of the enemy." In this period, however, the VC seems to have continued to reach the villages, albeit with a greater degree of difficulty.

The operational problems caused by fielding a two-battalion task force were largely resolved in December 1967, when a third battalion was added and maintained for the next three years. This gave the task force commander much greater flexibility, while mobility and reach were enhanced through the addition of extra Iroquois helicopters from Australia. A squadron of Australian Centurion main battle tanks added greater lethality, and provided a boost to the Australians in dealing with enemy bunker complexes. This also meant that operations could now be conducted outside Phuoc Tuy province, with one of the three battalions remaining to provide for the security of the positions at Nui Dat and the Horseshoe and maintain a ready reaction force. The operations mounted in 1967 had forced VC main force units into some of the more remote areas of Phuoc Tuy. Developments in the wider war now also influenced the conduct of the Australians' war.

The period between January 1968 and the launching of the Tet Offensive, and June 1969 saw extensive out-of-province operations in Bien Hoa, Long Binh, and

Long Khanh provinces in conjunction with both US and ARVN forces. During the Tet Offensive two battalions, 2RAR and 7RAR, were deployed to defend the approaches to Saigon and Bien Hoa, while companies from 3RAR remained in Phuoc Tuy and drove the Viet Cong out of positions they had occupied in the towns of Baria and Long Dien. During the resurgence of enemy activity in May 1968, the task force was again deployed to protect Long Binh and Bien Hoa, encountering concentrations of North Vietnamese as they positioned themselves on the enemy's main withdrawal routes. Two intense actions were fought at Fire Support Bases Coral (1RAR) and Balmoral (3RAR) that had been located between Saigon and War Zone D. Supported by intense and accurate rocket and mortar fire, the attack by a PAVN battalion against Coral on the night of May 13 saw one Australian artillery position temporarily overrun; the enemy was cleared out in stiff hand-to-hand fighting, but nine Australians were killed and 26 wounded that night.

Another seven were killed and 17 wounded in a second, heavy assault three nights later. In the second half of the month, PAVN units attacked 3RAR at Balmoral. As a result of the earlier engagements, the Australian battalions had been reinforced with Centurions, and these were deployed effectively in stemming subsequent North Vietnamese assaults. This operationally intense month resulted in overall Australian losses of 26 killed and 110 wounded. The third period of operations outside Phuoc Tuy occurred largely in January to April 1969, with the Australians deployed against enemy bases in the My Tho and Hat Dich areas, as well as around Bien Hoa again. An important development in this second phase of the Australians' war, in terms of NVA/VC behavior and capability, was the

North Vietnamese soldiers, captured after heavy fighting at Fire Support Base Balmoral in Bien Hoa province, stand blindfolded waiting to be taken away from the battle area by helicopter. Troops from 3RAR repulsed an estimated two battalions of North Vietnamese soldiers who stormed the base for four hours on May 28, 1968. (Australian War Memorial, Richard William Crothers, CRO/68/0575/VN)

increasing reliance upon bunker systems and the attendant problems these posed for the task force. In the first phase, in Phuoc Tuy, concentrations of NVA/VC forces had been encountered in camps, or occupying cave complexes in the Long Hai hills, with relatively crude field defenses, but by the end of 1967 this had begun to change. Bunker systems posed challenges for the task force for the remainder of its time in the province, although the addition of tanks to the order of battle provided an important additional counter to the advantages accorded through fighting from well-designed and concealed fixed positions. Initially, however, there had been little or no training in infantry–armor coordination, and it took time for appropriate tactics and techniques to evolve, with an inevitable price in casualties. Even as late as 1971, however, a bunker system could prove a difficult tactical proposition for assaulting infantry, especially if the armor was unavailable for some reason.

The third phase, between July 1969 and the withdrawal of the task force in October 1971, saw a return to a mix of main-force operations and pacification, heavily influenced by the advent of Vietnamization and the increasing certainty of US and allied withdrawal from the war. By this time the NVA/VC main force units were mostly confined to the northern fringes of the province and operations against them occurred along the border. There was still occasional heavy fighting in these areas. At Binh Ba in June 1969, a company from 5RAR drove a reinforced company of North Vietnamese from the area, destroying the village in the process in a battle that saw the Australians combine tanks, APCs, and helicopters in support. Increasingly, however, Australian operations concentrated on pacification, patrolling, and ambushing around the villages in order to disrupt the local cadres and guerrillas as contacts with significant numbers of main force soldiers became increasingly infrequent. As one young officer recalled, "this was Vietnam, weeks of trudging and then a contact of a few seconds, over almost before it began."

Such "infrastructure" operations called for skill, tenacity, and great patience. Fleeting contacts and brief, if intense, firefights were much more typical of the

Members of 2RAR/NZ on a rice-denial patrol in Phuoc Tuy province during December 1970. Their aim is to prevent Viet Cong fighters from getting supplies during the twice-yearly rice harvest. (Australian War Memorial, William James Cunneen, CUN/70/0890/VN)

experience of Australian soldiers than were the handful of big, and much better-known, set-piece engagements such as Long Tan, Coral, and Binh Ba. Unlike in World War II, for example, in which Australian soldiers had experienced long periods training in rear areas before being committed to operations, in Vietnam the infantry soldiers spent long periods in the field, interspersed by relatively brief periods at the Horseshoe or Nui Dat for rest and refitting, before returning to the field. Units and sub-units of 1ATF had roughly 3,500 enemy contacts in the course of the war, of which about 160 involved assaults by the Australians on bunkers, camps, and other defended locales. The range of engagement was almost invariably short – usually less than 20m – and brief. In keeping with the advantages enjoyed by all the allied forces in Vietnam, soldiers in the task force often expended prodigious quantities of ammunition, especially in set-piece assaults against bunkers. They could also call on a full suite of fire support options, including helicopter gunships, field, medium and heavy artillery, fixed-wing air support and, on occasion, naval gunfire offshore. In ambush they came increasingly to utilize the Claymore command-detonated, anti-personnel mine with great effect. Ambushes were often set at night, to impede Viet Cong movement, and the main focus was on obtaining intelligence, rather than an emphasis on body count for its own sake.

In November 1970, 8RAR completed its tour and was not replaced, with 1ATF reverting to a two-battalion structure. This increased the workload on the remaining battalions and reduced operational flexibility. This was partly resolved by locating one battalion at Nui Dat for operations in the west of the province, and basing the other at the Horseshoe, responsible for the eastern half. Within these battalion areas of operation, the rifle companies had their own AOs, and operational tasks in the last two years of the Australian commitment were dispersed and devolved to this level. Increasingly, when NVA/VC forces tried to move about the province, they paid the price. A good example of this was provided by an action by B Company, 7RAR around Xuyen Moc in late December 1970. Working with a troop of APCs, the infantry ambushed a large party of Viet Cong, killing 21, including several senior cadres, and further disrupting the VC's provincial infrastructure as a result. When VC main force units attempted to re-enter the province in mid-1971, knowing that the Australians would soon withdraw, they were forced out again by a series of operations mounted by 3RAR and 4RAR/NZ. NVA/VC strength in the province was reduced to approximately 1,400 effectives, a third of what it had been when the task force had arrived in 1966.

The task force withdrew from Phuoc Tuy in October–November 1971, and although the NVA/VC's ability to influence and coerce the population had been considerably reduced, this did not long survive 1ATF's departure. As the commander of the main force D445 Battalion after 1969, Lieutenant Colonel Nguyen Duc Thu, recalled, "the presence of Australian troops and American troops in Phuoc Tuy [allowed] the Government of South Vietnam ... to control the population. But with the withdrawal of the American troops and the Australian troops we turned the tables."

AIR AND NAVAL OPERATIONS

The principal Australian commitment to the Vietnam War was on the ground, but small contributions were also made by the other two services. These are dealt with separately here because there was very little cooperation between them during the war. Just as 1ATF worked within a US command environment, so the detachments of the RAN and RAAF worked within structures provided by the US 7th Fleet and the US 5th Air Force. Both services underwent major capital equipment acquisition programs in the 1960s, and service in Vietnam helped them familiarize themselves with new capabilities and their application on active service.

The RAAF based a transport unit in Vung Tau in August 1964, flying the twin-engine Caribou tactical transport plane. Known as "Wallaby airlines" from its call sign, No. 35 (Transport) Squadron (as it became) flew cargo and passengers all over the country, and regularly engaged in aerial resupply within the US airlift system. From April 1967, No. 2 Squadron, flying aging Canberra bombers, was based at Phan Rang as part of the US 35th Tactical Fighter Wing. Restricted to South Vietnamese airspace, it flew high-altitude night missions and low-altitude daylight missions in a close ground support role, one to which the aircraft proved particularly suited. The RAAF had begun to acquire Iroquois utility helicopters in 1964, and although these were designated for cooperation with the Army, the Air Force had declined to utilize them in this way. The airmobile nature of operations in Vietnam saw No. 9 Squadron deployed with the task force in mid-1966, but there were numerous problems between airmen and soldiers over issues of command and control and aircraft tasking and availability that were never entirely resolved during the war. The Royal New Zealand Air Force supplied a limited number of pilots from mid-1968, in order to help meet the aircrew shortage in this category. The legacy of ill will generated by this

The HMAS *Hobart* off South Vietnam in 1970. (Australian War Memorial, P00180.019)

experience resulted in the transfer of a new generation of battlefield helicopter from the RAAF to Army control in the mid-1980s.

Like the RAAF, the RAN contributed a range of ships and units, numerically quite small in comparison with the enormous US presence but of undoubted value as "niche" capabilities. HMAS *Sydney*, a light fleet carrier converted to a fast troop transport role, supported the Australian task force. Nicknamed the "Vung Tau ferry," *Sydney* transported troops and equipment between Vietnam and Australia from mid-1965 until the final evacuation of Australian personnel in 1972. Four destroyers participated in interdiction and naval gunfire support tasks on the gun line offshore: the three newly acquired, US-built Charles F. Adams class ships, and one older, British-pattern destroyer. The modern ships fitted easily into the US logistic system, and operated smoothly within the command and control structure. A sour note was sounded in June 1968, however, when HMAS *Hobart*, operating against North Vietnamese shore emplacements, was attacked by aircraft of the US Air Force by mistake, killing several members of the crew.

Ashore, the RAN deployed Clearance Diving Team 3 from February 1967 to April 1971 for explosive ordnance demolition tasks and port security at Vung Tau and throughout the Mekong Delta. The unit often worked in conjunction with US Navy SEALs, and in the last months of its operational tour was transferred to Da Nang, where it was again responsible for security within the port. No role could be found for the aging carrier and flagship of the Australian fleet, HMAS *Melbourne*. It was configured for an anti-submarine warfare role, but many of its aircrew and ground crew were converted to the Iroquois utility helicopter and flew as part of an unusual combined unit of the US Army – the 135th Assault Helicopter Company. Based at Black Horse, they flew intensive rounds of troop transport, resupply, medical evacuation, and gunship support missions with US, ARVN, South Korean, and occasionally Australian units on the ground.

CONCLUSION

Vietnam was Australia's longest war, and among its most divisive and controversial. Experience in South Vietnam had again emphasized the light infantry role within the Australian Army; had introduced it to various technologies not available to it before 1966, such as helicopter gunships and troop transports; and had allowed it to relearn some old lessons from earlier conflicts, such as the utility of tanks in the infantry support role in close jungle terrain. The commitment to Phuoc Tuy required an unparalleled peacetime expansion of the Army, one which was not maintained for long after the commitment ended and national service was suspended. The professionalism and skills of the three services were again confirmed, while institutionally the Australian Army emerged intact, with none of the drug, race, and discipline problems that wracked the US services. The Australian Task Force had come to dominate its area of operations in Phuoc Tuy province, but this alone could not ensure a long-term result favorable to the South Vietnamese government or American aims in the country.

Chapter 9

The Conduct of the War
Strategy, Doctrine, Tactics, and Policy

Lewis Sorley

It has often been asserted that the military leaders responsible for conduct of the Vietnam War were never given a clear-cut mission or objective for conduct of the war. While that may be so in a technical sense, there was never any doubt as to the ultimate goal – assisting the South Vietnamese to develop the capacity to maintain their independence in the face of Communist aggression. How to achieve that, militarily and diplomatically, was, however, a constant topic of debate and contention through the long years of American involvement, first as advisors to the South Vietnamese and then as combat participants on an ever increasing scale.

Most analyses of the war to date have portrayed the years of major American involvement as a uniform whole. This has been true both of journalistic accounts and those of historians. The result has been an inability to understand the war and why it turned out as it did, for the earlier years under the command of General William C. Westmoreland and the latter years under General Creighton Abrams differed in almost all important respects.

THE WESTMORELAND YEARS

General Westmoreland took command of American forces in Vietnam in June 1964 after having served since January of that year as deputy to General Paul D. Harkins. The United States was then still serving primarily in an advisory role to the South Vietnamese, along with providing important support in terms of logistics, communications, and intelligence. In the spring and summer of 1965, all that changed dramatically when US ground forces, both Army and Marine, were deployed to Vietnam in large numbers, numbers that over the next several years continued to increase in response to repeated requests from Westmoreland for more and more troops. At the peak, these forces reached 543,400 in Vietnam itself and many thousands more in supporting air and naval forces in the region of Southeast Asia.

President Richard M. Nixon, here visiting troops in Vietnam, took political risks to help the South Vietnamese militarily, including the 1970 incursion into Cambodia and the renewed bombing of North Vietnam in 1972. (NARA)

General William C. Westmoreland, commander of US forces in Vietnam 1964–68, conducted a war of attrition in which body count was the measure of merit. (NARA)

Many analysts of the war have remarked how it was closely controlled from Washington, a view usually illustrated by accounts of such matters as bombing targets chosen or approved at White House luncheons and the like. It is true that the US commander in Vietnam itself had not only to report through a convoluted chain of command, but also lacked control over air and naval forces operating in the theater outside South Vietnam. And throughout the war, a large and constantly changing set of rules of engagement did limit how and where battles might be fought. But a seldom considered aspect of the war, one critical to an understanding of it, is that – despite these fragmented responsibilities, and despite lack of unified command in Vietnam over all elements of the allied forces – the Commander, United States Military Assistance Command, Vietnam had a virtually free hand in deciding how to dispose and employ the forces under his command within South Vietnam.

Westmoreland understood the war to be primarily a classic military conflict, in which the objective was destruction of enemy combat units. His self-styled approach was to conduct what he termed a war of attrition, with his objective being to inflict as many casualties on the enemy as possible. The expectation was that the enemy had a breaking point, and that when he had absorbed sufficient casualties, he would cease his aggression against the South and allow them to live in peace.[1]

The measure of merit in such a war was body count, meaning simply the numbers of the enemy killed (along with those assumed to have been permanently disabled and those captured or induced to rally to the ARVN/US side). Westmoreland's preferred tactics were what he called "search-and-destroy" operations. These forays, often employing very large (multi-battalion and sometimes multi-division) forces, typically took place in the deep jungles adjacent to South Vietnam's borders with Laos and Cambodia. Their objective was to find NVA/VC forces and bring them to decisive combat.

Both were difficult tasks. The elusive NVA/VC forces were adept at evading battle except on their own terms, and on terrain that favored their forces. The NVA and VC could also largely control not only the frequency of combat engagements, but also their duration and the losses sustained. This was primarily due to the US/ARVN's self-imposed political restrictions that kept friendly forces from entering NVA sanctuaries across those borders. The NVA/VC not only established major lines of communications and base areas in the border regions, facilities immune to allied ground attack, but withdrew into such sanctuaries when they desired to disengage from battle.

These search-and-destroy operations were costly in terms of time, effort, and materiel, but often disappointing in results. Ambassador Henry Cabot Lodge reflected some of the frustration this situation induced in a June 1966 cable to Lyndon Johnson. "The best estimate is that 20,000 men of the Army of North Vietnam have come into South Vietnam since January," he wrote, "and as far as I can learn, we can't find them."[2]

Secretary of Defense Robert McNamara, here seen with Westmoreland, presided over a massive build-up of US forces in Vietnam but later confessed that early on he had lost confidence in allied ability to prevail in the conflict. (NARA)

When General Abrams first arrived to be the deputy commander, Lieutenant General Bruce Palmer Jr. took him aside. "I just poured out my soul about my feelings about Vietnam, the almost impossible task we had, given the national policy, limited objectives, and so on," Palmer recalled. "I told him I really had basic disagreements with Westy on how it was organized and how we were doing it." In what must have been a very difficult conversation, since both officers were West Point 1936 classmates of Westmoreland's, Abrams listened carefully, then replied, "You know, I'm here to help Westy and, although I privately agree with many things you are saying, I've got to be loyal to him. I'm going to help him."[3]

A landmark survey conducted after the war showed that army generals who had commanded in Vietnam were quite critical of the search-and-destroy tactics emphasized by Westmoreland. Nearly a third stated that the concept was "not sound," while another 26 percent thought it was "sound when first implemented – not later." As for the execution of search-and-destroy tactics, a majority of 51 percent thought it "left something to be desired," an answer ranking below "adequate" in the survey instrument. "These replies," observed the study's author, Brigadier General Douglas Kinnard, "show a noticeable lack of enthusiasm, to put it mildly, by Westmoreland's generals for his tactics and by implication for his strategy in the war."[4]

Westmoreland nevertheless succeeded, by dint of enormous effort and determination, in inflicting massive casualties on NVA/VC forces. But the anticipated objective was not achieved. The NVA/VC forces did not lose heart, nor cease aggression against South Vietnam. Rather, they continued to pour more and more forces into the war. Westmoreland often predicted that the NVA was going to run out of men, but in the event it turned out to be the United States that did so – or at least found it extremely difficult to deploy more troops in the face of reluctance to call up reserve forces and pressures to reduce draft calls.

Westmoreland's single-minded focus on what some have called "the war of the big battalions," bent on inflicting casualties on the NVA/VC's conventional forces, meanwhile detracted from attention to two other key aspects of the war. These were pacification (and especially rooting out the covert NVA/VC infrastructure that, through terror and coercion, kept the rural population of South Vietnam's hamlets and villages under domination) and improvement of the South Vietnamese armed forces to enable them to progressively take over responsibility for conduct of the war.

"Westmoreland's interest always lay in the big-unit war," said his senior intelligence officer, Lieutenant General Phillip B. Davidson. "Pacification bored him."[5] And, in his enthusiasm for taking over the main force war, Westmoreland in effect pushed the South Vietnamese out of the way, thus also abdicating his assigned role as the senior advisor to those forces and essentially stunting their development for a crucial four years.

An important manifestation of this neglect was failure to upgrade South Vietnam's armament, which was decidedly inferior to that fielded by NVA/VC forces who early on wielded such modern and effective weapons as the AK-47 assault rifle. In contrast, the M-16 rifle provided a key case in point. As stocks of this new and very effective weapon became available, Westmoreland gave his own American forces first priority, letting the South Vietnamese wait. Since American forces also enjoyed more of every kind of combat wherewithal – helicopters, artillery, air strikes, armor – than the Vietnamese, this issue policy for the M-16 made the disparity even greater. As late as the 1968 Tet Offensive, remembered Lieutenant General Dong Van Khuyen, South Vietnam's chief logistician, "the crisp, rattling sounds of AK-47s echoing in Saigon and some other cities seemed to make a mockery of the weaker, single shots of Garands and carbines fired by stupefied friendly troops."[6]

Thus the South Vietnamese during the Westmoreland years typically found themselves outgunned by NVA/VC forces and at a tactical disadvantage, leading to commensurately unfavorable battlefield performance and outcomes. Low morale and poor reputations were the inevitable results. Retired general Bruce Clarke visited Vietnam during February 1968 and afterward prepared a trip report in which he observed that "the Vietnamese units are still on a very austere priority for equipment, to include weapons." That adversely affected both their morale and

President Lyndon Johnson, here awarding medals to soldiers in Vietnam, was eventually driven from office by failure to bring the war to a satisfactory conclusion. (Lyndon Johnson Library)

effectiveness, he observed. "Troops know and feel it when they are poorly equipped."[7] Abrams agreed, vigorously pointing out at a September 1968 staff meeting that "the Vietnamese have been given the lowest priority of anybody that's fighting in this country! And," he added, "that's what we're trying to correct."[8]

There came a point, in the spring of 1967, when Washington's tolerance for repeated Westmoreland requests for more US forces (once described by Westmoreland as his "relatively modest requirements") ran out. A request for 200,000 troops submitted then was, after long consideration, essentially denied, with only a token number of additional troops authorized for deployment.

When, a year later, Westmoreland and the chairman of the Joint Chiefs of Staff General Earle Wheeler came up with a plan for 206,000 more US forces to be raised, the request – coming as it did in the wake of the NVA/VC's startling Tet Offensive, which Westmoreland had portrayed as a clear-cut ARVN/US victory – precipitated a major policy review in Washington. This led not to provision of that large increment of additional forces, but to a revised strategy for prosecution of the war and – not incidentally – replacement of Westmoreland as US commander in Vietnam.

This outcome was clearly to some degree the result of Westmoreland's having rendered, over a period of some months leading up to Tet 1968, very optimistic judgments concerning the situation in Vietnam. On a visit to the United States in the autumn of 1967 he had been particularly sanguine, saying that he had never been more encouraged in his four years in Vietnam and that we had reached a point where the end had begun to come into view. When, only a couple of months later, the Tet Offensive erupted all over Vietnam, producing graphic images on America's television sets, many concluded that either Westmoreland had not known what he was talking about or that he had not been leveling with the American people. It was hard to know which judgment was the more devastating.

When later analysis confirmed Westmoreland's immediate post-Tet insistence that the battle was an ARVN/US victory, that story never quite caught up with the original near-panic the attack had caused in many domestic sectors, notably the White House itself. A bitter joke of the time held that the Tet Offensive confirmed the domino theory even though only one domino – Lyndon Johnson – had fallen as a result.

ABRAMS IN COMMAND

General Creighton Abrams had been serving as Deputy COMUSMACV since May 1967, devoting himself primarily to efforts to upgrade South Vietnam's armed forces. When Abrams became COMUSMACV in late June 1968 (after having for some time been in *de facto* command, a circumstance made clear by the message traffic of the period), he brought to the post a radically different understanding of the nature of the war and how it ought to be prosecuted. Recalled General Fred Weyand, "The tactics changed within 15 minutes of Abrams's taking command."

What Weyand saw was a dramatic shift in concept of the nature and conduct of the war, in the appropriate measures of merit, and in the tactics to be applied.

General Creighton W. Abrams commanded US forces in Vietnam 1968–72, waging "one war" in which military operations, pacification, and improvement of South Vietnamese armed forces were of equal importance and priority. (US Army)

Abrams had the advantage of working with two exceptional public servants of like mind on the war, incisive intellect, becoming personal modesty, and sterling character, qualities that matched his own. Ellsworth Bunker had become United States ambassador to the Republic of Vietnam in April 1967, shortly before Abrams arrived as Deputy COMUSMACV, and held that post for a remarkable six years. Ambassador William Colby succeeded to the post of Deputy to the COMUSMACV for Civil Operations and Revolutionary Development Support (the US apparatus for support of the Vietnamese pacification program) in mid-fall of 1968, soon after Abrams took over the top command, and shaped and guided the successful pacification program for the next three critical years. Said Abrams, in tribute to what Colby was providing as 1968 neared an end: "This pacification program really bears no resemblance to what was going on last year – as far as results and so on."[9]

This leadership triumvirate was committed to Abrams's concept of "One War," an approach in which combat operations (much modified in concept and implementation from the earlier large-unit approach), pacification, and improvement of South Vietnam's armed forces were of equal importance and priority. Previously fragmented approaches to combat operations, pacification, and mentoring the South Vietnamese armed forces now became "one war" with a single clear-cut objective – security for the people in South Vietnam's villages and hamlets.

The "one war" insight also provided the answer to a false dichotomy that has grown up in discussing the war, with contending viewpoints arguing that it was a guerrilla war on one hand or a conventional war on the other. The fact is that it was both, in varying degrees and at different times and places. The "one war" approach recognized and accommodated this pervasive though shifting reality.

When Abrams was Vice Chief of Staff, he had signed off on a study, initiated by Chief of Staff General Harold K. Johnson, entitled "A Program for the Pacification and Long-Term Development of Vietnam." The document thoroughly repudiated Westmoreland's concept, strategy, and tactics for fighting the war. "People – Vietnamese and American, individually and collectively – constitute both the strategic determinants of today's conflict and 'the object … which lies beyond' this war," the study maintained.[10] That object was not destruction but control, and in this case particularly control of the population. Thus the imperative was clear: "The United States … must redirect the Republic of Vietnam–Free World military effort to achieve greater security."[11] Therefore, read the study's summary, "the critical actions are those that occur at the village, the district and provincial levels. This is where the war must be fought; this is where the war and the object which lies beyond it must be won."[12]

General Earle Wheeler (left) served as chairman of the Joint Chiefs of Staff for six years (1964–70) during the war in Vietnam. (Lyndon Johnson Library)

The study also made clear that body count, the centerpiece of Westmoreland's attrition warfare, was not the appropriate measure of merit for such a conflict. What counted was security for the people, and search-and-destroy operations were contributing little to that.

As might be expected, Westmoreland rejected out of hand the findings of the PROVN study. When Abrams succeeded to the top command, however, he set about implementing the study's prescriptions, even bringing out a principal member of the study team to serve as his long-range planner at MACV, where he reported directly to Abrams.

Abrams began by rejecting body count as the key measure of merit. "I know body count has something about it," said Abrams in a typical comment on the matter, "but it's really a *long* way from what is involved in this war. Yeah, you have to do that, *I* know that, but the *mistake* is to think that's the central issue."[13] Amplifying, he added, "I don't think it makes any difference how many losses he [the NVA/VC] takes. I don't think *that* makes any *difference*."[14]

Abrams was insistent on the key role of the pacification program. "I know the fighting's important," he told his senior commanders. "But all of these things in the pacification … building the village and the hamlet, and really building a base there and so on. I really think that, of *all* the things, *that's* the most important. That's where the battle ultimately is won."[15]

In early May of 1969 Abrams told his staff: "I must say I don't see any reason to shift in any way the major thrust of what we're trying to do. That is, the azimuth we're on in the *major* effort, that is the pacification program."[16] When General Earle G. Wheeler, chairman of the Joint Chiefs of Staff, came to visit in early autumn, Abrams told him it was the unanimous view of his senior commanders that "the place to put your money now, in terms of energy, effort, imagination, and all the rest of it is into this pacification program – enhancing the security, enhancing the effectiveness of government out among the people."[17]

As Vietnam "old hand" George Jacobson observed, "there's no question that pacification is either 90 percent or 10 percent security, depending on which expert you talk to. But there isn't any expert that will doubt it's the *first* 10 percent or the *first* 90 percent. You just can't conduct pacification in the face of an NVA division." Providing that security became the key operational objective.

Tactically, the large-scale operations that typified the earlier years now gave way to numerous smaller operations such as patrols and ambushes, both day and night, designed to find NVA/VC troops and crucial caches of materiel, then seize the supplies and interdict troop movement toward the populated areas. As early as August 1968, Abrams noted that the entire 1st Cavalry Division was operating in company-size units, suggesting "that gives you a feel for the extent to which they're deployed and the extent to which they're covering the area."[18] The implication was that, instead of a smaller number of operations by large, and therefore somewhat unwieldy, units, current operations featured fuller area coverage by widely deployed and more agile small units. Once contact was established with NVA/VC forces, larger and more powerful forces could be concentrated at the critical point.

With ARVN/US[19] forces thus positioned to block access to the population, the NVA/VC was forced to either fight on unfavorable ground or allow pacification to proceed unimpeded, a complete reversal of the earlier years when ARVN/US forces were mostly thrashing around in the deep jungles.

Abrams had also discovered the NVA/VC's reliance on a logistics "nose," the technique of pushing the wherewithal needed to fight a battle out in front of the troops rather than, as traditional armies would do, supplying them from the rear by means of a logistical "tail." In this approach, necessitated by lack of transport and secure lines of communications, Abrams had identified a major NVA/VC vulnerability.

"Where Westmoreland was a search-and-destroy and count-the-bodies man," wrote a perceptive journalist, "Abrams proved to be an interdict-and-weigh-the-rice man."[20] The reference was to Abrams's insistence on the value of discovering and seizing the NVA/VC's pre-positioned supplies, including the rice needed to feed his troops, thereby preempting or diminishing the force of planned offensives.

Abrams continually stressed working against all elements of the NVA/VC "system." By this he meant the supply system, recruiting system, infiltration system, propaganda system, main forces, local forces, guerrillas, infrastructure, transportation, base areas, lines of communications, political cadres, administrative cadres, support from the population. Guided by this concept of getting into the NVA/VC system, the major battles now had a coherence they had lacked in the earlier days of the war.

These preemptive tactics were paying off in many ways, one of the most dramatic being – as Ambassador Bunker reported to the President – reduction by one-third of Americans killed in action during 1969 while inflicting virtually the same losses on NVA/VC forces as the year before.[21] The statistics demonstrated that the drop in American losses was a function of superior tactics rather than any decline in the tempo of combat.

More and better intelligence, and better use of it, were also key factors in the successes now being achieved. In October 1968, General Phil Davidson, the MACV J-2[22], told a visiting senior official of his conviction that "the intelligence is many times better than what it was six months ago."[23] He cited a breakthrough in communications intelligence, a newly found capability to monitor and track the movement of NVA/VC infiltrators down the Ho Chi Minh Trail which enabled ARVN/US forces to, as Abrams put it, "arrange a proper reception." And, Davidson told a conference on intelligence collection, in contrast to previous years, "the commander is pleased with his intelligence, acts upon it, and has forced the staff to act upon it. That is what has changed in the last four or five months."[24]

When General Weyand returned to Saigon in mid-1970 to become Deputy COMUSMACV, he asked General Abrams what the mission was. Abrams' response was instructive. "Who the hell knows?" he retorted. "You know what has to be done. I know what has to be done. Let's get on with it." By that point in America's involvement in the war, although the objective remained the same, the approach to achieving it had been drastically altered. No longer would large

Secretary of Defense Melvin R. Laird (left) pressed for rapid withdrawal of US forces from Vietnam, reversing the build-up that had occurred during the earlier years. (NARA)

numbers of American ground forces assist in conduct of the war. They were being progressively and relentlessly withdrawn. South Vietnamese forces, greatly expanded in number and with – finally – modern weaponry comparable to what the NVA/VC had, were taking over more and more of the combat responsibility.

Perhaps surprisingly, this was going rather well. Much of the expansion, and certainly the key aspect of it, was in the Territorial Forces, known as Regional Forces and Popular Forces, drawn from the local populace and responsible for defending their home territories. These elements provided the "hold" in the "clear and hold" approach favored by Abrams. Observed the legendary John Paul Vann of these increases: "An enduring government presence in the countryside was thus established."[25] Senior South Vietnamese officers agreed. "Gradually, in their outlook, deportment, and combat performance," said Lieutenant General Ngo Quang Truong, "the RF and PF troopers shed their paramilitary origins and increasingly became full-fledged soldiers." So decidedly was this the case, Truong concluded, that "throughout the major period of the Vietnam conflict" the RF and PF were "aptly regarded as the mainstay of the war machinery."[26]

Four million Vietnamese citizens – women, old men, and children – were recruited into a People's Self-Defense Force and provided with 600,000 weapons (which they took turns using), thereby supplementing the Territorial Forces and, more importantly, constituting an overt commitment to the government side. Virtually all of President Thieu's advisors had counseled against creating such a force, but Thieu argued in response that the government had to rest upon the support of the people, and it had little validity if it did not dare to arm them.[27] The self-defense forces used those weapons not against their own government, but to fight against Communist domination, in the process establishing conclusively that the Thieu government did have the support of its people.

Meanwhile the pacification program, with President Thieu functioning as, said William Colby, "the number one pacification officer" in the country, was making steady progress. Abrams reinforced the importance of this program at every opportunity. "The body count does not have much to do with the outcome of the war," he stressed to senior commanders. "Some of the things I do think important are that we preempt or defeat the enemy's major military operations and eliminate or render ineffective the major portion of his guerrillas and his infrastructure – the political, administrative and paramilitary structure on which his whole movement depends." And, added Abrams, "it is far more significant that we neutralize one thousand of these guerrillas and infrastructure than kill 10,000 North Vietnamese soldiers."[28] Abrams thought it was absolutely the case that "the VCI [Viet Cong infrastructure] *permits the main forces to operate*."[29]

Restoration of security permitted farmers to harvest their crops and get them to market. Miracle rice strains (such as IR-8) were introduced, greatly increasing the yield of every hectare under cultivation. Genuine land reform resulted in distribution of a million and a half acres of land to nearly 400,000 farmers under the "Land to the Tiller" program. "In one fell swoop," noted John Vann, that program "eliminated tenancy in Vietnam. All rents were suspended."[30]

Ambassador Ellsworth Bunker, well situated to make comparative judgments in that he served in his post in Saigon during the last year of Westmoreland's tenure and continued after Abrams took command, said perceptively that "clear and hold" as the tactical approach "proved to be a better policy than the policy of attrition. The policy of attrition simply meant under the circumstances a very prolonged type of warfare, whereas if you can clear and hold and keep an area secure and keep the enemy out, psychologically as well as from a military point of view you have got a better situation. In effect, you shifted the initiative from the enemy to you."[31]

Very significantly, in stark contrast to the massive build-up of the earlier period, the years of Abrams's command were characterized by progressive withdrawal of virtually all American ground forces from Vietnam. Another disparity cut the same way. In contrast to the near blank check of the earlier years, increasingly stringent budgetary limitations now severely affected available forces and how they could be supported and employed.

In due course Abrams changed what he could – *everything* he could. He inherited an awkward chain of command, lack of unified operational control over South Vietnamese and other allied forces, an elaborate and wasteful base camp system, an exposed string of static border camps, severe geographical and procedural restrictions on conduct of the war, and greatly diminished domestic support. These he had to live with. The rest he changed.

DOCTRINE

Doctrine for such a complex and multi-faceted war was, in many cases, a work in progress. Airmobile warfare, with arrival on the battlefield of the helicopter on an unprecedented scale, was the key innovation. In armed versions as gunships and unarmed as vehicles for troop lift, command and control,

reconnaissance, resupply, radio relay, and the all-important medical evacuation, a huge fleet of rotary wing aircraft became the signature image of American forces in Vietnam. The Army's early 1960s experimentation with what evolved into an airmobile division, deployed to Vietnam as the 1st Cavalry Division (Airmobile), was very timely in terms of the build-up of American forces in Vietnam. Eventually nearly all US units of division size became adept at airmobile operations and were provided at least minimal helicopter support for their conduct. Complex schemes for employing mixtures of scouts, aerial gunships, and infantry elements, all heliborne, became part of the evolving doctrine for a new kind of warfare.

Airmobile warfare was the principal technological innovation of the war, with helicopters in large numbers performing multiple roles. (NARA)

In one dramatic demonstration of how this new capability could have strategic significance, in October 1968 General Abrams directed that the 1st Cavalry Division be moved from its operating location in I Corps in the north of South Vietnam to new positions in III Corps, much closer to Saigon, there to block an emerging NVA/VC offensive aimed at the capital. The distance to be covered was some 570 miles. Abrams made the decision late one afternoon. "Bring them down," he ordered. "When?" asked his staff. "Tomorrow."

Earlier the 1st and 25th US Infantry divisions had been moved out of war zones C and D, near the Cambodian border, to help South Vietnamese Army forces on pacification in the more populated areas. Then Abrams received intelligence that some four NVA divisions were getting ready to launch an attack against the populated areas. He did not want to pull the other two divisions out of the pacification support role, setting back that effort.

Abrams thus told Major General George Forsythe, commanding general of the 1st Cavalry, to take his highly mobile division and "ride the enemy with your spurs all the way down to the point where, if and when they do get down to the populated areas, they will be a relatively ineffective fighting force." Forsythe understood that Abrams wanted him to "harass them, cover, delay, and force them to change their time schedule and chew them up as they were coming down."

The first battalion moved was in place on October 31, 1968, with a battalion a day arriving thereafter. By November 12, the whole division was operational in the new area. There they set up a kind of hedgehog pattern to intercept the advancing NVA elements. When some got through, the 1st Cavalry just lifted its whole set of firebases up, jumped over the enemy, and confronted him again with the same hedgehog. November passed, then December and January. On February 26, recalled Forsythe, the remnants of one battalion of the NVA 5th Division attempted an attack on Bien Hoa airfield, where 126 of its soldiers wound up surrendering at the wire. At that point, Forsythe reversed gears and rode what was left of the attacking forces all the way back to the border.[32] This was airmobile warfare at its zenith.

Despite difficult terrain conditions, tanks and armored personnel carriers played an important part in the war, especially during the latter years when General Abrams was in command of US forces. (US Army)

Doctrine for employment of armored forces also underwent significant change during the course of the Vietnam War. Early on, General Westmoreland had resisted deployment of armored units. In July 1965, a time when the large-scale build-up of US ground forces in Vietnam was just getting underway, he

cabled the Army Chief of Staff that "except for a few coastal areas, most notably in the I Corps area, Vietnam is no place for either tank or mechanized infantry units."[33]

Widespread and effective employment of armored personnel carriers by the South Vietnamese demonstrated, however, that there was much more trafficable terrain for armored vehicles than the Americans thought, and subsequently even Westmoreland sought more such units. When Abrams, the most famous American battalion-level tanker of World War II, ascended to command in Vietnam, armored forces enjoyed a high priority and were widely employed to good effect. During the drawdown, in fact, Abrams protected his armored units as long as possible because he found them so versatile and useful.

Although both South Vietnamese and US forces included tank units, the armored personnel carrier became in many ways the star of the armored show. This was due in large measure to the evolution of its role, with doctrine in effect being developed on the battlefield and only later incorporated into field manuals. Up-armored (in imitation of modifications originally conceived by the Vietnamese), carriers mounted more weapons and assumed more roles, even some that were essentially tank-like. The many versions of the armored personnel carrier (as troop carrier, light "tank," armored ambulance, supply vehicle, command post, mortar carrier, cargo hauler, bridge launcher, flamethrower, TOW missile platform, and on and on) made it a ubiquitous presence on the battlefields of Vietnam.[34] Except for the helicopter, which of course came into its own during the Vietnam War, no vehicle underwent more of a combat metamorphosis than the humble armored personnel carrier.

REFLECTIONS

Ironies abound in the story of American involvement in the Vietnam War. One of the saddest involves selection of the overall commander of US forces. In January 1964, when Westmoreland was sent out to understudy Harkins and then succeed him as COMUSMACV, he was President Lyndon Johnson's choice from among four candidates proposed to him. The others were General Harold K. Johnson (who instead became Army Chief of Staff), General Creighton Abrams (who became Vice Chief of Staff), and Lieutenant General Bruce Palmer Jr. (who succeeded Johnson as Deputy Chief of Staff for Military Operations). The choice of Westmoreland was a fateful one in terms of how the war would be fought.

We know from subsequent evidence that Johnson, Abrams, and Palmer were of one mind on the nature of the war and how it should be prosecuted, while Westmoreland had a wholly different outlook. Fatefully, Westmoreland and his unavailing approach were chosen. Then, when Abrams was sent out in May 1967 as Deputy COMUSMACV, it was planned that he succeed Westmoreland within a matter of weeks. Intervening events acted to postpone that change of command for more than a year, an interval in which the Tet Offensive of 1968 took place and the course of the war changed dramatically.

Critiques of how the war was conducted can find plenty of grist. Lyndon Johnson, a truly great politician, was a sad failure as a war president and commander-in-chief. He received really terrible advice from his Secretary of Defense, Robert S. McNamara, and from the long-serving chairman of the Joint Chiefs of Staff, General Earle G. Wheeler. He stayed far too long with an inept field commander in Westmoreland, apparently not appreciating that, despite repeated assurances to the contrary, Westmoreland's approach was not succeeding. His unwillingness to call up reserve forces failed to capitalize on the link to public support those forces provided, a benefit probably equal to or greater than their military value.

McNamara, conceiving himself to be a management genius, had no feel for war and its inherent wastefulness, or for the essential part the willingness to overwhelm the enemy plays in the successful prosecution of a war. His lack of candor in dealing with the Congress and the public contributed hugely to the "credibility gap" which plagued both the Johnson administration and Richard Nixon when he came into office. His antagonism toward senior military leaders matched his unwillingness to heed their advice or, if he found that advice lacking, to replace them.

By the time the Nixon administration assumed responsibility for conduct of the war, much of the public and Congressional support (and even media support) of the earlier years had dissipated, wasted by Westmoreland's fruitless pursuit of a war of attrition.

It appears that President Nixon and his National Security Advisor, Henry Kissinger, came to office persuaded that within a matter of months they could negotiate a settlement with the North Vietnamese. When that proved to be a vain hope, they were faced with disengaging in a way that would not waste the sacrifices of those – American and South Vietnamese alike – who had fought, bled, and often died in the fight to maintain South Vietnam as a free and independent state.

Nixon proved to be a courageous war president, willing to take political risks in approving such operations as the 1970 incursion into Cambodia and the massive reinforcement of American air and naval forces which sustained South Vietnam in throwing back the enemy's 1972 Easter Offensive. He also proved himself adept at balancing off the need to (as he viewed it) placate anti-war forces at home by progressive withdrawal of US forces from Vietnam with the need to keep those forces there long enough to give the South Vietnamese time to prepare to assume the total burden of their own defense.

Melvin Laird as Secretary of Defense proved far more able than the widely heralded McNamara. Laird was also, however, a highly skilled politician (veteran of many terms in Congress as a representative from Wisconsin), and his interpretation of the political winds was that the administration needed to get out of Vietnam as rapidly as possible. He thus pushed for ever larger and earlier withdrawals of forces, contending for the President's ear with Kissinger and, probably, the President's own inclinations for a more measured pace. As it turned

William E. Colby made an important contribution as head of American support for pacification of South Vietnam's rural hamlets and villages. (William E. Colby Collection, Virtual Vietnam Archive, Texas Tech University)

out, Laird usually got his way in the end and, wonder of wonders, the South Vietnamese nevertheless proved up to the challenge.

Thus there came a point at which the war was won. The fighting wasn't over, but the war was won. The reason it was won was that the South Vietnamese had achieved the capability, with continuation of promised American support, to sustain themselves indefinitely as a free and independent nation. President Nixon promised President Nguyen Van Thieu – repeatedly, both in writing and through high-level intermediaries – three key things.

The first was that if, after completion of the Paris Accords supposedly ended the fighting, the North Vietnamese violated terms of the agreement and continued their aggression, then the United States would reintroduce military power to punish those violations. Second was that if there were a resumption of fighting the United States would, as provided for in the Paris Accords, replace on a one-for-one basis South Vietnam's losses of major combat systems (such things as tanks, artillery pieces, and aircraft). And third was that the United States would continue robust financial assistance for the foreseeable future.

In the event, thanks to actions of the Congress, the United States defaulted on all three commitments. The result was predictable. As CIA Chief of Station Tom Polgar cabled from Saigon: "Ultimate outcome hardly in doubt, because South Vietnam cannot survive without US military aid as long as North Vietnam's war-making capacity is unimpaired and supported by Soviet Union and China."[35]

Chapter 10

On the Ground
The US Experience

Bernard Edelman

Over the past few years, Bernard Edelman has interviewed and discussed the war with dozens of Vietnam veterans, many of whom are his friends, while writing profiles for a web site, veteransadvantage.com. For this chapter, he reviewed his notes and chose incidents and stories to illustrate and illuminate the experiences of troops sent halfway across the globe to do their nation's bidding in Vietnam. He interviewed several Marines with whom he returned to Vietnam in 2001, and also integrated excerpts of letters from Dear America: Letters Home from Vietnam, *the book he edited for The New York Vietnam Veterans Memorial Commission.*

> Above all, Vietnam was a war that asked everything of a few and nothing of most in America.
>
> *Myra MacPherson, 1984*

Few Americans who came of age during the turbulent, convulsive years of the 1960s had ever heard of "Indochina" or "Vietnam." They did not study its history in school or learn about its peoples in *National Geographic*. Yet this place halfway across the globe would erupt in mid-decade as the hot spot in the Cold War. Along with racial upheaval and watershed civil rights legislation, political assassinations and landmark "Great Society" programs, Vietnam came to dominate the daily headlines and the nightly news – and the psyche of America. For the almost 3 million men and 10,000 women who volunteered or were conscripted into military service and sent to the Vietnam theater of operations, it would be a place – a war, an experience – that would alter their lives, profoundly and irrevocably.

They arrived, initially as full companies and battalions, later as individuals – replacements – in a land of steamy triple-canopy jungle and endless rice paddies; of treacherous mountains and pristine beaches; of breathtaking beauty and

This grunt embodies the conflicting emotions of many of those who fought, particularly as the war dragged on. Note the bullet around his neck – and the peace sign on his helmet. This photo was taken in 1969. (© Mark Jury)

A GI waiting for a flight sits in front of a map of Southeast Asia at an airport terminal in South Vietnam in 1970. Most soldiers had little direct knowledge about how the war was being fought, except in their own AO or TAOR. (© Bernard Edelman)

wrenching sadness; of stultifying heat and the unrelenting monsoon rains – and an enemy as stealthy and cunning as he was motivated.

The active American military effort in the Republic of Vietnam lingered for nearly a decade and saw more than 58,000 Americans lost to the war. Five times that number were wounded in action. For some three in ten who served there, what they saw and did has exacted an ongoing psychological toll: tens of thousands have been disabled by post-traumatic stress disorder; a malady that in earlier wars was called soldier's heart or combat fatigue. Most, but not all, of these were infantrymen – "grunts," in GI-speak.

For the infantryman, Vietnam was no walk in the sun. Michael Patrick Kelley, a machine-gunner with Delta Company, 1st Battalion, 502nd Infantry, 101st Airborne Division, was drafted the day he graduated from college. "We saw very little contact during my tour despite the fact we were out in the bush incessantly looking for Chuck and his boys," Kelley said. "That was the serendipitous result of two things: rivers of blood spilled by US troops who'd fought so hard before us; and a change in the enemy's strategy following their staggering post-Tet '68 manpower losses. In our AO [Area of Operations], I later learned, the enemy broke up into three-man cells and made it a point to avoid major contact of any kind."

There were few troops with even an inkling of the Big Picture or first-hand knowledge of anything that might be happening beyond their AO. "I could write home only what I'd experienced in our TAOR west of Da Nang," said Sergeant Jerry Balcom. "It was always get up, move out, go here, do this – on 'search-and-destroy' operations, patrols, road sweeps, ambushes, perimeter security. That was what our war was about."

What Mike Kelley remembers most about his war was how extremely difficult and uncomfortable it was beating the bush looking for "Chuck": the Viet Cong, also referred to, with varying degrees of respect, as Charlie, Charles, Victor Charles, and the VC. Kelley describes what it was like out in the bush, "humping the boonies":

You were always filthy, always soaking wet, freezing or roasting your butt off; leeches in the trees and in the grass; leeches in the streams; mosquitoes buzzing in your ear; bugs of every sort crawling all over you; spiders the size of your hand in webs at eye level across the trails; jungle rot on your arms; ringworm in your crotch; hunks of congealed grease in your cold c-rats; real rats crawling over you at night; sleeping on rocks; sleeping in the mud; trying to sleep in the rain; never sleeping; sweat pouring down your face, perpetually fogging your glasses and soaking your fatigues when it wasn't raining; trying to figure out ways to make your 60- to 80-pound rucksack comfortable on your shoulders; throwing away gun ammo to lighten your load; wishing you hadn't thrown away gun ammo; straight uphill; straight downhill; slipping and sliding in the muck; weapons rusting; ammo dirty; gasping for breath; so exhausted you could hardly lift an arm day after day after day; dysentery; chronic diarrhea; fevers; common colds; hot beer; hot Diet Fresca; cold food; deafened and driven to tears by artillery fire; deafened by popped Claymores or LAWs; lonely as hell; homesick as hell; occasionally scared beyond words; pulling guard night after night with 5,000-pound weights on your eyelids; no paper for letters; no resupply 'cause of the rain; out of toilet paper; out of bug juice; starving; thinking about killing somebody for their peaches and pound cake.

"And," he jokes, "those were the good days."

Mike Kelley's worst bad day, the one incised in his memory, was the evening of September 16, 1970. His platoon had moved to the top of a hill so they could be extracted by chopper after a grueling 40-day mission. "While we were putting out our Claymores, my platoon medic stepped on a big mine next to me, although I really didn't know what had happened at the time.

"When I woke up in the Intensive Care Unit at the 85th Evac Hospital at Phu Bai the next day (I guess), I didn't realize that anybody else had been hurt," Kelley said. "Doc Smitty was still in surgery then, and I really didn't feel much pain or discomfort at all. I didn't feel very bad – until they wheeled Smitty out and put him in the bed next to mine.

"When I saw Doc and realized who it was, I was really flattened! They'd taken off both his legs above the knee, his genitals, and much of both hands. Above the waist he looked perfectly normal. Below the waist, he was pure hamburger.

"Though I would see a lot of horrific sights during my ten months in the hospital," Kelley said, "nothing shocked me like my first look at Smitty. It seemed impossible anybody that badly mangled could still be alive." Smitty didn't stay alive for long, however. His kidneys failing, Stephen T. Smith died on a C-130 flight to Saigon, where the only dialysis machine in the war zone was located.

Marco Polo Smigliani, who was born in a village called Poggiofiorito in Italy and emigrated to the United States in 1958, joined the Marines and was sent to Vietnam, where he found himself manning a machine-gun in the A Shau Valley with the 1st Battalion, 9th Marines, 3rd Marine Division in an operation called *Dewey Canyon*.

"It was just a living hell," he said. "I was very scared. We were right on top of the North Vietnamese, right on top of their base camp. Every day people were getting killed and wounded."

From February 23 to March 6, Private First Class Smigliani was wounded four times. He took a piece of shrapnel in his head and neck. He was hit by an AK-47 round in the left arm; as he went to the aid of another grunt, an RPG exploded, almost blowing off his arm. Waiting for a medical evacuation helicopter (called a medevac, or dust-off), clutching a .45 in his lap in case one of the NVA

Marine John Wilson shoulders a rocket launcher on a reconnaissance patrol south of the DMZ in 1966. Twelve days after this photograph was made, he was killed in action, one of more than 58,000 Americans lost to the war. (Larry Burrows, *Life* /©Time Inc)

regulars probing the perimeter broke through, he wondered: "Will I make it out of here alive?" As he was being medevac'd, he almost didn't; he was again hit by shrapnel, this time in his legs. Like Mike Kelley, he would spend ten months recuperating back in the States – and he considered himself "the luckiest guy in the world" that he hadn't bled out in the muck and mire of the A Shau.

Others were not so lucky. PFC Ray Griffiths was sent to Vietnam just after Christmas in 1965. He served in the same unit as Marco Smigliani would three years later. In a letter to his friend Madeline Velasco, he wrote:

> It's good to have someone to tell your troubles to. I can't tell them to my parents or Darlene because they worry too much, but I tell you truthfully, I doubt if I'll come out of this alive.
>
> In my original squad I'm the only one left unharmed. In my platoon there's only 13 of us. It seems every day another young guy 18 and 19 years old like myself is killed in action. Please help me, Mad. I don't know if I should stop writing my parents and Darlene or what.
>
> I'm going on an operation next month where there is nothing but VC and VC sympathizers. The area is also very heavily mined. All of us are

scared 'cause we know a lot of us won't make it. I would like to hear what you have to say about it, Madeline, before I make any decisions.

Oh, and one more favor. I'd like the truth now. Has Darlene been faithful to me? I know she's been dating guys, but does she still love me best? Thanks for understanding. See ya if it's God's will. I have to make it out of Vietnam though, 'cause I'm lucky. I hope. Ha ha.

He didn't. PFC Raymond C. Griffiths was killed, on the Fourth of July 1966, a few weeks after he wrote this letter. He was 19 years old.

In Vietnam, as in any war, the difference between life and oblivion could literally be inches. "On the night of January 18, 1969, at 0130 hours," recalls Ed Vick, a lieutenant (junior grade) in the brown-water Navy,

under the light of a quarter moon, we were traveling up a really narrow part of the Mekong River – a 300-yard gauntlet, really – when the entire riverbank erupted. I was standing on the coxswain's flat with a gunner when the first rocket passed between us.

Then a second rocket hit us below the water line. The gunner in the stern was blown up. The stern was awash. We were sinking. We were dead in the kill zone. It was the most terrifying night I'd experienced.

Luckily for Ed Vick and his remaining crew, their sister boat pulled in behind them and they managed to get all hands on board before the Seawolves, the Navy's attack helicopters, arrived, making firing runs at the riverbank.

Jack Farley was not lucky. First Lieutenant Farley was assigned as a forward observer with Company D, 2nd Battalion, 27th Infantry: the Wolfhounds. For nine months in 1966–67, few of his days or nights were without hazard.

One day at Fire Support Base Pershing, "Charlie hit us with 82mm mortar fire. One round exploded within 'gimme range,'" shrapnel peppering his body. He remembers "flying through the air. My glasses flew off and I reached out for them and grabbed 'em before I landed. I crawled five feet to the parapet. A medic peeked his head over and asked me if I was okay. I remember clear as day thinking, What would John Wayne say?

"Doc," I told him, "go look after the other men."

No one else had been hit, however. As he wrote to his father a few days later, "It took five pints [of blood] for the docs to get a pulse."

1Lt Farley returned home with four Bronze Stars, three with "V" device (for valor), the Army Commendation Medal, two Purple Hearts, and a shattered body. He spent 14 months at Walter Reed Army Medical Center in Washington, DC recovering from his wounds and learning to walk all over again: His right leg had been amputated above the knee. Farley was one of more than 300,000 GIs who were wounded in Vietnam, and one of more than 5,000 who lost one or more limbs – and survived, in part, because of the increasingly sophisticated use of medevacs.

WAR WITHOUT END

Of those who served in Vietnam, relatively few spent their entire tours – 12 months if you were in the Army, 13 for Marines – in the bush. In this war without a front, a guerrilla war against a crafty and elusive enemy, a pervasive angst set in among the troops. "I remember being just so annoyed, so frustrated," said Marine Sgt. Balcom, who spent 20 months in-country. "We'd take some hill at a great cost in blood. We'd leave. And then we'd have to take it all over again." His point echoed that of Philip Caputo, a Marine officer turned journalist, memoirist, and novelist. He recounted returning in 1971 to the area where he had served. If he had had any doubts, he knew the war was folly when grunts were still fighting over the same village he and his men had fought over six years earlier.

Few photographs better portray the hellish conditions in which Americans fought in Vietnam. Here a wounded Marine, Sgt Jeremiah Purdie, is brought to the relative safety on a hilltop position south of the DMZ in 1966. One of the iconic images of the war, it was published in 1971 after the death of the photographer who captured this image, Larry Burrows. (© Larry Burrows Collection)

While American forces arguably won the major battles of the war, supported by artillery and by airpower almost unchallenged in the South, the bulk of the combat occurred in small-unit firefights during ambushes and search-and-destroy missions. Booby traps – camouflaged pungi pits studded with sharpened, dung-tipped lengths of bamboo; grenades and bombs that blew up when the trip-wire was tripped – were just as feared, and took almost as many lives as AK-47 rounds and B-40 rockets. Many booby traps were configured to maim, which had the added value to the NVA/VC forces of occupying the efforts of his comrades and giving them the opportunity to shoot down medevacs and helicopter gunships.

Every place had its dangers. Jerry Balcom spent stretches during his tour in battalion headquarters. While not as hazardous as the bush, "Nobody was ever safe," Balcom said. "No one was immune from hot shrapnel or VC bullets. In the bush we'd get ambushed; in 'the rear with the gear,' we'd get mortared and rocketed often, and were hit by sappers before first light." On perimeter watch one night, Charlie attacked. A tracer round "went over my head by a matter of inches," he said. But for more than 47,000 Americans, the bullet or booby trap, the mortar or bomb, the rocket or grenade, did not miss; and for more than 10,000 others, accident or disease caused them to be sent home in an aluminum casket.

In a letter to his friend Jim Buckley, who had recently taken a freedom bird back to "The World," as GIs referred to "back home," Balcom wrote:

> I'm sorry I'm unable to bring you glad tidings, buddy, but I think you'll probably want to know this news.
>
> Our friend, our happy, crazy, almost always laughing pal, Dave Ranson, was killed during a firefight at 0600 this morning. An RPG [Rocket-Propelled Grenade] took his head, and several others were hurt. Jim, that guy had so much going for him – a beautiful girl to marry, school to finish, RELAD [Release from Active Duty] orders, and under 40 days to go... This ********** war is taking too many good guys. Perhaps I'm selfish, but a few have been friends and I know you've felt the same. There's nothing more to say. I thought you'd like to know...

It was in the rear "where we started having drug problems and racial problems," Balcom said. It was different in the boonies, where grunts had to be focused and alert, and everyone was "green." Ben Williams, a grunt with Hotel Company, 2nd Battalion, 3rd Marines, 3rd Marine Division, could not recall if one of his sergeants was black or white. "In the field we were all the same; we depended upon one another," Tex Williams said. Everybody bled red.

The war, though, was fought mostly out in the field – in the bush, or "boonies." One of the truisms of the war was that "We own the day; Charlie owns the night." And much of American military strategy was to engage Charlie whenever and wherever he could be pinned down to fight.

Roy Moon, a Navy corpsman who served with Williams in Hotel Company – all corpsmen were US Navy personnel assigned to Marine units – spent just about all of his 13-month tour of duty in the field, humpin' the boonies. Doc Moon had been drafted, but chose instead to join the Navy because "the odds were real good that I'd wind up in 'Nam as a grunt, and I really didn't want to go there." Moon hails from Wayne County, West Virginia, the state with the highest death rate in Vietnam, 84.1 per 100,000; the national average was 58.9 per 100,000.[1]

He wound up there anyway. Assigned as a deckhand on a destroyer, he was sent one day to work in the sick bay. The solitary corpsman on board, impressed with Moon's savvy, requested that he be assigned there. He was. Six months later, he was sent to corpsman's school, and then to field medic's school. "I knew then where I was goin'."

Arriving in Da Nang in September 1967, he was flown the next day to Dong Ha in I Corps, just south of the DMZ, the Demilitarized Zone, the no-man's land at the 17th Parallel separating North from South Vietnam, and assigned to 3rd Platoon, Hotel Company. He joined his new unit on the road near Con Thien, where Hotel Company was guarding a bridge. At first, they patrolled the flat lands and rolling rice paddies along the coastal plain, where what impressed him was "how the people could produce so much rice with so little equipment." The enemy there was not the Viet Cong, but the booby traps they'd planted. "Not

A GI holds protectively a badly wounded buddy. In Vietnam, out in the field racial conflicts were minimal. Soldiers were neither black nor white, but green. You depended on your comrades to cover you, and they depended on you to do the same. (Larry Burrows, *Life* © Time Inc)

A radio operator calls for a medevac to extract a soldier wounded in an ambush by the Viet Cong near Saigon in 1969. (Empics/Oliver Noonan Associated Press)

being able to see what could kill you," Doc Moon said, was really scary. When they were sent further north into I Corps – South Vietnam was divided into four tactical zones by the military; I Corps, which started at the DMZ, was the bloodiest–he was relieved: at least there you could see your enemy.

To this day, scenes from his tour are indelibly etched in his mind. There was the time "when Jerry Wooley got hurt. It's just like a picture, an image that's always there: I can see the area we were heading into. I can see where everybody is in the column. I see Jerry step on that mine. I see the smoke. And I see the body fall out of the smoke." Doc Moon raced ahead to his friend, whose wounds were more than extensive. Doc accompanied Jerry, who was conscious, on the dust-off. He refused Jerry's request for morphine, knowing that although it would mask the pain, it would also cause a drop in adrenaline, and Jerry would die.

Thanks to Doc's efforts, Jerry Wooley pulled through. But he'd lost three limbs and could never quite come to terms with his diminished physical state. A few years later, Doc learned, he took his life.

Skip Burkle – Frederick M. Burkle, MD – did his share of healing and saw his share of dying. In July 1968, he was 28 years old, married, with three very young children, the Senior Resident in Pediatrics at Yale University hospital. He received a "greetings" letter from Uncle Sam: his draft notice. Two weeks later, Lieutenant Burkle found himself in Vietnam, at a place called Delta Med, a Forward Casualty Receiving Facility for the 3rd Marine Division in Dong Ha. He was six miles from the DMZ.

On his first night there, Skip Burkle knew his life had changed forever. "It was chaotically busy," he recalled.

> I stumbled about to find a place to sleep. I felt totally out of place, awkward and in the way. I was given my first set of camouflage fatigues off a wounded Marine. His blood-stained name tag remained on them.
>
> That night, exhausted, soaking wet with sweat, I somehow fell asleep in a bunker, on a cot closely lined up next to a dozen others. I never felt so alone. Soon after drifting off into some vague state of sleep, we were abruptly awakened by the roar of choppers landing immediately outside, and by fine pellets of sand and gravel propelled like shrapnel through the cracks in the bunker.
>
> I had no idea what was happening. I got up and followed the others. In the triage bunker, what seemed to be pandemonium, with the incessant roar of the chopper engines, with dust flying all around, was in fact almost a symphony of coordinated activity.
>
> I stood there, transfixed, recognizing that I had to do a tracheotomy. I could only utter: "We need a surgeon here." In milliseconds, without a word being said, a corpsman sliced open the skin on the blooded neck and trachea and expertly forced a tube into the Marine's airway. A surgical drape was rapidly placed over the man's face and his litter was quickly removed out the triage entrance and onto a chopper hovering two feet off the pad. I later learned it took him to a hospital ship about 30 minutes away in the South China Sea.
>
> Almost total silence returned in what seemed to be only seconds from when I first heard the arriving choppers. I stood mute, as corpsmen worked feverishly around me, cleaning up, hosing water to wash the blood into a drain around my feet. I was neither noticed nor needed.

After his baptism of blood, Burkle adapted quickly to his new circumstances. Some of his experiences during his year in-country were inspiring. One evening, as the gate to the perimeter was being shut, a young ARVN soldier handed a corpsman a newborn, Burkle recounted.

> The infant was comatose, septic, suffering seizures and meningitis. I gave the baby antibiotics, steroids. Nothing was working. I decided to do a full-body exchange of blood; it was the only procedure I thought of that might save the baby's life.
>
> Three-quarters of the way through the procedure, by then it was daybreak, and we had been under fire all night, it looked like the baby was going to make it. When the perimeter gate was opened, the baby's parents came in. They brought a tiny white wooden coffin, they were so sure their baby would be dead. The mother just knelt down in front of us, with tears streaming down her face. Her child had survived.

Hospital personnel help a wounded GI into the emergency room at the 91st Evacuation Hospital in Chu Lai. The use of helicopters to evacuate the wounded saved countless lives that might otherwise have been lost. (© Mark Jury)

Other experiences at Delta Med were haunting: "The worst was the guys you knew you couldn't help," he said. "One day, the triage bunker was filled with the dying, young Marines whose flesh and organs had been ripped by bullets and shrapnel. "One casualty started calling out, *Mommy, Mommy, Mommy*, and soon there was just a cacophony crying, *Mommy, Mommy, Mommy*. There was no one among us who didn't have tears in our eyes."

On another not so fine day, Burkle was inserting a chest tube into a badly wounded Marine when the compound came under attack. He remembers:

> I can't leave him. A chopper comes in loud, blowing little chunks of dirt and
> gravel into the bunker. As we pull him up from the dirt floor to place him
> on the litter for evacuation, the chest tube is stepped on and pulled out. We

stand there, motionless at first. A corpsman says, "Doc, it's the only one we have!" To save the Marine's life, I wipe it off and shove it back into the hole. Immediately I thought that I had violated one of the basic tenets of medicine and the Marine would end up suffering from my decision.

The troop was medevac'd out, but Skip Burkle "worried about what I'd done for the longest time. It wasn't until 15, 17 years later that, during a trauma training course, a similar scenario was presented and the correct approach was to do what I had done. It was then that I realized, Oh my God, it's all right now."

Some things, though, can never be all right. Rick Weidman, the son of a career military man, didn't want to "miss my war," despite his misgivings. While attending Colgate University, he had become "convinced that, by the time we'd committed ground troops, we had already lost. It was the wrong war fought in the wrong way at the wrong time, for all the right motivations of the American people."

Still, Weidman would not miss "his" war. While most of his classmates "ducked or dodged the draft," he gave up his deferment and "volunteered" for the draft, insisting, however, that the only MOS (Military Occupational Specialty) he would accept would be 91B: Medic. "I believed then and I believe now, if you are going to reap the choicest fruits of our society, you had better be willing to lift the highest burden."

Early in October 1969, PFC Weidman was sent to Vietnam. He was assigned to the 23rd Medical Company, 196th Light Infantry Brigade, part of the Americal Division. For most of his tour, he worked at the aid station at a firebase called Hawk Hill.

On his second day there, he experienced his first mass casualty arrival. Three days later, he performed his first intubation on a GI with a sucking chest wound. Three nights later, "with VC right at our wire, with birds [helicopters] flying in and out," he and his fellow medics tended to scores of badly wounded GIs.

"I don't know how many guys we had torn up," he said. Much of the night was a blur of activity, a chaos of small-arms fire and explosions permeated by the unmistakable smell of cordite, grease, and blood. After the last bird lifted off, headed to the evacuation hospital at Chu Lai, Rick Weidman smoked a Camel. For the first time that night, he took a look at himself. "My face, my hair, my uniform, my boots were all covered in blood. Where there wasn't blood there was mud, and mud mixed with blood."

Standing there smoking, he realized that he had no emotional reaction to all the bleeding and the dying. His thoughts were focused: "What can I do, how fast can I do it, and how can I do it better in the future?" The emotional numbing had begun.

Like Rick Weidman, Paul Giannone didn't have to shoot at anybody in Vietnam. He arrived there in April 1969, a freshly minted 91B. Whatever bravado he had nurtured faded when he learned he had been assigned to the 29th CA. "I kind of really panicked," he said. "I thought CA stood for Combat Assault. And this unit was up in I Corps, which at that time was Marine country. I mean, I was just shakin' in my boots. They flew me up to Da Nang, and a sergeant picked me up at the airport. When I questioned him about CA, he laughed. 'You're with Civil Affairs,' he said."

For the next year, Giannone was based at Hoi An, an ancient port city south of Da Nang. His platoon worked mostly with refugees in rural health care, and he wasn't particularly thrilled with the assignment. At one point, frustrated, he volunteered for the infantry. "My orders actually came through, but in the interim I had seen a couple of people killed. It just shocks you, your first dead. You start realizing that, hey, this is for real. When you go down, you're not gonna come back up again. Or if you do, your guts are splattered all over the place or you're missing a leg or an arm." He managed to get his orders rescinded.

For a time during the first of his two tours he was assigned to the political prison in Hoi An to do what he called

band-aid stuff. The capacity of this prison was around 400, but there were between 1,400 and 1,600 men, women, and children, from newborns to people in their eighties, shoved in there. People were pretty much being openly tortured. Beriberi and scurvy were rife, but I was not permitted to bring in drugs, or even fresh fruit and vegetables to really help anybody.

One day, I came across a premature baby in the dispensary. That was a real hellhole. There were birds up on the ceiling defecating on the patients. The floor *was* the beds, just a writhing mass of bodies. It was obvious to me that if we didn't get this infant out of there she was going to die. But they wouldn't release her because she was a Viet Cong – because her mother, they said, was a Viet Cong. Now, a lot of the people in there were just on the wrong side of the government. I argued. I screamed. I even offered to take the baby with me. I told them I could find people who would take care of her. But no, this baby was a Communist. And one day I came in and she was dead.

Scotch couldn't assuage the pain, or the anger. Eventually, he came to see the war through Vietnamese eyes, a state of consciousness – and conscience – experienced by only a minority of GIs.

Sometimes you felt it was all so futile; sometimes you thought to yourself, What are we saving them for? More war? Are we saving these kids so they can go on to become soldiers?

I don't know if any of us looked at what we were doing as "winning hearts and minds" 'cause that was such a hollow thing. I think most of us were just trying to save as many Vietnamese civilians as we could. That was our bottom line. We may have been stuck in a bad situation, but we were trying to help people who were stuck in a worse situation. And they didn't get to leave the war zone.

Vince McGowan also worked to help the people our government insisted we were fighting for as we turned "swords into plowshares." For much of his tour,

That there is no glory in war is illustrated in this image of a grunt at Firebase Eunice during the incursion into Cambodia in April–May 1970. Troops had spent 36 days without relief in the jungle searching for COSVN, headquarters of the National Liberation Front. (© Bernard Edelman)

the New York City-born and -bred sergeant was the Non-Commissioned Officer In Charge of one of the few real tactical successes of the American effort in Vietnam: a 12-man Combined Action Program (CAP) run by the Marine Corps in the village of Binh Nghia.

"We were a showcase unit," McGowan said. "We worked with the Vietnamese regional and popular forces. We won most of the firefights in which we were engaged. We helped this village reach a degree of democratic rule. We helped write the book on how CAP units should operate. And the techniques we used were eventually incorporated into Marine Corps tactics."

For McGowan, a brash high-school dropout who "found himself" in Vietnam, and who was fascinated by the strange and exotic culture he found himself immersed in, running the CAP unit gave him the opportunity "to engage people in a mission that really was important." Growing up where he did, in a place where "a few guys on the block can control everything," he saw a parallel in villages like Binh Nghia, where "a few guys – the Viet Cong – could dominate a 'silent majority' without a groundswell of popular support."

Working with and getting to know the villagers and gaining their trust was, to McGowan, as vital to achieving success as was perfecting small-unit tactics – patrolling every night, seeking to engage the VC and fighting them on their own terms. One day, he recalled,

some of the village leaders gathered in a small town we called "Nuoc Mam," after the pungent fish sauce the Vietnamese seem to use in everything they cook. The VC attacked. The army unit with responsibility for that town did not know what to do. An army colonel ordered us to do nothing. But these were our people – our villagers – there. So two of us – the rest of the guys were out on patrol – packed up our gear and ran the three miles to the town. I must've been carrying 25 grenades, 1,500 rounds of ammunition, three LAWs.

We attacked the VC, who weren't expecting any real resistance. We were relentless. They used civilians as shields, but we had to press on. No quarter was given; no quarter was taken. We routed them.

A few months later, with Binh Nghia pacified, the decision was made on high to let the local militia take over. McGowan and his squad went on to establish another CAP unit on the My Lai peninsula. But for McGowan, 15 months in Vietnam were enough. "I had started to like it there too much," he said. After he returned to The World, it wasn't long before Binh Nghia reverted to Viet Cong control.

LIGHT AT THE END OF THE TUNNEL

For grunts, indeed for most who served in the war zone, there was not, there could not be, a singular "experience" of Vietnam. It is quite impossible to divine a definitive description. As James R. McDonough propounded in the prologue of his book, *Platoon Leader*, "The style of the war changed from year to year, from unit to unit, from place to place. There were no typical experiences. If anything was typical about the Vietnam experience, it was that it was different for everyone involved."

Perhaps the only constant about combat was summed up by Fred Zabitosky, a Special Forces sergeant who received the Medal of Honor for extraordinary valor deep in enemy territory in 1968. "There is no such thing as patriotism in a combat situation," he said. "You do not think about medals, promotions or even the flag. You do not think about why you are there or even your family. You think strictly about the people you are with and what you can do for each other." This sentiment, of course, is hardly unique to soldiers who fought and bled and died in the jungles and rice paddies and hamlets of Southeast Asia.

Perhaps the most salient change, as the war trudged on, was the sentiments of the troops who were there. Their feelings mirrored that of many in America who came to distrust the pronouncements of the generals and the politicians. These feelings became acute in the wake of the Tet Offensive that commenced on January 31, 1968. Even though American troops reacted and decimated the Viet Cong, killing upwards of 40,000 of the enemy, the war had reached a tipping point. After having been assured and reassured that we were winning, Americans' faith was ruptured. Two months later, President Lyndon Johnson announced that he would not seek reelection. But peace was not to be achieved any time soon, and almost as many GIs were killed during the presidency of his successor, Richard Nixon, who ran as the "peace candidate" in 1968, the bloodiest year of the war and one of the most traumatic in American history.

American soldiers salute the flag-draped caskets of their fallen brothers. KIAs from the field were brought to Graves Registration in body bags; they were shipped home in aluminum caskets. (© Larry Burrows Collection)

It was during the first of the 17 official campaigns of the Vietnam War that occasional stories about American "advisors" working with the Army of the Republic of Vietnam against Communist guerrillas began appearing on the front pages of newspapers and the covers of newsweeklies. Then, optimism reigned, born of both a sense of invincibility from the American experience in two world wars and the oft-repeated contention of America's political and military leaders that they could see "the light at the end of the tunnel." GIs, they believed, were on the path to victory against the ragtag Viet Cong.

This cliché burned bright in the minds of many of those troops who were part of the build-up – the Americanization of the fighting – that began in March 1965. As Marine Lance Corporal Jack Swender wrote in a letter that September to his uncle and aunt: "Some people wonder why Americans are in Vietnam. The way I see the situation, I would rather fight to stop communism in South Vietnam than in Kincaid, Humbolt, Blue Mound, or Kansas City... I think it is far better to fight and die for freedom than to live under oppression and fear." Three months later, Lance Corporal Swender, 22, was killed fighting for the cause he believed in.

Two years later, as more and more Americans poured into South Vietnam and took over the brunt of the fighting, the light shone no brighter than it had in 1965, despite official pronouncements to the contrary. Back in The World, anti-war demonstrations – in cities, in the nation's capital, on college campuses – mocked this elusive light and denounced the political and military leaders whose decisions seemed to have no effect on an intractable enemy. Some troops were angered by the demonstrations; others embraced them. But the bottom line for the men in the field was, to borrow from a rock song by Crosby, Stills, Nash, and Young: "Keep on keepin' on."

"Here in Vietnam the war goes on," Marine Captain Rod Chastant, 25, wrote in a letter to his brother in September 1967. "Morale is very high in spite of the fact that most men think the war is being run incorrectly. One of the staggering facts is that most men here believe we will *not* win the war. And yet they stick their necks out every day and carry on with their assigned tasks as if they were fighting for the continental security of the United States." Until he was killed in action one month after he extended his tour of duty, Capt. Chastant carried on in the highest tradition of the United States Marine Corps.

Rod Chastant's sentiment was echoed by Sergeant Phillip Woodall, who wrote to his father in April 1968, two months after the Tet Offensive, which failed militarily yet succeeded politically: "This war is all wrong. I will continue to fight, win my medals and fight the elements and hardships of this country. But that is because I'm a soldier and it's my job and there are other people depending on me."

When President Nixon announced that the United States would begin a phased withdrawal of its troops, the "Vietnamization" of the war – the turning over of responsibility and fighting to the Vietnamese forces, the ARVN – began. Still, American losses continued to mount. Some lieutenants and captains, seeing little point in engaging the NVA/VC forces, led their units out on patrol but didn't patrol: they didn't want to shed blood in an encounter that was essentially meaningless. In some units, grunts rebelled against gung-ho officers and "lifer" sergeants who they believed were taking unnecessary risks for personal aggrandizement. Out on patrol, they threw grenades not at the enemy but at their own officers; "fragging," as it came to be known, was widely reported in the media, although it was never as widespread as the press reported.

Most troops, however, continued to do as they were bid, even if they saw no point in doing it. In a letter dated October 30, 1969, First Lieutenant Robert Salerni wrote:

> After nine months I have mixed feelings about our involvement here. I can say, however, that the so-called Vietnamization of the war, while perhaps overplayed, is coming about. [The ARVNs] are taking more casualties than the Americans these days... Maybe all the time we've bought for these

people with American blood will finally begin to pay dividends. In any event, the Vietnamization seems to me the way to get us out of here, not simply to get up and let the VC have this country.

In a letter penned in late July 1970, Specialist 5 Tom Pellaton wrote to a friend:

You may have read about Fire Support Base Ripcord, southwest of Hue. The 101st ... had another defeat like Hamburger Hill... You will get the whitewashed version of what happened, I'm sure. But let me tell you, we were driven off that hill after overwhelming casualties. We lost over 80 men KIAs [Killed in Action] in less than two weeks and over 420 wounded. A full battalion of men. And for what? There is absolutely nothing out there in the jungle but mountains and triple canopy. Nothing but NVA [North Vietnamese Army; technically, they were PAVN, People's Army of Vietnam] who have built roads and who outnumber us in the province two or three to one.

Yes, it is no longer a case of the big imperialistic American aggressor killing the pure VC patriots. Instead, the VC are almost completely out of the picture. Instead, we [are fighting] highly trained, well-equipped NVA regiments and divisions. The South Vietnamese are doing very well militarily here. The 1st ARVN Division does as well as, if not better than, the 101st Airborne Division. The popular and regional forces keep the VC pretty much under control, but the fact remains that we are very much outnumbered and our best weapon cannot be used for political reasons. Napalm is almost out of the picture.

You may be surprised at my seemingly changed position. Talking of napalm, etc. When you see people, Americans, dying for lack of protection, for phony Vietnamization (it's not working because there just are not enough ARVN troops – they lose about a regiment a month in AWOLs and desertion) and for lack of good leadership (the infantry units were needlessly pinned down by the NVA at Ripcord because they stayed in a one-night defensive position for five or six nights in a row, which is *never* done. The whole thing is to move around and not let the NVA know where you are. Instead, they sat and took mortar rounds every night, with their 74 KIAs *every* day!).

My position has not really changed. There is no reason to be here – and there is even less reason to see Americans dying here. Many of the rear-echelon troops (higher-ranking officers and enlisted men) seem to be immune to their death. It still makes me limp with rage – overcome with sorrow! There seem to be so many people that are insensitive to this killing, even many of the political left who call the American GI "animal," etc. But the fact remains that both sides are suffering a catastrophic loss! I don't know if I've expressed myself very well, but perhaps you can sense my frustrations...

The collective national attitude back then toward soldiers and veterans, as instruments of an increasingly unpopular war in many quarters, rankled First Lieutenant Jack Farley. "Nobody cared," he said. "Nobody wanted to hear what it was about." Soldiers like Jack Farley had fought, and many had suffered grievous wounds, and the country did not embrace them on their return. Which hurt many, perhaps, as deeply as their wounds.

In the field, grunts did not fight for God, mother, or apple pie: they fought for each other. "You do not think about why you are there or even your family," said Medal of Honor recipient Fred Zabitosky. "You think strictly about the people you are with and what you can do for each other." (© Bernard Edelman)

* * *

Today, those who served in Southeast Asia have been "rehabilitated." No longer are we the drugged-out, crazed baby killers too often reviled by those who opposed the war – and too long portrayed as such by the popular media. Indeed, more than a few veterans returned home to demonstrate against a war that was as unwinnable as it was misguided and mismanaged. Today, many veterans still suffer psychological trauma as well as physical disabilities incurred during their military service. Still, the vast majority of those who came home got jobs, married, raised a family, became model members – leaders – of their communities. Perhaps nothing attests to this rehabilitation as the plague of Vietnam veteran wannabes, imposters, poseurs who never were what they cannot be. And those who served are, in increasing numbers, seeking out their brother and sister veterans, holding reunions, returning to the place where they lived the most intense time of their lives, some just to visit, others to help with the healing, of a former enemy, and of themselves.

Chapter 11

"Swatting Flies with a Sledgehammer"
The Air War

Professor Ronald B. Frankum, Jr.

AIR WAR OVER NORTH VIETNAM

During the Vietnam War, the United States air campaigns encompassed more than just the geographical extent of that country and included a variety of missions beyond bombing the North Vietnamese. The effort was broken down into a series of air operations that covered North and South Vietnam, Laos, and Cambodia. In addition to the offensively minded bombing sorties, American air assets were responsible for interdiction of NVA/VC forces, ground support of allied troops, armed and photographic reconnaissance, medical and tactical airlift, and specialized missions such as defoliation and search-and-rescue. It is easy to dismiss the real advantages of the American air effort in the war when focusing only on the perceived failures of the bombing mission. However, by assessing the air campaigns in total, it is clear that the war which was fought in harsh and rugged conditions could not have been carried out or lasted as long as it did without the significant contributions of the aircraft and personnel of the United States armed forces.

In November 1950, the Military Assistance and Advisory Group, which served as the clearinghouse for American military and technical support to the French Union forces in Indochina, added an Air Force Section to its mission in order to better coordinate its efforts with the French in their struggle against the Viet Minh.[1] While this date is seldom listed as one of significance during the American experience in Vietnam, it does mark the beginning of the United States air war. American air assets performed a number of missions, including support for the French Air Force in Indochina during the First Indochina War. They were also involved in the creation, training, and maintenance of the Vietnamese Air Force during the period of nation building, and the beginning of more active air missions such as reconnaissance and defoliation by the early 1960s. However, it

Marine Medium Helicopter Squadron 164 and infantrymen of the 2nd Battalion, 5th Marine Regiment during Operation *Mead River*, about eight miles southwest of Da Nang, November 20, 1968. (Virtual Vietnam Archive, Texas Tech University)

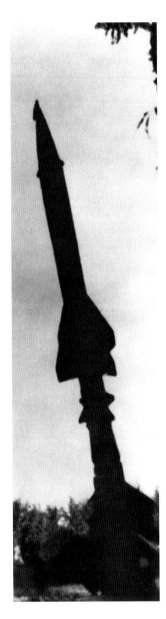

The North Vietnamese air defense system evolved into one of the most sophisticated in the world with the introduction of the SA-2 surface-to-air missile and a variety of antiaircraft artillery. (Virtual Vietnam Archive, Texas Tech University)

was not until the questionable Gulf of Tonkin incident in 1964 that the United States began to flex its muscles over Vietnam. When Congress approved the Gulf of Tonkin Resolution on August 7, 1964, it gave the president the authority to defend American forces and installations in Vietnam against attack and use whatever force necessary to assist South Vietnam in its war. President Lyndon Johnson then initiated a series of the most impressive air operations ever seen in the world. In response to the Gulf of Tonkin, Johnson ordered punitive air strikes against the naval facilities that supported the North Vietnamese boats thought to have been used in the attack, as well as the oil storage facility at Vinh. Operation *Pierce Arrow*, as the mission became known, succeeded in destroying 25 percent of the intended targets. While considered a success, the air operation did not impede the Vietnamese insurgents, known as the Viet Cong, who continued to escalate their attacks on South Vietnamese and American facilities and personnel over the next six months.

The myriad of events that occurred between August 1964 and February 1965 could have been enough for the United States to launch additional, punitive air sorties against North Vietnam. However, it was not until the February 7, 1965, Viet Cong mortar attack on Camp Holloway in the Central Highlands, which resulted in serious American casualties, that the United States decided to respond. In response, the Johnson administration launched Operation *Flaming Dart*, which targeted North Vietnamese facilities that had been suspected of supporting the increasing Viet Cong attacks. Air strikes against the Dong Hoi, Vit Thu Lu, Chap Le, and Vu Con barracks were conducted to demonstrate to the North Vietnamese that they would not go unpunished for supporting attacks against Americans in South Vietnam. A reconnaissance mission estimated that the targets had been effectively destroyed, but this did not deter the Viet Cong, who attacked the American billet in Qui Nhon on February 10, killing 23 Americans and wounding another 21. A second round of air sorties under *Flaming Dart* destroyed a significant portion of the Chanh Hoa barracks and prompted American officials to push forward a new, sustained bombing campaign. This was designed to force the North Vietnamese to suspend their support for the Southern insurgency, and negotiate a peaceful conclusion to the hostilities in Southeast Asia.

Even while the effects of *Flaming Dart* were being evaluated, the Joint Chiefs of Staff proposed an air campaign, which became known as Operation *Rolling Thunder*, to interdict supplies and personnel infiltrating into South Vietnam from the North. The air campaign would have another purpose, as Secretary of State Dean Rusk explained: "Strikes into North Viet Nam should be considered as serving the political purpose of indicating to the North that they cannot expect to rely upon a sanctuary in the face of their increased infiltration and operations in South Viet Nam."[2] The JCS established a list of 94 targets from which the Air Force and Navy would attack for two days per week over eight weeks. Operation *Rolling Thunder* would become one of the most significant air campaigns in United States history, and an intense point of contention in America's experience during the Vietnam War.

Air campaigns over North Vietnam

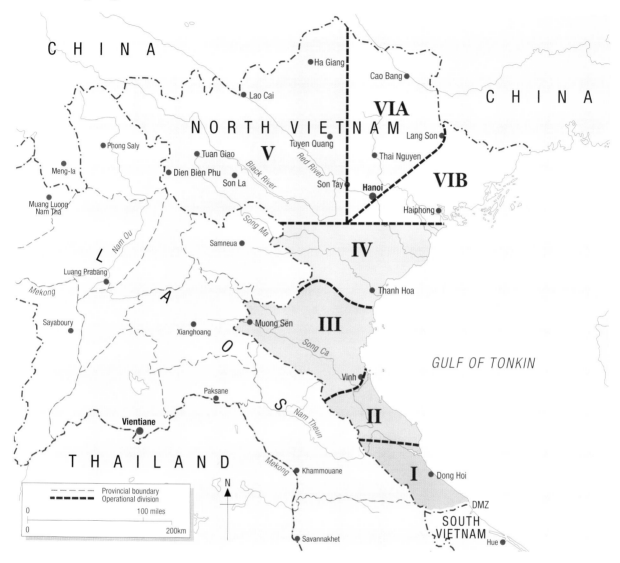

Despite delays caused by weather and South Vietnamese politics, the eight-week program began on March 2, 1965. United States aircraft struck at lines of communication between Hanoi and Vinh, as well as radar and communication facilities that supported infiltration. The air strikes were militarily successful, but, like so much of the Vietnam War, they failed to achieve the political goals desired by the United States. The United States expected the North Vietnamese to pull back when faced with overwhelming firepower but, instead, it continued its support for the Viet Cong and its struggle to incorporate South Vietnam into its fold. As the end of the eight-week program neared, it was understood that the United States had to maintain the pressure upon the North Vietnamese to induce

With additional sorties planned for *Rolling Thunder* and an increased requirement for air assets in support of operations in South Vietnam and Laos, the area of responsibility over North Vietnam was divided into "route packages" between the Air Force, Navy, and MACV.

North Vietnamese antiaircraft artillery in Ha Bac province during Operation *Linebacker I*, May 23, 1972. (Virtual Vietnam Archive, Texas Tech University)

them to negotiate acceptable peace terms. This translated to an extension of the initial air campaign, and propelled the United States into a more significant and lasting commitment to the defense of South Vietnam.

Throughout the early months of *Rolling Thunder*, the American air strikes concentrated on damaging installations, barracks, and supply depots. Of particular interest was the destruction of transportation choke points between the 17th and 20th parallels. Even when choke points were destroyed, the damage did not eliminate transportation; rather, it only hindered it. The North Vietnamese were very adaptable to changing conditions. If a bridge was destroyed, it would not take long for the establishment of an alternative, if more arduous, route fueled by human and animal power. When, on April 11, 1966, the first B-52 bombers struck North Vietnam at the Mu Gia Pass, which was one of three major supply routes to Laos and the Ho Chi Minh Trail, the 585 tons of bombs produced impressive results. However, a reconnaissance mission the next day discovered that the craters had been filled with dirt and rock, and trucks were moving through the pass. The air campaign to destroy railways, roads, and bridges was strategically sound; but in Vietnam where many people had survived for years without such conveniences, the hardship of a destroyed bridge was minimal.

After the initial success of *Rolling Thunder*, the Johnson administration proposed the first of what would become seven major bombing pauses. The pause, which began on May 13, 1965 to coincide with the days of Buddha's birthday, resulted from a hint from the North Vietnamese that it would consider negotiation toward a peaceful resolution.[3] It became clear very early in the pause that the North Vietnamese officials had little interest in compromise, and would only consider a resolution to the crisis on their own terms. On April 8, 1965, North Vietnam premier Pham Van Dong established four points that had to be met before a peaceful resolution to the conflict could be considered. They included: Vietnamese independence; non-intervention by foreign powers; political settlement; and reunification. The last of these points was non-negotiable for the United States, and the air campaign resumed on May 18.[4]

When it set the precedent of a bombing pause and the threat of restarting air strikes as a part of its strategy in the air war, the United States made a significant mistake. The North Vietnamese used the time to restructure and supplement their air defense system and repair much of the damage caused by *Rolling Thunder*. They also correctly interpreted the division within the Johnson administration over how the air campaign should proceed, as well as what constituted progress. The American strategy of using the carrot-and-stick failed to impress the North Vietnamese, and it did not alter North Vietnamese support for the Southern insurgency. The frequent bombing pauses and the gradual build-up in intensity of the air campaign did allow the North Vietnamese to construct what would become one of the strongest air defense systems in the world.

After the first bombing pause, the North Vietnamese introduced the Soviet-built SA-2, a surface-to-air missile, around Hanoi. The SA-2, while not the most effective weapon in air defense, did change the nature of the air war over North Vietnam. The SA-2, when combined with antiaircraft artillery, proved to be an effective deterrent. AAA was used primarily for low-altitude attack, while SA-2 missiles were more effective at high altitude. The blending of these weapons systems assured that United States airpower would face some type of concentrated threat when entering North Vietnamese air space. By 1966, an integrated air defense system, which included the Soviet-built MiG fighter, formed a protective ring around strategic centers in North Vietnam. While it can certainly be argued that the threat was ineffective, given the total number of sorties flown over North

Vietnam, it did provide the North Vietnamese with a way of combating the unseen enemy, and raising morale when an American aircraft was shot down.

It is clear that *Rolling Thunder* affected North Vietnamese strategy, and it most certainly caused them to divert valuable resources away from offensive action, but the air campaign did not result in the psychological damage American officials had hoped for, nor did it bring an end to the war. It is ironic that the intensity of *Rolling Thunder* might have had a reverse psychological effect on the Vietnamese people. The air campaign forced the North Vietnamese to mobilize its entire population.

Critics of *Rolling Thunder* also often point to the numerous restrictions placed on the air sorties over North Vietnam as a reason why the air campaign did not have the desired effect. From its first phase in March 1965, *Rolling Thunder* was limited by restrictions. At first it was geographic – only targets between the 17th and 19th parallels – but even when this was lifted, other restrictions came into force. Air sorties were ordered to avoid populated regions, which included a protective 30-nautical-mile ring around Hanoi and a ten-nautical-mile ring around Haiphong. The border with China was off limits, in order to avoid any direct or accidental contact with Communist China, which might expand the war. Finally, authorized air strikes could not attack non-military targets such as dykes, dams, questionable civilian structures, and hydropower plants. Air sorties on military targets at or near such targets were severely limited. These significant restrictions were among the many that plagued the air campaign, even though the limits followed a logical pattern given the objectives of the air campaign. The objective was not to win the war but to force the North Vietnamese to negotiate peace.[5] These restrictions hindered air strikes against a mobile force that relied on nineteenth-century modes of transportation, and exploited American restraint to its advantage. Coupled with the restrictions was an evolving air defense system that protected the bulk of North Vietnam's capacity to wage war and counteract the American build-up of forces in South Vietnam.

By 1968, the United States had been actively involved in the Vietnam War for three years, and had committed a significant amount of its resources toward the conduct of *Rolling Thunder*. While the war continued without end, major political and psychological setbacks emerged after the 1968 Tet Offensive and Johnson's decision not to seek another term in the White House. Meanwhile, the United States Air Force offered a more positive view of its air campaign over North Vietnam. According to bomb damage assessment reports, *Rolling Thunder* had made significant inroads into diminishing the North Vietnamese ability to sustain its wartime infrastructure. It was estimated that 22 percent of its industry, 47 percent of its transportation system, 65 percent of its petroleum, oil, and lubricant capacity, 58 percent of its electrical power plant capacity, and 73 percent of its military facilities had been destroyed or made inoperable.[6] *Rolling Thunder* had achieved remarkable results, but it had not accomplished its primary mission. Despite the 643,000 tons of bombs delivered (in the Pacific Theater during the World War II, the US had dropped 537,000 tons), it did not stop infiltration of

North Vietnamese resources to the South, nor did it force the North Vietnamese to negotiate. The North Vietnamese and the Viet Cong were able to launch the largest coordinated attack of the war during Tet 1968, which caused many to question the effectiveness of the air campaign, and in fact American strategy in Vietnam as a whole.

On March 31, 1968, Johnson shocked the nation when he announced that he would not seek nor accept his party's nomination for the presidency. In the same speech, though lost in the pronouncement, was a new strategy to suspend air strikes north of the 19th Parallel, with the intention of resuming negotiations to end the war. This move was primarily political, designed to induce the North Vietnamese to go to the peace table. It was also practical, because the number of targets left above the 19th Parallel was limited, and interdiction strikes between the 17th and 19th parallels were more effective. The psychological effects of these two announcements was to reinforce the North Vietnamese determination to carry on the war until it achieved a successful resolution. The American overture of peace through the suspension of bombing in 1968 was the culmination of a failed strategy. It demonstrated the unique inability of American officials to understand the nature of total war in North Vietnam, and the historical precedents of the *longue-durée* in Vietnamese wars for independence. The North

President Johnson used his Tuesday lunch sessions to determine Operation *Rolling Thunder* air strikes based upon recommendation from both military and political leadership. This type of micro-management sometimes focused on political repercussions of air strikes rather than military significance. (Virtual Vietnam Archive, Texas Tech University)

US Navy OV-10 "Black Pony." (Virtual Vietnam Archive, Texas Tech University)

Vietnamese, once again, used the latest bombing pause to repair bomb damage and improve their infrastructure for a future push south.

While the United States continued to focus its air campaign on interdiction through 1968, any momentum gained through three and a half years of *Rolling Thunder* had been lost. A few days before the 1968 presidential election, on November 1, Johnson ordered the suspension of all air operations over North Vietnam. The move was designed to bolster the candidacy of Hubert Humphrey, who was losing the presidential race to Richard Nixon. Like much of the air campaign, this last move was too little, too late.

It would be nearly another three and a half years before North Vietnam would once again be the object of intense bombing. The last and most effective air campaign of the war occurred in 1972, when North Vietnamese forces invaded South Vietnam in what became known as the Easter Offensive. President Richard Nixon responded to the offensive by initiating Tactical Air Command Operational Plan 100, referred to as *Constant Guard*, to provide ground support for the beleaguered South Vietnamese armed forces and the remaining American personnel under attack. Supplementing the defenses was a new air campaign against the North. On April 6, 1972, the United States launched Operation *Freedom Trail*, which concentrated on targets south of the 20th Parallel that supported the invasion. This air campaign, and the one that followed, were different from *Rolling Thunder* in that many of the restrictions imposed had been lifted and guidelines relaxed. Another difference was that *Freedom Trail* was not gradual. For more than one month, this air campaign bombed northern targets with intensity.

On May 9, Nixon announced the beginning of Operation *Linebacker*, which replaced *Freedom Trail* and expanded the bombing north of the 20th Parallel.

While there were still restrictions on targets near the Chinese border and within Hanoi, *Linebacker* was relatively free of constraint. With this air campaign, and the mining of the major port of Haiphong, American airpower helped to stem North Vietnam's offensive, and assisted in pushing back the invading forces to near their starting points. With the failure of its invasion, North Vietnam indicated that it was willing to resume the negotiations that had been going on in Paris for over three years. When it became clear that this indication was nothing more than a ploy to gain time to recover from the failed invasion, Nixon ordered another round of bombing, to begin on December 18.

Also known as the Christmas bombings, Operation *Linebacker II* lasted until December 29. This air campaign was unique in that there were no restrictions placed upon target selection for nearly 2,700 sorties, which delivered approximately 20,000 tons of munitions. The operation had its intended effect: the North Vietnamese agreed to resume negotiations and agreed to the final Paris Peace Agreement on January 27, 1973. Both *Linebacker* operations were successful in achieving their results. *Linebacker I* was pivotal in the defeat of the Easter Offensive, while *Linebacker II* brought North Vietnam back to the negotiating table. Many within military and civilian circles argued that it was unrestricted American airpower that caused these successes. While that is true to

The A-37 was one jet aircraft used by the South Vietnamese Air Force in ground support and armed reconnaissance. (Virtual Vietnam Archive, Texas Tech University)

The C-47 served in several capacities during the war. It primarily served as a transport but was also modified for surveillance, electronics, and gunship service. Using its three 7.62 mini-guns that could fire up to 6,000 rounds per minute, the AC-47 was ideal for armed reconnaissance. (Virtual Vietnam Archive, Texas Tech University)

OPPOSITE
Laos was divided into five military regions and divided into two major air campaigns: in the north, interdiction and ground support missions were predominant, while the southern regions focused primarily on interdiction.

a certain degree, it is also important to note that North Vietnamese strategy altered drastically when it launched the Easter Offensive. The large-scale, conventional attack was susceptible to air strikes, and suffered as a result. The success of *Linebacker I* was due, in large part, to the exposure of North Vietnamese personnel and weaponry, which offered lucrative targets to the American air sorties. *Linebacker II* did force the resumption of peace talks, but the North Vietnamese quickly turned that to their advantage by negotiating favorable terms, including the withdrawal of American armed forces from Southeast Asia. It would take a little over two years for North Vietnam to overrun the South. With the United States, and its air assets, out of the fight, the war's conclusion was inevitable.

THE AIR CAMPAIGN IN LAOS

The air war transcended the borders of Vietnam into Laos and Cambodia, where similar insurgencies threatened the two royal governments. While each air campaign was considered a sideshow to the war in Vietnam, both provided vital assistance to America's allies who were each fighting a growing Communist threat. The air war in Laos was significantly connected to the air campaigns in North Vietnam, South Vietnam, and Cambodia. The Royal Laotian Government required American assistance in fighting its own insurgents, the Pathet Lao, while the southern region of Laos served as a conduit between North and South Vietnam and Cambodia via the Ho Chi Minh Trail.

Air campaigns over Laos

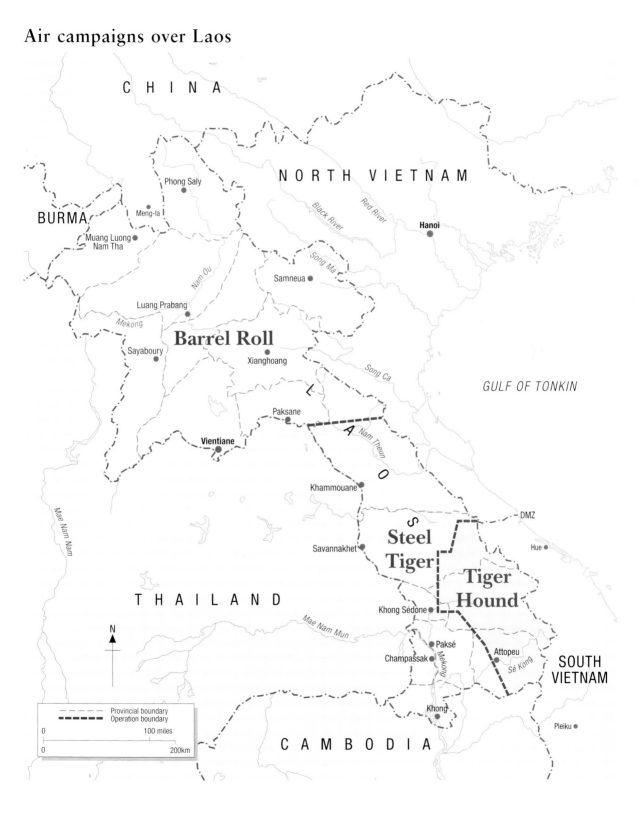

C H I N A

BURMA

Phong Saly

Meng-la

N O R T H   V I E T N A M

Black River

Red River

Hanoi

Muang Luong
Nam Tha

Samneua

Song Ma

Nam Ou

Luang Prabang

Barrel Roll

Mekong

Sayaboury

Xianghoang

Song Ca

GULF OF TONKIN

L

Paksane

A

Nam Theun

O

Vientiane

S

Khammouane

DMZ

**Steel
Tiger**

Savannakhet

Hue

**Tiger
Hound**

Mae Nam Nam

T H A I L A N D

Khong Sédone

N

Mae Nam Mun

Paksé

Attopeu

Champassak

Mekong

Sé Kong

SOUTH
VIETNAM

Khong

Provincial boundary
Operation boundary

0   100 miles

0   200km

C A M B O D I A

Pleiku

223

As a result, the air war was divided into two distinct missions: ground support in the north and interdiction in the south.

After the August 1964 Gulf of Tonkin incident, the United States decided once again to increase involvement in the struggle between the Pathet Lao and forces loyal to the Royal Laotian Government. American aircraft had already been engaged in northern Laos, flying armed reconnaissance missions in support of neutralist generals Kong Le and Vang Pao, both of whom were loyal to the Royal Laotian Government. The Government forces relied on American firepower, through Operation *Barrel Roll*, to serve as an equalizer to the better-equipped and motivated Pathet Lao, North Vietnamese, and occasional Chinese forces involved in the fight.

Interdiction was the predominant type of air sortie in the south. Operation *Steel Tiger*, which began on April 3, 1965, focused on interdicting the Ho Chi Minh Trail. Using existing intelligence, aircraft bombed the trails and roads, conveys, and depots established in military regions III and IV. Despite the high number of sorties flown and tonnage dropped, North Vietnamese traffic through Laos actually increased. The Ho Chi Minh Trail was of the highest strategic value for the war in Vietnam, and resources were diverted to the region to maintain trail activity. On December 6, 1965, part of the *Steel Tiger* area of responsibility was handed over to General Westmoreland to better coordinate air and ground interdiction missions. Operation *Tiger Hound* concentrated on interdiction, but also focused on the need to bottleneck North Vietnamese supplies at the major passes between North Vietnam and Laos. Even if the United States could not destroy the Trail complex, it could at least slow down the progression of supplies and personnel.

When Johnson halted bombing missions over North Vietnam in November 1968, Laos was the beneficiary of a surplus of aircraft and personnel. As a result, the United States shifted operations to Laos and initiated Operation *Commando Hunt* on November 15, 1968. The objective of this air campaign was interdiction and focused on the region between the 16th and 18th parallels. The Ho Chi Minh Trail, which had developed from a series of foot-trails to a well-established network of roads, trails, and pathways with truck stops, storage facilities, and rest areas, was the primary target. *Commando Hunt* created a serious obstacle to the movement of personnel and supplies down the Ho Chi Minh Trail, but it did not achieve its ultimate objective of shutting down the transit system. The air operation did throw off the North Vietnamese timetable for its 1969 offensive, and provided a period of time for Nixon's Vietnamization program to develop. In the end, however, it did not prove to be a deciding factor in the war's conclusion.

American air asserts were next challenged during the failed *Lam Son 719* operation in which the United States attempted to test Vietnamization using South Vietnamese troops to capture the strategic Laotian town of Tchepone. United States efforts were hampered by the December 1970 Cooper-Church Amendment to the defense appropriations bill, which prohibited American troops from entering Laos or American advisors from accompanying their ARVN counterparts

into action. However, the amendment did not include air assets. While the ground operation failed, American helicopters managed to extract a number of soldiers from their precarious positions deep within Laotian territory, losing more than 100 of the aircraft in the process.

The Laotian air campaigns are noteworthy for the several variables that restricted American action. As a result of the 1962 Geneva Agreements that underwrote Laotian neutrality, most of the United States missions were not publicized. This secret war in Laos made it difficult to expose North Vietnamese violations of Laotian neutrality, as American personnel and aircraft were not technically allowed in that air space. Topography and weather also played an important role in the air campaigns. Laos was a rugged country with a primitive road network and a monsoon season that dictated the opportunity, and type, of air sorties. The wet season, April to November, isolated troops on both sides as the dirt roads turned to mud and the rivers became impassable. The numerically inferior Royal Laotian Army used American air mobility during this season to launch offensive operations against the Pathet Lao. Transporting the royal forces by air, American aircraft bypassed the quagmire created by the monsoons to engage isolated Pathet Lao units who were often cut off from retreat or reinforcement. During the dry season, November to April, United States airpower

L-19 [O-1] "Bird Dog" served as a forward air control and observation aircraft during the war. (Virtual Vietnam Archive, Texas Tech University)

was used defensively to help against the numerically superior and offensively minded Pathet Lao and NVA troops.

While the air campaign in Laos failed to achieve its objectives, it was a necessary part of the United States' war in Vietnam. Laos was strategically significant to the war in Vietnam and was also experiencing an insurgency within its borders. To aid South Vietnam but neglect Laos would have been an anathema to American foreign policy. There were over 500,000 American sorties and 2 million tons of munitions delivered on Laos during the course of the air campaign. While this was not enough to maintain the government or interdict the Ho Chi Minh Trail, it did force the North Vietnamese to divert a tremendous amount of resources to the region to maintain the Pathet Lao and keep the Trail open. It is certain that the North Vietnamese needed these resources for the war in South Vietnam and the diversion proved costly for the North Vietnamese war effort.

As the American war in Vietnam wound down, so did the air war in Laos. On February 21, 1975, the United States signed a cease-fire agreement with the Pathet Lao. By August, the Pathet Lao had overrun the country and established the Lao People's Democratic Republic.

THE AIR WAR IN CAMBODIA

Cambodia also presented a unique challenge to the United States in Southeast Asia. Under Prince Norodom Sihanouk, Cambodia had pledged neutrality in the Vietnam War but, through its actions, had established a close, and profitable, alliance with North Vietnam. By allowing North Vietnamese supplies and personnel to transit the country, as well as ignoring the establishment of Viet Cong base areas along the Cambodian–South Vietnam border, Cambodia had exposed itself to the brunt of American escalation. The Johnson administration failed to react to these blatant violations of neutrality, and did not make any response to the changing stance of Sihanouk. It was not until Richard Nixon entered the White House that American airpower was brought to bear on Cambodia. While the air campaign in Cambodia was effective, it arrived too late to change the course of the Vietnam War, and helped to push Cambodia toward a dark and torturous future.

In July 1968, General Creighton Abrams, who had assumed command of MACV, requested an air campaign to destroy the North Vietnamese sanctuaries that had been established within a three- to ten-mile area inside the Cambodian border. Operation *Menu*, broken down into missions called Breakfast, Lunch, Supper, Dessert, and Snack, commenced on March 18, 1969. Because Cambodia still proclaimed neutrality in the war, *Menu* remained secret until May 2, 1970 when *The New York Times* ran a story about the damage inflicted by the air campaign. During *Menu*, American and South Vietnamese aircraft delivered approximately 120,000 tons of bombs on the North Vietnamese base areas. While the sanctuaries were not permanently destroyed, the bombing did disrupt the planned 1969 offensive against South Vietnam, which was to originate from Cambodia.

Air campaigns over Cambodia

On April 30, 1970, Nixon announced that the United States had begun a limited incursion into Cambodia, with the objective of locating and destroying North Vietnamese and Viet Cong personnel and base areas. The incursion had come at the request of Lon Nol and Prince Sisowath Sirik Matak, who had succeeded in replacing Sihanouk on March 18, 1970. During the offensive, there were 12 named air operations concentrating around two of the points of incursion, the Parrot's Beak and the Fish Hook.[7] North Vietnamese and Viet Cong personnel, base areas, and supply depots were located and destroyed; however, the main fighting forces were not. Airpower did play a decisive role, however, in limiting American and South Vietnamese casualties during the 60-day operation.

As the incursion continued, the Joint Chiefs of Staff formulated a new air campaign designed to interdict North Vietnamese and Viet Cong forces attempting to enter South Vietnam via Cambodia. Operation *Freedom Deal*, which absorbed

During the 1970 incursion into Cambodia, air sorties concentrated on ground support around the Parrot's Beak and Fish Hook, and armed reconnaissance in the northeastern region of the country to destroy fleeing North Vietnamese and Viet Cong forces.

Menu, concentrated on the area of greatest concern for the Cambodian Army and American armed forces. *Freedom Deal* was marked by the conflicting nature of the air war. It relied on quick and accurate intelligence to strike at the enemy, but also took great care not to damage or destroy culturally significant structures or artifacts in the region. In many respects, the United States tried to fight a culturally sensitive war against an enemy who used this restriction to its advantage. As the North Vietnamese and Viet Cong began to avoid *Freedom Deal* strike areas, General Abrams expanded and renamed the operation to *Freedom Action*.

Freedom Action began on June 20, and stopped at the end of the month when the last of the American forces withdrew from Cambodia. This air campaign, which delivered approximately 384,000 tons of munitions combined with the incursion, did disrupt North Vietnam's ability to use Cambodia as a launching point for further attacks directed against South Vietnam. After 1970, the United States used its airpower to aid the Royal Cambodia Government in its battle against the Khmer Rouge, a Communist insurgency similar to the Viet Cong in South Vietnam. After the incursion, the Khmer Rouge became more of a threat to Cambodia's stability as the North Vietnamese provided greater assistance to the group. While American airpower continued to serve as an equalizer, it did not diminish the insurgency. FANK forces became dependent on American military assistance and airpower in their fight. When this support was halted as a result of the Public Law 93-53, which prohibited the funding of United States operations in Cambodia after August 15, 1973, the Khmer Rouge swept through Cambodia. Lon Nol's forces surrendered on April 17, 1975 and, when Phnom Penh fell, the Khmer Rouge, under the leadership of Pol Pot, ushered in a reign of terror unprecedented in that country's long history.

AIR WAR IN SOUTH VIETNAM

While the air campaigns in Laos, Cambodia, and North Vietnam required an extraordinary effort to maintain, they did not match the variety of air assets used in South Vietnam. The United States dominated the skies and, as a result, was able to effectively utilize airpower not only for attack and ground support but also in a variety of ways that buttressed the American effort in Southeast Asia. Airmobility, search-and-rescue, defoliation, and tactical airlift all played a significant role in the air war and allowed the United States to use its resources effectively. The greatest advantage the United States held was in firepower, which became an important part of the ground support mission in South Vietnam.

The nature of the United States' build-up in South Vietnam, one of gradualism, coupled with the strategy of attrition (that is, destroying more of the enemy than he can replace) increased the significance of ground support missions in South Vietnam. Over a six-year period, from 1963 to 1968, American forces in Southeast Asia increased from 16,000 to 543,000. After the introduction of combat forces in March 1965, the mission changed from advice and defense to limited, and then active, engagement of the enemy. The objective of the air war in South Vietnam was to apply continuous pressure on the enemy as American forces

built up strength, and to support the overall attrition strategy. As a result, airpower was present in all named military ground operations throughout the war. Because the North Vietnamese and Viet Cong seldom concentrated in force for a long period of time, direct military engagements were brief and the delineation of battlefronts was often blurred. American airpower, often in the form of ground support missions, helped the United States forces identify, locate, and then destroy enemy targets while lessening the exposure to American troops. Within this air campaign, Arc Light missions became one of the United States' most potent, if not controversial, weapons.

Using B-52 bombers, the Strategic Air Command initiated Arc Light missions on June 18, 1965 in South Vietnam. The B-52 was noteworthy for the amount of munitions it could deliver over a target. As General Westmoreland described them, Arc Light missions were designed, "to assist in the defeat of the enemy through maximum destruction, disruption, and harassment of major control centers, supply storage facilities, logistic systems, enemy troops, and lines of communication in selected target areas."[8] The number of B-52 sorties supporting Arc Light missions increased during the war. By 1968, using the model F series, a flight of three B-52s over a pre-determined target could deliver approximately 114,750lb of munitions. The North Vietnamese and Viet Cong stationed in South Vietnam did not have an effective defense against the B-52, and rarely did they receive warning of a planned attack. Surprise and the overwhelming firepower made the Arc Light missions a valuable weapon in the war, but there were some

Arc Light Raid, January 1969. Missions over South Vietnam, like this Arc Light raid, expended more than 3.5 million tons of conventional ordnance between June 18, 1965 and August 18, 1973. (Virtual Vietnam Archive, Texas Tech University)

B-52 bomber. (Virtual Vietnam Archive, Texas Tech University)

disadvantages. B-52s were not designed for precision bombing but, rather, to carry nuclear warheads against the Soviet Union. Carpeting an area with 153 750-lb bombs (each B-52F carried 51 bombs) often meant over-saturation of the target and sometimes resulted in the destruction or death of unintended targets. The mission, however, was vital to American strategy in Vietnam, and helped serve as a critical component to the American war in Southeast Asia.

If the B-52 represented American firepower in Vietnam, the helicopter became the symbol of American airmobility in the Vietnam War. Its introduction to the battlefield changed the strategy and tactics of how to fight a war. The helicopter was introduced into Vietnam in December 1961 as a means to move ARVN troops. As the war escalated, its role increased. The UH-1 Iroquois was the most recognized helicopter of the war. The "Huey" was a utility helicopter and was modified for a number of missions beyond transportation, including fire support, search-and-rescue, medical evacuation, defoliation, and reconnaissance missions. Another helicopter employed in the war was the AH-1 Cobra.

Usually organized into assault helicopter companies or within two airmobile divisions, the helicopter was a formidable weapon of the air war because of its significant firepower capability. Helicopters served as a troop multiplier when the United States was building up its forces, and an equalizer to the many obstacles and hazards presented by Vietnam's topography. The helicopter made it possible for American forces and their allies to operate in the rice paddies, highlands, jungles, and bush of Vietnam.

The ability to move troops over inhospitable terrain quickly often resulted in surprising enemy forces. Rather than have to exhaust a force by land movement, the helicopter brought fresh troops to the field of battle and extracted casualties. The helicopter, as well as a dedicated fleet of fixed-wing transport aircraft, enabled the resupply of remote sites and forces operating in areas inaccessible by land.

Airmobility allowed the United States to take the battle to the enemy, even if it meant that the North Vietnamese and Viet Cong would have the option of choosing the terrain on which to engage the United States. As a result, there was no place in South Vietnam that was free from the threat of an American operation.

Another air campaign in South Vietnam involved the dispensing of herbicides to clear vegetation used by the North Vietnamese and Viet Cong to their advantage. By destroying the brush around heavily used roads, base camps, and villages, North Vietnamese and Viet Cong forces were exposed to American and South Vietnamese firepower. These defoliation missions also destroyed food supplies used by the Southern insurgents to sustain themselves during the war. The first defoliation mission occurred on November 28, 1961, in response to Viet Cong ambushes in the Mekong Delta. The United States Air Force modified six C-123 aircraft for the mission, which was deemed successful enough for continuation. The herbicide missions came under a new operation called *Ranch Hand*, which began on January 12, 1962. While the United States attempted many different types of defoliation missions, to include hand- and helicopter-mounted spray units, the slow-moving, but steady, C-123 proved to be the most efficient aircraft for the mission. *Ranch Hand* continued until 1971, spraying millions of acres with herbicides. The mission was successful in exposing enemy locations, destroying enemy food resources, and providing safer access along contested roads and canals. The effects of the herbicides have been controversial in the postwar period: some evidence has suggested that the chemicals used in the

Used in close combat support and a variety of other offensive sorties, US Army AH-1 "Cobra" became one of the most feared aircraft of the war in South Vietnam. Its 7.62mm mini-gun could fire between 2,000 and 4,000 rounds per minute and it was equipped with a 40mm grenade launcher and two 26-round rocket pods. (Virtual Vietnam Archive, Texas Tech University)

The C-123 "Provider" was modified to dispense defoliants during Operation *Ranch Hand*. The United States sprayed approximately 19 million gallons of herbicides in Southeast Asia, 60 percent of which was Agent Orange. The name of the agent was derived from the colored band on the 55-gallon drum containing the chemicals. (Virtual Vietnam Archive, Texas Tech University)

herbicides have caused long-term disease in those exposed to the spraying. While that controversy continues to elicit intense debate, it is fair to say that the defoliation of enemy terrain lessened the threat of casualty to American soldiers and their allies during the war. If the defoliation operation raised questions about the application of airpower during the war, other missions highlighted the usefulness of American air assets.

SEARCH-AND-RESCUE

There is perhaps no more inspiring story of duty and courage than those involved in search-and-rescue in Vietnam. Those members of the Aerospace Rescue and Recover Service and supporting personnel risked their lives to save downed pilots and assist those injured in the line of duty. They also provided reassurance that aid was never too far away for those in distress.

Search-and-rescue missions began in Vietnam on April 1, 1962, and lasted the duration of the war. As the air war escalated, search-and-rescue operations expanded to Laos and Cambodia, and included non-military organizations such as Air America, Civil Air Transport, and Continental Air Service. Personnel earned numerous distinctions, including one Medal of Honor earned by Airman First Class William H. Pitsenbarger for his action near Cam My on April 11, 1966.[9] When the 1st Infantry Division engaged the enemy and began suffering casualties, Pitsenbarger's unit was called in to assist. He rode a hoist over 100 feet to the jungle floor where he then coordinated rescue and medical efforts. Pitsenbarger continued evacuating the wounded, refusing his own extraction until all were recovered, even after one of the two helicopters assisting the effort was damaged and forced to leave the battlefield. When the Viet Cong assaulted the position, Pitsenbarger, while defending himself, continued to aid the wounded, often exposing himself to enemy fire. Despite being wounded three times, Pitsenbarger continued his duties. The fighting was so fierce that the unit suffered 80 percent casualties. When the perimeter was breached, Pitsenbarger was fatally wounded.

Pitsenbarger's decision to stay with the troops and help the wounded, rather than evacuate, resulted in his death. As his Medal of Honor citation reads, "His bravery and determination exemplify the highest professional standards and traditions of military service and reflect great credit upon himself, his unit, and the United States Air Force." The courage and sacrifice of the search-and-rescue teams was remarkable; Airman First Class William H. Pitsenbarger was one of the many thousands whose job it was to ensure that the wounded soldier or airman received the fastest and best care available.

* * *

Whether the air war during the Vietnam War was successful is a matter of perspective. If one includes all of the air campaigns in Southeast Asia, combat as well as non-combat sorties, a positive answer is more likely. Aircraft, in a ground support role, allowed the United States to pursue a strategy of attrition, but that strategy was fraught with error. Laos and Cambodia surely would not have survived as long as they did without air assets to serve as troop multipliers and provide ground support but, in the end, each suffered a similar fate to South Vietnam.

The use of aircraft in non-military missions provided significant advances for modern warfare. Medical airlift, search-and-rescue, and tactical airlift were extremely successful, and provided services to the armed forces that were without precedent. However, neither the bombing campaigns against North Vietnam nor the interdiction missions influenced events as the United States had hoped. The air war did not stop North Vietnamese aggression, nor did it save the South. Even if one concedes that these actions were not specific to the objectives of the air campaigns, it is fair to assess the air war within these parameters. Success and failure are often measured in inches; in Vietnam, such fine distinctions are lost in the tragedy of war.

A-1 Skyraider. (Virtual Vietnam Archive, Texas Tech University)

Chapter 12

Battle for the Mekong
The River War in Vietnam

Professor R. Blake Dunnavent

The French imperial conquest of Indochina saw the first operations by Western navies on Vietnam's inland waterways. Despite these early efforts, extensive riverine operations did not emerge until after World War II, when a demoralized France chose to reassert colonial rule in Indochina. The French experience in the First Indochina War, which encompassed all of Indochina from the borders of China in the north to the canals that border Cambodia in the south, provided the United States Navy with some of its concepts for projecting seapower onto Southeast Asia's inland waterways. When the French began combat operations against the Viet Minh, Ho Chi Minh's Communist military forces in Indochina, military leaders quickly grasped the significance of controlling the fertile Red River Delta in the north and the Mekong Delta in the South. These watery regions not only provided the bulk of the rice to the Vietnamese people, but also a haven for enemy forces to extract taxes from the poor peasants and a means to transport weapons, materiel, and manpower to critical locations for the Viet Minh's war against the French.

Prior to the first official salvos of the war in December 1946, the French Far East Naval Brigade successfully seized My Tho and Can Tho using river craft in October 1945. Recognizing the potential of the marriage between ground and naval forces, in November General Philippe Leclerc created the Naval Infantry River Flotilla to operate on the Mekong and Bassac rivers. This riverine amphibious unit later evolved into the *divisions navales d'assaut* (naval assault divisions) or *dinnasauts*, which the French deployed onto Indochina's rivers and canals throughout the conflict. These units were composed of American World War II landing craft varying in sizes and firepower. When the French withdrew their forces following the debacle at Dien Bien Phu, the South Vietnamese Navy adopted many of these craft and the tactics developed by the *dinnasauts*.[1]

The agreements reached at Geneva in 1954 officially terminated France's role in Southeast Asia and divided Vietnam into two halves. Separated by the 17th

A US Navy monitor leads two armored troop carriers down a canal during a patrol in the Mekong Delta, November 1967. (US Naval Historical Center)

Parallel, North Vietnam became the Democratic Republic of Vietnam, controlled by the Communists, and South Vietnam became the American-backed Republic of Vietnam. American naval personnel arrived in South Vietnam as part of the Military Assistance and Advisory Group and became conduits for supplies for the burgeoning VNN. When the MAAG assimilated into the Military Assistance Command, Vietnam in 1964, naval advisors, part of the Naval Advisory Group, not only provided logistical support to the VNN, but also actively advised South Vietnamese sailors and officers in combat. With the growing US naval presence in South Vietnam, interest in riverine warfare surfaced in Navy Department research reports, studies, US Naval War College theses, and MACV studies. All of these sources encouraged the development of a riverine force capable of countering Communist influence in the Mekong Delta and the remainder of the shallow waterways of South Vietnam.[2]

OPERATION *MARKET TIME*

As American involvement in the war waxed, it quickly became obvious that Communist forces were using the long and vulnerable coast of South Vietnam for the seaborne infiltration of supplies to the insurgent Viet Cong. In order to meet this threat, in 1965 the US established Task Force 115, the Coastal Surveillance Force, and inaugurated Operation *Market Time*. The plan called for a three-pronged barrier designed to intercept and interdict Communist supply vessels, and included both air surveillance and naval patrols in an effort to seal the coastline. Operation *Market Time* forces patrolled nine "sectors covering the 1,200-mile South Vietnamese coast from the 17th parallel to the Cambodian border and extending forty miles out to sea."[3] These forces intercepted trawlers en route from North Vietnam to Communist forces in the South. *Market Time* units also searched the myriad of coastal water craft, such as sampans and junks, that plied the waters off South Vietnam to impede smuggled Communist weapons and supplies and prevent them from reaching NVA/VC ground forces. Communist forces heavily relied on this seaborne infiltration to supply the insurgency with logistic support.

The workhorse of TF 115, the fast patrol craft or Swift boat, "was adopted from the Sewart Seacraft Company's vessel designed to ferry crews to offshore drilling rigs in the Gulf of Mexico."[4] The MK-1 Swift boat was 51 feet in length and had a draft of three feet six inches. It maintained twin .50 caliber machine-guns on top of the pilot house and one .50 caliber machine-gun mounted above an 81mm mortar aft. It displaced 19 tons, maintained a crew of five, and was powered by geared diesel engines which turned two propellers, giving this welded, aluminum-hulled craft a top speed of 25 knots. Between 1965 and 1966 over one hundred of these vessels were constructed. The following year, eight MK-IIs were produced with the same armament and propulsion, but with a length of 51 feet four inches and displacing 19.5 tons. With this armament, and capable of transporting ground troops, the Swift boat later served as a critical asset in riverine operations. While they did not totally seal off the South Vietnamese

coastline, the *Market Time* sea and air patrols achieved a great level of success, and threatened the viability of the critical Communist logistic network. As a result the Viet Cong shifted their focus away from the vulnerable waters of the open sea, to the numerous rivers and canals of IV Corps Tactical Zone. Thus the Communists sought to move supplies down the waters of the mighty Mekong River and its many tributaries, hoping to lose themselves amid the bustling river traffic that flowed through the narrow and shallow channels in the nearly 3,000 miles of wetlands that already served as a nearly inviolable Viet Cong stronghold.[5]

A US Navy river patrol boat cruises in an inlet in the southern tip of South Vietnam in search of craft carrying personnel and supplies to the Viet Cong, June 22, 1966. (US Naval Historical Center)

OPERATION *GAME WARDEN*

On December 18, 1965, US Navy leaders established the River Patrol Force, designated TF 116, to conduct Operation *Game Warden*. Naval leaders ordered *Game Warden* forces to curtail enemy infiltration and logistics on the Mekong Delta's major arteries, the Mekong, Bassac, Co Chien, Ham Luong, and My Tho rivers. The River Patrol Force was also tasked with patrolling the Long Tau Shipping Channel, which was the main water route to Saigon. This critical waterway meandered through the dense foliage of the Rung Sat Special Zone which provided an excellent refuge for enemy forces to attack ships. Because the

Operation *Game Warden*

PCF was unable to navigate all of South Vietnam's shallow waterways, *Game Warden* forces required a shallow draft, but still fast craft to begin extensive patrols. Primarily adopted from the Hatteras Yacht Company's design, the river patrol boat became synonymous with the River Patrol Force and additional riverine operations throughout South Vietnam. The MK-I PBR was 31 feet in length and had a draft of two feet two inches – except at high speeds, when the PBR drew just nine inches of water. Each PBR mounted twin .50 caliber machine-guns in a turret forward, port and starboard mountings for M-60 machine-guns and one 40mm automatic grenade launcher, and a single .50 caliber machine-gun aft. It displaced 14,500 pounds, maintained a crew of four, and was powered by geared diesel engines which propelled two Jacuzzi water jets, giving this fiberglass-hulled craft a top speed of up to 30 knots. In 1966, around 160 MK-I PBRs were constructed. The following year, 81 MK-II PBRs were produced with the same armament and propulsion, but with a length of 31 feet, 11 inches and displacing 16,000lb.[6]

Although command of *Game Warden* operations fell to NAG, by early 1966, US naval forces had primarily shifted to a direct combat role that necessitated the establishment of an operational headquarters within MACV. As a result, on April 1, 1966, Naval Forces, Vietnam was created. The commander of Naval Forces, Vietnam directed that *Game Warden* units be organized into river divisions that operated from various land bases at Nha Be, Cat Lo, My Tho, Vinh Long, Can Tho, Sa Dec, Long Xuyen, Da Nang, Binh Thuy, Tan Chau, Ben Tre, and Tra Noc, but also from landing ship tanks anchored in river mouths. Although these river units successfully patrolled and engaged the enemy on the major waterways, *Game Warden* forces were critically weakened by a lack of visibility. The rivers and tributaries of the Mekong Delta are often narrow and winding, and lined with thick foliage, which allowed Communist forces nearly unimpeded ability to travel on land and left the PBRs vulnerable to rocket attacks from VC forces dug into the undergrowth. The inability of *Game Warden* forces to deal with such threats led COMNAVFORV to recognize the need for the PBRs to have close air support during riverine operations. Initially, the River Patrol Force used detachments of Bell UH-1B (Huey) Iroquois helicopters deployed by the Army. On April 1, 1967, though, the Navy formed Helicopter Attack Light Squadron 3 (HAL-3), dubbed the Seawolves, composed of 24 Hueys dispatched earlier by the Army. Each Seawolf carried 14 2.75 inch rockets, a 40mm grenade launcher, either a quad of flex-mounted M-60 machine-guns or two 7.62mm mini-guns, two door-mounted M-60 machine-guns, sometimes a door-mounted .50 caliber machine-gun, and small arms. The Seawolves provided close air support and reconnaissance for *Game Warden* units plying the brown waters of South Vietnam.[7]

Although the Navy eventually codified tactics into tactical doctrinal manuals, initially *Game Warden* forces implemented tactics learned while on operations. The two most typical tactics were the day and night patrols which were dictated by the Rules of Engagement established by the South Vietnamese government. Initially, ROE dictated that *Game Warden* forces could only fire upon targets that had engaged them first. Later, these ROE permitted *Game Warden* forces to engage fleeing craft. The ROE were typically forwarded to *Game Warden* forces directly or attached to operation orders from NAVFORV. Because of this, "adherence to the latter meant constant updates and revisions to ROE. Although not technically tactics, the parameters established within ROE directly affected tactics."[8] Typically, on day patrols, the PBRs would operate in pairs staying within radar range and usually midstream. When encountering a sampan or junk, the crews maneuvered their craft at an angle that permitted most of the PBR's array of weapons to be fixed on the approaching craft. In addition, the crews attempted to not moor alongside the suspicious craft, and the PBR not conducting the investigation of identification cards and search of the craft would be in a position to provide cover fire against the two banks as well as the suspect craft. Night patrols were somewhat different, because all civilian vessels were under a curfew issued by the South Vietnamese government. This meant that any water craft discovered active at night was considered an enemy target. Operating in pairs as on day patrols, the two-boat unit would approach at high speed, then, when within range, the crews would turn on searchlights, thus illuminating the suspicious contact, and direct all the passengers to come into the open. If these orders were not heeded, the patrol officer had permission to fire on the non-complying target. Another night tactic was to cut the engines, then drift onto the bank and wait to ambush those who broke the curfew: enemy personnel moving in the jungle close to, or attempting to cross, the waterway.[9] This meant that the enemy found transiting logistics to its forces more difficult as everywhere they ventured on South Vietnam's major waterways US Navy and VNN craft patrolled the brown water. Even if *Game Warden* forces were not present when the enemy began moving men and supplies, TF 116 or VNN units could suddenly appear and impede enemy operations.

THE MOBILE RIVERINE FORCE

The River Patrol Force, like Operation *Market Time*, achieved considerable success interdicting the insurgents' lines of communications in the Delta. However, lacking a ground component, the River Patrol Force remained quite vulnerable to enemy attacks launched from shore. Additionally, COMUSMACV and COMNAVFORV agreed that to make a true difference in the course of the war in the Delta, American ground forces would have to actively seek out and eliminate enemy ground forces on land as well as interdict their supplies afloat.

In early 1967, these leaders established TF 117, the Mekong Delta Mobile Riverine Force, also known as the Riverine Assault Force, to accomplish this task. After selecting the ground component, the US Army's 2nd Brigade of the 9th Infantry Division, the MRF was divided into Mobile Riverine groups Alpha and Bravo, with each group maintaining two squadrons and each squadron containing two river assault divisions. The ground components performed search-and-destroy operations once ashore, implementing typical army fire and movement tactics, using the MRF flotilla as their fire support and extrication elements. Two command and communications/control boats, which were converted World War II mechanized landing crafts or LCM-6s, became the MRF's flagships. The spoon-bowed CCBs had radar and radios to maintain contact with all of the river craft and operated as command posts for the naval and ground forces. Each CCB's armament consisted of two M-60 machine-guns, one 20mm cannon, and two .50 caliber machine-guns aft, with a .50 caliber machine-gun and 40mm cannon in a turret forward.

The squadrons' battleships, known as monitors, were heavily armored spoon-bowed LCM-6 conversions similar to the CCBs. Five monitors were in each squadron and mounted two .50 caliber and M-60 machine-guns and one 20mm cannon aft, an 81mm mortar amidships in a pit, and a 40mm cannon and .50 caliber machine-gun in a turret forward. Some of the monitors mounted flamethrowers forward to incinerate enemy positions and were referred to as "Zippos." Other river craft, "dubbed "douche boats," were equipped with high-pressure water jets that could disintegrate enemy positions, including cement bunkers. The "douche boat" also performed an originally unanticipated support function: its water jets easily gouged out wet docks to expedite on-the-scene repairs for damaged river craft. Both the CCB and monitor were 60 feet long, displaced up to 75 tons, and had a draft of three and a half feet. Powered by geared diesel engines which turned two propellers, both of these craft could make up to eight knots. The principal craft of the MRF were the 26 armored troop carriers. The ATCs were also converted LCM-6s, but were 56 feet long and had a draft of three and a half feet. They were armed with a 20mm cannon, two .50 caliber machine-guns, and either four .30 caliber or M-60 machine-guns and could accommodate 40 combat troops. Each ATC displaced 66 tons and was powered by geared diesel engines that turned two propellers, giving this craft a top speed of eight and a half knots.

Assault support patrol boat (ASPB), damaged by North Vietnamese action in the Mekong Delta area, June 1968. The crew is returning fire while attempts are made to keep the boat afloat. (US Naval Historical Center)

Specially converted ATCs served as the brown-water fleet's tankers, helipads, and medical aid stations. The MRF's minesweeper and destroyer was the assault support patrol boat. Unlike the PCF and PBR, which the Navy adopted from civilian designs, the ASPB was specifically modeled for the River Assault Force. The ASPB was 50 feet long, had a draft of three feet, nine inches and was armed with a 20mm cannon in a turret forward, two 40mm grenade launchers, one .50 caliber machine-gun amidships, and an 81mm mortar and .50 caliber machine-gun aft. Displacing 28 tons, the ASPB was powered by geared diesel engines that turned two propellers, giving this unique craft a top speed of 15 knots.[10]

To conduct search-and-destroy operations in the Mekong Delta, the MRF operated from bases ashore and afloat. The major land facility at Dong Tam was originally a marshy area which both services' construction units dredged and filled to create the land upon which the base was built. This location provided a logistical area and headquarters for the 2nd Brigade, 9th Infantry Division. To provide flexibility on South Vietnam's major waterways, NAVFORV created the Mobile Riverine Base which was composed of two tugs, two LSTs, one salvage craft, one landing craft repair ship, two barracks ships, and one barracks barge. To further enhance the capabilities of the MRF to adapt to enemy movement, the Navy developed the Mobile Support Base, constructed from four ammunition pontoons, which provided all of the same facilities as the MRB.[11]

THE RIVER WAR IN I CORPS: OPERATION *GREEN WAVE* AND TASK FORCE CLEARWATER

As *Game Warden* forces began the arduous, yet successful, duties of engaging and curtailing insurgent movement on IV CTZ's major waterways, COMNAVFORV decided to enhance MACV's military presence in South Vietnam's northern provinces in I CTZ. In September 1967, COMNAVFORV deployed ten PBRs to operate on the Cua Dai River. Based at Da Nang, these patrol craft conducted Operation *Green Wave* for three weeks, until circumstances dictated abandoning this endeavor. Although unsuccessful, this strategic consideration intrigued the Commander, III Marine Amphibious Force, Lieutenant General Robert E. Cushman. He believed that NAVFORV PBRs could be deployed to escort South Vietnamese and American shipping on the Perfume and Cua Viet rivers. With this in mind, Cushman asked COMNAVFORV if there were adequate resources to dispatch to I CTZ to accomplish this task. COMNAVFORV responded by directing two PBR sections north to escort and patrol Naval Support Activity Da Nang logistic supply craft. Following a brief period of organizational restructuring, NAVFORV's PBRs began operations on January 9, 1968. Luckily for the US Marine Corps, the Navy's river units started operations before North Vietnamese forces assaulted and laid siege to Khe Sanh in late January. After construction of landing strips at the terminus of the Cua Viet River, this inland waterway became the logistical lifeline to the besieged Marines. When the Tet Offensive began on January 31, the deputy commander of MACV requested additional naval assets from NAVFORV. To facilitate MACV's request, on

An inshore patrol craft passes the city of Ca Mau, January 1969. (US Naval Historical Center)

February 24 COMNAVFORV ordered additional naval forces, including LCMs and Seawolves, to I CTZ. These assets became Task Force Clearwater, and were divided into the Dong Ha River Security Group and the Hue River Security Group.[12]

SEALORDS

Following the Tet Offensive, COMUSMACV wanted more vigorous naval operations conducted in the Delta. To accommodate this request, COMNAVFORV carefully scrutinized and analyzed operations *Market Time* and *Game Warden*, as well as MRF reports noting that the NVA/VC forces had once again altered strategy. With the catastrophic defeat of its forces during the Tet Offensive, the NVA/VC had stepped up infiltration of men and supplies from nearby Cambodia, yet they had shifted their movement away from the major rivers onto South Vietnam's smaller and less traveled waterways.

On October 18, 1968, COMNAVFORV assimilated units from TFs 115, 116, and 117 into TF 194 for the barrier interdiction campaign known as Southeast Asia, Lake, Ocean, River, Delta Strategy, or SEALORDS for short. SEALORDS was created to blockade infiltration routes along the Cambodian border and to seek out enemy forces along these smaller canals and streams. Materials infiltrated

SEALORDS campaign

from Cambodia fell into four principal logistical groups: "arms and ammunition, foodstuffs, medical supplies and raw materials"[13] and, to a small degree, men. The enemy forces carried this materiel across the border on their backs, or on relatively inconspicuous water craft such as sampans. COMNAVFORV directed the MRF to launch "riverine strike sweeps," Coastal Surveillance Force PCFs, dubbed *Market Time* Raiders, to perform "river incursions," and *Game Warden* components to execute "riverine raiding and blocking operations."[14] Once SEALORDS was established, some of the MRF units were assimilated into the new barrier strategy. Following the inception of Vietnamization, the MRF was disestablished in August 1969.

SEALORDS built on the success of previous riverine operations by transplanting the experience and skills gained by the task forces onto the smaller waterways and canals to frustrate NVA/VC forces. However, the units used in SEALORDS were now operating on many virgin waterways where the NVA/VC's hegemony had never been contested, forcing the adoption of new tactics in new hostile environments. Also, SEALORDS forces had more latitude than *Game Warden* units had had in 1966 and 1967, because the government of South Vietnam had less strict Rules of Engagement by 1968.

On November 1, 1968, the SEALORDS campaign began when TF 194 units transported, then provided fire support for, a battalion of the Vietnamese Marine Corps along the Rach Gia–Long Xuyen Canal in Kien Giang Province. On November 5, COMNAVFORV established Operation *Search Turn*. The area of operation comprised the Cai San Canal to the Bassac River, then northwest along this river to the Rach Gia–Long Xuyen Canal, then down this canal to the Gulf of Thailand.[15]

Next, COMNAVFORV looked toward the border waterways of Cambodia and South Vietnam, where insurgent forces were filtering into IV CTZ practically uncontested. COMNAVFORV ordered initial transits on the Rach Giang Thanh River and Vinh Te Canal to determine the feasibility of permanent operations on these inland waterways. Following these forays, coupled with the successful implementation of *Search Turn*, COMNAVFORV established Operation *Foul Deck* on November 21, 1968. In February 1969 COMNAVFORV changed the name of *Foul Deck* to *Tran Hung Dao*, in recognition of the Vietnamese contribution to the combined effort. At 105 yards wide, the Rach Giang Thanh River was navigable by PBRs year round. The Vinh Te Canal was about 40 miles long and its width averaged about 38 yards. Throughout monsoon season, from June to November, both the canal and river were easy to navigate. During the dry season, however, from mid-April to early June, the water level of the canal dropped below one foot, meaning sampans were the only possible means of transit. Due to these limitations, COMNAVFORV assigned PCFs from TF 115 to the Rach Giang Thanh River and directed TF 116 PBRs to the Vinh Te Canal.[16]

After the creation of these two barriers, on December 6 COMNAVFORV expanded SEALORDS with the establishment of Operation *Giant Slingshot*. COMNAVFORV directed TF 194 forces to operate on the Vam Co Dong and Vam Co Tay rivers which flowed on either side of the Cambodian territory known as the Parrot's Beak. Due to its close proximity to Saigon, the capital of South Vietnam, the insurgents used this region extensively to infiltrate men and supplies. The right portion of the slingshot began north along the Vam Co Dong (east) River, near the capital of Tay Ninh province, Tay Ninh, and ran to the Vam Co River south near Ben Luc. Within this portion of the AO, the winding Vam Co Dong extended about 93 miles through a flat, primarily rice-producing region scattered with only a few coffee, sugar, and tea plantations. Although a small number of hamlets were located along the river, most of the populace north of Ben Luc lived in Tay Ninh City. The water level in this river was regulated by the rainy season, from May to October, and was not affected by the Mekong's overflow. This permitted PBRs to transit the river year round. The left element of the slingshot began on the Vam Co Tay (west) River, at the capital of Kien Tuong province, Moc Hoa, and went south. The Vam Co Tay, from its confluence to the Cambodian border, was about 102 miles in length. Like the river's eastern branch, the Vam Co Tay meandered and constantly changed shape. The densely covered nipa palm-lined banks created poor visibility for the PBRs, which could navigate the river throughout the year. When the rains caused excess flooding from the Mekong, the overflow seeped into the northern canals and finally drained through the Vam Co Tay. In the dry season, the southern portion of the river dropped to a depth of 13 feet, while the northern portion dropped as low as three feet.[17]

Although *Giant Slingshot* forces patrolled fairly efficiently, the LSTs and YRBMs could not travel the entire length of the rivers to provide support for the river boats. Therefore, a new means of support was needed for these forces. An initial PBR and support base established at Ben Luc was the jumping-off point for the new logistical concept. This new concept was the Advance Tactical Support Base, which NAVFORV constructed on or near existing American or South Vietnamese bases. Several of the ATSBs had afloat elements as well as shore installations. The afloat portions of the bases consisted of hollow ammi pontoons which supported living quarters and housed water and fuel. These pontoons could be towed in a short time to any location for support or to evacuate for mortar, rocket, or artillery attacks. To defend these bases, naval personnel erected concertina wire along the perimeter, scattered with Claymore mines and trip flares, as well as machine-gun pintles. Some utilized surveillance equipment such as radar and magnetic sensors to detect enemy movement. COMNAVFORV developed *Giant Slingshot* ATSBs along the Vam Co Tay at Tan An, Tuyen Nhon, and Moc Hoa, while ATSBs were established at Ben Luc, Go Dau Ha, and Tra Cu on the Vam Co Dong.[18]

In late 1968, COMNAVFORV examined the SEALORDS campaign and recognized that a gap existed in the barriers along the Cambodian border. In order to close this brown-water wall, COMNAVFORV established Operation *Barrier Reef* on January 2, 1969. Located in the Plain of Reeds, the new barrier connected *Giant Slingshot* and *Tran Hung Dao*. In March, COMNAVFORV enhanced this operation by splitting it into *Barrier Reef East* and *Barrier Reef West*. *Barrier Reef East*'s AO extended from Tuyen Nhon along the Lagrange and Ong Lon canals to Phuoc Xuyen, while *Barrier Reef West* units patrolled the Dong Tien Canal and the remainder of the Ong Lon Canal to the Vam Co Tay River. The Lagrange–Ong Lon Canal intersected other canals in the region, each averaging 27 to 55 yards in width. The banks were primarily composed of silt and clay at a fairly steep height, but navigable year round by PBRs.[19]

With the growing number of naval operations associated with SEALORDS, COMNAVFORV recognized that the Seawolves were able to provide only limited close air support for the riverine forces. The Navy wanted an aircraft that could provide more ordnance than the Seawolf, but still maintain the accuracy of the helicopter gunship. NAVFORV noticed that the Air Force and Marines used the OV-10 Bronco as an observation platform; if outfitted with an array of weapon systems, this small prop-driven aircraft could fill this attack role. In April 1969, NAVFORV activated Navy Light Attack Squadron 4 (VAL-4), dubbed the Black Ponies. The Bronco's fixed wing allowed quick reaction time, and its armament included four M-60 machine-guns, two 19-round 2.75-inch rocket pods, eight 5-inch rockets, a Mark IV 20mm gun pod and a SUU-11 7.62mm gatling gun. The 14 Black Ponies dispatched to the Delta were divided into two detachments, one based at Binh Thuy to aid SEALORDS forces and the other at Vung Tau to support the RSSZ and *Game Warden* units. Each detachment consisted of five aircraft, with an additional pool of four at Binh Thuy for maintenance purposes. The Black Ponies provided a 24-hour scramble alert status to support Navy units requiring air cover or suppression fire throughout the Delta day and night. In addition, VAL-4 launched preplanned attacks and provided an overhead cover role for river craft plying virgin waterways or for ground troops.[20]

The .50 caliber machine-gunner of a PCF peppers an enemy position along the shore of a Lower Ca Mau peninsula river in April 1969. (US Naval Historical Center)

Wanting to continue the aggressive posture of the Navy's in-country forces, COMNAVFORV analyzed incoming data and noticed that, although SEALORDS was working, some parts of South Vietnam still lacked an American or South Vietnamese naval presence. After careful consideration, COMNAVFORV selected the Cua Lon River, located on the Ca Mau peninsula in An Xuyen province, which still provided a sanctuary for NVA/VC forces. More importantly, the South Vietnamese Navy commander wanted to take back the peninsula because of the economic value of the area to South Vietnam. On June 27, 1969, COMNAVFORV activated Operation *Sea Float*. Slightly different than the ATSBs of *Giant Slingshot*, *Sea Float* was a mobile advance tactical support base built on 11 ammi pontoons, which permitted the entire facility to be anchored on the Cua Lon River rather than constructed on the riverbank. Extensive security precautions, which included general quarters drills, and the placing of machine-guns, rockets, and mortars all over the *Sea Float* structure, were necessary to ensure the endeavor's safety in this

Gunners aboard two PCFs watch for enemy ambush positions as their craft tow a third damaged by enemy fire during an incursion in the Lower Ca Mau peninsula, April 1969. (US Naval Historical Center)

hostile environment. COMNAVFORV assigned many different river craft to this MATSB. Eventually, *Sea Float* forces required additional logistics, which prompted COMNAVFORV to establish Operation *Solid Anchor* on the riverbank near *Sea Float*. COMNAVFORV ordered *Sea Float/Solid Anchor* forces to search all sampans and water traffic on the Cua Lon and Bo De rivers. However, water craft were not taken under fire unless the occupants committed hostile actions toward the friendly forces. COMNAVFORV granted permission to completely destroy existing bunkers or structures of known enemy construction. In September, COMNAVFORV established another operation on the Ca Mau peninsula to continue the Navy's offensive presence on the southernmost tip of South Vietnam. Named *Breezy Cove*, this operation was located on the Ong Doc River north of *Sea Float*. Similar to *Giant Slingshot*, COMNAVFORV created an ATSB and deployed one RIVDIV, a monitor, two ASPBs, and three ATCs.[21]

Basic riverine tactics on the barriers mirrored those for *Game Warden*. Initially, and according to ROE, SEALORDS forces used day and night patrols. The day patrols sailed up the waterways and inspected water craft, fired on suspicious craft, and returned fire from the banks when enemy forces chose to engage the American brown-water craft. Eventually, American forces abandoned night patrols in favor of the Waterborne Guard Post. This shift stemmed from the realization that in the remarkably low ambient noise level of the waterways at night, PBRs and PCFs, no matter how quiet they may have been at low RPMs, still generated too much noise. Therefore, it was exceedingly difficult to surprise suspected or known NVA/VC positions. The WBGP tactic usually involved two river boats. While moving in midstream, the second boat captain would slowly shut down his engines and drift into the bank. The lead boat would proceed a short distance ahead then it also would shut down and drift quietly into the bank. The boats would then loosely tie up so the current would not carry them away. The crews then waited to ambush anyone they detected moving on the water or land near the ambush site. The NVA/VC's tactics were dictated by their need to retain a certain level of mobility within the SEALORDS AOs; US and VNN forces denied them this. NVA/VC forces attempted to avoid contact whenever possible. In the early months of the SEALORDS campaign, the NVA/VC relied on typical water traffic to shield their movements during the day. As SEALORDS daytime patrols became more frequent and checks of routine traffic more effective, it became apparent to both sides that the best time to infiltrate was under the cover of darkness. Usually the boats on nighttime WBGPs were taken under fire only when NVA/VC troops wanted them to break their guard posts, or when they were unaware that US/RVN patrols were in the area. The US/RVN forces benefited from the infiltration units' lack of familiarity with the area, which caused them to rely upon locals to guide them. Increasing familiarity with the AO and with NVA/VC methods of operation led to a continued process of fine-tuning SEALORDS tactics.[22]

The US Navy's index for measuring the effectiveness of the SEALORDS barriers, and all of the other operations, was the number of firefights. In a time when body count was the rule of the day, it is easy to understand why the Navy selected this form of documentation; however inadequate this measurement may appear, it nevertheless offers some data for interpretation.

The most obvious interpretation is that the recorded firefights proved the barriers were working, because they at the very least disrupted infiltration. When US/RVN forces engaged NVA/VC forces, whether sampans or infantry, it cost the North Vietnamese time, manpower, and supplies. For example, if a PCF came upon a hostile sampan and it was taken under fire, the contents of the craft would either be destroyed or captured. This in turn would cause a chain reaction in the NVA/VC supply system. The units for whom the supplies were destined would not receive the shipment because it was intercepted; thus they would probably experience shortages of ammunition and/or other supplies. This, in turn, would result in a reduction of the tempo of local operations or possibly the postponement of planned attacks.

As early as March 1969, reports corroborated this hypothesis. COMNAVFORV recorded that "each month new reports are received which tell of [enemy] infiltration attempts which were abandoned when a patrol craft suddenly appeared around the river bend." Intelligence reports also stated that a large backlog of supplies had accumulated in Cambodia and was not being moved. Further, infiltration routes had been changed to avoid SEALORDS forces. Such changes were noted on the *Giant Slingshot* barrier in September 1969. The North Vietnamese, responding to the threat of WBGPs and extensive patrolling of the waterways at night, in desperation, attempted many crossings during the day, when sampan traffic was at its height.[23]

By November 1969, the Cambodia-based logistics logjam caused by SEALORDS was creating serious problems in North Vietnamese planning for the winter–spring campaign. This was confirmed in January 1970 by a surrendered NVA soldier who claimed "that a 300-man unit which needed weapons and supplies had been prevented from crossing in to the 'Seven Mountains' area for several weeks by Navy forces." Clearly, the SEALORDS interdiction forces cut down infiltration of North Vietnamese supplies, but success depended upon inter-service cooperation.[24]

Aid from various ground forces also strengthened the barrier operations. The cooperation of friendly forces such as Civilian Irregular Defense Groups, Provincial Reconnaissance Units, Regional Forces/Popular Forces, National Police Field Force, Vietnamese Marine Corps, ARVN units, the US Army and SEALs, was vital to NAVFORV. These forces could be carried by water craft or helicopter for specific operations or routine clear-and-sweep patrols. Ground units provided the manpower the SEALORDS campaign needed to search out the enemy in their base camps, and to provide additional security to ATSBs, MATSBs, and other naval facilities in the Delta.

While firefights suggest the flow of North Vietnamese logistics was being disrupted, the primary measure for the effectiveness of SEALORDS was the pacification of the delta. For pacification to take hold, an increased level of

security was necessary. This meant that the local population could freely move on the waterways and in the land area itself. To provide a brief examination, three provinces are used to demonstrate the progress of pacification. They were chosen because one, Kien Tuong, was part of a SEALORDS operation, *Giant Slingshot*; one, Phong Dinh, was located southwest of the Border Interdiction Campaign; and the last, An Xuyen, was on the southernmost tip of South Vietnam on the Ca Mau peninsula, where Operation *Sea Float* was located.

The device used by the Central Intelligence Agency and MACV to measure pacification was the Hamlet Evaluation System. The HES was created by the CIA to estimate the level of security in the thousands of hamlets in South Vietnam. American district advisors filed monthly reports estimating the level of security in each hamlet. Each hamlet was assigned a letter designation: A, B, C, D, E, or V. If a community was under full Communist control it was assigned the letter "V," while an "A" designation signified a hamlet not under Communist control which

A crewman of a river patrol boat scans the river bank during patrol on the Alfa Canal, February 1969. (US Naval Historical Center)

included "an elected leadership living calmly in the village which was equipped with a school, local defense unit, a bustling market, and confidence." Designations "B" through "E" indicated an incremental decrease in security levels. William Colby, deputy to COMUSMACV for Civil Operations and Rural Development Support (and later director of the CIA), pointed out that these rankings could fluctuate as a result of the advisors' failure to visit all the hamlets in a district, or the inexperience of new advisors. Therefore "the figures were merely indicator trends, not absolute reports of the facts." The HES reports provide a suggestion of the level of security and the general success or failure of each province's pacification program.[25]

Prior to Operation *Giant Slingshot*, there was practically no freedom of movement on Kien Tuong's waterways. After only one month of operations, a district advisor reported that PBR patrols had disrupted some forms of NVA/VC activity. In May 1969, district advisors reported that Navy operations had curtailed movement and infiltration on province waterways. Corroborating these reports was the fact that no hamlets in the province were classified "V," and only a handful were in "D" and "E" categories. From April to December 1968, Kien Tuong averaged about 57 hamlets in the top three (ABC) security ratings, while the number of less secure "DE" hamlets fluctuated from three to 31. By March 1970, no hamlets were classified in the lower "DE" rating, all 61 hamlets registering in the more secure "ABC" categories. This assessment remained

Table 1: The number of A, B, C, D, E and V hamlets for Kien Tuong province

Month/Year	A*	B*	C*	D/E	V
April 1969	–	52	–	31	0
May 1969	–	53	–	8	0
July 1969	–	56	–	4	0
August 1969	–	56	–	4	0
September 1969	–	58	–	3	0
October 1969	–	58	–	3	0
November 1969	–	58	–	3	
December 1969	–	58	–	3	0
January 1970	0	37	19	5/0	0
February 1970	1	47	10	3/0	0
March 1970	7	36	18	0/0	0
April 1970	3	42	16	0/0	0
May 1970	7	40	14	0/0	0
July 1970	1	58	2	0/0	0
February 1971	1	50	10	0/0	0
March 1971	0	54	7	0/0	0
April 1971	1	58	2	0/0	0
May 1971	1	56	4	0/0	0
December 1972	3	53	5	0/0	0

*Only ABC totals are given for 1969. These are listed under "B."

unaltered through December 1972 (see Table 1). These statistics strongly suggest that the local population felt safe enough to accept GVN control and to separate themselves from NVA/VC influence.[26]

Phong Dinh was an interior province not bordering Cambodia, and thus experienced a situation somewhat different from Kien Tuong. In April 1969 the number of "ABC" hamlets numbered 119, while 71 were classified "V" (see Table 2). The number of hamlets classified "ABC" rose gradually throughout 1969, reaching 160 in January 1970. These remained static until July 1970; by December of the same year the province averaged about 90 percent "ABC" hamlets. While the number of more secure hamlets increased, the "V"-ranked hamlets began a steady decline from 43 in July 1969 to 31 in February 1970, then to a record low of eight in July 1970. A rise in "ABC" hamlets was desired, but a decline in "V" hamlets might more effectively prove that the NVA/VC was losing its control in this and other provinces.[27]

A Zippo monitor uses one of its flame throwers to clear overgrowth from a river bank, May 1970. (US Naval Historical Center)

Table 2: A, B, C, D, E and V hamlets for Phong Dinh province

Month	A*	B*	C*	D/E	V
April 1969	–	119	–	79	71
May 1969	–	120	–	72	53
July 1969	–	130	–	63	43
August 1969	–	131	–	72	32
September 1969	–	147	–	59	29
October 1969	–	166	–	43	28
December 1969	–	166	–	47	21
January 1970	27	90	43	42/2	33
February 1970	27	94	42	41/2	31
March 1970	27	82	51	45/2	30
April 1970	26	82	51	52/5	23
May 1970	26	83	48	61/4	16
July 1970	32	85	43	55/	8
December 1970			90.2% ABC hamlets		

*Only ABC totals are given for 1969. These are listed under "B."

Table 3: The number of A,B,C,D, E, and V hamlets for An Xuyen province

Month	A*	B*	C*	D/E	V
April 1969	–	62	–	44	195
May 1969	–	70	–	34	74
August 1969	–	81	–	35	60
September 1969	–	92	–	28	56
October 1969	–	106	–	24	45
December 1969	–	114	–	18	44
January 1970	0	69	33	25/3	46
February 1970	0	72	35	21/3	45
March 1970	0	84	35	13/0	44
May 1970	0	78	33	22/2	41
July 1970	9	78	34	17	33
December 1970	13	90	32	26	15

*Only ABC totals are given for 1969. These are listed under "B."

An Xuyen province offered convincing examples of the success of pacification in the Delta. Prior to any SEALORDS operations in the area, the Ca Mau peninsula experienced almost total NVA/VC control. When the Coastal Raiding and Blocking Group began transits onto the waterways, the NVA/VC responded fiercely. To increase the impact of US Navy and VNN forces on the area, COMNAVFORV established *Sea Float* in June 1969. Reaction to this new base, in a once hostile area, came immediately. Only a few months earlier the district advisor recorded nearly 200 "V" hamlets and only 62 "ABC" hamlets. In August, shortly after the creation of *Sea Float*, "V" hamlets had dropped to 60 while "ABC" hamlets jumped to 81 (see Table 3). Then in September 1969, *Breezy Cove*, on the Song Ong Doc, was activated to augment and strengthen US/GVN presence in An Xuyen. By December 1970, "V"-rated hamlets had dropped to 15, while "ABC" hamlets had risen to 135, with 103 in the "AB" categories.[28]

These three provinces provide a basis for understanding the final outcome of the SEALORDS campaign. Although only three provinces have been examined in detail, available statistics indicate levels of security and pacification increased throughout the Delta. To one of the commanders within the SEALORDS campaign, another, more easily observable proof of pacification was the general flourishing of the countryside. In the early 1960s, NVA/VC territory appeared brown and dead; following the establishment of SEALORDS, "from the cities [one] could see, as time went on … it was getting greener and greener the farther [one] went out." When this commander returned in 1971, he noted that the Delta was green as far as the eye could see. He credited this development to the presence of the Navy, which kept the NVA/VC from bothering the local populace; thus they were "able to grow their crops and move [them] to market without being harassed by anybody." In the judgment of COMUSMACV, the SEALORDS campaign made a major contribution to the pacification of the Delta. For the first time, COMUSMACV added, a screen had been provided to disrupt the flow of Communist supplies from Cambodia, and this greatly reduced US/GVN casualties.[29]

Regardless of the Navy's new, aggressive posture, domestic political ramifications stemming from the Tet Offensive forced President Lyndon B. Johnson to begin withdrawing American forces from South Vietnam in late 1968. When Richard Nixon won the 1968 presidential election, he promised to terminate the conflict in Southeast Asia. Nixon's administration dubbed the withdrawal program "Vietnamization," which entailed transferring the war back to the South Vietnamese military. The Navy responded with Accelerated Turnover to the Vietnamese, or ACTOV, to accomplish this goal. COMNAVFORV ordered the chief of NAG to begin training South Vietnamese personnel so that the VNN's manpower would slowly assume all of the duties of SEALORDS and the other naval components under NAVFORV. The US Navy constructed training bases and special schools to accelerate the turnover of NAVFORV duties to the VNN. When NAVFORV stood down in 1973, the VNN became solely responsible for all operations on South Vietnam's inland waterways.

America's role in the Vietnam War had ended. The US Navy's brown-water personnel began as advisors and ended as advisors. NAVFORV's operations and campaigns, such as *Game Warden* and SEALORDS, proved successful in pacifying the Delta and other regions of South Vietnam. The local population which once traveled in fear on the canals and rivers of South Vietnam could easily transit these waterways and conduct commerce vital to the economy of the Republic of Vietnam. A testimony to the successes of the US Navy and VNN came after the collapse of Saigon in 1975, when the Delta was the last location to fall to Communist forces.

Chapter 13

Tactics in a Different War
Adapting US Doctrine

Gordon L. Rottman

Search and destroy, tunnel rats, sappers, walking point, cloverleafing, busting brush, jitterbugging: none of these phrases were found in the US Army field manuals of the 1960s, despite President Kennedy's 1961 message to Congress, "We need a greater ability to deal with guerrilla forces, insurrections, and subversion. Much of our effort to create guerrilla and anti-guerrilla capabilities has in the past been aimed at general war." Therefore, when the first US Army and Marine infantry units arrived in Vietnam in the spring of 1965, doctrine and tactics were still very much oriented towards general warfare, such as that in Europe and Korea – facing large conventional forces fighting in the open.

The US armed forces were obligated to be fully prepared for a large-scale conventional war, possibly involving nuclear and chemical weapons. Limited wars of liberation and guerrilla warfare were of only secondary concern to America's vast military machine. Despite the enormous effort funneled into technology to counter guerrillas, ranging from seismic sensors to people-sniffers to night vision devices, for almost the next decade infantrymen underwent training focused nearly exclusively on conventional tactics. It is true that conventional tactics provide the basis for counterinsurgency, or any other specialized tactics. It is also true that a degree of Vietnam-oriented training was incorporated into the training of soldiers, NCOs, and officers. Nevertheless, this training barely scratched the surface of real circumstances in Vietnam. The infantryman fresh out of the training pipeline had never undertaken significant ambush and counterambush training; manned night listening posts; conducted cross-country movement and land navigation in a company column; practiced off-loading and loading a helicopter under combat conditions; or for that matter, even ridden in a helicopter. Cultural orientation was virtually unheard of.

Once on the ground, units adapted and coped. Operational summaries and lessons learned studies were available, but for the most part units developed their own tailored tactics and techniques. As far as could be seen, there was little

Crossing linear obstacles such as streams, roads, gullies, and Arc Light bomb-blasted swathes of craters and tangled debris slowed movement and caused an accordion stop-and-go effect. (US Army)

While terrain conductions in Vietnam were extremely rugged, there really is no terrain feature that is not passable by motivated and well-led infantry. Here an ARVN company crosses a flooded stream with all its equipment. (Nguyen Ngoc Hanh)

standardization, in some instances even between companies of the same battalion, much less between divisions in Vietnam.[1]

This dearth of standardization, owing to a lack of specific tactical doctrine at higher echelons, is understandable. While the environment that troops fought in in Vietnam is commonly portrayed as jungle, this was actually seldom the case. South Vietnam ranged from the mountainous north through the winding valleys, rolling hills, and plains of the Central Highlands, dense triple- and double-canopy forests further south, and the sprawling canal- and river-coursed marches of the Mekong Delta. All of these terrains included forests, large bamboo-covered locales, and fields of man-high elephant grass. These forest stands were dense and difficult to navigate, but not as difficult as near-impenetrable rain forests or jungles. There were, of course, areas that were very nearly impassable. Hills, ridges, gullies, ravines, swamps, exceedingly dense underbrush, and bamboo could be found almost anywhere, and all of these greatly hampered foot movement. Visibility was limited, but in most instances a soldier could see two to four of his comrades when deployed on line, and often more of his unit was visible. Some 20–30m of relatively unobstructed visibility was common.[2]

The climate had just as much effect on small-unit tactics as the terrain. It was hot, humid, and either too dry or too wet. There always seemed to be one extreme or another – insufficient water for drinking or too much, causing immersion foot or other problems – depending on whether it was the November–April dry season (or northeast monsoon) or the June–October wet season (or southwest monsoon). Soldiers claimed that there were three seasons – wet, dry, and dusty – occurring at hourly intervals. Heat exhaustion could affect even the well-acclimatized, and hospitals complained that most of the wounded required extensive rehydration. Mosquitoes, dry land and water leeches, ants, scorpions, centipedes, snakes, and flies were troublesome, but more nuisances than hazards. Malaria, dengue fever, dysentery, diarrhea, and "undiagnosed fevers," were common ailments. Stories of snake and tiger attacks were more often just that – stories – and seldom occurred.

The brutal climate was aggravated by a diet of C-rations and infrequent B-ration hot meals, long hours of "busting brush," lack of sleep because of 50 percent alert (one man off, one on for two-hour intervals), daily stress, and perpetual alertness, even when no contact was made.

Another reason tactics and techniques varied widely between units was the emphasis placed on initiative in leaders and the American leadership concept that can be simply described as, "Tell me what you want done and I'll do it, but don't tell me how to do it." This was a very American notion, but admittedly, many commanders kept a tight rein on their subordinates, micro-managing maneuvers and operations. Even then, it was still left up to company commanders and platoon leaders how they deployed their men when moving and engaging in combat. This flexibility was essential, as aspects of terrain, vegetation, and NVA/VC deployment and actions were highly variable. No amount of detailed specified movement formations or tactical maneuvers could accommodate all the variables of any given situation.

Visibility was a major factor in small-unit tactics. It was essential for soldiers to see their nearest comrades, and some degree of intra-visibility was also crucial among sub-units within the same company. Even with the benefit of radios at squad level, visual contact was critical to maintain orientation, prevent gaps from developing, coordinate fires and maneuver, and prevent friendly fire incidents. Once soldiers were receiving fire and had gone to ground their visibility was even more limited, often to no more than a few meters. This of course made control of any unit more difficult, and delivering effective return fire.[3]

Contact was typically initiated at a range of 12–20m. This negated the long-range advantage of weapons intended for a European battlefield. The sudden close-range engagements in Vietnam required a high volume of automatic weapons and high-explosive-fragmentation fire. This was provided to infantrymen in the form of the semi-automatic 7.62mm M14 rifle, and from 1966/67 the semi- and full-auto 5.56mm M16A1 rifle. The M16A1 had a major impact on tactics. Regardless of the weapon's flaws (less rugged than its predecessor, need for painstaking cleaning, minor mechanical problems – mostly corrected), its light and compact design was ideal for the chaotic terrain, its light ammunition allowed much more to be carried, and its high rate of fire proved beneficial. However, the light bullet lacked effective penetration through dense brush, bamboo, and foxhole parapets. The introduction of the M16A1 meant that the rifle squad lost its 7.62mm M14A1 automatic rifles. Therefore, the platoon's two 7.62mm M60 machine-guns assumed even more importance, because of their effective penetration and high volume of fire.

Another weapon that proved highly valuable was the 40mm M79 grenade launcher. This light, compact weapon fired high-explosive-fragmentation rounds at point and area targets, as well as multiple-projectile ("buckshot") rounds and a wide variety of pyrotechnic signals. The two M79s per squad meant the loss of two rifles; grenadiers were armed with pistols for self-defense, contributing nothing to squad firepower.

Soldiers were burdened with extra ammunition, three or more days' rations, demolitions, Claymore mines, trip flares, ammunition for other platoon weapons, and pyrotechnics. In a conventional environment, soldiers are resupplied daily. In Vietnam, it was often every three to six days.

There was no need for antitank weapons, as they were of little use for defeating bunkers because of their excessive weight, and their heavy and bulky ammunition. The platoon's two 90mm M67 recoilless rifles were placed in storage, as were most company and battalion jeep-mounted 106mm M40A1 recoilless rifles. Some 106mms were used in firebases as anti-sniper weapons and for harassing fire. Only the light, compact single-shot, disposable M72 light antitank weapon saw continued use as an anti-sniper and anti-bunker weapon.

Mortars were another weapon that saw much less use than previously. They were invaluable for fire support base defense, but the weight and bulk of the weapons and their ammunition meant that they very seldom accompanied units in the field. Mortars, to be effective, require a large ammunition supply. In some instances, though, mortars were flown into night locations for defensive fires and illumination, and flown out again in the morning.

Visibility in forests was extremely limited, no more than 20m, and often much less. Even this squad pausing in a clearing within a bamboo grove could see no more than 10m. (US Army)

FIRE SUPPORT

Another aspect of the war that reduced the need for mortars was the availability of field artillery. As the battlefield was not linear, there were no front lines facing each other; no enemy fixed positions; no headquarters, artillery positions, supply dumps; none, in fact, of the targets found on a conventional battlefield. The US/ARVN forces' problem was to place fire into large areas because of the widely dispersed enemy, resulting in "free fire zones." The NVA/VC were faced with the opposite, to place firepower into a small area – US/ARVN bases. The US/ARVN forces had artillery designed for accurate fire in a conventional war, while the NVA/VC had less accurate rockets and mortars delivering only moderate firepower. Instead of artillery forces battering away at each other, ample artillery was available to support units making sporadic contacts scattered over an area of operations. This was accomplished by establishing a series of mutually supporting fire support bases. These might be atop hills and ridges, or on flat ground or set in clearings suitable for helicopter landing zones. Firebases might be maintained in a semi-permanent status, protecting lines of communication and population centers. Despite this, many were established for short periods, weeks or just a few days, to support specific operations. Such bases typically held one or two batteries (one each 105mm and 155mm howitzer batteries or just only two 105mm howitzers), protected by a rifle company.

Heavier and longer-ranged artillery was available in the form of 175mm guns and 8-inch (203mm) howitzers. The heavy artillery was usually located at semi-permanent firebases containing an artillery battalion-plus, or at brigade or division bases. The "one-oh-five," or "dime-nickel" as it was called on the radio, provided most fire support, a "contact fire mission." It was accurate to seven miles and had a high rate of fire. The "one-five-five" or "dime-nickel-nickel" was excellent for suppressing suspected NVA/VC positions not in immediate contact with US/ARVN forces, blanketing a ridge line for example. It was not as accurate as the 105mm, but laid down some heavy metal to nine miles. It was also ideal for harassing and interdiction fire. Harassment and Interdiction was delivered at random times and locations, usually at night when NVA/VC forces were moving, targeted at areas where troops might be moving or bivouacked. The "one-seven-five" was also used for H&I and long-range suppression. It was strictly an area fire weapon[4] as it sacrificed accuracy for long range – 20.3 miles. The "8-incher," on the other hand, was considered the most accurate of all artillery pieces, consistently hitting point targets at 10.4 miles. However, its 200-lb rounds could only be delivered to units who were beyond 100m of NVA/VC forces. Naval gunfire support, available in coastal regions, was not as accurate as field artillery fires; it required a precautionary safe distance of 600m.

American units simply did not operate out of range of their 64 artillery battalions.[5] Given this fact, the ability to heliolift artillery into remote clearings and quickly establish a firebase provided a great deal of flexibility in the support of infantry operations. Since the infantry were likewise rapidly inserted at different points throughout an area and the artillery almost as quickly emplaced to support them, NVA/VC forces were kept off balance and had to be prepared for an American thrust from any direction. This required a wide dispersal of both personnel and supply dumps (caches). However, the NVA/VC had the ability to move and concentrate forces rapidly.

Artillery targets were pre-planned to support an operation. The unit would know the locations or projected locations of supporting firebases, and the calibers of the guns. This allowed the unit to plot targets capitalizing on the different weapons' capabilities and positioning; it was preferable to assign targets to batteries which were on a gun-to-target line perpendicular to its route or deployment line. This is why multiple firebases were generally scattered throughout an area of operations. All gun positions were set up to allow 360 degrees of fire.

Pre-planned targets were plotted along roads and trails, around clearings and villages, on likely enemy ambush sites, at stream crossing sites, and in areas where the enemy might assemble for attacks. At night, companies established defensive positions, referred to as "remain over night" positions. Final defensive concentrations (DEFCON) were plotted to surround the RON with a wall of steel. Fires were plotted on possible NVA/VC assembly, attack, and supporting weapons positions, as well as withdrawal routes.

Air support was almost as responsive as artillery support. Close air support, in the form of fighter-bombers, could be on-station within an hour, often less owing to flights being held in holding patterns over "hot" areas. Attack helicopters – gunships – also provided valuable fire support. A light-fire team, with a gunship and a light observation helicopter, or a heavy-fire team, with an additional gunship, provided accurate rocket, machine-gun, and grenade fire.

CAS could accurately deliver 500-lb, 750-lb, and 1,000-lb general-purpose and napalm bombs. To facilitate CAS, it was essential that US/ARVN positions be marked; and even so, cluster bombs were seldom used close to US/ARVN troops, because of the danger of the wide dispersal of bomblets. Infantrymen could not talk directly to CAS fighter-bombers; coordination was conducted through an airborne forward air controller aboard a Birddog spotter aircraft. He was equipped with radios allowing direct contact with infantrymen and fighters, and would orbit over an assigned area relaying requests for CAS. When the strike flight arrived on-station he would already have identified the location of the US/ARVN unit and marked the target with white phosphorous rockets. He then served as an air traffic controller to vector the "fast-movers" in and relay corrections from the "ground-pounders."

Colored smoke grenades and rocket-propelled smoke streamers and star cluster flares – "pop-ups" – were used to mark US/ARVN ground positions for aircraft. This may seem a simple matter, but their use involved numerous considerations. "Smokes" were available in red, yellow, green, violet, and white. Red was restricted to signaling that a unit was in contact or to warn off landing helicopters because of enemy fire. White was not used, as it might be confused with WP rounds marking NVA/VC targets. Green was generally not very visible against the terrain, and yellow could be hard to see in dried grass and dust. Violet

was mostly used against dried-out vegetation, and yellow amongst green vegetation. When marking a US/ARVN location, the aircraft were never told what color smoke would be used. The ground unit notified the aircraft that it was popping smoke and the pilot announced what color he saw, with the ground unit confirming. It was not uncommon for the NVA/VC to monitor radio traffic and try to confuse aircraft by popping smoke of the same color. Flares, tracers, handheld strobe lights, colored marker panels, and signal mirrors were also used to mark positions to aircraft.

CAS normally could not be brought in as close to US/ARVN positions as artillery, and it was essential that attack runs be made perpendicular to the unit's long axis, rather than overhead or toward it. However, helicopter gunships could deliver their comparatively light ordnance much closer to US/ARVN positions. Another advantage of using the gunships was that the ground unit could talk directly to the LOH accompanying them, or even to the gunships themselves.

For successful fire support actions, reliable radio communications were necessary. This could not be guaranteed in Vietnam's rugged terrain. Rifle companies used the AN/PRC-25 or 77 radio. These were basically the same radio, the latter having a fitting for a secure voice scrambler and refinements that meant it was more reliable and needed less power. However, it did not have a longer range

Fire support, especially by field artillery, was critical. Rifle companies often operated independently and typically numbered only 80 men. The terrain they operated in meant that if they were engaged they could not expect rapid back-up. Helicopter-delivered troops could only reinforce them if landing zones were nearby and there was always a danger that the enemy might ambush them. (US Army) than the "25" as was often assumed. The man-packed radio was carried at company and platoon levels, and was heavy at 23.5lb with battery. Batteries lasted a day or less, depending on how much transmitting was done, and they were always part of resupply deliveries. When on the move the radio-telephone operator used a three-foot tape antenna with a planning range of five miles. However, a ten-foot "fishing pole" antenna could be fitted for longer range when necessary, or a "jungle antenna" could be used. This was a locally fabricated wire-frame affair hoisted on a tree limb. Range was erratic, as was contact, especially from beneath triple-canopy growth and in the mountains. Helicopters were used as airborne radio relays, and relay sites were established on top of hills. The rugged terrain and weather seriously hampered communications, and the hot weather reduced battery life.

It is important to note that any soldier, regardless of rank or duty position, could request and coordinate fire support, artillery, CAS, or helicopter support, and all infantrymen were trained to do so. This was a key factor in saving units when casualties among leaders mounted, or small patrols or outposts made contact with NVA/VC forces.

AIRMOBILITY

The helicopter was arguably the single most important component affecting tactics in Vietnam. The French possessed only 54 helicopters in all of Indochina. By contrast, operating in Vietnam in 1968, the US Army fielded almost 130 aviation companies.[6]

Helicopters principally served in an air assault role, delivering troops onto the battlefield at unexpected times and locations. They also provided command and control over widely dispersed ground units. This allowed commanders to "orchestrate" their units and concentrate their forces. A battalion commander could be on-station (that is, orbiting overhead) over a unit in contact within minutes. This had its good and bad points. The company commander on the ground focused on fighting, while his airborne commander coordinated fire support in all its forms and redirected other units to include inserting troops by helicopter to attack, encircle, or block the enemy force. He also directed resupply and medical evacuation (medevac) flights – also know as "dust-offs." On the downside, airborne commanders sometimes lost an appreciation of the ground, its obstacles to movement, and time–distance factors. Some tried to micro-manage the fight from above, not only unable to appreciate the ground commanders' difficulties, but also unable to even see them.

The airmobile assault could deliver a company or battalion onto a remote LZ with unprecedented speed, over-flying difficult terrain and NVA/VC troops, arriving from unexpected directions, and enhancing the element of surprise. How fast combat power could be built up – "piling on" – depended on the size of the LZ, weather, distance from the pick-up zone, the number and type of available choppers, and the rated lift capability that day.[7]

The size of the LZ determined how many helicopters could be landed at once. Common weather conditions affecting airmobile operations included fog, monsoon rains, and thunderstorms, which could cancel flights or force detours and delays. Since there were never enough helicopters available to lift a complete large unit, multiple lifts were usually made. The distance between the PZ and LZ, plus refuel time, were major factors in planning an air assault as was the time necessary to build up the force on the ground. Most assaults were conducted by UH-1D/H Huey helicopters carrying a limited number of troops. Once the LZ was secured, larger CH-47 Chinooks could lift three times the number as a Huey.

Helicopters also provided rapid reinforcement of units in the field or endangered bases, withdrawing and repositioning troops; undertaking visual reconnaissance, medevac, and resupply; moving critical equipment and repair parts from one location to another; and a myriad of administrative movements. Besides providing unprecedented speed and mobility, helicopters reduced the number of convoys exposed to one of the NVA/VC's main offensive means, ambush. The armed UH-1B/C-series and AH-1G Cobra attack helicopters contributed aerial fire support to the infantry's airmobile maneuver capability.

The 1st Cavalry Division (Airmobile) pioneered the concept of airmobility, and was the first US division committed to Vietnam.[8] The division possessed sufficient helicopters to simultaneously lift one-third of its infantry and artillery. It also possessed significant aerial rocket artillery capabilities. The division quickly demonstrated both the value of airmobility and the tactical flexibility it offered. In 1969, the 101st Airborne Division was converted to airmobile. The Americal Division also received an aviation group, giving it almost the same capabilities as an airmobile division. All other divisions possessed only a single aviation

Unprecedented tactical mobility and speed of deployment was provided to US/ARVN forces by helicopters; however, aimobility was not the answer to all tactical problems and its limitations had to be recognized and accommodated. These troops are boarding a 228th Chinook Aviation Battalion for transport into action near An Khe. (US Army)

With a sufficiently sized landing zone and enough aircraft, a rifle company or even a battalion could be inserted on the ground within minutes. The VC and NVA had to undertake extra precautions and actions to counter this capability. Here men of 'B' Troop, 1st Squadron, 9th Cavalry, 1st Cavalry Division assault onto a mountain top overlooking the A Shau Valley. (US Army)

battalion, but numerous non-divisional aviation units provided support. Every infantry unit became as proficient in airmobile operations at all levels as the dedicated airmobile divisions. The Marine Corps had already possessed a significant helicopter capability to exploit the vertical flank in the conduct of amphibious operations. They too became just as adept in airmobile operations.[9]

An airmobile operation[10] involved more than merely flying vast numbers of infantrymen into a jungle clearing. The launching of such an operation first required an objective. Often this involved the attempt to entrap an NVA/VC unit known to be in the area. US conventional doctrine focused on seizing terrain to dominate the battlefield, not on enemy units. As with much else, this doctrine had little applicability in Vietnam. The NVA/VC was mobile and agile. They seldom fought to retain terrain, and US/ARVN forces would not occupy terrain that they had cleared for any length of time. The objective was to locate and destroy NVA/VC forces. Such an operation might involve several battalions, with companies being inserted over a broad area. Specific units were assigned to secure hilltops for surveillance; occupy blocking positions in valleys, on known trails and natural movement routes; and attack suspected NVA/VC base camps and other sites. Some units would sweep through suspect areas, and others would cordon and search villages. Timing and coordination were critical to ensure that NVA/VC forces were trapped. Prior to this, firebases would be established around the area, and others would be set up once the operation had been launched. Prior to establishment of firebases, air cavalry and long-range reconnaissance patrol units would have scouted the area for signs of NVA/VC activity.

The unit to be airlifted assembled on an airstrip or a jungle PZ lining up by "stick" – the number of men that could be lifted in a chopper that day. Companies were divided into sticks of men. In theory a Huey could carry 11 troops, but in practice, various factors meant that often only six to eight could be carried. They would fight as sticks if the LZ were under attack, reorganizing into squads and platoons when able. "Lifts" would take off, escorted by gunships, and return for the rest, sometimes ominously carrying wounded.

Artillery and air strikes blasted the LZ as the choppers approached. The coordinated fires were lifted and gunships swooped in, rocketing and strafing the wood lines around the LZ. In some areas, suitable LZs were scarce to none. Heavy bombs might be used to blast a hole in the jungle, and engineers with chainsaws and demolitions rappelled in to clear a one-ship LZ. In some instances, river sandbars were used. Other areas were dotted with any number of clearings. Local VC were often posted at clearings to report the arrival of Americans, and sometimes NVA/VC units were situated to cover LZs. They became adept at assessing where US/ARVN forces might be inserted, especially once an operation commenced. This was not difficult, given the scarcity of LZs in most areas, and the earlier terrain assessment.

The troops disembarked from the choppers rapidly and established a perimeter, which thickened as additional lifts arrived. Once the force was complete, it moved out to its objective. A security force might be left to hold the LZ, which served as a supply and medevac base if other LZs were scarce. It could also become a firebase.

There was always the risk of a "hot" LZ resulting in a pitched battle centered around the usually exposed area, with incomplete units on the ground, and vulnerable helicopters attempting to insert additional troops, provide fire support, resupply and medevac. In worse case situations, they might also be extracting ground elements. Other ground forces might be inserted in the vicinity of such a fight to attack from a different direction, or engage withdrawing NVA/VC forces. Artillery and air assets would be redirected, and even relocated, to support the developing battle.

When NVA/VC forces did disengage and withdraw, airmobile forces undertook pursuit, a traditional cavalry mission. This entailed occupying blocking positions, inserting forces to intercept withdrawing troops, and repositioning artillery. Pursuing ground forces could also be kept resupplied, or leapfrogged ahead of the enemy. Brigades and divisions often maintained airmobile alert forces on standby to exploit situations and reinforce units in contact.

THE GRUNT'S WAR

Regardless of command and control capabilities, reasonably reliable communications, the latest weapons, massive fire support, the speed and flexibility of heliborne operations, and responsive logistics, the infantryman's war in Vietnam was fought at a low, savage level. It was not a war of grand maneuvers, sweeping offensives across a country, or liberating cities. The front line was the direction in which one was facing. Booby traps inflicted a huge death toll, but were not scattered at random through the forests. They were found around US/ARVN bases, along routes patrols might follow, and on approaches to NVA/VC bases and villages. There may have been an annual MACV campaign plan, and division- and brigade-level operations, but to the infantryman it was a war fought by companies. It was a small-unit war of endless patrolling, ambushes, and close-range firefights of the most vicious kind.

The American infantryman, the "grunt," was the primary element that made any tactic effective, but he had to be backed by fire support, provided tactical mobility, and sustained by an effective logistics system. (US Army)

One dynamic affecting tactics was unit organization. It was not uncommon for companies of normally 180 men to field 80 or even fewer troops. Normal 44-man rifle platoons could number only 20-plus men.[11] Besides a scarcity of replacements, at any one time troops were on sick call, R&R, detailed for firebase security, etc. More often than not, a platoon's three ten-man rifle squads numbered seven or eight. The 11-man weapons squad often ceased to exist, with the two machine-guns integrated into rifle squads and the 90mm recoilless rifles not needed. Platoon sergeants and squad leaders were typically a grade or two lower than authorized. Tactics were kept simple, owing to inexperienced leaders and the dense terrain, which restricted intra-visibility. It was common for a platoon to be organized into two larger squads and when contact was made, the platoon leader and platoon sergeant each took direct control of a squad. The company weapons platoon virtually disappeared. Usually possessing only two or three 81mm mortars, they were more often held in firebases.

Battalion organization changed as well. Infantry battalions consisted of a headquarters company with service and combat support elements, and three rifle companies. Battalions added a fourth rifle company and a combat support company by late 1968. This fourth rifle company provided a company to defend the battalion firebase without reducing the number of companies conducting field operations. The battalion scout platoon, assigned to the combat support company, often operated separately, providing an additional maneuver element.

Terrain and climate as factors affecting tactics have been discussed. The enemy of course was a dominating factor. NVA regulars and VC main forces were quality

Armor, such as this M48A3 tank, was another form of fire support. Many thought armor would be unusable in Vietnam, but much of the land on which actions were fought could accommodate tanks and armored personnel carriers. Five (two Marine) US tank battalions, ten mechanized infantry battalions, and nine armored cavalry squadrons served in Vietnam. (US Army) units, although the latter were mostly filled with North Vietnamese, even before the 1968 Tet Offensive decimated the VC. These forces were conventional light infantry. They were not guerrillas, although they employed many guerrilla techniques. From 1965 on, Vietnam was a low-intensity conventional conflict. The enemy may not have employed armor, artillery, or aircraft, but operations on both sides were divisional or multiple-division actions. It is a mistake to call NVA and VC main force troops guerrillas merely because they employed unconventional tactics. Local VC guerrillas supported them and this was still an aspect of the war, but for the most part American soldiers were fighting light conventional forces which had adapted their tactics to the terrain and the firepower and mobility of US/ARVN forces. Local force VC and their supporters conducted harassing actions and sabotage; collected intelligence; disseminated propaganda; collected "war taxes" from locals; impressed locals for labor; served as guides; and provided other support to transiting NVA and main force units.

While actions were mostly small in scale, operations were managed at brigade and division levels, with multiple battalions deployed and orchestrated by higher headquarters. Battalions deployed their companies and platoons widely, in an effort to find dispersed NVA/VC forces. These "minor" contacts could grow into larger actions as the division marshaled its forces. Additional companies and even battalions were airmobiled into the area; artillery was brought to bear; and attack helicopters were dispatched. It was not uncommon for a handful of men closely engaged on the ground to be supported by unseen hundreds more.

NVA/VC forces were able to disperse their forces widely and amass them for sudden attacks, often in unexpected areas; then rapidly disengage and return to favored sanctuaries in Cambodia and Laos. Because of overwhelming US/ARVN firepower, mastery of the air and the airmobility that provided, control of major population centers and lines of communication, the VC/NVA fought as low-profile light infantry. They were not able to employ armor and artillery until near the war's end, when they gained the operational initiative. The rugged forested terrain provided the necessary concealment to move, conduct attacks, and withdraw. Out of necessity, they employed comparatively light weapons.

US/ARVN forces employed sweeps, cordon and search, and search-and-destroy tactics to locate elusive NVA/VC forces and their hidden supplies and materials. "Search-and-destroy" operations were later redesignated "search-and-clear" to counter negative associations.[12] This was countered by wide dispersal of forces and supply dumps, concealing dumps, establishing bases in remote areas, caching supplies in hidden sites, and hiding personnel and facilities in tunnels. Covert reconnaissance and hit-and-run attacks on US/ARVN installations and outposts were common. Ambushes, raids, small-scale harassing attacks, and road mining were the primary means of engaging superior forces. These attacks were executed only when the NVA/VC had the tactical advantage. They would strike and withdraw, seldom allowing themselves to become decisively engaged. Another tactic was to hug US/ARVN units: that is, to engage and move in as close as possible. The terrain usually made this a necessity, but it was also absolutely

Search and Destroy

Fire support bases and combat operations bases supported a combination of ground sweeps, reconnaissance operations, and airmobile insertions against an NVA base area.

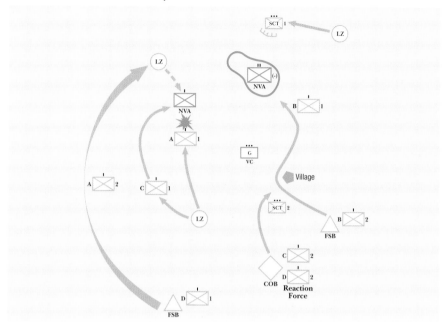

essential for survival and a successful engagement; closing in to 50m or less negated US/ARVN artillery and air strikes.

How a unit moved was critical. Conventional tactics called for units of any size to move in geometric formations, with their three sub-units arrayed in orderly formation. The terrain and vegetation in Vietnam seldom permitted this, and such formations were also slow and noisy, with each man breaking his own trail. Units moved instead in columns, generally one, two, or sometimes three parallel columns in close proximity, within visual contact.

The denser and rougher the terrain, the less practical multiple columns became. Each column was preceded by a point squad, but its rear had to remain in visual contact with the main body. A rear guard was necessary, and might occasionally establish an ambush on its back-trail in the event the column was being tracked. Flank security was important, but often impractical. Individual flankers had difficulty keeping pace with the column and maintaining visual contact. A very real concern was flankers being mistaken for the enemy. Movement was slow owing to the terrain and climate, the necessity for cautious movement, and heavily burdened troops. A column often moved in an accordion effect as it encountered obstacles: gullies, streams, and denser brush belts. One common technique was for a company to halt in an area where the NVA/VC was active, with its platoons a few hundred meters apart. Platoons would send out squads to the flanks to search a wider area, then loop back to the platoon position in a "cloverleaf."

In the middle of the forest, ambushes were rare. The NVA/VC could seldom accurately predict the course a US/ARVN unit would take. Contacts in the jungle

Because of the limited penetrating power of the 5.56mm M16A1 rifle, and the lack of squad automatic weapons, the rifle platoon's two 7.62mm M60 machine-guns became key weapons. (US Army)

were more often chance contacts, with two moving elements colliding. In some instances, one element might detect the other first, and establish a hasty ambush or launch a flank attack. Contacts were at close range and without warning.

If the NVA/VC troops did not begin to break contact soon after engagement, then US/ARVN forces inferred that the intent was to inflict as much damage on their unit as possible and a plan existed to counter this. The NVA/VC preferred to avoid decisive prolonged engagements with US/ARVN forces, owing to their ability to respond rapidly with firepower and airmobile reaction. A unit receiving fire from a village, for example, from which the NVA/VC did not soon withdraw, were most likely being drawn into a trap. Inexperienced and aggressive commanders could easily find themselves surrounded by a superior force. As experience was gained, commanders learned to be more wary. They would maneuver to the flanks after fixing the NVA/VC with fire, and maintain an awareness of their own flanks and rear. Rather than immediately attacking an apparently inferior NVA/VC force, they took the time to call for artillery and air support, and await the arrival of reinforcements and blocking forces. In the same vein, the NVA/VC knew that if the US/ARVN force had not fallen for the bait, they would soon have to break contact or they themselves would become trapped.

NVA/VC ambush techniques were well developed and well planned. Most were executed on roads against large US/ARVN units, on foot or aboard vehicles. Battalion- and even regimental-size ambushes were executed. Supply convoys were desirable targets, as they allowed the opportunity to capture supplies. The L-shaped ambush was the preferred technique. The "L"'s long arm was positioned parallel

Ambush theory and practice

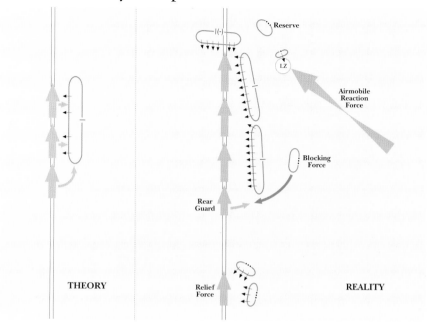

with the column's axis to pour in fire from the flank. The short arm crossed the column's path and would halt it with enfilading fire down its axis. The ambush force would typically establish a reserve behind the "L"'s long arm to respond to counter-attacks the ambushed column might launch. It might also be committed against the column's rear. Often another ambush or blocking force was positioned further down the column's path from the direction it had come. This force might have been held well back from the road to prevent its detection as the column passed. It would then move up to the road to block escapees from the kill zone and ambush a relief force. The fact that the relief force would almost undoubtedly be ambushed often prevented one from being dispatched for some time. An airmobile reaction force would be launched if available and had the best chance if landed in the right place and used aggressively. Often, though, LZs in the area were ambushed. Other airmobile forces might be inserted to block the enemy's withdrawal routes.

Whether on foot or mounted, a force moving on a road deployed tactically, with wide dispersal between vehicles and sub-units. An advance guard preceded the main body by no more than three minutes, flank security was deployed (though this was not always possible), and a well-armed rear guard followed. The commander was positioned well forward, but not with the point. For motorized columns, armed and armored escort vehicles were distributed throughout the convoy. Ambushes could be defeated, but it was more successful to employ effective tactics and techniques to counter them before they were initiated.

The NVA/VC followed Mao Tse-tung's doctrine: "When the enemy advances, withdraw; when he defends, harass; when he is tired, attack; when he withdraws, pursue."[13] They also followed the principle known as "one slow, four quick steps." The slow first step involved a thorough and deliberate planning process, with each action rehearsed and every fighter familiar with his duties and the terrain. The four quick steps of execution were: 1) move into the area of operations rapidly; 2) assault immediately before discovery; 3) withdraw from the battlefield swiftly with captured weapons and materials as well as casualties; and 4) scatter into small groups and move to secure areas.

US/ARVN units often developed specialized tactics for specific enemy and terrain situations in their areas of operation. These often fell into disuse when the unit moved to a new area with different situations, and new techniques were developed. In the Mekong Delta, the VC built bunker lines along canals, often backed by open rice paddies. Once these positions were discovered, either through aerial reconnaissance or when the VC ambushed water traffic, artillery-supported airmobile platoons would be rapidly inserted in numerous points around the area to "seal" it in a process called "jitterbugging." "Bushmaster" operations saw the insertion of platoons into sparsely vegetated areas in the last two hours of daylight. The platoons occupied ambush positions after dark to interdict VC movement. A central command post was established and the platoons were within 750m of each other to provide mutual support if one initiated an ambush. An offshoot of the "bushmaster" was "checkerboard." Platoons would remain for a full day after their first night in one location, and then break down into squads occupying a grid square pattern. Squads moved continuously from square to square to locate small enemy elements. Since it was only a two-day operation they carried only ammunition and rations, allowing them to move easily. There were scores of such tactical innovations developed by units throughout the war.

CONCLUSION

Small-unit tactics and techniques were in a constant state of evolution in Vietnam, as both sides sought to gain advantages and lessen their own limitations. As with so many other aspects of the war, there was no firm and fast doctrine.

Vietnam was a war of innovation and adaptation. It was like no other war the US had fought, owing to the ideologically and politically charged atmosphere. There were advances in technology, new weapons, and equipment, but there was no real US doctrine to support this kind of war in this kind of land. US military doctrine was oriented toward a large-scale, conventional, European war of massed, armored maneuver forces, possibly seeing the use of nuclear, biological, and chemical weapons. Only lip service was given to creating an extensive new doctrine at all echelons that was specific to Vietnam. Instead, in the American tradition, the military sought a quick solution to problems through technology and field innovation.

New weapons and equipment were rushed through development. Some items of equipment were almost desperate attempts to find a fast and easy solution to a problem, and had little chance of meeting expectations. Others were valuable enhancements, especially in the areas of communications, mobility, and firepower, but they too failed to change the balance or the outcome. In the area of tactics, innovation, initiative, and improvisation actually had more success. Units freely developed their own tactics and techniques by trial and error. Even with the 365-day rotation and a constant turnover in leadership at all echelons, units were able to develop, implement, and improve their tactics and techniques. It was an evolutionary process, though. The NVA/VC changed its own tactics, or found ways to counter American efforts.[14]

Successful tactics and techniques were not always passed on to other units, even within the same division. It was recognized that what worked for one unit in a given area, against a local enemy force, might not work someplace else. Change had another benefit: it kept the NVA/VC off balance. And it was necessary for survival: the enemy would rapidly inflict damage on any unit allowing itself to establish routines and patterns.

Much of what was learned was never codified, never integrated into an effective counterinsurgency doctrine. The raw basics and essentials of small-unit actions and techniques, however, were absorbed into and adapted to fit conventional doctrine. From airmobile operations to the gritty details of patrolling and ambushing, innovations dating from the Vietnam War can be seen in today's small-unit tactics, and still serve soldiers and Marines well.

Fighting in Vietnam was not just limited to jungles and rice paddies. Infantrymen experienced in close combat on terrain with limited visibility sometimes had to immediately adapt to fighting in major urban areas. This trooper is sweeping with his platoon into the imperial city of Hue in 1968. (US Army)

Chapter 14

The "Living-Room War"
Media and Public Opinion in a Limited War

Professor Daniel C. Hallin

The role of the media has provoked as much contestation as any aspect of the Vietnam War. Richard Nixon, for example, reflecting on the war in his memoirs, placed the blame for the failure of American policy squarely on the media:

> The Vietnam war was complicated by factors that had never before occurred in America's conduct of a war... [T]he American news media had come to dominate domestic opinion about its purpose and conduct... In each night's TV news and each morning's paper the war was reported battle by battle, but little or no sense of the underlying purpose of the fighting was conveyed. Eventually this contributed to the impression that we were fighting in military and moral quicksand, rather than toward an important and worthwhile objective. More than ever before, television showed the terrible human suffering and sacrifice of war. Whatever the intention behind such relentlessly literal reporting of the war, the result was a serious demoralization of the home front, raising the question whether America would ever again be able to fight an enemy abroad with unity and strength of purpose at home.[1]

James Reston, columnist, and, during part of the Vietnam War, Washington bureau chief for *The New York Times*, wrote, "Maybe the historians will agree that the reporters and the cameras were decisive in the end. They brought the issue of the war to the people, before Congress or the courts, and forced the withdrawal of American power from Vietnam."[2]

Supporters of American intervention in Vietnam portray the media as the villains of the story: they turned the public against the war, and caused the collapse of American will to prevail in a war that could and should have been won. Opponents portray the media as the heroes: they told the public the real truth about a failed policy, and forced policymakers to face reality. The former

Representatives of American news media interview US soldiers during action in South Vietnam. (TRH Pictures)

view has been widely held within the American military, and the latter among journalists. As sharply as they disagree in political terms, however, the two camps in this debate share many assumptions about the media's role in the war: that media coverage of the war was broadly critical of US policy, and that the media played a decisive role in turning the public and policymakers against it. They also generally share the assumption that television brought the "true horror of war" into people's living rooms, changing the dynamics of public opinion in wartime forever.

This conventional wisdom about the media and Vietnam is deeply rooted in American collective memory and widely disseminated around the world. Historians, however, have been essentially unanimous in rejecting it. Public support for the war in Vietnam did, of course, decline dramatically over the years, and in a democracy it is inevitable that this will have profound effects on policy. And of course the media play a central role in the dynamics of public opinion. But their role was both more ambiguous and less decisive than the conventional wisdom holds. In the early years of the war, through about 1967, media coverage was for the most part supportive of American policy in Vietnam. The media's role must be considered as part of the process by which policymakers mobilized support for a foreign conflict about which the public was initially very skeptical. Later, coverage shifted to include more political controversy and more "negative" information, and this is certainly part of the story of how the US came to reverse course on the Vietnam War. The historical evidence does not, however, suggest that the media were the central, driving force of this change. The media themselves shifted in response to other powerful forces in American society, and in many ways must be seen as more followers than leaders in the American change of course in Vietnam. This is particularly true of television, which – despite the common view that the camera brought the true horror of war into the American living room – was particularly cautious about reporting that might generate controversy with audiences, advertisers, or government; it presented a mostly sanitized view of the war; and was relatively slow to venture into more critical reporting.

THE DEBATE BEGINS

The Vietnam War first entered the American public sphere in a significant way in 1963. By modern standards, the US presence there was already quite large, growing to 17,000 advisors by October 1963. In the context of the Cold War, however, a deployment of this magnitude did not generate much political debate, and Vietnam was very much a backwater in media terms, with only a handful of reporters present in Saigon representing the wire services, news magazines, and a very few newspapers. A major media controversy did develop during this period, one which would establish the lines of debate about the media and Vietnam that would prevail down to the present. The controversy was touched off by the battle of Ap Bac in January 1963. US advisors expressed their frustration to reporters that South Vietnamese troops had performed poorly, and critical reports appeared in much of the US press. Later that year,

The Buddhist monk Thich Quang Duc immolates himself on a Saigon street corner in 1963 in protest at the attempted suppression of the rights of Buddhists in South Vietnam. (TRH Pictures)

attention shifted to the political conflict between President Ngo Dinh Diem and opponents of his regime. This conflict produced the first iconic media image of the war – the photo of a Buddhist monk immolating himself in protest of the Diem regime – amid a good deal of critical reporting about the Diem government and the progress of US policy. Officials in the Kennedy administration accused the journalists of undermining US policy with this reporting, and launched a public-relations offensive which involved encouraging established journalists to go to Vietnam to counter the coverage of the young reporters stationed there. This led to some internal tension within the press, most notably at *Time* magazine, whose correspondents resigned after the magazine, owned by Henry Luce (who had strong opinions on US policy in Asia), criticized the Saigon press corps.

The events of 1963 are legendary in both versions – heroic and anti-heroic – of the conventional narrative of the media and Vietnam. The reality is a little less dramatic, however. First, media coverage in this period essentially reflected the views of US officers and officials, who became increasingly divided, both in Vietnam and in Washington, about whether the war was indeed going well, and whether to continue supporting the Diem government. It illustrates a general pattern media scholars would later confirm as a kind of law of foreign policy reporting: that significant critical reporting generally appears in the US media if and only if political elites are divided over policy.[3] Second, even the younger reporters responsible for the most critical reporting questioned the tactics, but not the basic premise, of US policy in Vietnam. David Halberstam of *The New York Times*, for example – who was the object of personal lobbying by President Kennedy, urging his removal by the paper – wrote in his 1965 book, *The Making of a Quagmire*:

I believe that Vietnam is a legitimate part of that global commitment. A strategic country in a key area, it is perhaps one of only five or six nations in the world that is truly vital to US interests.[4]

SELLING THE AMERICAN COMMITMENT

Vietnam largely faded from the news columns following the ouster of Diem. It reentered in August 1964 with the Gulf of Tonkin incident, and within a year would come to dominate the news in the new era of a media-saturated society. By mid-1964, it was clear to US policymakers that the war was indeed not being won in South Vietnam, and that a much more extensive and direct American role in the war would be necessary. This was politically delicate, however. President Johnson had been assuring the public that he would avoid sending troops to Vietnam, and opinion polls showed considerable uneasiness about the prospect of major war there. The administration downplayed the beginning steps of the "escalation" of American involvement, presenting them as retaliatory strikes (for instance following the Gulf of Tonkin attack) or as continuations of existing policy which did not require political discussion. This went on until July 1965, when Johnson finally called on the public to rally behind a major American commitment.

Media coverage generally accepted administration statements at face value during this period. Much of what was reported on the basis of official sources – like the occurrence of the second Gulf of Tonkin attack, to which the US ostensibly retaliated – turned out to be false or misleading, and this is a period in which the media clearly did not live up to the widely accepted ideal of a

The Associated Press photographer Huynh Thanh My covers a Vietnamese battalion pinned down in a Mekong Delta rice paddy about a month before he was killed in combat on October 10, 1965. (Empics/AP Photo)

"watchdog" press. This was true for two major reasons. First, the Cold War conceptual framework which guided administration policy in Vietnam was almost entirely taken for granted in American politics in this period, and this was true just as much among journalists as among other prominent political actors. Early in 1962, for example, *The New York Times* printed a big map across the Week in Review section with the heading "Communist Expansion in Asia Since the End of World War II – and the Military Situation in Vietnam." Nixon's comment about the media presenting the war with "little or no sense of the underlying purpose of the fighting" may have been true in 1971. For many years before, however, one of the media's principal functions was to explain the war to their readers within a narrative of US resistance to global Communist expansionism. Within this framework, alternatives to a policy of intervention were not really thinkable.

In the early 1960s, moreover, the professional routines of journalism centered around a particular understanding of "objective reporting" which assigned the journalists a relatively passive role. In practice, "objective" reporting meant reporting what was said by government officials without comment by the reporter. If officials were engaged in a policy debate, this would produce "balance." If not – and at this time the Johnson administration was united, and the Republicans not inclined to challenge the President on the war – it meant that the media were more or less transmission belts for official statements. The crucial decision to commit the US to a major war in Vietnam was thus made with relatively little public debate, and the Johnson administration was able to "manage" news coverage relatively effectively to ensure that this would be the case.

CHANGE TO A "LIVING-ROOM WAR"

Vietnam became a "living-room war"[5] from the middle of 1965, as American troops entered combat in large numbers. The press corps correspondingly surged from about 40 accredited correspondents in 1964 to about 400 by mid-1965. In 1964, in an effort to reduce tensions that had developed with the press corps, the US military had adopted a policy called Operation *Maximum Candor*. This initiative involved a greater effort to accommodate the media, through access to American forces and facilities, expanded briefings and other efforts to provide information. Reporters generally enjoyed considerable freedom of movement and access to US forces, though there were controversies over restrictions on access to air bases, and, increasingly, over the quality of information given in official briefings – over the policy, for example, of characterizing casualties in particular battles only as "light," "moderate," or "heavy." The imposition of censorship of the sort applied in World War II and part of the Korean War was discussed – many journalists themselves favored it – but rejected for a variety of practical and political reasons. It was replaced by a set of guidelines journalists were required to accept as a condition of accreditation, which restricted reporting of information that could affect operational security. Violations of these guidelines or controversies over their application were quite uncommon.[6]

Morley Safer reports on the
burning of a Vietnamese village
in 1965. (Photo by CBS Photo
Archive/Getty Images)

Morley Safer reports on the burning of a Vietnamese village in 1965. (Photo by CBS Photo Archive/Getty Images)

From the beginning, some critical and controversial reporting appeared in the press and television. Two occasions generated the greatest controversy. The first was Morley Safer's August 1965 report on the burning of the village of Cam Ne, which showed US Marines setting fire to the village with Zippo lighters, and included Safer's concluding comment: "Today's operation shows the frustration of Vietnam in miniature. There is little doubt that American firepower can win a military victory here. But to a Vietnamese peasant whose home means a lifetime of backbreaking labor, it will take more than presidential promises to convince him that we are on his side." The second was a series of reports by *New York Times* correspondent Harrison Salisbury, reporting on the effects of US bombing of North Vietnam, which questioned US claims that civilian casualties were minimal. These were relatively isolated reports however; Salisbury was attacked by many of his colleagues in the press, and nothing like Safer's report would appear in television over the next year or two.

For the most part, media coverage of the Vietnam War from 1965 through 1967 followed conventions of reporting established in World War II, and was neither critical in tone nor graphic in its depiction of combat. World War II reporting was based on two sets of reporting conventions. The first emphasized the "big picture," understood in terms of military strategy. The second emphasized the individual American soldier, and had a human interest rather than an analytic perspective. The same conventions dominated Vietnam reporting. The lead story in a newspaper on most days, as well as the television anchor's introduction to network reports on Vietnam, would feature a battlefield roundup based on the daily press briefing in Saigon. These were generally upbeat in tone: as Morley Safer's Cam Ne story indicates, reporters almost universally assumed that American firepower would eventually produce victory in Vietnam. Of battles reported on television in which a judgment was reported on success or failure, 62 percent were described as "victories" for the US.[7] Reporting on US troops emphasized their professionalism and high morale. The image of the enemy was also very traditional, heavily focused on atrocity stories and peppered with terms like "savage," "brutal," and "murderous."

During World War II, the press served to mobilize public opinion in support of the war effort both by making the war seem understandable, within a perspective of military strategy, and by cementing the bonds of sentiment between the public

Ten year old Phan Thim Kim Phuc runs in terror from a napalm attack on her village, 1972. (TRH Pictures)

at home and the soldiers in the field. Vietnam coverage did essentially the same thing in the early years of the war. One element that did not fit the story line carried down from World War II was the story of political conflict in Saigon. The South Vietnamese government continued to be shaky, and in 1966 what was essentially a civil war within a civil war took place there. This did get substantial coverage, and may have been a factor in the gradual erosion of public support for the war.

Vietnam was the first war extensively covered by television. There was some television coverage of Korea, but the technology of the fifties made it difficult to shoot sound film under combat conditions, and television news was in any case not the institution it would be after 1963, when CBS and NBC introduced half-hour nightly news broadcasts.

How did television change the public's relation to war? It made it more immediate, not in a temporal sense (television reports were mostly five days old when they aired in this period) but in the sense that television makes people feel "close" to events. It also may have shifted the balance somewhat from strategic and political reporting to an intensified emphasis on the individual soldier, since television is particularly dependent on an "up close and personal" style of reporting. But the impact of television should not be exaggerated. Television was less likely than the print media to depart from conventional understandings of war, and was

Walter Cronkite interviews the commanding officer of the 1st Battalion, 1st Marines, during the battle for Hue City in 1968, while his CBS camera crew use a jeep for a dolly. (NARA)

slower to shift toward more skeptical reporting of Vietnam. The television camera, moreover, was very far from showing the "true horror of war night after night" in people's living rooms. The typical television report would show only fleeting images of combat or casualties, usually not more than outgoing fire or air strikes seen from a distance. In part, this was due to the nature of the war itself, to the fact that so many operations turned out to be nothing more than what the troops called a "long hot walk in the sun." In part it resulted from strong concern on the part of the networks that graphic coverage would offend audiences and advertisers.

South Vietnamese General Nguyen Ngoc Loan executing a Viet Cong prisoner in the streets of Saigon. (TRH Pictures)

THE FRAME SHIFTS

By 1967, some evidence of change in media frames was beginning to appear. In political coverage, especially, there was increasing emphasis on debate about how long the war would last, and whether the Johnson administration was leveling with the public about its progress. The term "credibility gap" dates to this period. The administration responded with a high-profile public-relations effort late in 1967, intended to convince the public – as a presidential election year approached – that the end of the war was indeed within sight. This initiative was upended by the Tet Offensive, launched by the Vietnamese Communists in January 1968.

The Tet Offensive was a dramatic, heavily covered media event, and clearly departed from the earlier pattern of Vietnam coverage in important ways. Journalists generally accepted the official interpretation that the offensive represented a military defeat for the Communists. Tet did not *look* like a US victory in the news, however. It was during the Tet Offensive that the "living-room war" did really turn violent, if only for a few weeks. As the fighting entered the cities where it was concentrated, readily accessible to journalists, and probably more meaningful to an urban audience, the volume of images of combat and casualties rose dramatically. These included another of the iconic images of the Vietnam War: that of South Vietnamese General Nguyen Ngoc Loan executing a Viet Cong prisoner in the streets of Saigon.

There were two periods when graphic images of the violence of war did appear with some frequency in the Vietnam coverage, Tet and the North Vietnamese "Easter Offensive" of 1972. In 1968, the images of intensified conflict seemed to belie the Johnson administration's claim that the end of the fighting was in sight. Journalists often interpreted Tet as a "pyrrhic" victory for the US, either because of the destruction it caused – something not normally emphasized in earlier reporting – or because of the political consequences for the Johnson administration. One particularly important element of Tet as a media event was the decision of Walter Cronkite – a veteran of World War II coverage and, according to some polls, the "most trusted man" in America – to cover the fighting first hand, at a time when anchors did not normally leave the anchor desk, and to close a special broadcast with a commentary calling for a change of policy on the war.

After Tet, coverage returned more or less to normal for the balance of 1968. But the shift in tone resumed in 1969, particularly after the middle of the year, when President Nixon began the withdrawal of American troops, and political divisions began to grow. The change should not be exaggerated. Many elements of the reporting remained similar. American troops were still presented very sympathetically most of the time; the enemy remained mainly faceless and sinister; American motivations for fighting in Vietnam were still interpreted as noble. The tone did shift significantly, however. The upbeat rhetoric of the early years gave way to more matter-of-fact descriptions of the action; 24 percent of battles were described as inconclusive in their results after Tet, as opposed to two percent before,[8] and journalists sometimes commented ironically on the eternal recurrence of the war. "It illustrates the frustrations of fighting here," reported one CBS correspondent (June 18, 1969), describing a search-and-destroy operation that years before would surely have been described as a "big victory." "The troops have held so many assaults here they've long ago lost count of the number… We enter, fight the enemy or find they've just left, we leave, and the Communists return." There was greater emphasis on the human costs of the war, as illustrated by a 1969 issue of *Life* magazine which featured photos of all the Americans killed in a week of combat. There was increased emphasis on the political debate at home. And there were a number of major stories that played key roles in the growing debate over the war. These included the story of the My Lai massacre and some other reporting on atrocities by US troops, beginning in 1969, as well as the publishing of the Pentagon Papers in 1971. The Pentagon Papers, printed in the face of threats of legal action by the Nixon administration, revealed the extent to which officials had misled the press and the public through much of the Vietnam War. They contributed to a significant shift in American journalism away from the more deferential reporting styles that had prevailed at the war's beginning.

MEDIA, POLICY, AND OPINION

On the surface, the significant shift in media framing of the war between 1967 and 1969 would seem consistent with the conventional wisdom about the media and Vietnam: the idea that the media were the decisive actor, that changes in media coverage produced the shift in opinion and policy. A closer analysis does not support that conclusion, however. The media, certainly, were part of the process by which opinion and policy on Vietnam changed, and journalists themselves were significant actors. Certainly one important factor in the shift in public discussion of the war was the fact that journalists who covered it over a period of years became increasingly skeptical that American policy could

An injured journalist is helped to safety in October 1966. Over 60 journalists were killed during 20 years of conflict in Vietnam. (Topfoto)

succeed. But it is also clear that the media were, to a large extent, responding to other actors, not driving the process of change by themselves.

Three forces had particular influence on the media. The first, referred to earlier in this article, was the balance of elite opinion. Journalists covering the war from Washington, especially, did so on the basis of sources, almost all of them US government officials located in the standard "beats" for gathering political news – the White House, the State Department, the Pentagon, and Capitol Hill. In 1964–65, these sources rarely expressed doubt or dissent on the war. This would gradually change. Early in 1966, the Senate Foreign Relations Committee, under Chairman J. William Fulbright, held hearings which represented the first significant domestic debate on the war. By 1967, considerable debate was taking place within the Johnson administration. In the Defense Department, for example, Secretary Robert McNamara's "systems analysts," responsible for "crunching the numbers" on the progress of the war, were increasingly leaning to the view that US policy in Vietnam could not succeed at a level of commitment that seemed sustainable. McNamara clashed with the Joint Chiefs of Staff and Lieutenant General Westmoreland, and left the administration. His successor, Clark Clifford, however, came to similar conclusions. In 1968, the issue of the war became an important factor in electoral politics. And after 1969, deep divisions existed at all levels of American politics, including sharp conflicts in the Nixon administration, where the secretaries of Defense and State came into conflict with the White House and National Security Advisor Henry Kissinger.

The role of the press in the formulation of policy tends to expand when channels of communication break down within an administration. This had occurred in 1963, when US advisors dissatisfied with policy found their views cut out of the US mission's reporting to Washington. It occurred again in the Nixon era, starting in mid-1969. It was, in part, the effort of the White House to plug "leaks" to the press connected with these divisions that led to the Watergate scandal.

A second important influence on the changing frame of war reporting was public opinion itself. Opinion polls have almost invariably shown initial public reluctance about a decision to go to war, followed by a strong "rally round the flag" effect, in which opinion shifts to support for war. This occurred in late 1965, when public support for the Vietnam War peaked at about 70 percent supporting the war and 25 percent opposed. Support then dropped early in 1966 – about the time the Senate Foreign Relations Committee held hearings – rebounded a bit later in the year, and then began a steady decline that lasted through the end of the war. By early 1967, a plurality disapproved of Lyndon Johnson's handling of the war, and by October 1967, a plurality told pollsters that they thought the US had made a "mistake" getting into Vietnam. Public opinion had thus *already* shifted substantially against the war *before* the most significant changes in media coverage began. This clearly undercuts the conventional wisdom that media coverage drove public opinion on the war. The evidence from opinion polls also undercuts the common notion that the Tet Offensive was the "turning point" of the war, or that Cronkite's special broadcast had a decisive influence. Tet was important in many ways, as a catalyst for public discussion of Vietnam policy. Opinion polls show some change in people's assessments of how well the war was going, and in the balance between those calling themselves "doves" and "hawks" early in 1968. But overall the evidence does not suggest that Tet changed the general trend toward declining support which was already underway.[9]

If media coverage did not drive public opinion, what did produce the decline in support for the war? Various hypotheses have been put forward, including the arguments that the level of support for the war was driven by the cumulative casualty toll,[10] or by cues from political elites,[11] who as we have seen were increasingly divided. To a significant extent it may simply have been a matter of time, a reaction to the fact that the war continued for years, with no clear end in sight.

What of the role of the anti-war movement? Significant anti-war demonstrations and "teach-ins" began early in 1965, while public debate in "mainstream" institutions was still very limited. Martin Luther King, Jr. announced his opposition to the war in April 1967. In the pre-1968 period, however, media coverage of the anti-war movement was limited in volume and generally hostile, often emphasizing an "aid and comfort to the enemy" frame.[12] After the success of Senator Eugene McCarthy (and, eventually, other anti-war candidates) in the 1968 elections, and as participation in anti-war activities expanded, news coverage became more extensive and less hostile, though protests were still typically reported more as disruptions of social order than as political statements. A typical news story on a war protest would focus on the presence or absence of violence; only 16 percent of television reports on anti-war rallies had soundbites from the speeches.[13]

The impact of the anti-war movement on policy and opinion is hard to judge. Though participation in the anti-war movement widened in the later period, the movement always remained unpopular with most of the mass public. It has been argued that the rise of protest and the growth of anti-war sentiment in the mass public have to be understood as parallel but separate developments, driven by different motivations.[14] Much of the anti-war movement saw American intervention as unjustified from the beginning; little of this point of view made it into news coverage. Mass public opposition was focused on the success of US policy, rather than its motivations or premises. It does seem likely, however, that the anti-war movement contributed to the shift in news frames by dramatizing to journalists that the war was indeed a political issue, and could not be treated (as in earlier reporting) as a matter of consensus.

A third important factor affecting news coverage was the decline of morale among American troops in Vietnam. American soldiers, as we have seen, were the main characters of the "living-room war." Their words and images dominated the reporting, especially on television. During the 1991 Gulf War, a common theme in public discussion was the idea that the nation had to atone for its failure to support the troops a generation earlier in Vietnam. In fact, American political culture has long treated the individual soldier as an icon of patriotism and a symbol of the "common man," around whom American national identity is built. This was no less true of Vietnam than of other wars, and a strong identification in news reporting with the ordinary soldier continued from the beginning of the war to the end. The image of the soldier was tarnished to some extent by reporting on atrocities, though the extent of this coverage should not be exaggerated; it is no accident that the My Lai story was broken by a small alternative news service, and not a mainstream news organization.[15] It is true, however, that the media's strong focus on the individual soldier began to cut both ways politically in the later part of the war, particularly after troop withdrawals began and it became clear that main objective of US policy in Vietnam was to find a way out. From the middle of 1969, news reports from the field in Vietnam, once dominated by expressions of enthusiasm from the troops, included an increasing volume of comments from soldiers that reflected either a desire simply to go home or, especially later in the war, criticism of the war itself as "senseless."

CONCLUSION

The dominant framework for understanding war in American culture is derived from World War II. An important element of that framework is the idea that war stands above politics, occupying a "sacred" space of the "civil religion" of patriotism. Americans remember World War II as the "good war" in part because the nation was unified. The value system of journalism, by contrast, centers around notions of balance and objectivity, and the notion of the press as an independent "Fourth Estate"[16] and "watchdog" of state power. In the case of World War II, journalists set aside normal reporting conventions to merge themselves in the war effort. World War II, of course was a "total war": the survival of the nation was clearly at stake, war was formally declared, and the entire society was mobilized around the war effort. When Johnson announced that the nation was going to war in Vietnam, he referred to "lessons of history," and strove to invoke the World War II understanding of war as a sacred national cause, just as President Bush would do a generation later in announcing war against the "Axis of Evil." Like Bush, Johnson was largely successful; political leaders of both parties, the mass public and the media for the most part rallied round the cause, none of them quite completely – opposition to the war in the polls was never lower than 25 percent, for instance – but enough to produce solid political backing for the war.

Vietnam, however, like all the wars the US has fought following World War II, was a limited war, not a total war. It was one policy political leaders tried to balance against other priorities; as it continued and costs mounted, consensus broke down. That process was extremely painful. For soldiers and their families, it is difficult to accept the notion of a limited war – difficult to accept the idea that you are risking your life for a cause to which the nation is not fully committed. This is in part what accounted for the decline of morale later in the war. For the American public at large, too, the contradiction between the cultural norm of what war should be and the reality of Vietnam was disillusioning. The contradiction between the rhetoric of total war used to mobilize public support and the reality of limited war is important to understanding the recurrent pattern of public opinion in post-World War II conflicts. It helps to explain the shift from strong support and a significant closing-down of political discussion at the beginning of a war, to disillusionment once a conflict becomes protracted.

For journalists, limited war creates ambiguity about what model of their role is appropriate. Over the course of the Vietnam War, they gradually shifted from what can be called the "sphere of consensus" to the "sphere of legitimate controversy."[17] This happened, to a large extent, in response to the forces outlined above: the growth of debate among political elites, the erosion of public support, and the disillusionment of American soldiers increasingly worried about being the "last casualty" in a fading war. Journalists shifted from deferential and celebratory reporting to the roles of neutral observer and watchdog which prevail in normal political reporting. With this shift, of course, the media contributed to the interlinked processes by which opinion and policy on Vietnam changed. The controversy over the media's role is intimately related to this shift, as the proper role of the media in covering the war became as controversial as the war itself.

The conventional wisdom that the media were decisive to the outcome of the Vietnam

War has prevailed in part because it is a convenient way to remember Vietnam. For policymakers like Richard Nixon or for military commanders, it is easier to blame the media than to face up to their own failings. For journalists, similarly, it is easier to remember their role as a heroic confirmation of the ideal of the press as Fourth Estate, rather than to face up to their own implication in the tragedy of Vietnam. And for the public, too, it is probably easier to tell the story of Vietnam either as a story of betrayal by particular actors like the media and the anti-war movement, or as a story about how the democratic process worked in the end, than to remember it as a serious error of collective judgment. The collective memory of the Vietnam War seems to focus more on the later than the earlier years of the war – as painful as the divisions of that period were, it seems easier for people to remember than an early era when the majority of the country acquiesced in the decision to go to war without serious question and debate. That is also, however, a critical part of the story of the Vietnam War.

Participation in the anti-war movement widened in the later years of the war, but the movement remained unpopular with most of the public. Some Vietnam veterans demonstrating against the continuation of the war publicly threw away their medals, as at this demonstration near the Capitol, on April 23, 1971. (Empics/AP Photo/John Duricka)

Chapter 15

The Final Act – And After
The Legacy of War

Arnold R. Isaacs

The last minutes of the Vietnam War seemed almost too stagy to be real, as if history were posing for a propaganda poster.

Under a blazing sun on the morning of April 30, 1975, a long line of Communist tanks rolled into the heart of Saigon, each with a red-and-blue Liberation flag fluttering from the top of its radio antenna. A few wide-eyed onlookers watched them go past. Otherwise the sidewalks were empty, puddled here and there with bits of military gear and uniforms shed by members of the defeated South Vietnamese Army. Standing in the open hatches, crewmen wearing leather tankers' helmets returned the spectators' stares.

A few blocks past the deserted US Embassy, the column reached Cong Ly Boulevard, opposite the high steel fence that stood in front of the Doc Lap Palace, seat of South Vietnam's presidents. Without slowing, the lead tank roared across the intersection and rammed into the palace gate. The gate held momentarily, rocking the tank backward for a second or two, then tore away from its hinges. The tank crashed through onto the palace grounds. As more tanks roared through the gap in the fence, a group of palace guards at the top of the driveway threw down their weapons and sat down, waiting to surrender. From one of the tanks, a lone soldier leaped down, carrying a Liberation flag on a short staff. He sprinted up the wide ceremonial staircase and disappeared into the building, reappearing a moment later on a small balcony just above the entrance. From there he waved the flag furiously over his head as if, one chronicler wrote, he wanted to signal his comrades all the way to Hanoi that their long struggle was over.

Inside, Duong Van Minh, sworn in less than 48 hours earlier as the last president of the Republic of Vietnam, waited with a few senior associates in a second-floor conference room. When a group of Communist officers entered the room, Minh stood and said formally, "We have been impatiently waiting for you since this morning, to hand over power." "You cannot hand over what you no longer have," the commanding officer replied scornfully.

Crowds of Vietnamese try to scale the wall of the US Embassy in Saigon on April 29, 1975, hoping to escape aboard one of the evacuation helicopters before Communist forces occupy the city. (Empics/AP Photo/Neal Ulevich)

Less than two months earlier, anyone predicting such a quick, dramatic, and decisive end to Vietnam's 30-year war would have been thought delusional. Not even the leaders in Hanoi imagined that the offensive they planned for that spring would yield total victory in less than eight weeks.

The first battles of that offensive came in early March, when Communist forces seized stretches of highways 19 and 21, the only two usable roads leading from the Central Highlands to the coast. Then, on March 10, North Vietnamese troops and tanks attacked Ban Me Thuot, a provincial capital in the Southern Highlands. By late the next day, Communist troops controlled the town. Three days later, President Nguyen Van Thieu flew secretly to the former US logistics base at Cam Ranh Bay to meet with his commander in the highlands region, Major General Pham Van Phu. Thieu's order was stunning: Phu should pull all regular South Vietnamese forces out of the entire highlands region, regroup on the coast, then send units back up to reopen Highway 21 and retake Ban Me Thuot. Local and provincial troops, mostly minority tribesmen, were not to be told about the order. They would be left where they were to screen the regular forces' retreat, then would be abandoned. The retreat was to take place along a long-unused secondary road called Highway 7-B, which ran 135 miles from Pleiku to the coastal town of Tuy Hoa. Mines left by both sides still lay under stretches of the road, and numerous bridges had been blown up and never rebuilt, but because the two main roads out of the highlands were cut, there seemed no other choice.

Following the meeting, General Phu flew back to his headquarters in Pleiku, but the next morning he left again for the coast. So did most of the senior officers on his staff, leaving the retreat to be carried out by subordinates, with virtually no planning or specific orders to unit commanders. As soldiers abandoned their positions, dozens of undamaged aircraft, hundreds of vehicles and artillery pieces, and mountains of ammunition and fuel were left behind to be captured by the North Vietnamese. Along the road, the retreating troops came under increasingly heavy attacks from Communist units closing in on the route. Many units ran out of food. With each day the retreat slipped deeper into chaos. Only a handful of hungry, demoralized troops ever reached the coast.

While the disaster was still unfolding in the highlands, President Thieu decided on another strategic retreat in the far north of the country. There too his commanders quickly lost control. Government troops pulled out of Quang Tri province on March 19. Hue was abandoned a week later. Da Nang, South Vietnam's second largest city, fell on Easter weekend. In the first three days of April, defending units collapsed as far south as Cam Ranh Bay, leaving the entire northern half of the country to the advancing North Vietnamese. The conquerors faced hardly any fighting: government forces were disintegrating faster than their enemy could pursue and engage them.

The Communists' advance paused in early April, while their commanders prepared for the final assault on Saigon. But – although the thought was difficult to absorb after so many years of stalemate – there was no possible doubt that the war was at last coming to an end. In the South Vietnamese capital, a strange, dreamlike air settled over the city as it waited for the end. On the evening of April 21, President Thieu tearfully announced his resignation, turning over his office to the frail, half-blind Vice President Tran Van Huong. A week later, Huong stepped down in favor of Duong Van Minh, who against all logic appeared to believe the Communists would halt their advance and negotiate with him instead of assaulting the city. Their answer came less than an hour after his inauguration, when North Vietnamese pilots, flying captured South Vietnamese fighter jets, bombed Tan Son Nhut Airport, signaling the start of the final battle. Before dawn the next morning, a withering artillery barrage closed the runways. A few hours later, US helicopters flew in from ships offshore to lift out the remaining Americans in the city, along with several thousand Vietnamese. The evacuation flights continued through the night, and as they flew between the city and the South China Sea, pilots could look down and see long lines of Communist tanks heading toward Saigon. So sure were they of an unopposed advance that they left their headlights on, illuminating their route across the dark land toward the victory that would soon be in their hands.

AMERICA'S AMNESIA

The United States had largely put Vietnam out of its mind after the last US troops withdrew in 1973. The war's sudden end brought it back to American television screens and newspaper front pages for a few weeks. However, Vietnam swiftly dropped out of sight again after Saigon's surrender. Remarkably, after the years of bitter division over the war, the conclusion did not unleash any significant new wave of argument or recrimination. Instead, Americans on both sides of the issue seemed mainly relieved. In part, the subject was just too painful: "We lost the war in Vietnam, and that's why we don't talk about it," one man said. But it also seemed that even after so many years of passionate debate, Americans still did not quite know what to say to themselves about Vietnam, and its troubling impact on their vision of their nation and themselves.

Americans are taught to think of war as narrative, something that begins, proceeds through a succession of battles, and then comes to an end. But the war in Vietnam, as experienced both by the men who fought it and by those watching from home, had no narrative structure. Its battles seemed random episodes of violence, not connected in any logical way. When the fighting ended somewhere, one could see the bodies and smashed villages, but almost never any change in the war, any indication that either side was closer to winning or losing. Battles were like grenades thrown in a stream – after the splash subsided and the noise died away and the dead fish floated downstream, the stream looked exactly as it had before, running between the same banks with the same force and appearance it had always had. That too helped explain why so many Americans fell so silent after the war was finally over – not just because the subject was painful and divisive, but because the event itself was so elusive and hard to understand.

The silence was particularly painful for many veterans. On the whole, it reflected confusion, not rejection. But it contributed to a powerful sense among returning soldiers that they were shunned by the country that had sent them to an unsatisfying and unsuccessful war. Instead of parades and flags, the most persistent symbolic experience of the soldier's homecoming from Vietnam was being taunted and spat on by anti-war protestors. Almost certainly, spitting happened far more often in fiction and folklore than in real life. But if the memory was often mythical, the hurt it represented was real. Also painful was the popular-culture stereotype of the Vietnam vet as a drug-ridden psychotic. And, since the war ended in failure, it was hard for former soldiers to find any meaning in their experience, or any reason for it. "I want it to have been worth *something*," one wounded veteran mourned after coming home, "and I can't make myself believe that it was."[1]

When the Vietnam Veterans Memorial in Washington was dedicated in 1982, some veterans associated it too with what they saw as the country's failure to respect and appreciate their service. "Black walls, the universal color of sorrow and dishonor. Hidden in a hole, as if in shame,"[2] one soldier complained. But the public and, in time, the great majority of veterans found the wall a place of solace and healing, even if its design was not traditionally patriotic. "It doesn't say whether the war was right or wrong. That's for everyone to decide on his own," a man whose son was wounded in Vietnam told the writer Myra MacPherson. "It just says, 'Here is the price we paid.'"[3] The wall overcame the country's deep

The Vietnam Veterans Memorial in Washington DC.
(Topfoto/Imageworks)

fissures over the war. Other words might still divide, but the names unified. "It is exactly the right memorial," said a retired general, "for that war."[4]

LEGACIES OF A LOST WAR

Thirty years later, the memory of Vietnam continued to hover over US military policies and doctrines on the use of force. Policymakers and strategists, like the country, were divided on what lessons to draw from the Vietnam failure. Some, blaming the defeat on timidity and unnecessary restraint, argued that bolder, more aggressive policies would be needed to protect American interests and prevail in future conflicts. Others, seeing Vietnam as a case of hubris in Washington and a failure to understand the limits of military power, concluded that the United States must be much more wary of intervening in foreign wars.

US military leaders in the post-Vietnam era embraced somewhat contradictory attitudes, less cautious in some respects and more cautious in others. Almost unanimously, commanders agreed that maximum military force should be used quickly, instead of gradually escalating as in Vietnam, and that military leaders should be allowed to fight as they thought best, without political constraints. At the same time, though, they were determined that no future generation of soldiers should be sent to fight without strong popular support at

Remembrance of wars past: US forces in Iraq fought in different terrain and vastly different circumstances than in Vietnam, but like their predecessors in that earlier war, soldiers such as these US soldiers standing guard outside of the local governor's office in downtown Fallujah were also facing a protracted conflict in an unfamiliar culture against an elusive enemy. As the Iraq war dragged on, critics and an uneasy American public increasingly saw troubling parallels with Vietnam. (© Thorne Anderson/Corbis)

home, or (since the public would presumably not keep supporting long, inconclusive wars) without the prospect of a fairly fast and unequivocally successful conclusion, followed by a quick disengagement of US forces. Since those conditions could rarely be guaranteed, military officers were for the most part extremely hesitant, often much more so than civilian policymakers, about involving American troops in complicated, faraway conflicts.

As Marine General Anthony C. Zinni observed shortly before his retirement in 2000, what American military leaders after Vietnam really wanted, if they had to fight another war, was a national crusade with moral clarity, united resolve on the home front, and an all-out effort aimed at total, unambiguous victory: in other words, a repeat of World War II. "We want to find a real adversarial demon – a composite of Hitler, Tojo, and Mussolini – so we can drive on to his capital city and crush him there. Unconditional surrender. Then we'll put in place a Marshall Plan, embrace the long-suffering vanquished, and help them regain entry into the community of nations. Everybody wants to do that... I would love to do that somewhere before I step down." But, Zinni added, the world of the late twentieth and early twenty-first centuries was not going to offer another World War II. Instead, the wars that American soldiers were likely to fight in were going to be exactly the kind their commanders did not like to think about or plan for:

confusing conflicts in obscure places, requiring US forces to deal with tangled political and humanitarian issues as well as military ones.

The first Persian Gulf War seemed, for a time, to fit the post-Vietnam model of a successful use of US military force. Along with vanquishing the enemy, President George H. W. Bush declared, the campaign in the desert had also vanquished the memory of the Vietnam defeat. "The specter of Vietnam," he proclaimed, "has been buried forever in the desert sands of the Arabian Peninsula."[5] But the ghost did not stay buried. It continued to haunt policy debates on interventions in Somalia, Bosnia, Haiti, Kosovo, and, most notably, over the war in Iraq. Before that war began, President George W. Bush and his advisors conveyed the expectation of a swift, satisfying victory, with US troops welcomed as liberators by a grateful Iraqi public. The quick capture of Baghdad and televised images of jubilant Iraqis celebrating the toppling of Saddam Hussein's statue (which was actually pulled down by off-camera US troops) briefly seemed to confirm that optimistic vision. As celebration gave way to growing violence and American soldiers continued to be killed and wounded, though, the impression of a clean, morally unambiguous victory began to fade. Gradually, though the comparison was strongly disputed by Bush administration officials, allusions to Vietnam began to appear in the public discussion of America's new war.

Three years of war in Iraq did not produce the mass protests or widespread campus turbulence that marked the Vietnam era, but activists nonetheless worked to bring an anti-war message to the public. Cindy Sheehan, whose son Casey was killed in Iraq, became a focal point for protest in the summer of 2005 when she camped out for weeks near President Bush's ranch in Texas, unsuccessfully seeking to speak with the president about the war. (Topfoto/Bob Daemmrich/Imageworks)

The differences between the two wars were vast. The terrain, the culture, political institutions, the makeup and nature of the enemy, the scale of military operations, and the historical roots of conflict in Vietnam were utterly unlike those in Iraq. The international environment had changed beyond recognition, and so had the American army, now a professional volunteer force instead of an army depending on draftees. Yet as the conflict in Iraq ground on, Americans increasingly began to find troubling parallels.

In both wars, the enemy was hard to find and not easy to distinguish from the civilian population. In both wars, the problems of fighting a dispersed insurgency were not easily solved, despite the Americans' overwhelming superiority in manpower and firepower. And in both wars, Washington's rhetoric seemed disproportionate to the reality, as when President Bush declared that "the year 2005 will be recorded as a turning point in the history of Iraq, the history of the Middle East and the history of freedom," and – in an updated formulation of the domino theory – that America's enemies in Iraq were planning to establish "a base from which to launch attacks against America, overthrow moderate governments in the Middle East and establish a totalitarian Islamic empire that reaches from Spain to Indonesia."[6] Most critically, in both wars there was no reliable way to measure whether the war was being lost or won, or exactly how success could be defined. American patience with the war in Vietnam had been worn away by the impression of an endless conflict without visible movement toward a decisive result. Along with the perception of stalemate, a majority of Americans came to believe that going to war in Vietnam had been a mistake. As the conflict in Iraq drew toward the three-year mark, with over 2,100 American soldiers killed and more than 15,000 wounded by the end of 2005, similar perceptions and a similar loss of public belief in the war had become a growing concern for the administration in Washington.

Like the rest of the country, veterans who had served in Vietnam were split on the war in Iraq. On both sides, though, watching a new generation of American soldiers fight a war that was losing support at home stirred painful memories. Some Vietnam vets felt passionately that the country had to stick with its soldiers until they succeeded. Just as passionately, others believed that if Iraq was a war that shouldn't be fought, sacrificing more lives in the name of those who had already been killed would be senseless and wrong. Still others were torn between those two viewpoints. He thought about Iraq with hope and dread, said Mark Treanor, who led a Marine platoon in Vietnam – hope that the country was doing the right thing and would do what it took to finish the job, and dread that if it was the wrong thing to do or if the public wasn't patient enough, the soldiers' lives that were lost there would have been wasted.

James Webb, the novelist and former Marine (and Treanor's Naval Academy classmate), was a vehement defender of the Vietnam War but believed Iraq was a mistake, and was sulfurous at the administration's efforts to equate criticism of the policy with disloyalty to the country or the troops. Recalling that the President and Vice-President, along with many other prominent architects and advocates of the Iraq War, had managed not to go to Vietnam, Webb noted coldly: "I don't need a bunch of people who hid under the bed during Vietnam to tell me what it means to be patriotic."

THE POW/MIA MYTH

Among Vietnam's legacies, one of the strangest and saddest was the enduring myth of scores or hundreds of American prisoners still held long after the end of the war. No credible evidence of those mythical prisoners was ever found (the one former POW who turned up in Vietnam after the war, Marine Private Bobby Garwood, was by all available evidence a willing defector, not an unwilling captive). None of the 591 American prisoners who came home in early 1973 ever identified a single prisoner who was known to be alive at the time of the exchange but did not return. Nor was there any plausible reason why the Vietnamese Communists would have chosen to keep prisoners for years and decades after their victory was achieved. Yet the fantasy took a powerful hold on the American imagination. It was perpetuated by a variety of interests: families of missing servicemen who could not relinquish hope that their loved ones were still alive; would-be adventurers with fantasies of bringing back lost heroes; con artists who raised millions of dollars for imaginary "rescue missions"; novelists and Hollywood scriptwriters who churned out scores of stories in which action heroes like Rambo blasted their way into the jungle to bring back America's missing heroes. The stories were wildly improbable but also wildly popular, possibly because they unconsciously expressed an underlying feeling that America had lost something in Vietnam – confidence, trust in its leaders, unity, and a national sense of righteousness – that it desperately wanted to get back.

The myth was promoted as well by those in the government and out who, for strategic or political or emotional reasons, opposed normalizing US relations with Vietnam. As long as there was any suspicion of POWs remaining in captivity, the argument went, normalization must not proceed until Hanoi had returned the remains of every missing American. That formulation sounded properly patriotic and unassailably the right way to settle the POW question once and for all. It was, however, a demand that the Vietnamese could not possibly meet. The missing included hundreds of airmen who were lost far out over the South China Sea, or blown to bits in midair explosions, or pulverized in aircraft that went down in remote jungles. The Vietnamese could not return those bodies; in many cases they didn't know anything about them. Thus, as long as a "complete accounting" was the non-negotiable condition for acting on all other issues, progress toward normalization was impossible. That meant the missing-in-action activists – the families and their supporters – and opponents of normalization both had the same interest in keeping the POW myth alive.

Periodically, sensational reports appeared, claiming to prove that American prisoners had remained in captivity after the war. None was ever confirmed, and in nearly every case, the supposed evidence was conclusively shown to be false. The fallacy of the POW myth went beyond those faked reports, however. Its arithmetic was false, and so was its terminology. For many years the MIA movement and its supporters asserted again and again that at the war's end there were approximately 2,500 Americans who could be designated as POW/MIA – Prisoner of War/Missing in Action – and referred to as "officially missing" and "unaccounted for." The number (which gradually declined to "about 2,000" as remains were found and repatriated), the acronym, and the phrases "officially missing" and "unaccounted for" were repeated in countless news reports and public statements, almost never qualified or questioned. All of them, however, were incorrect.

There were not 2,500 officially missing and unaccounted-for Americans during the war. After the POW release in early 1973 following the US–North Vietnamese cease-fire agreement, the US Defense Intelligence Agency listed 1,303 American servicemen as missing in action – 1,238 who were already classed as MIA and another 65 who had been thought to be POWs but were neither freed in the exchange nor included on Hanoi's list of prisoners who had died in captivity. The number of true mysteries was much smaller than that, since in many of the MIA cases there was convincing but not quite conclusive evidence that the men had died. How, then, did it happen that for more than two decades, it was almost universally accepted that the total number of MIAs was nearly twice as many as were declared missing during the war?

The answer lay in a puzzling Defense Department decision to combine the wartime list of missing servicemen with another list of 1,118 men who were known to have died but whose remains could not be retrieved to be sent home and buried. The official status of those men during the war was KIA-BNR: Killed in Action, Body Not Recovered. Adding them to the postwar "unaccounted for" list didn't just distort the numbers, it distorted the language as well. The KIA-BNRs were not unaccounted for, since in the vast majority of cases the services knew exactly what had happened to them. Nor were they missing in action, since these men were known dead (by definition, MIA status meant that a man's fate after his disappearance was not known). Still further distortion lay in the acronym POW/MIA, the preferred term of the MIA movement that was adopted by the Defense Department as well. As used in wartime by the armed services, the two categories were mutually exclusive. POW status meant that there was some information that a man had survived and been taken prisoner; MIA meant that there was *no* evidence for either survival or capture after someone disappeared. Hyphenating the two and speaking as if they were a single group obliterated that distinction, inflated the number of possible prisoners, and thus falsely strengthened the impression that scores or hundreds of Americans might still be held captive.

The misleading numbers and illogical words both served to blur the only conclusions that were truly justified by the known facts: though there could never be 100 percent certainty, evidence and logic were both very strongly against the theory that the Vietnamese had deliberately kept prisoners after 1973; and it was probable to the point of certainty that the overwhelming majority of missing men had died when they first disappeared.

The MIA story was so flimsy and illogical (as was the associated fantasy of a vast cover-up by the US government) that its power over a 20-year period remains difficult to explain. Lazy, credulous journalism bore some responsibility, as did political leaders who for many years were too timid to challenge even the most absurd claims for fear of appearing unsympathetic to the families of missing American heroes. Even so, it seemed curious that so much postwar attention was given for so long to imaginary prisoners and preposterous conspiracy theories, instead of trying to discern what really happened in Vietnam and what it meant. Only after the United States and Vietnam reestablished diplomatic relations in 1995 did the issue begin to fade from public view – in part because the organizations that promoted it had lost one of their chief reasons for existence, which was to prevent normalization from happening.

Late that year the US Defense Department quietly acknowledged that two decades of demands for a "complete accounting" – defined by one Pentagon official as having "a live person or his identifiable remains" for every name on the list[7] – had been pursuing a logical impossibility. Of the 2,200 then considered "unaccounted for" (using that term to mean only that no body had been recovered), the department now admitted that in well over 500 cases "we judge no actions by any government will result in the recovery of remains." Most of those losses, the department added, "were not known to the Indochinese governments" at all.[8] The new statement rested on little if any new information. In the great majority of cases, the facts had been known and the same conclusions could have been reached when the men were lost. It wasn't learning the truth that had taken more than 20 years; what took that long was finding the political courage and the honesty to tell it.

DANGEROUS JOURNEYS

Vietnam's human suffering did not end with its war. A new tragedy unfolded as growing numbers of Vietnamese took to the sea to escape oppression and economic misery following the Communist victory. Their flight brought a new phrase into the world's vocabulary: "boat people."

The exodus mushroomed in the late 1970s, in large part because the Vietnamese authorities deliberately pressured the large ethnic Chinese community to leave the country. More than 300,000 refugees landed on the shores of Thailand, Malaysia, and other Southeast Asian nations on the rim of the South China Sea in 1978 and 1979. A quarter-million more arrived between 1980 and 1984. No one knew how many others died when overcrowded, unseaworthy boats broke apart, or in attacks by marauding pirates along the Thai and Malaysian coasts. Some calculated that half of all those embarking were lost at sea. Even if that was an overestimate, deaths still numbered in the hundreds of thousands.

The sea journey was only the beginning of the refugees' ordeal. Malaysia, Thailand, and the other countries in the region were unwilling hosts, fearing that the rest of the world would tire of resettling an endless flow of Vietnamese, and that the "first asylum" countries would be permanently stuck with a large population of refugees who had nowhere else to go. In some cases, Thai and Malaysian authorities went so far as to tow refugee boats back out to sea, but on the whole, if reluctantly, they did give temporary shelter to the arriving refugees. Conditions in the refugee camps were grim, however, not by accident or for lack of resources but purposely, to discourage more refugees from coming – a policy euphemistically called "humane deterrence."

In the earlier phases of the crisis, though refugees had to wait for months in the camps, they were reasonably assured of eventual resettlement. US procedures were slow but Washington still considered that anyone fleeing Vietnam was eligible to come to the United States as a refugee from Communism. Other countries, notably France, Canada, and Australia, raised their quotas to accommodate the tide of boat refugees. But as more and more boats continued to come, resettlement countries began to roll up the international welcome mat. From the early 1980s on, refugees faced years in the camps, instead of months, and greater uncertainty whether and where they would ever find permanent

This dramatic shot shows a boat full of Vietnamese refugees swamped off the Malaysian coast. (UNCHR/K. Gaugler)

refuge. Some agreed to go back voluntarily to Vietnam, but many refused, deciding that even an indefinite stay in refugee camps was better than returning to the hardships they had risked their lives to escape.

SETTLERS FROM A LOST LAND

Those boat people whose journey ended in the United States became part of a Vietnamese-American community that would number more than 1.1 million at the turn of the twenty-first century. Like millions of earlier immigrants, the Vietnamese set about creating a place for themselves in their new homeland while also trying to preserve their traditions and identity – a quest that brought rewards but also sorrows.

Adapting to American life was a struggle for some, easier for others, but three decades after the war, many Vietnamese Americans were solidly entrenched in the American middle class. Names such as Nguyen and Tran were sprinkled among other American family names on class and graduation lists, in directories of professional associations, and in news stories about high-tech inventors and entrepreneurs, state legislators and other elected officials – on casualty reports from Iraq, too, and even the National Football League roster. Success in America did not erase all the burdens of a painful past, however. Beside the normal difficulties of adjusting to a new culture, many Vietnamese, particularly those who had served in the South Vietnamese government or armed forces, felt that their lives and suffering had been erased from history. In the war they saw portrayed in American news media and books and films, the Vietnamese and their sacrifice were all but invisible. America had given them shelter but honored only its own 58,000 dead, not the more than 200,000 South Vietnamese soldiers who had also been killed or the many thousands who spent years after the war in harsh prison camps. In American eyes, or so it felt to many Vietnamese Americans, they were seen only as victims, "devoid of struggle, history, heritage and past," as one put it.[9]

Nor could Vietnamese in the United States put the war behind them as easily as other Americans. Most Americans had not just material luxury "but also the luxury of historical amnesia," wrote a young man named Vu Nguyen in Orange County, California. "With the exception of veterans and their families, perhaps, most Americans can forget – have forgotten – Vietnam… My family – like many Vietnamese-American families – can't forget why we are here." Nguyen, the son of a former South Vietnamese pilot, wrote those words in the midst of a sharp dispute in the Little Saigon district of the city of Westminster, where residents demonstrated for weeks in early 1999 against a video store owner named Tran, who had provocatively posted a photograph of the Communist leader Ho Chi Minh in his store. Nguyen's article in a local weekly was titled "Why I Hate Ho Chi Minh." When he looked at Tran's "shrine" to the father of Vietnamese Communism, Nguyen explained,

> [I] see my father taking his wife, his brother and me – his 2-month-old
> son – in a military Jeep through sniper fire and past the bodies of unlucky

friends and relatives to get to Tan Son Nhut Airport in April 1975.

I see my mother carrying me over barbed-wire fences while being shot at by Communist troops as her husband prepares to take off in a stolen cargo plane, cramming in as many people as possible, to escape certain execution.

I see my parents trying to adjust to their new surroundings without being able to speak a lick of English.

I see my dad taking a job in Arlington, Texas, killing rats beneath people's homes just to make ends meet... I see the look of distress on my dad's face as his father lay dying in Vietnam in 1997 because he couldn't go home to say goodbye for fear of being jailed – or worse – by the Vietnamese government.[10]

At this Vietnam War Memorial in Westminster, California the United States flag flies above one displaying the Missing in Action symbol, and alongside the flag of the RVN. (Photo by David McNew/Getty Images)

The war in Vietnam might have become dated for other Americans, Nguyen went on, but not for his family: "We still fight the war every day."

In Nguyen's parents' generation, some still preserved a dream, if not a real hope, of reversing the war's outcome and recapturing their country from the Communists. The flag of the Republic of Vietnam, with its three horizontal red stripes on a yellow

field, was still raised on ceremonial occasions and at sites such as the Vietnam War Memorial in Westminster, where bronze statues of an American and a South Vietnamese soldier stood under the flags of both countries. When Van Tran became the first Vietnamese American elected to California's State Assembly, one of his first acts was to propose a resolution to recognize the former South Vietnamese flag – "the flag that we cherish, that we fought for and that we believe in," Tran declared, "as opposed to one representing a dictatorial and repressive regime."[11]

Inevitably, a new generation that was more at home in America and more distant from the wartime experience was less emotional about issues left over from the war. The resulting generation gap was wide and often painful on both sides. Even Vu Nguyen, who had written so movingly about his hate for Ho Chi Minh and his family's struggle for survival, also acknowledged that the demonstrations against the video store had not served any purpose. "The Vietnam that my parents talk about is dead," he told the producers of a documentary film about Little Saigon. "It doesn't exist anymore."[12]

An elderly couple photographed at the Camp Pendleton refugee center in California in 1975. They were part of the first wave of Vietnamese refugees who reached the United States after fleeing in the chaos of the war's last days. (Tony Aloi)

THE PRICE OF VICTORY

The Vietnam that did exist had its own struggles with the past and its own painful gap between generations.

The years following what was called "liberation" were, as the Communist party leaders themselves eventually admitted, disastrous. Instead of a better life after their enormous sacrifice during the war, the great majority of Vietnamese endured a decade of even greater privations. Having achieved their dream of unifying the country, the aging revolutionaries who dominated the party leadership imposed a Stalin-style Five Year Plan that was supposed to rebuild it. Instead, a combination of outmoded Marxist–Leninist doctrine, catastrophically bad management, and vast corruption made the plan utterly unworkable. Living standards, already poor, plummeted. Rice and grain rations were cut to below wartime levels, leaving millions in hunger. Fish, traditionally the main protein source in the Vietnamese diet, disappeared because fishermen had no fuel and because so many boats had vanished in the exodus of boat people. Shortages sent food prices soaring beyond the reach of most ordinary wage earners – and huge numbers of people were earning no wages at all, including a million men in the South who had been in the defeated South Vietnamese Army and militia. Party leaders blamed the country's plight on wartime damage and the postwar US trade embargo. But in the public's ears and possibly in their own, those claims sounded increasingly hollow.

The new rulers failed to bring anything resembling true reconciliation with those who had been on the losing side. In an act of ugly vengeance, the victors bulldozed dozens of military cemeteries and obliterated their dead enemies' graves – in Vietnamese culture, a devastating loss for the families of the dead. There was vengeance against the living, too. Scores of thousands of former South Vietnamese soldiers and officials were kept in prison camps, many for years, for what their

Tens of thousands of North Vietnamese soldiers and truck drivers killed along the nearby Ho Chi Minh Trail are buried in Truong Son National Cemetery in the former Demilitarized Zone. (Steve Raymer/National Geographic Image Collection)

These smartly dressed young people of Hanoi represent the new generation of Vietnam, born after the war. (Steve Raymer/National Geographic Image Collection)

captors called "reeducation." Also imprisoned were religious leaders and dissidents who had opposed the former regime but were now deemed to be too dangerously independent-minded to be left free. Liberation did not even bring enduring peace. On Christmas Day of 1978, after months of clashes along the Vietnamese–Cambodian border, Hanoi sent 100,000 troops to overthrow the Khmer Rouge government. It took only two weeks for Vietnamese forces to capture Phnom Penh, the Cambodian capital, but resistance continued in the countryside, and ten years of guerrilla war followed, with a steady trickle of casualties.

In the mid-1980s, no longer able to deny how drastically its policies had failed, the Communist Party changed course. The Sixth Party Congress in 1986 chose 71-year-old Nguyen Van Linh, who had been kicked out of the Politburo four years earlier for his unorthodox views, as the party's new secretary general. Linh introduced a reform program called *doi moi* (renovation), which relaxed state controls, encouraged private business, and welcomed foreign investors. Under Linh and his successors, Vietnam's economy finally began to improve. The reforms posed a dilemma for the party, however. It clung to its Leninist ideology and rejected any sharing of power, but the more people could find livelihoods in the private sector, the less control the party had over their lives – and their thoughts. Ho Chi Minh and the heroic legend of the struggle for national unification still commanded respect, but for more and more Vietnamese, the party and its myths were increasingly irrelevant to present conditions and their daily lives.

"I can work what I like. I am free," a young man named Tung jubilantly told one of the first customers in his brand-new Internet business in Hanoi. To Tung, as to many of his contemporaries, his country's leaders were living in the past. After explaining to his visitor that the government regulated Internet access and blocked sites it deemed politically sensitive, Tung added with a rich laugh: "Our government thinks the Internet can be good for spies. But spies are for wartime. We are not in a war. We have peace."[13]

Reform and wider scope for personal choices did not just weaken the grip of the Communist Party. It also weakened customs, traditional relationships, and a sense of shared responsibility to the society. Not only old-style Communists found the new values troubling. "Money is spoiling the young generation," said a Catholic nun in Saigon (as most residents still called it years after it was officially renamed Ho Chi Minh City). "Very many young people are now so greedy of money, of wealth. I don't like that."[14] Many felt similarly, but after the poverty and despair of the first decade after liberation, Vietnamese overwhelmingly welcomed the new era of hopefulness and greater personal freedoms.

While reviving the economy, the reformers also pursued Vietnam's long-standing hope for normal relations with the United States. The American side, not Hanoi, was chiefly responsible for the 20-year delay, but in July 1995 President Clinton finally announced that relations would be resumed. "Whatever divided us before," the president said in an oddly passionless ceremony, "let us consign to the past." Some veterans and others condemned his decision, others approved, but compared to earlier debates on Vietnam, this one was short-lived and without emotional fire. For the great majority of Americans, it seemed, the division in their own country was ready to be consigned to the past, too. "To recognize Vietnam is not to dishonor the memory of our fallen or missing comrades," one veteran wrote. "It is to recognize the truth. The war is over."[15]

Not completely over, as subsequent events would show. Echoes of Vietnam and its era reverberated in the debate on Iraq, in angry controversies during the 2004 presidential election over President Bush's and his opponent John Kerry's military records and Kerry's anti-war activities, and in the continuing cultural and political battles over national values. That those echoes still sounded so long after the war suggested that the argument had never really been just about Vietnam, but was part of a much longer, never-ending debate about just what America is, and who Americans believe they are.

ENDNOTES

Chapter 1

1   See Lewis Sorley, "Creighton Abrams and Active-Reserve Integration in Wartime," *Parameters* 21/2 (Summer 1991), pp.35–50.

2   Lieutenant General James Helmly, Memorandum on the Readiness of the United States Army Reserve, December 20, 2004, Author's collection.

3   For a full bibliography of works on the Vietnam War, see Edwin Moise's "Vietnam War Bibliography," at http://www.clemson.edu/caah/history/FacultyPages/EdMoise/bibliography.html. The bibliography is unmatched and is both annotated and constantly updated to include the most recent works in the field.

4   For a complete treatment of Vietnam's past and the story of French imperialism and its effect on the country, see Joseph Buttinger, *The Smaller Dragon: A Political History of Vietnam* (New York: Praeger, 1958); and Joseph Buttinger, *Vietnam: A Dragon Embattled*, 2 vols (New York: Praeger, 1967). Though newer works of history exist, these exhaustive studies form a critical base for further understanding.

5   For further reading on the intricate nature of the struggles of Vietnamese nationalism, see William Duiker, *The Rise of Nationalism in Vietnam, 1900–1941* (Ithaca: Cornell University Press, 1976).

6   For a revealing study on British actions in the region during the era, see Nicholas Tarling, *Britain, Southeast Asia and the Onset of the Cold War, 1945–50* (Cambridge and New York: Cambridge University Press, 1998).

7   The British remained interested observers throughout the Vietnam War, and papers in the British National Archives in Kew represent an underutilized source for understanding Vietnam. Though the collections are scattered from the files of the Foreign Office to the files of the War Office, papers exist on a myriad of topics ranging from ambassadorial critiques of American tactics, to the workings of the British Jungle Warfare school in Malaya (which trained scores of South Vietnamese officers), to the comings and goings of Sir Robert Thompson – lauded for his actions in Malaya and constant advisor to the Americans in Vietnam.

8   The best recent work on the Diem regime is Phillip Catton, *Diem's Final Failure: Prelude to America's War in Vietnam* (Lawrence, KS: University Press of Kansas, 2002). The expanding historiography of the field also includes Robert Topmiller, *The Lotus Unleashed: The Buddhist Peace Movement in South Vietnam, 1964–1966* (Lexington, Kentucky: The University Press of Kentucky, 2002).

9   The most complete study of the ARVN is Thomas R. Cantwell, "The Army of South Vietnam: A Military and Political History, 1955–1975," Doctoral Dissertation, University of New South Wales, 1989. In addition, this author is preparing a study on the ARVN for publication with New York University Press entitled *Vietnam's Forgotten Army: Heroism and Betrayal in the ARVN.*

10   George Moss, *Vietnam: An American Ordeal*, 3rd edition (Upper Saddle River, NJ: Prentice Hall, 2002), p.441.

11   Stanley Karnow, *Vietnam: A History* (New York: Viking, 1983), p.185.

12   Quote taken from President Dwight Eisenhower's inaugural address, January 20, 1953; http://www.re-quest.net/history/inaugurals/eisenhower/.

13   Karnow, *Vietnam*, p.265.

Chapter 2

Much of this chapter is taken from the sources listed by this author in his *The Last Valley: Dien Bien Phu and the French Defeat in Vietnam* (London: Weidenfeld & Nicolson, 2004; Cambridge, MA: Da Capo Press, 2004). Additional material draws upon G. Longeret, J. Laurent, and C. Bondroit, *Les Combats de la RC 4* (Paris: Indo-Editions, 2004).

1   The universalist Cao Dai sect, founded in the 1920s by a seer named Ngo Minh Chieu, was centred on Tay Ninh northwest of Saigon. Numbering between one and two million adherents, it was a baffling mixture of Confucianism, Buddhism, Taoism, and the outward trappings of Catholicism. The slightly less numerous Hoa Hao sect of Chau Doc province was founded by an occultist Buddhist monk in 1939. Both movements were to some extent encouraged by the Japanese during their occupation.

2   Regional units were full-time guerrillas, operating only within their own districts and provinces, and received relatively light issues of relatively elderly weapons. Regular units were the elite of General Giap's main force which operated nationally.

Chapter 3

1   Officially disbanded in November 1945, the Indochinese Communist Party (ICP) was always secretly in action, publicly under the name the Viet Minh Front (Viet-Nam Doc Lap Dong Minh – The League for the Independence of Viet-Nam), that was created in South China in 1940. The Second Congress of the ICP (February 1951) was separated into three Communist parties, one each for Vietnam, Laos, and Cambodia. The Vietnam Labor Party thus appeared; and its branch in the South was named The People's Revolutionary Party. In December 1976, the Fourth Congress reused the name The Vietnamese Communist Party.

2   The Geneva Agreements allowed for the free movement of people and military men to choose the North or the South; so about 42,000 military men had moved from South to North.

3   In 1964 and 1965, most of the units moving South were battalion-sized units from the IV and III military zones. In 1966 and 1967, about half of them were the size of regiments, trained and equipped by the General Staff. From late 1971 into 1972, armored vehicles, heavy artillery, and two divisions were sent South.

4   During the Vietnam War (known as "the American War" to the North Vietnamese) more than 80 percent of the population in the North lived in the countryside; thus over 80 percent of the soldiers in the People's Army were peasants.

5   General Thanh is a very close friend of this author and openly shared his observations in June 1967.

6   Before 1960, from 1950 to 1954, during the Dien Bien Phu campaign and in the Northwest Region, Chinese military advisors had a major role in the battlefield command.

7   Sun-Tzu was the legendary Chinese philosopher on military thought; he wrote "Art of War" – the earliest known military treatise of mankind – in the sixth century BC.

8   Kissinger and Nixon had thought that the friendship between Beijing and Washington would dramatically weaken the North Vietnamese fight against America. However, this was a false calculation.

9   They spent nine years fighting the Khmer Rouge (1978–89), in a war in which more than 50,000 comrades died and 300,000 were wounded.

10   He meant that the human cost of General Giap's military strategy was more than the American public would have tolerated.

Chapter 4

1 John Prados, *The Blood Road: The Ho Chi Minh Trail and the Vietnam War* (New York: John Wiley & Sons, 1999), p.45; Military History Institute of Vietnam, *Victory in Vietnam* (trans. Merle L. Pribbenow) (Lawrence, KS: University Press of Kansas, 2002), p.115. Cf. Hoang Khoi, *The Ho Chi Minh Trail* (Hanoi: The Gioi Publishers, 2001).
2 Prados, *The Blood Road*, p.108.
3 Ibid., pp.207–212.
4 Ted Shackley with Richard A. Finney, *Spymaster: My Life in the CIA* (Dulles, VA: Potomac Books, 2005), pp.242–245; Prados, *The Blood Road*, pp.320–321.

Chapter 5

1 Timothy N. Castle, *At War in the Shadow of Vietnam: U.S. Military Aid to the Royal Lao Government, 1955–1975* (New York: Columbia University Press, 1993), p.25.
2 Australian Embassy Paris to External Affairs Office, Canberra, February 28, 1967, Savingram 9, Series No. 1838/334, Control Symbol 3016/11/161 part 11, National Archives of Cambodia, Canberra.
3 Alfred W. McCoy, "America's Secret War in Laos, 1955–1975,"in Marilyn B. Young and Robert Buzzanco (eds.), *A Companion to the Vietnam War* (Malden, MA: Blackwell, 2002), p.292.
4 Fred Branfman, *Voices from the Plain of Jars: Life Under an Air War* (New York: Harper & Row, 1972). McCoy, "America's Secret War in Laos," pp.294–296.
5 Timothy N. Castle, *One Day Too Long: Top Secret Site 85 and the Bombing of North Vietnam* (New York: Columbia University Press, 1999), p.3.
6 McCoy, "America's Secret War in Laos," pp.290–291.
7 H. R. Haldeman, *The Haldeman Diaries: Inside the White House* (New York: G. P. Putnam, 1994), p.143.
8 William Shawcross, *Sideshow: Nixon, Kissinger, and the Destruction of Cambodia*, revised edition (New York: Simon and Schuster, 1987).
9 Ben Kiernan, "The Impact on Cambodia of the U.S. Intervention in Vietnam," in Jayne S. Werner and Luu Doan Huynh (eds.), *The Vietnam War: Vietnamese and American Perspectives* (Armonk, NY: M. E. Sharpe, 1993), p.225.
10 W. Randall Ireson and Carol J. Ireson, "Laos," in Douglas Allen and Ngo Vinh Long, (eds.), *Coming to Terms: Indochina, the United States, and the War* (Boulder, CO: Westview Press, 1991), pp.143–145.
11 Peter W. Rodman, *More Precious than Peace: The Cold War and the struggle for the Third World* (New York: Charles Scribner's Sons, 1994), p.461.

Chapter 6

1 Harry F. Noyes, "Heroic Allies," *Vietnam* (August 1993).
2 QLVNCH, *Quan Su 4*, 1972 (ARVN, *Military History 4*, (1972)).
3 Philip C. Clarke, "The Battle that Saved Saigon," *The Reader's Digest* (March 1973).
4 Lewis Sorley, "Reassessing the ARVN," *Vietnam* (April 2003).
5 George J. Weith & Merle L. Pribbenow, "Fighting is an Art," *The Journal of Military History* 68 (January 2004).

Chapter 8

1 The Australia–New Zealand–United States (ANZUS) Treaty was signed in 1951 in order to persuade Australia and New Zealand to accept a "soft" peace treaty with Japan. It became, and for Australia remains, the key security relationship for the Pacific dominions during the Cold War.

Chapter 9

1   William C. Westmoreland, *A Soldier Reports* (Garden City, NY: Doubleday, 1976), p.153.

2   William Conrad Gibbons, *The U.S. Government and the Vietnam War, Executive and Legislative Roles and Relationships, Part IV: July 1965–January 1968* (Princeton, NJ: Princeton University Press), p.358, citing cable Saigon 5378.

3   Gen. Bruce Palmer Jr., Oral History Interview, General Creighton Abrams Story, US Army Military History Institute.

4   Douglas Kinnard, *The War Managers* (Hanover: University Press of New England, 1977), p.45.

5   Lt. Gen. Phillip B. Davidson, LBJ Library Oral History Interview, as quoted in Mark Moyar, *Phoenix and the Birds of Prey* (Annapolis, MD: Naval Institute Press, 1997), p.49.

6   Lt. Gen. Dong Van Khuyen, *RVNAF Logistics* (Washington, DC: US Army Center of Military History, 1980), p.57.

7   Gen. Bruce C. Clarke, Letter to Brig. Gen. Hal C. Pattison, December 29, 1969, Clarke Papers, US Army Military History Institute.

8   Lewis Sorley (ed.), *Vietnam Chronicles: The Abrams Tapes, 1968–1972* (Lubbock: Texas Tech University Press, 2004), p.48.

9   Sorley, *Vietnam Chronicles*, p.86.

10 *PROVN Study* (Department of the Army, 1 March 1966), vol.I, p.v.

11 Ibid., p.vii.

12 Ibid., p.1.

13 Sorley, *Vietnam Chronicles*, p.382.

14 Ibid., p.266.

15 Ibid., p.315.

16 Ibid., p.188.

17 Ibid., p.273.

18 Ibid., pp.27–28.

19 Allied with South Vietnam were the United States and a number of other nations contributing combat forces, most notably the Republic of Korea (South Korea), Thailand, Australia, and New Zealand. Essential support for South Vietnam came largely from the United States, with small contributions from a number of other nations.

20 "Indochina: A Cavalryman's Way Out," *Time* (February 15, 1971), p.26.

21 Bunker Reporting Cable #84, February 10, 1970.

22 J-2 is the staff designator for the intelligence officer on a joint staff.

23 Sorley, *Vietnam Chronicles*, p.59.

24 Ibid., p.69.

25 John Paul Vann, Remarks, Lexington, Kentucky, January 8, 1972, Vann Papers, Patterson School of Diplomacy and International Commerce, University of Kentucky.

26 Lt. Gen. Ngo Quang Truong, *Territorial Forces* (Washington, DC: US Army Center of Military History, 1978), pp.34, 127.

27 William E. Colby, *Lost Victory* (Chicago: Contemporary Books, 1989), p.243.

28 As quoted in Beverly Deepe, *Christian Science Monitor* (October 23, 1968).

29 George McArthur, Interview Notes of December 18, 1970. Emphasis in the original.

30 Vann, Remarks, Lexington, Kentucky, January 8, 1972, Vann Papers.

31 Amb. Ellsworth Bunker, Oral History, unpublished transcript of interviews by Stephen Young, p.45.

32 Maj. Gen. George Forsythe, Senior Officers Debriefing Program Interview, US Army Military History Institute.

33   As quoted in Gen. Donn A. Starry, *Armored Combat in Vietnam* (New York: Arno Press, 1980), p.56.

34   For more on this topic see Lewis Sorley, "Adaptation and Impact: Mounted Combat in Vietnam," in George F. Hofmann and Donn A. Starry (ed.), *Camp Colt to Desert Storm: The History of U.S. Armored Forces* (Lexington: University Press of Kentucky, 1999), pp.324–359.

35   As quoted in Olivier Todd, *Cruel April* (New York: Norton, 1987), p.145.

Chapter 10

1   http://thewall-usa.com/stats/index.html.

Chapter 11

1   For more information about the Viet Minh and Viet Cong, see Robert K. Brigham, "Viet Nam Doc Lap Dong Minh Hoi [Vietnam Independence League]" and "National Front for the Liberation of South Vietnam (NFLSV)," in Spencer C. Tucker, (ed.), *The Encyclopedia of the Vietnam War: A Political, Social, and Military History* (New York: Oxford University Press, 2000).

2   Paper Prepared by Secretary of State Rusk, February 23, 1965; as reprinted in Foreign Relations of the United States [hereafter referred to as FRUS], *1964–1968, vol.II: Vietnam, January–June 1965* (Washington: United States Government Printing Office, 1996), p.357.

3   Document 288: Telegram from the Department of State to the Embassy in Vietnam, May 10, 1965. FRUS, *1964–1968, vol.II: Vietnam, January–June 1965*, pp.629–630.

4   Document 304: Notes of a Meeting, May 16, 1965. FRUS, *1964–1968, vol.II, Vietnam, January–June 1965*, pp.665–668; see also Justus M. Van Der Kroef, "The War Seen from Hanoi," *Vietnam Perspectives*, 1/3 (1966), pp.22–31.

5   See W. Hays Parks, "Rolling Thunder and The Law Of War," *Air University Review*, 33/2 (1982), pp.2–23.

6   CHECO Report, James B. Overton, "ROLLING THUNDER – January 1967–November 1968 – Continuing Report" (October 1, 1969), p.22.

7   For more information, see CHECO Report, David I. Folkman Jr. and Philip D. Caine, "The Cambodian Campaign – April 29–June 30, 1970 – Special Report" (September 1, 1970).

8   CHECO Report, Warren A. Trest, "USAF SAC Operations in Support of SEAsia – Special Report" (December 17, 1969), p.3.

9   US Army Center of Military History Website, http://www.army.mil/cmh-pg/mohviet2.htm (accessed November 21, 2005).

Chapter 12

1   Bernard B. Fall, *Street Without Joy* (New York: Schocken Books, 1972), p.44; Robert McClintock, "The River War in Indochina," Richard M. Meyer, "The Ground-Sea Team in River Warfare," in Naval History Division, *Riverine Warfare: Vietnam* (Washington, DC: Naval Historical Center, 1972), pp.7–17; Edwin B. Hooper, Dean C. Allard, and Oscar P. Fitzgerald, *The United States Navy and the Vietnam Conflict, vol.1: The Setting of the Stage to 1959* (Washington, DC: Naval History Division, 1976), pp.96–98.

2   Edward J. Marolda and Oscar P. Fitzgerald, *The United States Navy and the Vietnam Conflict, vol.2: From Military Assistance to Combat, 1959–1965* (Washington, DC: Naval Historical Center, 1986), p.306; Edward J. Marolda, *By Sea, Air, and Land: An*

Illustrated History of the U.S. Navy and the War in Southeast Asia (Washington, DC: Naval Historical Center, 1994), pp.20–30, 162; R. Blake Dunnavent, *Brown Water Warfare: The U.S. Navy in Riverine Warfare and the Emergence of a Tactical Doctrine, 1775–1970* (Gainesville: University Press of Florida, 2003), pp.110–113.

3   Marolda, *By Sea, Air, and Land*, pp.143–144.

4   Spencer C. Tucker (ed.), *Encyclopedia of the Vietnam War: A Political, Social, and Military History* (California: ABC-CLIO, 1998) vol.1, pp.403–404.

5   Tucker, *Encyclopedia of the Vietnam War*; Dunnavent, *Brown Water Warfare*, p.113; Marolda, *By Sea, Air, and Land*, pp.143–144; Clarence E. Wunderlin, Jr. "Paradox of Power: Infiltration, Coastal Surveillance, and the United States Navy in Vietnam, 1965–1968," *The Journal of Military History* 53 (July 1989), pp.275–289; Richard T. Miller, "Fighting Boats of the United States," in Naval History Division, *Riverine Warfare: Vietnam*, p.229.

6   Dunnavent, *Brown Water Warfare*, p.113; Miller, "Fighting Boats of the United States," p.232.

7   Marolda, *By Sea, Air, and Land*, pp. 162–167; Dunnavent, *Brown Water Warfare*, pp.113–115; Miller, "Fighting Boats of the United States," p.232; Erwin J. Bulban, "Navy Using Armed Helicopters in Vietnam," *Aviation Week and Space Technology* 88 (May 20, 1968), p.69.

8   Dunnavent, *Brown Water Warfare*, p.129.

9   Appendix III, Revised Rules of Engagement–Game Warden, COMNAVFORV Monthly Historical Center, October 1966, OANHC; Victory Daniels and Judith C. Erdheim, *Game Warden* (Alexandria, VA: Center For Naval Analyses, January 1976); Keith R. Tidman, *The Operations Evaluation Group: A History of Naval Operations Analysis* (Annapolis, MD: Naval Institute Press, 1984), p.295; Thomas J. Cutler, *Brown Water, Black Berets: Coastal and Riverine Warfare in Vietnam* (Annapolis, MD: Naval Institute Press, 1988), pp.166–167.

10 Cutler, *Brown Water, Black Berets*, pp.240–246; Dunnavent, *Brown Water Warfare*, pp.116–117; Marolda, *By Sea, Air, and Land*, pp.198–209.

11 Dunnavent, *Brown Water Warfare*, pp.116–117; Marolda, *By Sea, Air, and Land*, pp.198–214; W. C. Wells, "The Riverine Force in Action, 1966–1967," in Naval History Division, *Riverine Warfare: Vietnam*, pp.139–140; Edwin B. Hooper, *Mobility, Support, Endurance: A Short Story of Naval Operational Logistics in the Vietnam War, 1965–1968* (Washington, DC: Naval History Division, 1972), p.154.

12 Dunnavent, *Brown Water Warfare*, pp.118–120; I Corps River Patrol Group, Task Force Clearwater, COMNAVFORV Monthly Historical Summaries and Supplements, February 1968, OANHC; Cutler, *Brown Water, Black Berets*, pp.273–282; S. A. Swartzrauber, "River Patrol Relearned," in Naval History Division, *Riverine Warfare: Vietnam*, pp.79–82.

13 Roger A. Shorack, "An Analysis of Interdiction Barrier Operations and Effectiveness on SEALORDS Operations Tran Hung Dao, Barrier Reef and Giant Slingshot," Navy Electronics Lab Center, San Diego, California, July 1970, *Records of the Military Assistance Command Vietnam*, Part 1: *The War in Vietnam, 1954–1973* (Library of the United States Army Military History Institute, Frederick, MD: University Press of America, 1988), R47; "VC Tactical Use of Inland Waterways in South Vietnam," *Records of the Military Assistance Command Vietnam*, Part 2: *Combined Intelligence Center Vietnam, 1954–1973*.

14 Operation SEALORDS Summary, COMNAVFORV Monthly Historical Summaries and Supplements, November 1968, OANHC; Dunnavent, *Brown Water Warfare*, pp.120–121.

15 Mobile Riverine Force (Task Force 117), COMNAVFORV Monthly Historical Summaries and Supplements, November 1968 OANHC; Operation SEALORDS Summary, COMNAVFORV Monthly Historical Summaries and Supplements, November 1968, OANHC; Dunnavent, *Brown Water Warfare*, pp.121–123.

16 Dunnavent, *Brown Water Warfare*, pp.121–124; Roger A. Shorack, "An Analysis of Interdiction Barrier Operations," R47.

17 Shorack, "An Analysis of Interdiction Barrier Operations," R47; Dunnavent, *Brown Water Warfare*, p.124.

18 Robert C. Powers, "Beans and Bullets for Sea Lords," United States Naval Institute *Proceedings* 97 (December 1970), p.96; Operation SEALORDS Summary, COMNAVFORV Monthly Historical Summaries and Supplements, March 1969, OANHC.

19 Operation SEALORDS Summary, COMNAVFORV Monthly Historical Summary, January, March 1969, OANHC; Shorack, "An Analysis of Interdiction Barrier Operations," R47; Dunnavent, *Brown Water Warfare*, p.125.

20 An unnumbered history of VAL-4, Box #144, VAL-4 History Apr 72, Vietnam Command File, OANHC; Light Attack Squadron Four (VAL-4), "OV-10 Bronco Fact Sheet," August 1969; Dunnavent, *Brown Water Warfare*, p.115.

21 Elmo Zumwalt, Jr., Elmo Zumwalt III, and John Pekkanen, *My Father, My Son* (New York: Macmillian Publishing Co., 1986), pp.63–64; Coastal Surveillance Force Summary, COMNAVFORV Monthly Historical Summaries and Supplements, June, September 1969, OANHC; Operation SEALORDS Summary, COMNAVFORV Monthly Historical Summaries and Supplements, December 1969, OANHC; Powers, "Beans and Bullets for Sea Lords," p.96; Dunnavent, *Brown Water Warfare*, p.127.

22 Cutler, *Brown Water, Black Berets*, pp.300–301; Shorack, "An Analysis of Barrier Interdiction Operations," R47.

23 Operation SEALORDS Summary, COMNAVFORV Monthly Historical Summary, March, September 1969, OANHC.

24 Operation SEALORDS Summary, COMNAVFORV Monthly Historical Summary, January 1970, OANHC.

25 William Colby, *Lost Victory: A Firsthand Account of America's Sixteen-Year Involvement in Vietnam* (Chicago: Contemporary Books, 1989), pp.190–191.

26 MACCORDS/RAD: Province Profiles, August 1968–December 1972 (partial statistics), Center of Military History, Washington, DC.

27 Ibid.

28 Ibid.

29 Admiral Elmo R. Zumwalt, Jr., interview with author, April 17, 1992; The Reminiscences of Rear Admiral Arthur W. Price, Jr. United States Naval Institute, Oral History Collection, Annapolis, MD, 1982.

Chapter 13

1 Brig. Gen. S. L. A. Marshall and Lt. Col. David A. Hackworth, *Vietnam Primer* (Washington, DC: Department of the Army, 1967).

2 Ibid.

3 Ibid.

4 In contrast to accurate fire directed at point targets, area fire was delivered to a defined area within which multiple scattered targets, such as a dispersed unit, were located.

5 Maj. Gen. David E. Ott, *Field Artillery 1954–1973*, Vietnam Studies series (Washington, DC: Department of the Army, 1975).

6   The US Army fielded a wide variety of aviation companies, each with 18–30 aircraft, assigned to divisions, brigades, and aviation groups and battalions. They included Airmobile Light (UH-1), Assault Support and Medium Helicopter (CH-47), Aerial Weapons (UH-1, AH-1 attack), Air Cavalry Troops, and various fixed-wing aircraft companies. Shelby L. Stanton, *The Rise and Fall of an American Army: U.S. Ground Forces in Vietnam, 1965–1973* (Novato, CA: Presidio Press, 1985).

7   Rated lift capability. In theory a UH-1H helicopter could carry 11 troops, but with the addition of door guns, ammunition, two gunners, and rated lift capability, only six or seven could be carried. Lift capability in terms of troops was determined by the altitude of the departure airfield, the temperature, and air density (affected by humidity).

8   Stanton, *Rise and Fall*.

9   Eugene W. Rawlins, *Marines and Helicopters, 1946–1962* (Washington, DC: US Marine Corps Historical Center, 1976).

10   Lt. Gen. John L. Tolson, *Airmobility 1961–1971*, Vietnam Studies series (Washington, DC: Department of the Army, 1973).

11   Stanton, *Rise and Fall*.

12   Ibid.

13   The NVA/VC frequently quoted Mao Tse-tung's military theory as contained in what is known as the "Little Red Book."

14   Lt. Gen. John H. Hay, Jr., *Tactical and Materiel Innovations*, Vietnam Studies series (Washington, DC: Department of the Army, 1974).

Chapter 14

1   Richard M. Nixon, *The Memoirs* (New York: Grosset & Dunlap, 1978), p.350.

2   J. Reston, "The End of the Tunnel," *The New York Times* (April 30, 1975), p.41.

3   L. Bennett, "Toward a theory of press-state relations in the United States," *Journal of Communication*, 40/2 (1990).

4   David Halberstam, *The Making of a Quagmire* (New York: Random House, 1965), p.319.

5   The phrase was popularized by M. Arlen. See his book *Living-Room War* (New York: Penguin, 1982).

6   M. Hammond, *Reporting Vietnam* (Lawrence, KS: University Press of Kansas, 1998); Twentieth Century Fund, *Battle Lines* (New York: Twentieth Century Fund, 1985).

7   D. Hallin, *The "Uncensored War": The Media and Vietnam* (New York: Oxford University Press, 1986), p.146.

8   Ibid., p.162.

9   J. Mueller, *War, Presidents and Public Opinion* (New York: Wiley, 1973); B. Roper, "What the Opinion Polls Said," in P. Braestrup (ed.), *Big Story* (Boulder, CO: Westview Press, 1977).

10   Ibid.

11   J. Zaller, *The Nature and Origins of Mass Opinion* (New York: Cambridge University Press, 1992).

12   T. Gitlin, *The Whole World is Watching* (Berkeley: University of California Press, 1980); D. Hallin, *The "Uncensored War"*; M. Small, *Covering Dissent* (New Brunswick, NJ: Rutgers University Press, 1994).

13   Hallin, *The "Uncensored War,"* p.200.

14   H. Schuman, "Two Sources of Anti-war Sentiment in America," *American Journal of Sociology*, 78/3 (1972).

15   Many Americans did not believe the news of the My Lai massacre. See E. Opton, Jr.,
      "It Never Happened, and Besides, They Deserved It," in N. Sanford, C. Comstock,
      et al., *Sanctions for Evil* (San Francisco: Josey-Bass, 1971).
16   Herbert Gans, *Deciding What's News* (New York: Vintage, 1979).
17   Hallin, *The "Uncensored War,"* pp.116–7.

Chapter 15

1   W. D. Ehrhart, *Passing Time: Memoir of a Vietnam Veteran against the War*
     (Jefferson, NC: McFarland & Co., 1986), p.18.
2   Rick Atkinson, *The Long Gray Line* (Boston: Houghton Mifflin, 1989), p.591.
3   Myra MacPherson, *Long Time Passing: Vietnam and the Haunted Generation*
     (Garden City, NY: Doubleday & Co., 1984), p.622.
4   John Douglas Marshall, *Reconciliation Road* (Syracuse, NY: Syracuse University
     Press, 1993), p.202.
5   Radio address, March 2, 1991.
6   Speech at the Philadelphia World Affairs Council, December 12, 2005.
7   *Washington Post* (October 18, 1995).
8   US Department of Defense report, *A Zero-based Comprehensive Review of Cases
     Involving Unaccounted For Americans in Southeast Asia* (November 13, 1995), pp.5,
     9.
9   Vanessa Hue, "Oakland Museum Show Stirs Trouble: Vietnamese Angry over Firing
     of Staffer Who Criticized It," *San Francisco Chronicle* (December 19, 2003).
10   *Orange County Weekly* (February 19–25, 1999).
11   *Los Angeles Times* (May 26, 2005).
12   R. Scott Moxley, "Fresh Division Appears in Little Saigon: A New Film – Saigon,
     USA – Shows Younger Vietnamese Americans Ready to Fight Their Own Battles,"
     Orange County Weekly (May 30–June 5, 2003).
13   Conversation with author, Hanoi, 1998.
14   Conversation with author, Ho Chi Minh City, 1998.
15   William Broyles Jr., "The War Is Over. Life Goes On," *The New York Times* (July
     16, 1995).

BIBLIOGRAPHY

Chronology

Karnow, Stanley. *Vietnam: A History* (New York: Viking, 1983)

Moss, George. *Vietnam: An American Ordeal*, 4th edition (New York: Prentice Hall, 2002)

Wiest, Andrew. *The Vietnam War, 1956–1975* (Oxford: Osprey, 2002)

Chapter 3

Clayton, Anthony. *France, Soldiers and Africa* (London: Brassey's, 1988)

Fall, Bernard. *Street Without Joy* (London: Pall Mall Press, 1961)

Ferrari, Pierre & Vernet, Jacques M. *Une Guerre Sans Fin: Indochine 1952–53* (Lavauzelle, 1984)

Gaujac, Paul (ed.). *Histoire des Parachutistes Francais* (Editions d'Albatros/Société de Production Littéraire, 1975)

Héduy, Philippe (ed.). *La Guerre d'Indochine 1945–54* (Société de Production Littéraire, 1981)

Labrousse, Pierre. *La Méthode Vietminh – Indochine 1945–54* (Charles-Lavauzelle, 1996)

Chapter 4

Dickson, Paul. *The Electronic Battlefield* (Bloomington: Indiana University Press, 1976)

Graves, Jim. "SOG's Secret War," *Soldier of Fortune Magazine* (June 1981)

Hoang Khoi. *The Ho Chi Minh Trail* (Hanoi: The Gioi Publishers, 2001)

Le Cao Dai. *Memoirs of War: The Central Highlands: A North Vietnamese Journal of Life on the Ho Chi Minh Trail, 1965–1973* (Hanoi: The Gioi Publishers, 2004)

Military History Institute of Vietnam. *Victory in Vietnam* (trans. Merle L. Pribbenow) (Lawrence, KS: University Press of Kansas, 2002)

Plaster, John L. *SOG: The Secret Wars of America's Commandos in Vietnam* (New York: Penguin Onyx Books, 1998)

Plaster, John L. *SOG: A Photo History of the Secret Wars* (Boulder (CO): Paladin Press, 2000)

Prados, John. *The Blood Road: The Ho Chi Minh Trail and the Vietnam War* (New York: John Wiley & Sons, 1999)

Prados, John & Stubbe, Ray W. *Valley of Decision: The Siege of Khe Sanh* (Annapolis: Naval Institute Press, 2004)

Shackley, Ted with Finney, Richard A. *Spymaster: My Life in the CIA* (Dulles, VA: Potomac Books, 2005)

Van Staaveren, Jacob. *The United States Air Force in Southeast Asia: Interdiction in Southern Laos, 1960–1968* (Washington: Center for Air Force History, 1993)

Chapter 5

Branfman, Fred. *Voices from the Plain of Jars: Life Under an Air War* (New York: Harper & Row, 1972)

Castle, Timothy N. *At War in the Shadow of Vietnam: U.S. Military Aid to the royal Lao Government, 1955–1975* (New York: Columbia University Press, 1993)

Castle, Timothy N. *One Day Too Long: Top Secret Site 85 and the Bombing of North Vietnam* (New York: Columbia University Press, 1999)

Chandler, David. *The Tragedy of Cambodian History: Politics, War, and Revolution since 1945* (New Have: Yale University Press, 1991)

Clymer, Kenton. *The United States and Cambodia, 1870–1969: From Curiosity to Confrontation* (London and New York: Routledge, 2004)

Clymer, Kenton. *The United States and Cambodia, 1969–2000: A Troubled Relationship* (London and New York: Routledge, 2004)

Deac, Wilfred. *Road to the Killing Fields: The Cambodian War of 1970–1975* (College Station, TX: Texas A & M University Press, 1997)

Guilmartin, John F., Jr. *A Very Short War: The Mayaguez and the Battle of Koh Tang* (College Station, TX: Texas A & M University Press, 1995)

Hamilton-Merritt, Jane. *Tragic Mountain: The Hmong, the Americans, and the Secret Wars fro Laos, 1942–1992* (Bloomington, IN: Indiana University Press, 1993)

Ireson, W. Randall and Ireson, Carol J. "Laos," in Allen, Douglas and Ngo Vinh Long (eds.). *Coming to Terms: Indochina, the United States, and the War* (Boulder: Westview Press, 1991)

Isaacs, Arnold R. *Without Honor: Defeat in Vietnam and Cambodia* (Baltimore: The Johns Hopkins University Press, 1983)

Kiernan, Ben. *How Pol Pot Came to Power: A History of Communism in Kampuchea, 1930–1975* (London: Verso, 1985)

Kiernan, Ben. "The Impact on Cambodia of the U.S. Intervention in Vietnam," in Werner, Jayne S. and Luu Doan Huynh (eds.). *The Vietnam War: Vietnamese and American Perspectives* (Armonk, NY: M. E. Sharpe, 1993)

Kiernan, Ben. *The Pol Pot Regime: Race, Power, and Genocide in Cambodia under the Khmer Rouge, 1975–79*, 2nd edition (New Haven: Yale University Press, 2002)

McCoy, Alfred W. "America's Secret War in Laos, 1955–1975," in Young, Marilyn B. and Buzzanco, Robert (eds.). *A Companion to the Vietnam War* (Malden, MA: Blackwell, 2002)

Savada, Andrea Matles (ed.). *Laos: A Country Study,* 3rd edition (Washington, DC: Library of Congress, 1995)

Shawcross, William. *Sideshow: Nixon, Kissinger, and the Destruction of Cambodia,* revised edition (New York: Simon and Schuster, 1987)

Stevenson, Charles A. *The End of Nowhere: American Policy toward Laos since 1954* (Boston: Beacon Press, 1972)

Warner, Roger. *Back Fire: The CIA's Secret War in Laos and Its Link to the War in Vietnam* (New York: Simon and Schuster, 1995)

Chapter 6

Clark, Philip. "The Battle that Saved Saigon," *The Reader's Digest* (March 1973)

Noyes, Harry. "Heroic Allies," *Vietnam* (August 1993)

Sorley, Lewis. "Reassessing the ARVN," *Vietnam* (April 2003)

Weith, George and Pribbenow, Merle. "Fighting is an Art," *The Journal of Military History* (January 2004)

QLVNCH, *Quan Su 4*, 1972 (ARVN, *Military History 4*, 1972)

Chapter 8

Dennis, Peter, and Grey, Jeffrey (eds.). *The Australian Army and the Vietnam War 1962–1972: The 2002 Chief of Army's Military History Conference* (Canberra: Army History Unit, Department of Defence, 2002)

Doyle, Jeff, Grey, Jeffrey and Pierce, Peter. *Australia's Vietnam War* (College Station: Texas A&M University Press, 2002)

Edwards, Peter (series editor). *The Official History of Australia's Involvement in Southeast Asian Conflicts 1948–1975*:

Edwards, Peter with Pemberton, Gregory. *Crises and Commitments: The Politics and Diplomacy of Australia's Involvement in Southeast Asian Conflicts 1948–1965* (Sydney: Allen & Unwin, 1992)

Edwards, Peter. *A Nation at War: Australian Politics, Society and Diplomacy during the Vietnam War 1965–1975* (Sydney: Allen & Unwin, 1997)

McNeill, Ian. *To Long Tan: The Australian Army and the Vietnam War 1950–1966* (Sydney: Allen & Unwin, 1993)

McNeill, Ian and Ekins, Ashley. *On the Offensive: The Australian Army in the Vietnam War 1967–1968* (Sydney: Allen & Unwin, 2003)

Coulthard-Clark, Chris. *The RAAF in Vietnam: Australian Air Involvement in the Vietnam War 1962–1975* (Sydney: Allen & Unwin, 1995)

Grey, Jeffrey. *Up Top!: The Royal Australian Navy in Southeast Asian Conflicts, 1955–1972* (Sydney: Allen & Unwin, 1998)

Langley, Greg. *A Decade of Dissent: Vietnam and the Conflict on the Australian Home Front* (Sydney: Allen & Unwin, 1992)

McNeill, Ian. *The Team: Australian Army Advisors in Vietnam 1962–1972* (Canberra: Australian War Memorial, 1984)

O'Brien, Michael. *Regulars and Conscripts: With the Seventh Battalion in Vietnam* (Sydney: Allen & Unwin, 1995)

Newman, S. D. *Vietnam Gunners: 161 Battery RNZA, South Vietnam, 1965–1971* (Tauranga: Moana Press, 1988)

Chapter 9

Colby, William. *Lost Victory: A Firsthand Account of America's Sixteen-Year Involvement in Vietnam* (Chicago: Contemporary Books, 1989)

Cook, John L. *The Advisor* (New York: Bantam, 1973)

Moore, Lt. Gen. Harold G. and Galloway, Joseph L. *We Were Soldiers Once ... and Young* (New York: Random House, 1992)

Moyar, Mark. *Phoenix and the Birds of Prey* (Annapolis: Naval Institute Press, 1997)

Pike, Douglas. *PAVN: People's Army of Vietnam* (Novato: Presidio, 1986)

Sorley, Lewis. *A Better War: The Unexamined Victories and Final Tragedy of America's Last Years in Vietnam* (New York: Harcourt Brace, 1999)

Sorley, Lewis. *Honorable Warrior: General Harold K. Johnson and the Ethics of Command* (Lawrence: University Press of Kansas, 1998)

Sorley, Lewis (ed.). *Vietnam Chronicles: The Abrams Tapes, 1968–1972* (Lubbock: Texas Tech University Press, 2004)

Starry, General Donn A. *Armored Combat in Vietnam* (New York: Arno Press, 1980)

Chapter 11

Carlock, Chuck. *Firebirds* (Summit, 1995)

Clodfelter, Mark. *The Limits of Air Power: The American Bombing of North Vietnam* (New York: Free Press, 1989)

Drew, Dennis M. *Rolling Thunder 1965: Anatomy Of A Failure* (Maxwell AFB, AL: Air University Press, 1998)

Frankum, Ronald B., Jr. *Like Rolling Thunder: The Air War in Vietnam, 1964–1975* (Lanham, MD: Rowman and Littlefield, 2005)

Guilmartin, John F., Jr. "Bombing the Ho Chi Minh Trail: A Preliminary Analysis of the Effects of Air Interdiction," *Air Power History*, 38/4 (1991), pp.3–17.

Parks, W. Hay. "Rolling Thunder and the Law of War," *Air University Review*, 33/2 (1982), pp. 2–23.

Churchill, Jan. *Classified Secret: Controlling Airstrikes in the Clandestine War in Laos* (Manhattan, KS: Sunflower University Press, 2000)

Schlight, John. *The War in South Vietnam: The Years of the Offensive, 1965–1968* (Washington: Office of Air Force History, 1988)

Sharp, Admiral U. S. G. *Strategy For Defeat: Vietnam In Retrospect* (San Rafael, CA: Presidio Press, 1978)

Smith, John T. *Rolling Thunder: The Strategic Bombing Campaign, North Vietnam 1965–1968* (Manchester, UK: Crecy Publishing, March 1995)

Thompson, James Clay. *Rolling Thunder: Understanding Policy and Program Failure* (Chapel Hill, NC: University of North Carolina Press, 1980)

Tilford, Earl H., Jr. *Search and Rescue in Southeast Asia* (Washington: Office of Air Force History, 1992)

Tilford, Earl H., Jr. *Crosswinds: The Air Force's setup in Vietnam* (College Station: Texas A&M University Press, 1993)

Chapter 12

Bulban, Erwin J. "Navy Using Armed Helicopters in Vietnam," *Aviation Week and Space Technology* 88 (May 20, 1968), p.69.

Cutler, Thomas J. *Brown Water, Black Berets: Coastal and Riverine Warfare in Vietnam* (Annapolis, MD: Naval Institute Press, 1988)

Daniels, Victory and Erdheim, Judith C. *Game Warden* (Alexandria, VA: Center for Naval Analyses, January 1976)

Dunnavent, R. Blake. *Brown Water Warfare: The U.S. Navy in Riverine Warfare and the Emergence of a Tactical Doctrine, 1775–1970* (Gainesville, FL: University Press of Florida, 2003)

Hooper, Edwin B., Allard, Dean C. and Fitzgerald, Oscar P. *The United States Navy and the Vietnam Conflict*, vol.1: *The Setting of the Stage to 1959* (Washington, DC: Naval History Division, 1976)

Hooper, Edwin B. *Mobility, Support, Endurance: A Short Story of Naval Operational Logistics in the Vietnam War, 1965–1968* (Washington, DC: Naval History Division, 1972)

Marolda, Edward J. and Fitzgerald, Oscar P. *The United States Navy and the Vietnam Conflict*, vol.2: *From Military Assistance to Combat, 1959–1965* (Washington, DC: Naval Historical Center, 1986)

Marolda, Edward J. *By Sea, Air, and Land: An Illustrated History of the U.S. Navy and the War in Southeast Asia* (Washington, DC: Naval Historical Center, 1994)

Naval History Division. *Riverine Warfare: Vietnam* (Washington, DC: Naval Historical Center, 1972)

Operational Archives, Naval Historical Center, Washington, DC. COMNAVFORV Monthly Historical Summaries and Supplements, 1968–1973

Operational Archives, Naval Historical Center. Vietnam Command File. An unnumbered history of VAL-4, Box #144, VAL-4 History April 1972

Powers, Robert C. "Beans and Bullets for Sea Lords," United States Naval Institute *Proceedings* 97 (December 1970), pp.95–97.

Tidman, Keith R. *The Operations Evaluation Group: A History of Naval Operations Analysis* (Annapolis, MD: Naval Institute Press, 1984)

University Press of America, Library of the United States Army Military History Institute, *Records of the Military Assistance Command Vietnam Part 1. The War in Vietnam, 1954–1973*

University Press of America, Library of the United States Army Military History Institute, *Records of the Military Assistance Command Vietnam Part 2. Combined Intelligence Center Vietnam, 1954–1973*

Wunderlin, Clarence E., Jr. "Paradox of Power: Infiltration, Coastal Surveillance, and the United States Navy in Vietnam, 1965–1968," *The Journal of Military History* 53 (July 1989), pp.275–289.

Zumwalt, Elmo R., Jr., Zumwalt, Elmo R., III, and Pekkanen, John. *My Father, My Son* (New York: Macmillian Publishing Co., 1986)

Chapter 13

Albright, John, Cash, John A. and Sandstrum, Allan W. *Seven Firefights in Vietnam*, Vietnam Studies series (Washington, DC: Department of the Army, 1970)

Garland, Lt. Col. Albert N. (ed.). *Infantry in Vietnam: Small Unit Actions in the Early Days, 1965–66* (New York: Jove Publications, 1985)

Hay, Lt. Gen. John H., Jr. *Tactical and Materiel Innovations*, Vietnam Studies series (Washington, DC: Department of the Army, 1974)

Marshall, Brig. Gen. S. L. A. and Hackworth, Lt. Col. David A. *Vietnam Primer.* (Washington, DC: Department of the Army, 1967)

Ott, Maj. Gen. David E. *Field Artillery 1954–1973*, Vietnam Studies series (Washington, DC: Department of the Army, 1975)

Rawlins, Lt. Col. Eugene W. *Marines and Helicopters, 1946–1962* (Washington, DC: US Marine Corps Historical Center, 1976)

Stanton, Shelby L. *The Rise and Fall of an American Army: U.S. Ground Forces in Vietnam, 1965–1973* (Novato, CA: Presidio Press, 1985)

Tolson, Lt. Gen. John L. *Airmobility 1961–1971*, Vietnam Studies series (Washington, DC: Department of the Army, 1973)

FM 7-10, *The Rifle Company, Platoons, and Squads* with Change 1, April 1970

FM 7-11, *Rifle Company, Infantry, Airborne Infantry and Mechanized Infantry*, January 1962

FM 7-15, *Rifle Platoon and Squads Infantry, Airborne and Mechanized*, March 1965

FM 31-21, *Guerrilla Warfare*, March 1965

FM 31-22, *Counterinsurgency Forces*, November 1963

FM 31-30, *Jungle Operations and Training*, September 1965

FM 31-35, *Jungle Operations*, September 1969

Chapter 14

Arlen, M. *Living-Room War* (New York: Penguin, 1982)

Braestrup, P. *Big Story: How the American Press and Television Reported and Interpreted the Crisis of Tet 1968 in Vietnam and Washington* (New Haven, CT: Yale University Press, 1983)

Braestrup, Peter. *Battle Lines: Report of the Twentieth Century Fund Task Force on the Miltiary and the Media* (New York: Priority Press, 1985)

Gitlin, T. *The Whole World Is Watching: Mass Media in the Making and Unmaking of the New Left* (Berkeley: University of California Press, 1980)

Hallin, D. *The "Uncensored War": The Media and Vietnam* (New York: Oxford University Press, 1986)

Hammond, W. *Reporting Vietnam: Media & Military at War* (Lawrence, KS: University Press of Kansas, 1998)

Mueller, J. *War, Presidents and Public Opinion* (New York: Wiley, 1973)

Opton, E. "It Never Happened, and Besides, They Deserved It," in Sanford, N., Comstock, C. et al. *Sanctions for Evil* (San Francisco: Josey-Bass, 1971)

Roper, B. "What the Opinion Polls Said," in Braestrup, P. *Big Story* (Boulder, CO: Westview Press, 1977)

Schuman, H. "Two Sources of Anti-war Sentiment in America," *American Journal of Sociology* 78/3 (1972)

Small, M. *Covering Dissent: The Media and the Anti-Vietnam War Movement* (New Brunswick, NJ: Rutgers University Press, 1994)

Wyatt, C. *Paper Soldiers: The American Press and the Vietnam War* (New York: Norton, 1993)

Zaller, J. *The Nature and Origins of Mass Opinion* (New York: Cambridge University Press, 1992)

Chapter 15

Bao Ninh, trans. by Phan Thanh Hao, *The Sorrow of War* (New York: Pantheon Books, 1995)

Borton, Lady. *Sensing the Enemy* (Garden City, NY: Dial Press, 1984)

Boucher, Norman. "The Other Vietnam Vets," *Boston Globe Magazine*, April 30, 1989

Broyles, William, Jr. *Brothers in Arms: A Journey from War to Peace* (New York: Knopf, 1986)

Cerquone, Joseph. *Uncertain Harbors: The Plight of Vietnamese Boat People* (Washington, DC: US Committee for Refugees, October 1987)

Clarke, Douglas L. *The Missing Man: Politics and the MIA* (Washington, DC: National Defense University Press, 1979)

Duiker, William J. *Vietnam: Revolution in Transition* (Boulder, CO: Westview Press, 2nd edition, 1995)

Duong Thu Huong (trans. by Phan Huy Duong and Nina McPherson). *Novel Without a Name* (New York: William Morrow & Co., 1995)

Ehrhart, W. D. *Passing Time* (Jefferson, NC: McFarland & Co., 1989)

Franklin, H. Bruce. *M.I.A., or Mythmaking In America* (New Brunswick, NJ: Rutgers University Press, rev ised edition, 1993)

Freeman, James A. *Hearts of Sorrow: Vietnamese-American Lives* (Stanford, CA: Stanford University Press, 1989)

Isaacs, Arnold R. *Vietnam Shadows: The War, Its Ghosts, and Its Legacy* (Baltimore, MD: Johns Hopkins University Press, 1997)

Isaacs, Arnold R. *Without Honor: Defeat in Vietnam and Cambodia* (Baltimore, MD: Johns Hopkins University Press, 1983 & 2000)

Karlin, Wayne; Le Minh Khue, and Truong Vu (eds.). *The Other Side of Heaven: Post War Fiction by Vietnamese and American Writers* (Willimantic, CT: Curbstone Press, 1995)

Larimer, Tim. "Vietnam's Vets Feeling Forgotten," *Washington Post* (Dec. 28, 1994)

Lopes, Sal (ed.). *The Wall: Images and Offerings from the Vietnam Veterans Memorial* (New York: Collins Publishers, 1987)

MacPherson, Myra. *Long Time Passing: Vietnam and the Haunted Generation* (Garden City, NY: Doubleday, 1984)

Mather, Paul D. *M.I.A.: Accounting for the Missing in Southeast Asia* (Washington, DC: National Defense University Press, 1994)

Palmer, Laura. *Shrapnel in the Heart: Letters and Remembrances from the Vietnam Veterans Memorial* (New York: Random House, 1987)

Raymer, Steve, and Martin, Paul. *Land of the Ascending Dragon: Rediscovering Vietnam* (Norwalk, CT: Gates & Bridges, 1997)

Sheehan, Neil. *After the War Was Over: Hanoi and Saigon* (New York: Random House, 1992)

Timberg, Robert. *The Nightingale's Song* (New York: Simon & Schuster, 1995)

US Veterans Administration. *Myths and Realities: A Study of Attitudes Toward Vietnam Era Veterans* (Washington, DC: Senate Veterans Affairs Committee, July 1980)

Walker, Keith. *A Piece of My Heart: The Stories of Twenty-Six American Women Who Served in Vietnam* (Novato, CA: Presidio, 1985)

GLOSSARY

AAA	Antiaircraft artillery
AATTV	Australian Army Training Team Vietnam (Australian)
ANV	Vietnamese National Army (see also ARVN) (South Vietnamese)
Anzac	Australia New Zealand Army Corps
ANZUS	Australia New Zealand United States defense organization
AO	Area of Operation (US Army)
APC	Armored Personnel Carrier (US)
ARVN	Army of the Republic of Vietnam (South Vietnamese)
ASPB	Assault Support Patrol Boat (US)
ATC	Armored Troop Carrier (US)
ATF	Australian Task Force (Australian)
ATSB	Advance Tactical Support Base (US)
AWOL	Absent without Leave (US)
Brown-water Navy	US Navy River Patrol Force (US)
CAS	Close air support (US)
CBU	Cluster Bomb Unit (US)
CCB	Communications/Control Boat (US Navy River Patrol Force or "brown-water" Navy) (US)
CEFEO	French Far East Expeditionary Force (French)
CG	Commanding General
CGDK	Coalition Government of Democratic Kampuchea (Cambodia under a Khmer Rouge/non-Communist coalition)
Chu Luc	General Giap's main force regulars in Tonkin
CIA	Central Intelligence Agency (US)
CIDG	Civilian Irregular Defense Group (South Vietnamese/US)
C-in-C	Commander-in-Chief
COMNAVFORV	Commander of Naval Forces, Vietnam (US)
COMUSMACV	Commander, United States Military Assistance Command, Vietnam (US)
CORDS	Civil Operations and Revolutionary Development Support (US)
COSVN	Central Office of South Vietnam
CTZ	Corps Tactical Zone (US)
DAO	Defense Attaché's Office (US)
DEFCON	Defensive concentration (US)
DK	Democratic Kampuchea (Cambodia under Khmer Rouge control)
DMZ	Demilitarized Zone (US)
DRV	Democratic Republic of Vietnam (North Vietnam)

FAC	Forward Air Controller (US)
FANK	Forces Armées Nationales Khmer (Cambodian Army)
FFV	Field Force Vietnam (US)
FOB	Forward Operating Base (US)
GVN	Government of South Vietnam (South Vietnam)
HES	Hamlet Evaluation System (US)
H&I	Harassment and Interdiction (US)
Huey	UH-1 Iroquois helicopter (US)
ICC	International Control Commission
JCS	Joint Chiefs of Staff (US)
JGS	Joint General Staff (South Vietnam)
KIA	Killed in Action (US)
LAW	Light Antitank Weapon (US)
LOH	Light Observation Helicopter (US)
LCM	Landing Craft Mechanized (US)
LST	Landing Ship Tank (US Navy)
LZ	Landing Zone (US)
MAAG	Military Assistance and Advisory Group (US)
MACV	Military Assistance Command, Vietnam (US)
MATSB	Mobile Advance Tactical Support Base (US)
Medevac	medical evacuation of wounded troops, also known as "dust-offs" (US)
MIA	Missing in Action (US)
MOS	Military Occupational Specialty (US)
MR	Military Region (French)
MRB	Mobile Riverine Base (US)
MRF	Mobile Riverine Force (US)
NAG	Naval Advisory Group (US)
NAVFORV	Naval Forces, Vietnam (US)
NCO	Non-Commissioned Officer
NLF	National Liberation Front
NVA	North Vietnamese Army (see also PAVN)
NVN	North Vietnam
NZTTV	New Zealand Training Team Vietnam (New Zealand)
PAVN	People's Army of Vietnam (see also NVA)
PBR	River Patrol Boat (US Navy River Patrol Force or "brown-water" Navy)
PCF	fast patrol craft or Swift boat (US Navy River Patrol Force or "brown-water" Navy)
PEO	Programs Evaluation Office (US)
pintle	mount for a machine-gun (US)

POW	Prisoner of War
PRK	People's Republic of Kampuchea (Cambodia under Vietnamese-installed government)
PROVN	A Program for the Pacification and Long-Term Development of Vietnam (US government)
PTSD	Post-Traumatic Stress Disorder
PZ	Pick-up Zone (US)
RAAF	Royal Australian Air Force (Australian)
RAD	River Assault Division (US Navy)
RAN	Royal Australian Navy (Australian)
RAR	Royal Australian Regiment (Australian)
RCL	Recoilless Rifle
RFs/PFs	Regional Forces and Popular Forces ("Ruffs and Puffs") (South Vietnamese/US)
RIVDIV	River Division unit (US Navy)
ROE	Rules of Engagement
RON	"Remain over night" positions (US)
RSSZ	Rung Sat Special Zone (US)
RT	Reconnaissance Team (US)
SAS	Special Air Service (Australia and New Zealand)
SEALs	Sea, Air, Land Teams, US Navy special operations force (US)
SEALORDS	Southeast Asia, Lake, Ocean, River, Delta Strategy (US)
SEATO	Southeast Asia Treaty Organization
Seawolves	US Navy attack helicopters
SOG	Studies and Observation Group (US)
SVN	South Vietnam
TAOR	Tactical Area Of Responsibility (Marine nomenclature for AO)
TF	Task Force (US)
TOW	Tube-launched optically-tracked wire-guided missile (US)
VAL-4	Navy Light Attack Squadron Four (US; also known as the "Black Ponies")
VC	Viet Cong
VM	Viet Minh
VNAF	Vietnamese Air Force (South Vietnam)
VNMC	Vietnamese Marine Corps (South Vietnam)
VNN	Vietnamese Navy (South Vietnam)
VPA	Vietnam People's Army (see also PAVN, NVA)
WBGP	Waterborne Guard Post (US)
WP	White Phosphorus (US)
YRBM	Yard Repair Berthing and Messing (non self-propelled) floating base (US Navy)

INDEX